BUILDING CULTURAL COMPETENCE

BUILDING CULTURAL COMPETENCE

Innovative Activities and Models

Edited by

KATE BERARDO

and

DARLA K. DEARDORFF

Foreword by

FONS TROMPENAARS

STERLING, VIRGINIA

COPYRIGHT © 2012 BY STYLUS PUBLISHING, LLC.

Published by Stylus Publishing, LLC
22883 Quicksilver Drive
Sterling, Virginia 20166-2102

Library of Congress Cataloging-in-Publication Data

Building cultural competence : innovative activities and models / edited by Kate Berardo and Darla Deardorff.
    p. cm.
    Includes bibliographical references and index.
ISBN 978-1-57922-803-3 (cloth : alk. paper) — ISBN 978-1-57922-804-0 (pbk. : alk. paper) — ISBN 978-1-57922-805-7 (library networkable e-edition) — ISBN 978-1-57922-806-4 (consumer e-edition)   1. Intercultural communication—Study and teaching—Activity programs.   2. Multiculturalism—Study and teaching—Activity programs.   3. Multicultural education.   I. Berardo, Kate.   II. Deardorff, Darla K.

HM1211.B85   2012
303.48'2—dc23

2011050374

13-digit ISBN: 978-1-57922-803-3 (cloth)
13-digit ISBN: 978-1-57922-804-0 (paper)
13-digit ISBN: 978-1-57922-805-7 (library networkable e-edition)
13-digit ISBN: 978-1-57922-806-4 (consumer e-edition)

Printed in the United States of America

All first editions printed on acid free paper that meets the American National Standards Institute Z39-48 Standard.

Bulk Purchases
Quantity discounts are available for use in workshops and for staff development.
Call 1-800-232-0223

First Edition, 2012

*Dedicated to all intercultural professionals seeking to advance the thinking
in our field, and in honor of all the pioneers of this field
who laid the foundation from which we build.*

CONTENTS

ACKNOWLEDGMENTS

Our thanks go primarily to our families for their unlimited patience with the time, energy, and multiyear process it required for us to move from concept to manuscript with this book. We would also like to thank Peggy Pusch in particular for her specific guidance in compiling this work, and all of our colleagues (you know who you are) for the support, challenge, and inspiration they provide. Finally, our thanks go to Jim Lance and the folks at Stylus for an incredibly seamless publishing process and to our fantastic contributors who worked often through several rounds of editing to deliver the best end product possible. It takes a village not only to raise a child, but also to write a book; this work is indeed a collective effort, and we are proud to have been part of it.

FOREWORD

What a delight to be able to write a foreword to *Building Cultural Competence*, a book that brings creativity and innovativeness to training tools, models, and activities. I full-heartedly agree with the authors on how amazing it is that an important field such as ours has made so little progress in the last 30 years. Further, the cry for intercultural competence becomes louder during a time when we don't have to travel anymore to find an increasingly diverse population and when training is needed now more than ever. This book therefore is quite timely in bringing fresh perspectives to developing intercultural competencies.

TOWARD TRANSCULTURAL COMPETENCE

The many sections of this book show clearly the developments our profession has been going through as a field and what learners need to be going through to develop intercultural competence. In the earlier sections, a lot of attention is given to cultural understanding. What is culture, and how does it apply to me? Later parts of the book deal with cross-cultural understanding leading to respect. Then the book focuses on how to deal effectively and appropriately with differences and comes to the core of what we call *intercultural competence*. Finally, some contributors provide training activities that show how to embed this process of maximizing diversity that we call *transcultural competence*.

To further the discussion, it is interesting to see how the activities and tools in this book align with the Transcultural Competence Profiler (TCP), which is normally completed online. For a free try, go to www .thtconsulting.com and use the password *Stylus*.

The four aspects of intercultural competence in the TCP are the following:

1. Recognition: How competent is a person to recognize cultural differences around him or her?
2. Respect: How respectful is a person about those differences?

3. Reconciliation: How competent is a person to reconcile cultural differences?
4. Realization: How competent is a person to realize the necessary actions to implement the reconciliation of cultural differences?

We are delighted to see for the first time some parallel models in this book and, even better, a set of practical tools and instruments to help the intercultural professional.

OVERVIEW OF THE TCP AND ITS RELATION TO THIS BOOK'S ACTIVITIES

Recognition

The book begins with a set of chapters to help readers understand core concepts related to culture and cultural understanding. New and adapted exercises build awareness of how cultures form, the importance of perspective-switching, and the nature of culture change. This section focuses on activities that help people understand these cultural differences.

Respect

How we define ourselves, culturally speaking, is the focus of the next section. This set of activities includes introductions, icebreakers, and exercises that take people on a learning journey to understand, articulate, and negotiate their cultural identities, which will help individuals respect cultural differences.

How respectful is a person about those differences? Respect serves as the basis for our attitudinal, cognitive, and behavioral orientation toward people who have diverse values.

In our profession, we focus some of our work on helping people recognize cultural differences. Stopping at the level of awareness and recognition only might support one's (negative) stereotypes. Respect for those differences is crucial for one's competence to deal with cultural differences.

Reconciliation

The next set of frameworks and exercises in this book are designed to help individuals moving across cultures to plan for and manage their transitions effectively. It updates one of the most established arenas of intercultural work with fresh thinking and ideas on how to best prepare people for cultural transitions.

I am very pleased that attention is given to going beyond understanding differences, a key component of cultural competencies in being able to resolve differences. In this section the contributors focus expressly on building creative problem-solving skills required to navigate the complexities of various cultural situations. Isn't it a good idea that Kate and Darla included a section on dealing with dilemmas? Well done!

Realization

The activities in the last section of this book have been developed expressly with the goal of building global teams as one of the ways to create realization. This section contains a single tool—one designed for professionals who do intercultural work. One of the best ways we can help others is to continue to help ourselves in the journey of intercultural competence building.

I was happily surprised and impressed by how much valuable thought and instrumental training tools have been developed in all stages of transcultural competence. I am hopeful that with the work of Kate, Darla, and their contributors, the next 30 years will be more progressive in dealing with the dynamics of the meeting of cultures and go beyond just explaining that we are different. Best wishes in developing cultural competence in others!

Fons Trompenaars
August 26, 2011

CHAPTER 1

HOW TO USE THIS BOOK

Kate Berardo and Darla K. Deardorff

I do not believe you can do today's job with yesterday's methods and be in business tomorrow.
—Nelson Jackson

We cannot solve our problems with the same thinking we used when we created them.
—Albert Einstein

Building Cultural Competence brings you a collection of tools and activities to help build cultural competence—from the basics of understanding core concepts of culture to the complex work of negotiating identity and resolving cultural differences. Often as facilitators and consultants, we encounter the question of how to develop individuals' intercultural competence. This development of cultural competence (or the many other terms used to describe successful interactions with those from different backgrounds; see Deardorff, 2009) is becoming an increasingly hot topic, not only in the intercultural field but in a variety of fields, including business and higher education, and research has shown that the acquisition of such key intercultural skills unfortunately doesn't just happen.[1] Rather, this cultural competence must be intentionally developed over time through effective learning experiences. Thus, this book is truly cutting-edge in proposing new and innovative training activities to help you develop learners' cultural competence.

Fundamentally, this is a book about staying relevant to organizations, clients, students, and learners by offering the latest and best the intercultural field has to offer by pulling together what's new and interesting from experienced coaches, trainers, and facilitators around the globe. It contains brand-new exercises, updates on classic models like the descrip-

tion, interpretation, evaluation (DIE; Nam & Condon, 2010) framework and the U-Curve model of adjustment, and adaptations—and dare we say improvements—of more conventional activities and exercises that can help build the intercultural competence of the people we work with.

The need for innovative new approaches to training and facilitating intercultural learning has been well established in research and is one of the main impetuses for writing this book (e.g., Berardo, 2008). As seasoned intercultural trainers, we found ourselves frustrated by the lack of innovation in our field, seeing many of the same activities being used for the past 20 plus years. As the epigraphs at the beginning of this chapter suggest, we felt it was time to see what was out there in terms of new ways of thinking and training in intercultural competence development, plus share some of our own activities we feel have worked particularly well in training settings.

As this book's editors, we have spent over two years working closely with each other on this project, soliciting innovative intercultural activities from around the world, carefully and thoroughly vetting the activities, and then selecting 52 of these to include in this book. Given our own training experiences and desire to have a very practical, usable resource, we hope this book can not only serve as a recipe book of activities but also as a desk reference you can flip through for inspiration and ideas to design your next program effectively. The contributors of the activities hail from over 10 countries and include many experts in the field who have had decades of training experience. These contributors represent a wide variety of experiences (i.e., many are global nomads themselves) and backgrounds in such professional fields as education, business, anthropology, and health care. These activities have been effectively used in settings ranging from corporations to the World Bank to nonprofits and to universities with participants of all ages from children to adults.

WHO SHOULD USE THIS BOOK?

Are you a consultant who wants to stay relevant with clients and meet their needs in regard to cultural competence development? Are you a human resources professional looking for truly innovative activities to use with your employees to help them work more effectively in diverse teams? Are you an education-abroad administrator seeking some learning experiences to better prepare your students for study abroad? This text is designed specifically for trainers and educators in higher education, business, and non-profit settings, and at all experience levels. These well-organized, at-a-glance exercises are easy to use and can be adapted to breathe new life into existing intercultural work.

HOW THE BOOK IS ORGANIZED

The next two chapters frame the art and science of building cultural competence in learning experiences. They are designed to provide an essential review of the key concepts and practices that help ensure success when engaging in the deep work of building cultural competence, and should be essential reading for any facilitators and coaches before undertaking any of the exercises in this book.

In Chapter 2 intercultural pioneer Janet M. Bennett first takes us through effectively facilitating a cultural competence learning experience. She artfully captures in words (a low-context medium) the nuance and essence of effective facilitation (a high-context concept). She covers what competencies are needed to effectively facilitate intercultural learning; how to balance different needs and preferences that stem from cultural differences, learning styles, and developmental needs in a program; and how to skillfully handle the variety of challenging situations we may

face when engaging in the transformative learning process behind building cultural competence.

In Chapter 3 Jeanine Gregersen-Hermans and Margaret "Peggy" D. Pusch skillfully assume the daunting task of capturing and condensing how to design and assess an effective cultural competence building learning experience into a single chapter. They compress their decades of facilitation and design experience into five key guiding principles for effective facilitation design and assessment and offer a number of checklists, question lists, and other practical tools to help practitioners put these guiding principles into action.

The Main Sections

Following these chapters are a collection of activities and models in nine sections that represent the main content of this book, organized by what they will help participants to learn in building their cultural competence and help you as a facilitator achieve in a learning experience. Box 1.1 provides a brief overview of each section in the book.

Each section contains two main types of contributions: activities and models. Activities include ice-breakers, introductions, exercises, games, case studies, and simulations that help build cultural competence. Models include tools and frameworks. Box 1.2 provides a legend to help you understand what these different types of activities and models are and what they contain.

What Is Included in Each Activity Description

All activities are written in the same format and include the information shown in Box 1.3 in a quick ready-to-use layout.

The tools and frameworks follow a slightly different format, as detailed in Box 1.4.

Quick Glance Guide at All Frameworks and Activities

Box 1.5 and Box 1.6 provide an overview of the different models and activities in this book.

USING THE BOOK'S MATERIALS IN LEARNING PROGRAMS

We suggest you use this book as

- a means to design entire learning experiences. Chapters 1, 2, and 3 can help you think

BOX 1.1   Overview of the Main Sections

Introduce Core Concepts	We begin with a collection of activities that help learners understand core concepts related to culture and cultural competence. This includes how to define culture creatively and understand the process of intercultural competence development. The new and adapted exercises presented here build awareness of how cultures form, the importance of perspective-switching, and the nature of culture change.
Understand Differences	This next section focuses on activities that help people understand how deeply and pervasively cultural differences influence us. Learners explore differences such as attitudes toward power and hierarchy in a variety of situations with this set of activities, from daily interactions to business ones, from current events to websites, and from hosting guests to filling out applications.
Explore Cultural Values	This set of activities focuses on helping learners understand their own and others' values, as a means to build self- and other-awareness, and is a critical first step in negotiating value differences.
Navigate Identity	How we define ourselves, culturally speaking, is the focus of this section. This set of activities includes introductions, icebreakers, and exercises that take people on a learning journey to understand, articulate, and negotiate their cultural identities.
Manage Cultural Transitions	This set of frameworks and exercises is designed to help individuals moving across cultures to plan for and manage their transitions effectively. It updates one of the most established arenas of our work with fresh thinking and ideas on how to best prepare people for cultural transitions.
Communicate Successfully	Knowledge of cultural differences needs to translate into action, and this set of innovative exercises helps people learn and practice how to communicate successfully in various intercultural situations.
Build Global Teams	While many activities in this book can be used with teams, the activities in this section have been developed expressly with the goal of building global teams. The exercises in this section include introductions, simulations, and a game that aim to facilitate team cohesiveness and trust.
Resolve Differences	Beyond understanding differences, a key component of cultural competence is being able to resolve differences. This section focuses expressly on building creative problem-solving skills required to navigate the complexities of various cultural situations.
Develop Professionally	This final section contains a single tool—one designed for professionals who do intercultural work. It can be used individually by readers of this book to plan their own ongoing development, and it can be used by facilitators who work with intercultural professionals in their career development planning. We end with this tool, recognizing that one of the best ways we can help others is to continue to help ourselves in the journey of intercultural competence building.

BOX 1.2 The Different Types of Contributions Presented in *Building Cultural Competence*

Activity Types

Introductions	Exercises that serve to introduce people to one another, culturally speaking
Icebreakers	Short exercises that introduce key topics and serve as intellectual warm-ups
Exercises	Experiential activities that may build cultural knowledge, attitudes, or skills
Games	Educational play that has a goal, rules, and often a competitive element
Case Studies	Specific situations that can be analyzed to provide intercultural learning
Simulations	Acting out an actual or fictional cultural situation as a means of learning

Model Types

Tools	Instruments that can be used and applied toward building cultural competence
Frameworks	Conceptual models that convey key ideas and processes related to culture

---

BOX 1.3 Format for Activities

Overview of the Activity	• A brief summary of the activity • The focus • Learning objectives • Appropriate audiences (adults, teenagers, or children) • Level of challenge to participants (low, medium, or high) • Time required for the activity (in hours and minutes) • Materials • Preparation (room setup, instructions for passing out materials, etc.)

Facilitating the Activity	• Step-by-step instructions for facilitating the activity, including
	  • setup of the activity
	  • managing the activity
	  • debriefing of the activity

Additional Information	• Additional information on successfully facilitating the activity, including
	  • key insights and learnings that should emerge from the activity
	  • variations (adaptations that can be made to the activity for different audiences or group sizes or for different purposes)
	  • facilitation tips and suggestions

Background Information	• About the exercise
Handouts and Additional Materials	• Copies of any handouts or other background information needed for the activity

---

through and plan the design of the session and subsequently help you choose the right activities to match your learning objectives.

- input for single exercises in programs. You will find the quick glance of models and activities helpful in this regard.

- a desk reference when you need inspiration and ideas for maximum impact with your learners.

- a connection point to a group of talented contributors so you can reach out, share how you have been working with these activities,

---

BOX 1.4   Format for Tools and Frameworks

Overview of the Tool or Framework	• A brief summary of the tool or framework • The focus • Learning objectives • Appropriate audiences (adults, teenagers, or children) • Level of challenge to participants (low, medium, or high) • Summary description of the model
Key Talking Points	• The main points that should be used to introduce the tool or framework so individuals can work with it
Suggested Uses	• Ways in which the tool or framework can be used during learning experiences
Key Insights and Learnings	• Typical learnings that emerge through the use of the tool or framework
Background Information	• About the tool or framework • About the contributor (see Contributors on p. 373)
Handouts and Additional Materials	• Copies of any handouts or other background information needed for using the tool or framework

---

and continue to collaborate on building cultural competence.

We trust and encourage you to take these activities as starting points and to adapt them further to ensure they work with your audiences and their specific needs. Be sure to pay attention to the variations with each exercise as well; here in particular is where you will find much creativity and innovation.

We could have certainly categorized these activities in any number of ways. We chose to list them by the dominant theme they address in building cultural competence. However, many of these activities address multiple themes and aspects of cultural competence development, so we encourage you to think holistically about these activities as you work through them.

Finally, it is important to be realistic with what can be achieved through one activity or exercise and to realize that intercultural competence is a process that develops over time. So simply using a few activities from this collection will not result in individuals' transformation.

REPRODUCING MATERIALS IN THIS BOOK

The necessary handouts for all the exercises are in this book. We encourage you to photocopy and use these handouts in your work—with one simple request: Please give credit where credit is due, respect the generosity of our contributors in sharing their work with you, and be sure to include the appropriate copyright and reference when you use an activity.

FINAL THOUGHTS

We'd like to leave you with a concluding quote as food for thought in the larger context of why we're in this work: Martin Luther King Jr. once said, "We must learn to live together as brothers, or perish together as fools." The work we all do is incredibly important in contributing in some way toward helping our fellow humans on this planet learn to live together, and in so doing, work together in addressing some of the larger issues that face us all in this 21st century. Thank you for joining us on this exciting and vital journey of intercultural competence development. We hope this will be a useful resource for you in your own work, and we wish you all the best as you help prepare others to live together successfully in the future.

NOTE

1. There is no consensus on the terminology, which varies by field and discipline, used to describe this concept, such as, for example, global competence, cultural intelligence, global learning, cross-cultural competence, and so on.

BOX 1.5   Quick Glance at Frameworks and Tools Included in This Book

Title	Key Focus	Summary Overview	Audience	Level of Challenge	Page Number
ICC Model by Darla K. Deardorff	Introduce core concepts	This is the first research-based framework of intercultural competence reflecting the consensus of leading intercultural experts that can be used to guide the structure of intercultural training, curriculum, and assessment, as well as help individual learners map their own intercultural competence.	Adults	Medium	45
Describe-Analyze-Evaluate (DAE) by Kyoung-Ah Nam	Introduce core concepts	This model is an alternative to what may be the most widely used intercultural exercise: describe, interpret, evaluate (DIE). DIE asks people to observe an unusual object or a photograph of an unfamiliar scene, and then describe what they see, interpret possible meanings, and finally evaluate by giving their value judgments. While the DIE exercise has been a favorite in intercultural communication, the ambiguity between interpretation and evaluation and the negative association of the word *die* in English have been a problem. This model proposes a DAE version using a significant Korean word, 대, DAE (in phonetics [dæ]), as a more positive and constructive acronym (Nam & Condon, 2010).	All Learners	Medium	53
OSEE Tool by Darla K. Deardorff	Introduce core concepts	This tool is inspired by the scientific method and provides a practical process for moving beyond assumptions.	Adults	Medium	58
Four Key Components of Transition Planning by Kate Berardo	Manage cultural transitions	The four key components of transition planning helps individuals understand and prepare for cultural transitions. By exploring what transition stress is, why it happens, how it may manifest itself, and what individuals can do about it, the process offers a thorough and personalized approach to helping participants manage cultural transitions.	Adults	Medium	183
The 5Rs of Culture Change by Kate Berardo	Manage cultural transitions	The 5Rs of Culture Change looks at five key changes we face when we move across cultures. It helps people understand why it is normal to experience ups and downs when moving across cultures and why stress is a part of the transition process.	Adults, Teenagers	Medium	193
The SCORE Communication Principles by Kate Berardo	Communicate successfully	The SCORE Communication Principles are a set of guidelines for communicating effectively and appropriately across cultures. It is designed to be an easy to remember checklist for communicating in global settings and can be used by speakers and listeners to minimize miscommunications.	Adults, Teenagers	Low	225
The Möbius Model by Emma Bourassa	Communicate successfully	This model demonstrates the evolution of understanding of cross-cultural communication. It uses a progression of images to relate to various experiences of intercultural communication and Bennett's (1993) developmental model of intercultural sensitivity to explore the complexity of intercultural communication as an ongoing process of learning and experimentation.	Adults	Medium	231
A 360 Degree View on Cultural Dilemmas by Kate Berardo	Resolve differences	This tool helps people solve complex intercultural challenges in a structured, holistic way. It provides a clear process and set of questions to reach more effective and appropriate solutions.	Adults	Medium	311
Multicultural Compass Model by Jacqueline Wasilewski	Resolve differences	The Multicultural Compass is a conceptual tool to help people decide how to behave when they have to choose between culturally marked behaviors.	Adults, Teenagers, Children	Medium	316
The Wheel of Intercultural Skills by Kate Berardo	Develop professionally	The Wheel of Intercultural Skills is a planning tool that helps individuals understand which skills and experiences are relevant and necessary for building a career in the intercultural field. Individuals can map out their current intercultural skill levels, plan for their future development, and evaluate current and future opportunities in the intercultural field with this tool. The wheel can be used as an aid in writing an effective résumé or curriculum vitae (CV), to track one's development over time, and as a personal assessment tool for workshops on careers in the intercultural field.	Adults	Medium	355

BOX 1.6   Quick Glance at Activities Included in This Book

Title	Contributor	Focus	Type	Summary Overview	Audience	Group Size	Time (in minutes)	Level of Challenge	Page Number
Four Analogies	Kate Berardo	Introduce core concepts	Icebreaker	Through the four analogies of an onion, iceberg, fish in water, and lenses, participants quickly and effectively learn how to think about culture, helping them to think creatively about what it means to work across cultural boundaries.	Adults, Teenagers, Children	1–100+	20	Low	61
Go Bananas!	Kimberly Pineda	Introduce core concepts	Icebreaker	By exploring different ways to peel a banana, individuals are reminded there are many right ways to do things across cultures.	Adults, Teenagers, Children	6–75	20	Low	69
Yes/No	Darla K. Deardorff	Introduce core concepts	Icebreaker	This quick activity helps introduce the concept of cultural conditioning.	Adults, Teenagers, Children	2–300+	10	Low	72
Point and Name	Darla K. Deardorff	Introduce core concepts	Icebreaker	This activity helps introduce the concept of cultural conditioning.	Adults, Teenagers, Children	15–300+	10–15	Low	74
Meeting on the Congo	Merry Merryfield	Introduce core concepts	Icebreaker	This activity teaches the need to understand the power of perspectives and worldviews as a key part of intercultural competence development.	Adults, Teenagers	15–30	30	Medium	76
The Form	Darla K. Deardorff	Understand differences	Icebreaker	This mini-simulation provides participants with a brief experience of difference.	Adults, Teenagers	2–50	15	Low	81
The Great Game of Power	Stephanie Pollack	Understand differences	Exercise	Participants one at a time arrange the objects in the room so that one chair becomes the most powerful object in relation to the other chairs, a table, and a bottle. Any of the objects can be moved, but none of them can be removed altogether from the space. A number of variations are created, allowing each person who so desires the opportunity to rearrange the objects. Each variation on why or why not the chosen chair has the most power is discussed. There is no right answer; it is about the conversation, which highlights various views of power and how relative they are to cultural context.	Adults, Teenagers	12–50	30–60	Medium	86
Strange Situations	Lothar Katz	Understand differences	Exercise	This activity explores the personal discomfort and potential conflict inherent to cross-cultural interactions in a lighthearted manner. It encourages participants to question their assumptions and explore those of others, rather than jumping to conclusions too quickly. At the same time, it serves as a great icebreaker at the beginning of a session.	Adults	6–30	30–60	Low	91
Narrative Insights	Lily A. Arasaratnam	Understand differences	Exercise	The short story becomes an interactive learning instrument in this exercise where participants read and reflect on a short story that addresses race issues and stereotyping. Through fictional interviews with characters, they discuss the issues addressed in the story, hold meaningful dialogues, and build key cultural competency skills like perspective taking and empathy.	Adults, Teenagers	4–40	40–65	Medium	98
Web Savvy: Cultural Differences	Jeanne Feldman	Understand differences	Case Study	This activity objectively examines cultural difference through the medium of Internet website design. Certain cultural tendencies actually manifest themselves physically in the way websites are structured and conceived.	Adults and University Students	6–20	120–180	Medium	104

(continued)

BOX 1.6   (continued)

Title	Contributor	Focus	Type	Summary Overview	Audience	Group Size	Time (in minutes)	Level of Challenge	Page Number
Culture in Current Events	Jennifer Evanuik	Understand differences	Case Study	Through this case study approach, participants apply aspects of intercultural communication to real-life events. Best used as a culminating exercise at the end of an intercultural training session, this activity will engage participants in a discussion of intercultural aspects in a context that is familiar to them.	Adults	3–40	20	Medium	111
Listening Deeply for Values	Kate Berardo	Explore cultural values	Exercise	In this exercise, people share stories of intercultural challenges they have made while others listen deeply for the values held by the storytellers. This exercise demonstrates that people often bring to the surface and communicate the values that drive them, and shows that the real task is to learn how to listen to others and ourselves to discover these values.	Adults	1–30	60–90	High	119
Human Values Continuum	Darla K. Deardorff	Explore cultural values	Icebreaker	This activity gets participants physically involved in thinking about their responses to value statements and generates discussion among participants. This is a good way to introduce the cultural values framework (Hofstede, 2001). It is also a good way to gain a cultural profile of the group.	Adults, Teenagers	4–50	10–15	Medium	126
Values Wheel	Rita Wuebbeler	Explore cultural values	Exercise	Participants build trust with and develop an understanding of each other by creating values wheels and sharing the values that are important to them at work.	Adults	6–12	20–30	Medium	128
Values Auction	Kristen Draheim	Explore cultural values	Exercise	After participants share proverbs from their childhood and explore the values these proverbs represent, they engage in an auction to buy the values that are most important to them. This exercise quickly and creatively helps participants identify which values are most important to them and shows how emotionally charged our values often are to us.	Adults	8–16	90	Medium	132
Building Utopiastan	Lisa Nevalainen, Maureen White	Explore cultural values	Simulation	This group role-playing challenges participants to prioritize underlying cultural values and to recognize culturally conditioned behaviors connected to cultural values.	Adults	5–50	90	Medium	136
Voices From the Past	Kate Berardo	Navigate identity	Introduction	Voices From the Past provides a creative alternative to standard introductions by having participants share key messages that influenced them, setting the tone for openness, depth, and exploration of values from the start of a program.	Adults	6–20	20–45	Medium	143
Voices of Diversity	Tatyana Fertelmeyster	Navigate identity	Introduction	Through structured introductions, participants move to a deeper level of personal connection with each other, and a constructive climate for addressing cultural diversity is created.	Adults, Teenagers	5–15	15–45	Medium	148
Identity Tag Game	Darla K. Deardorff	Navigate identity	Introduction	This activity helps participants explore their own cultural self-awareness while getting to know each other better.	Adults, Teenagers	2–300+	20–30	Low	151
Cultural Artifact	Darla K. Deardorff	Navigate identity	Icebreaker	This activity helps participants explore their own cultural self-awareness while getting to know each other better.	Adults, Teenagers	2–300+	15	Low	155

BOX 1.6 (continued)

Title	Contributor	Focus	Type	Summary Overview	Audience	Group Size	Time (in minutes)	Level of Challenge	Page Number
Crafting a Vision Statement	Barbara F. Schaetti, Sheila Ramsey, and Gordon Watanabe	Navigate identity	Exercise	This activity uses the writing of a vision statement as a powerful tool for helping participants set their commitments and align their identities in the context of a training program's larger learning goal.	Adults, Teenagers	6–60	60–120	Medium	158
Before and After: The Dilemma	Laura Di Tullio	Navigate identity	Exercise	In this activity, participants use textual and visual hints to explore the concept of identity over time and across space. In philosophy, identity is a dilemma. If something really changes, it cannot be the same thing before and after the change; if it is not one and the same thing before and after the change, nothing has really changed (Gallois, 2011). This activity invites participants to explore the notions of identity and change in time and in space and to discuss whether and how change affects their own values and belief frame of reference as they move across cultures.	Adults	2–20	50	High	169
Me You Identity Poems	Fanny Matheusen	Navigate identity	Exercise	In this activity, individuals create biograms (identity poems) for each other as a tool to explore how we see ourselves, how others see us, and how this affects our interactions across cultures. The poems reflect what people know of each other after working together in a group, which often is surprisingly little. We use poems because they appeal to our imagination, which helps in intercultural communication. The symbolic language we use in the poems is multilayered in significance.	Adults, Teenagers	6–16	45	Medium	174
Sherlock Holmes	Nagesh Rao	Navigate identity	Exercise	Playing Sherlock Holmes is a cultural self-awareness exercise in which participants learn how they make sense of the world around them, how judgments are made based on the meanings created, and how communication and dialogue can play a role in cocreated meanings.	Adults	15–30	60–90	High	179
Different Days, Different Ways	Bruce La Brack	Manage cultural transitions	Exercise	This exercise allows individuals to anticipate and reflect upon the impact of making the transition to another culture and explore the differences between their typical home schedule and a typical day abroad by comparing their schedule of daily activities with a 24-hour grid.	Adults, Teenagers	1–60+	30–60	Low	200
Duct Tape Hands	Stephanie Pollack	Manage cultural transitions	Exercise	In this exercise, participants experience firsthand some of the challenges of cultural transitions as a means to open a discussion on effective cultural adjustment.	Adults, Teenagers	8–40	25–40	Medium	208
Making a House a Home	Nancy Longatan	Manage cultural transitions	Exercise	Through a series of questions, individuals reflect on what it means to set up a new home abroad, discussing practical considerations and the deeper meaning of home. Questions facilitate a discussion on how individuals can set up their new home in a way that supports their transition.	Adults	1–8	30–60	Low	211
You, Me, and Transition Makes Three	Kate Berardo	Manage cultural transitions	Guided discussion	This exercise, specifically designed for couples moving abroad, helps each person in the relationship identify and express what causes his or her stress, how this stress manifests itself, and what the person and those around that person can do to help manage stress. It promotes necessary conversations between couples on	Adults	2	60–90	High	215

(continued)

BOX 1.6 (continued)

Title	Contributor	Focus	Type	Summary Overview	Audience	Group Size	Time (in minutes)	Level of Challenge	Page Number
				how they can support one another during stressful times.					
Hats Worn, Torn, Reborn	Kate Berardo	Manage cultural transitions	Exercise	Role changes are an often overlooked cause of transition stress. This exercise helps people explore how various roles they play—friend, colleague, parent, or child—may change as they move across cultures and how to proactively plan for these changes.	Adults	1–10	45–90	Medium	220
Three Chairs	Darla K. Deardorff	Communicate successfully	Exercise	This activity, done in triads, illustrates how communication styles affect our communication with others, especially those from different cultural backgrounds.	Adults, Teenagers	3–99	20–25	Medium	238
Visual Communication Patterns	Emma Bourassa	Communicate successfully	Exercise	In this activity participants investigate different communication styles by analyzing and trying on a communication pattern, which may challenge assumptions that speaking the same language is the most important aspect of intercultural communication. This game leads to negotiating meaning in communication styles and can lead to a deeper conversation on the values that determine specific cultural patterns of communication.	Adults, Teenagers	10–40	15–30	Low	241
Speed Dating Across Cultures	Maria Jicheva	Communicate successfully	Role playing	Speed Dating Across Cultures is a communication and influencing exercise in which individuals pair up and practice short role playings and try out different styles to do this effectively. This is a highly energizing and fun exercise that avoids afternoon slow training moments. It helps translate cultural dimensions into easily understandable terms for practical everyday scenarios, thus bringing them to life.	Adults	8–50	60–90	High	248
Snowball	Stephanie Pollack	Build global teams	Introduction	This creative alternative to traditional introductions helps participants get to know one another and deeply dive into important topics quickly.	Adults, Teenagers	8–35	25–50	Low	261
Inside Circle, Outside Circle	Basma Ibrahim DeVries, Barbara Kappler Mikk	Build global teams	Introduction	In this activity participants form one large circle and are then invited to step forward to make a general statement about themselves (e.g., "I speak two languages."). All others who who can say the same thing about themselves then step into the middle, and participants see who has stepped to the inside circle and who has remained in the outside circle. Once everyone has had a chance to observe who has stepped into the circle, inside circle members can step back and rejoin the outside circle until the next person makes a statement. The movement in this activity helps create a visual picture of the interplay of different ideas, interests, experiences, and challenges that participants have encountered. This activity can be used in multiple ways and for multiple purposes: introductions of participants and their interests, generating cohesiveness in groups, and showing similarities and differences on a variety of levels.	Adults, Teenagers	10–20+	15–60	Medium	265
Cultural Competence diversophy®	George Simons	Build global teams	Game	Through an interactive and enjoyable game of cards, participants explore the awareness and practices needed to develop cultural competence and discover how to build them.	Adults	4+	60	Medium	268

BOX 1.6 (continued)

Title	Contributor	Focus	Type	Summary Overview	Audience	Group Size	Time (in minutes)	Level of Challenge	Page Number
Virtual Construction Site: A Virtual Team Problem-Solving Simulation	Rita Wuebbeler	Build global teams	Simulation	Teams build structures blindly, based on instructions given to them by team members who are sitting back-to-back with them, which simulates the challenges of virtual communication in a multicultural team environment.	Adults	8–24	50–60	Medium	296
Team Simulation	David Goddard	Build global teams	Simulation	This simulation can be used in various sizes of groups to help participants realize the impact of culture on teamwork and develop strategies to work efficiently in diverse teams.	Adults	12–60	90	Medium	299
Market Expansion	Monika Chutnik, Marta Nowicka	Build global teams	Simulation	Various leadership styles are differently received depending on the cultural backgrounds of team members and the country where the team is based. This exercise makes it possible to experience reactions to different leadership styles and to understand them depending on one's own and the team's cultural setup.	Adults	10+	60	Medium	303
Push Back	Darla K. Deardorff	Resolve differences	Icebreaker	This activity gets participants physically engaged in conflict to introduce ways to resolve cultural difference.	Adults, Teenagers	2–200+	5–10	Low	324
On the Train	Gundula Gwenn Hiller	Resolve differences	Case study	Through a nuanced critical incident, participants learn to identify and resolve situational, cultural, and individual factors that influence intercultural interactions.	Adults, Teenagers	1–30	45	Medium	326
Meteorite	AFS Interkulturelle Begegnungen e.V.	Resolve differences	Simulation	This simulation involves inhabitants of three cities with three very different perspectives. Through this simulation, participants practice communicating clearly, as well as understanding the value of different perspectives.	Adults, Teenagers	6–18	30	Medium	331
Archivum 2060	Maja Woźniak	Resolve differences	Simulation	In this simulation, two teams from different cultural institutes plan an art exhibit, archivum 2060. Without knowing it, these teams have different ideas about how to arrange the artwork in three exhibition rooms. One team believes the pieces of art should be grouped by category and the other believes the artwork should be grouped by color. The two groups meet to decide how to arrange the artwork, and an interesting discussion ensues, allowing a rich reflection on intercultural competence.	Adults, Teenagers	3–15	60–90	High	339

REFERENCES

Bennett, M. J. (1993). Towards a developmental model of intercultural sensitivity. In R. Michael Paige (Ed.), *Education for the intercultural experience* (pp. 21–72). Yarmouth, ME: Intercultural Press.

Berardo, K. (2008). *The intercultural profession in 2007: Current professionals, practices, and challenges in the field.* Retrieved from http://www.culturosity.com/SIETAR.htm

Deardorff, D. K. (2009). *The SAGE handbook of intercultural competence.* Thousand Oaks, CA: Sage.

Hofstede, G. (2001). *Culture's consequences: Comparing values, behaviors, institutions and organizations across nations.* Thousand Oaks, CA: Sage.

Gallois, A. (2011, Spring). *Identity over time. Stanford encyclopedia of philosophy.* Retrieved from http://plato.stanford.edu/archives/spr2011/entries/identity-time/

Nam, K-A, & Condon, J. (2010). The D.I.E. is cast: The continuing evolution of intercultural communication's favorite classroom exercise. *International Journal of Intercultural Relations, 34*(1), 81–87.

CHAPTER 2

THE DEVELOPING ART OF INTERCULTURAL FACILITATION

Janet M. Bennett

Let us begin this chapter on how to be an effective and appropriate facilitator by making it clear that *no one* can tell you how to be an effective and appropriate facilitator. That said, it is long overdue in our profession to have a stimulating dialogue about facilitation skills unique to our field, approaches modified for their cultural context and impact. For decades we have borrowed methods from other disciplines, whether outdoor activities in the sixties, encounter groups in the seventies, human resources in the eighties, games and simulations in the nineties, online adventures in the new century, or tried-and-true lectures for all times. Each may have its place. However, *that place is culturally contexted.*

OUR FOCUS

It is not our goal to review the history of the field (Pusch, 2004), nor will we examine the usefulness and limitations of distinct methods in our work (Fowler & Blohm, 2004; Kohls, 1995). Intercultural training design models, the underlying theories that give an educational foundation to our efforts, have also been explored elsewhere (Bennett, 2003, 2008; Bennett & Bennett, 2004). This chapter is not about new methods and design strategies but rather explores a few modest thoughts on the adaptations we make to create a culturally responsive learning environment, whether we are teaching about culture or across cultures or on any topic. These are the unwritten, and frankly often unresearched, bits of tacit knowledge passed from one facilitator to another. And of course, as such, they are subject to reconstrual by all experienced facilitators who have succeeded quite well, thank you, without these particular whispered bits.

A basic instructional design model (Hodell, 1997) details the essential steps required to create new learning opportunities: analysis, design, development, implementation, and evaluation. In the case of Hodell's model, development and implementation are ultimately about facilitation, which is the focus in this chapter, with particular attention to *culturally responsive* development and implementation. Once a careful needs assessment and analysis have been completed, and a conceptually grounded design has been created (as discussed in Chapter 1), how does our intercultural context affect our development of the program, our implementation of that design, and the overall facilitation of the training?

WHAT COMPETENCIES DO WE NEED?

To be a successful facilitator across cultures, or to train others about culture, the competent facilitator needs a skill set, mind-set, and heart set that sometimes seem so demanding as to be unobtainable. Michael Paige's (1993) seminal article on facilitator competencies suggests a lengthy list of desirable skills and characteristics, and the chart of facilitator competencies in Box 2.1 provides some concrete details.

WHAT IS FACILITATION?

The word *facilitation* often connotes having a guide on the side rather than a sage on the stage, as the oft-quoted American phrase goes. The implication is that if the facilitator stays off the stage, learners will find their own answers to questions; this is no doubt true—at times. But an intercultural facilitator is both a bit of sage and a bit of guide, and has quite a few other roles as well. We are beginning to collect data that suggest a knowledgeable sage has a great deal to offer the learner experiencing new cultures (Paige & Goode, 2009; Vande Berg, Connor-Linton, & Paige, 2009). And the notion that all learning includes experiential learning has some truth to it (Chapman, McPhee, & Proudman,

2008). However essential experiential learning may be, it is nevertheless not sufficient to achieve intercultural competence in a vacuum. According to George Kelly (1963), learning from experience requires more than being in the vicinity of events when they occur (p. 73). Intercultural learning is an integration of the experience and our ability to *construe* that experience. Some interculturalists call this *sense making*, and urge sojourners to find cultural mentors to support their learning (Osland & Bird, 2000; Osland, Bird, & Gundersen 2007; Vande Berg et al., 2009). Such transformative learning often occurs more readily when a qualified facilitator is present.

A facilitator is therefore in a position to heighten intercultural learning. For example, he or she can move the learner beyond simple explanations for behavior: "My counterpart overseas lied to me when he said the report would be done by the first of the month." Instead, the facilitator of intercultural learning can probe issues of saving face and indirectness (Ting-Toomey, 1999).

BOX 2.1   Intercultural Facilitation Competencies

The effective intercultural facilitator has the ability to:

- comprehend the role of training and facilitation in the host culture;
- communicate clearly to nonnative speakers of the language used in the program;
- facilitate multicultural groups (including taking turns, participation, use of silence, etc.);
- "code shift" from one communication style to another;
- paraphrase circular or indirect statements for linear and direct group members;
- express enthusiasm for the topic in culturally appropriate ways;
- suspend judgment of alternative cultural norms;
- recognize culture-specific risk factors for trainees (loss of face, group identity, etc.);
- develop multiple frames of reference for interpreting intercultural situations;
- demonstrate good judgment in selecting the most appropriate interpretation in a transcultural situation;
- ask sensitively phrased questions while avoiding premature closure;
- avoid ethnocentric idioms, slang, and aphorisms;
- interview a cultural informant to obtain needed information on subjective culture;
- recognize ethnocentrism in goals, objectives, content, process, media, and course materials, as well as group interaction;
- motivate learners based on their own values;
- deliver programs in a variety of methods;
- interpret nonverbal behavior in culturally appropriate ways;
- monitor the use of humor for cultural appropriateness;
- display cultural humility;
- operate at ethnorelative stages of development; and
- be culturally self-aware.

How does this work? In a program, the facilitator can design experiences to maximize curiosity. During the event, he or she can reduce anxiety for the learners in the new context. As the sage on the stage, the facilitator can prepare them for the intercultural situation by selecting concepts, scaffolding those concepts to structure a foundation for the experience, providing frameworks for real-time issues that develop, and suggesting alternative perspectives. As the guide on the side, the facilitator can probe the experiences for greater depth, connect experiences to concepts, coach respectful curiosity, and support skills development. Intercultural facilitators are both guides and sages.

HOW DO WE MOTIVATE OUR LEARNERS?

Raymond Wlodkowski (2008) offers us yet another framework for considering our facilitation process: his time-motivation continuum for structuring motivational strategies for adult learners. He suggests it is beneficial to change the approach to motivation we use in our work, depending upon where we are in the course schedule—beginning, middle, or end. He notes that at the beginning of a program, we must establish inclusion, building an environment early in the process that communicates a welcoming atmosphere in which participants feel respected and connected. Further, he notes it is necessary to develop a positive attitude among the learners and to diffuse any negative preconceptions individuals may have about the topic, previous learning, or their ability to connect with the materials. During the middle of the program, the facilitator best motivates learners through strategies that provide meaningful engagement and challenge, including the participants' own values and perspectives during the learning opportunity. Finally, at the end of the learning event, participants want to know they learned something and can apply it in their own world, so strategies that focus on mastery and validations of their accomplishment are the most motivating. In all, Wlodkowski sequences 60 distinct motivational strategies (pp. 382–385), each with a selection of activities that promote engagement. One outcome of this approach is that facilitators can readily recognize that what we do to motivate a group of Chinese engineers is distinctly different from what we do to motivate a group of German professors; what we do to motivate them at the beginning of a program is different from what we do near the end.

WHAT ARE THE CORE CONCERNS OF A CULTURALLY RESPONSIVE FACILITATOR?

While there are no doubt countless ways a facilitator needs to adapt to the intercultural context, three areas are core to successful facilitation/learning:

- adaptation to balance challenge and support,
- adaptation to different cognitive styles and learning styles, and
- adaptation to culture-specific preferences.

These adaptation responses are grounded in a learner-centered orientation to programs. As educators we can rely on the theoreticians to inform our content, but when it comes to successful facilitation, we start with the learner. How will he or she learn most readily? What lowers the learner's anxiety and frees up his or her curiosity? We know something about this—not everything, but something.

How Do We Adapt Programs to Balance Challenge and Support?

Risk reduction is part of an inclusive climate and may involve transforming our monocultural techniques. Calling on people by name, targeting the silent observer to respond to the next question, requiring role playing, conducting activities that give minimal time to reach a conclusion, creating artificial competition—all may create discomfort for certain cultures. As we seek to engage in risk reduction for learners, interculturalists must recognize that much of what we do pushes individuals outside their comfort zone, whether we are talking about sexual orientation or the various aspects of culture shock in India.

Our learners may feel inherently threatened by even our most basic concepts. While I was conducting a training session on using third person intermediaries to resolve conflict, I found some participants horrified that anyone on earth could do such a thing and quite resistant to the idea that this abomination could occur in their organization. To an interculturalist, conflict interventions are routine; to those unfamiliar with this strategy, the idea assaults core values of honesty and forthrightness. I needed to balance this challenge with a substantial amount of support, with practical comparisons of American use of third person intermediaries. In the United States, we pay for mediators and lawyers, while the rest of the world often uses intermediaries for free.

And isn't pushing people beyond their comfort zone vital for new learning to take place? Well, yes and no. Yes we need to challenge our learners; if we don't, they may sleep or get bored, but in any case they learn little. However, if we over-challenge them, they also learn little. They tend to flee the learning environment psychologically and become resistant, or they vote with their feet and leave physically, or they suggest *you* depart from future learning events. Based on a simple but useful concept from Nevitt Sanford (1966), Bennett (2008) suggests that balancing challenge and support in the program reduces resistance, limits frustration, and enhances the potential for deeper learning.

The idea of risk management is further substantiated in the anxiety/uncertainty management theory developed by Bill Gudykunst (1995), who suggests that effective intercultural communication requires that our uncertainty (cognitive, involving knowledge and predictability) and our anxiety (affective, involving emotional disequilibrium) are balanced between our minimum and maximum thresholds. If we maximally challenge, we limit learning. If we minimally challenge, we limit learning. In other words, what is the optimal level of challenge? How can we develop equilibrium between what we teach and how we teach it to potentiate insight?

It must be acknowledged that some facilitators are quite committed to the idea of high risk, high gain learning. If you push the learners far beyond their comfort zone, they suggest, the group will experience stress that replicates the intercultural experience. This in turn fosters learning by simulating the real-life rigors of intercultural interaction. There are various rationales for this, including the French Foreign Legion syndrome ("I learned on my own; you will learn best on your own."), the Titanic syndrome ("Let's plan a disaster and see how the trainees handle it."), and the Clean Slate syndrome ("Preparing the learners ruins the freshness of the experience."). While definitive research comparing the comfort versus discomfort proposition does not yet exist, various models support the notion that creating programs that balance challenge and support has a better potential of positive outcomes for many learners (Bennett & Bennett, 2004; Pettigrew, 2008).

How Do We Adapt to Thinking and Learning Styles?

Part of this balancing includes careful attention to the style differences of the members of the group. Two style differences in particular affect our facilitation: cognitive styles and learning styles. The thoughtful facilitator will likely spend the rest of his or her life observing, assessing, and responding to style differences in these areas. No sooner does it seem somewhat clear how members of familiar cultures think, learn, and communicate, when suddenly our classrooms are occupied by less familiar cultures, and we are left to decipher new cultural perspectives. Globalization guarantees a lifetime of these learning opportunities for us as facilitators, and we fail to enjoy this quest at our own peril as professionals.

Often based on cultural influences, individuals bring different cognitive styles to the learning room. They have distinctly different logics, characterized by Nisbett (2003) as Eastern and Western thinking styles. For instance, he suggests that Westerners develop a scientific mind-set from the earliest age:

> The rhetoric of scientific papers consists of an overview of the ideas to be considered, a description of the relevant basic theories, a specific hypothesis, a statement of the methods and justification of them, a presentation of the evidence produced by the methods, an argument as to why the evidence supports the hypothesis, a refutation of possible counterarguments, a reference back to the basic theory and a comment on the larger territory of which the article is a part. . . . this rhetoric is constructed bit by bit from nursery school through college. (p. 74)

In contrast, Easterners tend to learn an entirely different set of logical principles that confound the Western observer. The formal rules differ, the basic assumptions vary, organizational patterns diverge, and dialectical approaches deviate. And this rhetoric is also constructed bit by bit from nursery school through college (Bennett, 2009).

Facilitating a session in a single cognitive style privileges one group of participants and leaves others at a higher risk of feeling excluded. For instance, traditional education in the United States, as well as other countries, often privileges cognitive styles that demonstrate critical thinking in terms of linear logic and separate ways of knowing (Belenky, Clinchy, Goldberger, & Tarule, 1986; Yershova, DeJaeghere, & Mestenhauser, 2000). If we want to balance thinking styles in the classroom, we can add metaphors to our logic, allegories to our lessons, stories to illustrate our significant points, and authentic cultural materials that reflect other ways of knowing.

Adaptation to learning styles is the second strategy we use to foster culturally responsive facilitation. While there are some controversies about the impact of culture on learning styles (Barmeyer, 2004; Edmondson, 2007; Irvine & York, 1995; Kolb, 1984, 2007; Oxford & Anderson, 1995; Smith, 2001; Yamazaki, 2005), nevertheless, adequate evidence exists for making sure we facilitate group interactions with a commitment to addressing culturally influenced learning styles.

What precisely does this mean? If we base our discussion on the most frequently used learning styles assessment in intercultural facilitation, Kolb's (2007) Learning Styles Inventory, it means we can readily identify our learners' different styles and respond to them accordingly. While we want to avoid rigidly characterizing anyone's style, it helps to be attentive to learning styles in the classroom so responses can be framed most effectively. Experience with learning styles allows us to hear a question, observe a behavior, or watch a reaction to an exercise and make some educated assessments of the learning style and respond in the presented style. The seemingly "over" participating student may simply be a concrete learner, eager to anchor his or her learning with stories and examples. We facilitate that student's learning by connecting his or her story to the ideas we are discussing. The silent, seemingly shy participant may be a reflective learner, enjoying contemplative, connective time. We give the learner time and space, lowering risk in the classroom. For the more abstract learner, we recognize that examples may be less useful, but citations and theoretical syntheses are deeply valued. And for the active learner, we may find that coaching a new perspective is helpful.

How Do We Adapt to Specific Cultures?

The third area of adaptation for facilitators involves culture-specific preferences, knowing enough about the culture we are working with to modify our facilitation role to meet expectations. For example, the American preference for first names is far from universal, as is casual attire and allowing food in class. These informal preferences in the learning environment in the United States paradoxically may cause discomfort in other cultures, where a more formal context is preferred and is indeed more relaxing because it is expected. Maintaining a hierarchical status in the class may be perceived as arrogant in one culture and a sign of well-deserved credibility in another. Individual achievement and lighthearted competition

may be sharply dissonant with a collateral culture where group ownership and thoughtful interdependence are more normative. Research on value orientations is plentiful, and understanding these contrasts serves us well as educators.

Finally, while seemingly obvious, the successful facilitator needs to be well read on current issues in the cultures of the participants in the course. Has a civil rights incident occurred locally? Has a Middle Eastern woman been profoundly affected by recent events? Has a lawsuit been filed? Has the group you are working with experienced learning that contradicts the intercultural perspective? This local knowledge can help us place the comments from our participants in context and help prevent our misinterpretation of their behavior.

HOW DO WE SELECT AND SET UP ACTIVITIES?

The process of selecting activities has traditionally consisted of identifying the latest collections of exercises and simulations and stringing the best of them together to create a stimulating program. Developments in intercultural instructional design and increasing audience diversity, however, have put those days behind us, and instead we are now typically faced with much more complex challenges, a few of which appear in the checklist in Box 2.2.

After attending to these primary questions, several other significant issues remain. One of the concerns is the level of language proficiency in the group: Is the range of vocabulary required for the activity manageable? A second concern is whether required aspects of the activity violate cultural norms. For instance, if the exercise requires directness, it may not succeed in a culture that emphasizes indirectness. A third concern is whether we have developed a classroom climate that supports the level of risk taking required by the activity. For example, if we open a program with a high-risk simulation, the group may not have developed adequate cohesion to handle the roles comfortably. Yet another concern is the availability of authentic cultural materials relevant to the age, class, gender, educational level, status, physical ability, and ethnicity of the participants.

The success of any particular module in a program is also dependent on how the facilitator sets up the activity and debriefs it. Thoughtful, systematic setups are worth the time involved, since they frame the intercultural learning expected. Box 2.3 provides

---

BOX 2.2   Selecting Learning Activities

Select an activity by assessing:

1. How appropriate is this activity for the concept being explored?
2. Does this activity balance the challenge of the content?
3. Does this activity further movement in the learning cycle by

   a. building on the learner's existing experience? (concrete)
   b. offering reflection and connection? (reflective)
   c. examining a concept or framework? (abstract)
   d. applying a concept in a pragmatic, relevant way? (active)

4. Is it appropriate in the pacing and sequencing of the learning?
5. Does it fit with the group's predominate cognitive, learning, and communication style, or does it contrast with the predominate style and thus serve the nondominant style?
6. How does this activity work for different cultures? Review the activity through the various cultural filters present in the classroom (nationality, ethnicity, race, gender, age, class, religion, physical ability, etc.). For whom will this activity seem most natural? For whom will it seem most alien? Is it sufficiently beneficial to those for whom it is alien to take that risk? Why or why not?
7. Will various culture groups likely resist this activity? How? Are the participants developmentally prepared for this activity and the content it teaches?

---

a brief checklist for setting up an activity. Equally critical is the debriefing, which emerges organically from the setup, addressing the stated objectives, the indicated concepts, and the established debriefing questions. In addition to focusing on the anticipated learning, the debriefing should also provide opportunities for unanticipated insights, observations from various cultural frames, and the random, rich spontaneous comments that often emerge in intercultural groups.

HOW DO WE RESPOND TO RESISTANCE?

In training facilitators, we find the issue that intimidates most new facilitators is how to address resistance in the group. The idea of resistance itself may be a barrier to effective facilitation, allowing us as "perfect" interculturalists to deride our participants as obviously engaged in counterproductive behavior (i.e., Could they be racist? Could they simply be ignorant?). Judith Katz (1992) has suggested there are no resistant learn-

---

BOX 2.3   Setting Up Activities

1. Introduce the activity, emphasizing (as appropriate) the cultural concept or framework being explored.
2. Relate the planned activity to participants' context, and establish its relevance.
3. Provide the participants with the necessary cultural data, history, or background to enhance their learning during the activity.
4. Deliver inoculations to address resistance and fear.
5. Clearly state the objectives for using the activity, as well as a specific question you expect them to answer or specific observations you expect them to make.
6. Supply the participants with written objectives, guidelines, and checklists, as appropriate.
7. Outline the specific debriefing questions you will use after the activity.

ers, only *fearful* learners. This remarkably simple frame shift allows us to construe resistance in an entirely different way: What is this learner afraid of? What is presenting a barrier to his or her learning? And most importantly, what can we do to facilitate the learner's comfort, reduce anxiety, and open up the learning environment to his or her concerns? After some probing, a seemingly resistant learner who had complained about "all the minorities stealing our jobs," confessed he was worried about his young son never getting a decent job. While the facilitator may never know what really prompted his protest, fear seems a fair enough bet, and responding in that vein is a nonadversarial approach that turns the heat down, not up. Developmentally, this may not be the right time to argue the data on stolen jobs. This is a time to keep the learner and his or her allies on board without adding to the resistance: "Your son has a better chance to get a job than most if he learns from you at an early age to interact across cultures successfully, including learning a second language."

Such an approach adheres to the fundamental principle that the effective facilitator rarely meets force with force. When we tangle with a participant in an adversarial way, the odds are that some of the participants will think, "Thank heavens someone finally took that person on!" Meanwhile, other participants will say, "Maybe I am next; I will just hide out in silence until this class is over." What may simply seem to be a difficult dialogue in some cultures may intimidate learners from other cultures where such interactions seem like altercations. As an Asian professor in computer technology once informed me, "Remember, any confrontation may be perceived as a personal confrontation and as such, may be an unrecoverable error. Your relationship may be terminated."

When we are working with a multicultural group—and who of us isn't?—the odds suggest that reducing anxiety is more likely to create a receptive climate for some of the difficult topics we may wish to explore.

So-called resistance usually emerges around fairly predictable issues. The learners may resist the *content* of the program or the *methods*. In the content area, typical responses may differ somewhat based on whether the topic is global differences or domestic issues.

Resistance to global topics often emerges from the participants' self-perceived expertise:

- "I have lived overseas for four years already!" (a global manager)

- "I never have culture shock." (a U.S.-based frequently flying consultant)
- "Just be yourself; that's all that really matters." (a study abroad student)

Or it may emerge from the perceived goals of the organization:

- "We don't have time for this. We're trying to do business here." (a busy executive)
- "Teeth don't have culture." (a professor in a dental school)
- "We're trying to treat cholera, not understand these people." (a humanitarian relief worker)
- "This is a virtual team. We have very little time together, so intercultural competence doesn't really come up." (a team manager)

On the domestic side, in discussing social justice issues or organizational inclusion, there are also challenges to the content being discussed:

- "This is all just political correctness." (a corporate supervisor)
- "Why are we spending taxpayers' money on this, when city government is already broke?" (a government manager)
- "We already have too many things to think about in our overcrowded classrooms without worrying about diversity." (an elementary school administrator)

These comments represent only a small sample of frequently heard statements of resistance to content; there are also many statements of resistance based on the methods you are using in your program:

- "Is this going to be all touchy-feely?" (a military leader)
- "We need more role plays." (a government executive)
- "I want to hear other people's stories." (a humanitarian aid worker)
- "Just give me the dos and don'ts; I don't need more than that." (a study abroad student)

To respond to the myriad comments that seem to constitute resistance, the fleet-of-foot facilitator needs to develop a collection of inoculations. Inoculations are used to prevent "dis-ease" in the group that may be caused by a reaction to an idea or method. As facilitators, we introduce a controlled form of the objection early in the program to reduce the reaction and therefore avoid the dis-ease. Inoculations are most often presented at the beginning of the program, to ward off the inevitable questioning of your professional credibility, the necessity of the program, and reactions to the content.

First, they can provide a safety net for the participants ("Ah, I am not the only person who has felt this way; our facilitator understands!"). A clear example of this is the use of the inoculation when facilitating highly experienced, perhaps even expert, audiences: "I know that all of you are very experienced in working across cultures, and in fact, you know much more about the specific cultures you have worked with than I ever will. But what I have to offer today is . . ."

Second, like the inoculations we tolerate to ward off disease, facilitation inoculations provide a small dose of the possible objections and an immediate antidote: "I suspect that some of you are wondering whether this program is full of touchy-feely activities, and I want to promise you that none of you have to confess your secret feelings today!"

Third, inoculations can address learning style differences: "We're going to start the morning by laying a foundation of the definitions and concepts, and then proceed to put those ideas into practice for your workplace."

As part of the needs analysis, the wise facilitator lists all the possible objections his or her particular audience may offer, and systematically develops responses to them prior to beginning the course. For instance, a group of new facilitators were developing inoculations for a class of busy supervisors who have little or no experience with intercultural learning, limited amounts of perceived diversity in their workplace, and little felt need to learn about it. What follows are a few of the sample inoculations and possible responses they developed during their train-the-trainers program as they assessed their own audiences' likely resistances.

INOCULATION: Some of you here today might think that this cultural competency program is a waste of time.
RESPONSE: However it is a part of our mission statement just like safety is. I believe this program will not only help us meet our mission statement but will make this organization an even better place to work for all of us, and I believe it is worth our time.

INOCULATION: Nobody is going to force you to like working with different people.
RESPONSE : What we want to do here today is to get you to a comfortable place in working with other people.

INOCULATION: Some of you may think this is just another Flavor of the Month program.
RESPONSE : However, our organization has adjusted its mission statement to include diversity as a core value. The organization is committed to creating a welcoming work environment for all employees. This commitment is here to stay.

INOCULATION: Some of you may have previously attended a diversity class and would rather go to the dentist than do that again.
RESPONSE : I believe this class is different. There will be no finger pointing, accusations, or group hugs. This class will open discussion on learning skills to help you to live and work in a world that continues to grow more diverse every day.

A FEW FINAL THOUGHTS

As we consider the changing arena of intercultural learning, allow me to offer a few final thoughts. The world of our work is transforming, and current trends suggest that our professionalism requires new levels of intercultural facilitation competence.

First, facilitation is becoming much more specialized. In the 1980s we may very well have entered classrooms where the discussion of culture was little short of revolutionary, and the question on the floor was, What is culture, anyway? Today we might just as easily face questions about the distinct communication patterns among the Yoruba, Ibo, and Hausa tribes.

Another trend suggests that among these tribes, the expatriate executive needs specific skills for performance appraisals, conducting meetings, interviewing, coaching, and mentoring. This reflects the trend toward very specific work-related programs that address significant professional functions.

Further (and isn't this gratifying?), there is a trend toward increasing numbers of well-educated, culturally experienced participants, who still seek and value additional development of their intercultural competence. This new audience demands highly sophisticated programming that directly addresses their specific needs. Such an audience was less typical only two decades ago.

A fourth trend reflects the interface between global and domestic intercultural issues. Those experiencing intercultural contrasts wherever they are may be seeing White male Serbians, Asian Brazilians, Black Italians, and bicultural/biracial individuals. This rainbow classroom means the facilitator has to be comfortably familiar with both cultural and racial issues, competent to move adeptly among the many concerns, and careful about making assumptions about participants.

So, yes, we are faced with the conclusion that the intercultural facilitator has to be a generalist and a specialist, global and domestic, able to dance to the many melodies the world presents. And this new understanding highlights the last trend, the demand for professionalization of intercultural facilitation. The world asks a lot of us now in terms of our own preparation, our own intercultural competence, our own advanced certifications. And it rewards us with a sense that our field can make a difference in this world that truly needs what intercultural competence is all about.

REFERENCES

Barmeyer, C. I. (2004). Learning styles and their impact on cross-cultural training: An international comparison in France, Germany and Quebec. *International Journal of Intercultural Relations, 28*(6), 577–594.

Belenky, M., Clinchy, B., Goldberger, N., & Tarule, J. (1986). *Women's ways of knowing.* New York, NY: Basic Books.

Bennett, J. M. (2003). Turning frogs into interculturalists: A student-centered development approach to teaching intercultural competence. In N. A. Boyacigiller, R. A. Goodman, & M. E. Phillips (Eds.), *Crossing cultures: Insights from master teachers* (pp. 157–170). New York, NY: Taylor & Francis.

Bennett, J. M. (2008). Transformative training: Designing programs for culture learning. In M. A. Moodian (Ed.), *Contemporary leadership and intercultural competence: Understanding and utilizing cultural diversity to build successful organizations* (pp. 95–110). Thousand Oaks, CA: Sage.

Bennett, J. M. (2009). Cultivating intercultural competence: A process perspective. In D. K. Deardorff (Ed.), *The SAGE handbook of intercultural competence* (pp. 121–140). Thousand Oaks, CA: Sage.

Bennett, J. M., & Bennett, M. J. (2004). Developing intercultural sensitivity: An integrative approach to global and domestic diversity. In D. Landis, J. M. Bennett, & M. J. Bennett (Eds.), *Handbook of intercultural training* (3rd ed., pp. 147–165). Thousand Oaks, CA: Sage.

Chapman, S., McPhee, P., & Proudman, B. (2008). What is experiential education? In K. Warren, D. Mitten, & T. A. Loeffler (Eds.), *Theory and practice of experiential education* (pp. 3–15). Boulder, CO: Association for Experiential Education.

Edmundson, A. (2007). *Globalized e-learning cultural challenges.* Hershey, PA: Information Science Publishing.

Fowler, S. M., & Blohm, J. M. (2004). An analysis of methods for intercultural training. In D. Landis, J. M. Bennett, & M. J. Bennett (Eds.), *Handbook of intercultural training* (3rd ed., pp. 37–84). Thousand Oaks, CA: Sage.

Gudykunst, W. B. (1995). Anxiety/uncertainty management (AUM) theory: Current status. In R. L. Wiseman (Ed.), *Intercultural communication theory* (pp. 8–58). Thousand Oaks, CA: Sage.

Hodell, C. (1997). *Basics of instructional systems development.* Alexandria, VA: American Society for Training and Development.

Irvine, J. J., & York, D. E. (1995). Learning styles and culturally diverse students: A literature review. In J. A. Banks & C. A. M. Banks (Eds.), *Handbook of research on multicultural education* (pp. 484–497). New York, NY: Macmillan.

Katz, J. (1992, May). *Cultural diversity: More than valuing differences.* Plenary speech presented at the meeting of the Society for Intercultural Education, Training, and Research International 28th Annual Congress, Jamaica.

Kelly, G. (1963). *A theory of personality.* New York, NY: Norton.

Kohls, L. R. (1995). *Training know-how for cross-cultural and diversity trainers.* Duncanville, TX: Adult Learning Systems.

Kolb, D. A. (1984). *Experiential learning: Experience as the source of learning and development.* Englewood Cliffs, NJ: Prentice Hall.

Kolb, D. A. (2007). *Kolb learning style inventory— version 3.1: Self-scoring and interpretation booklet.* Boston, MA: Hay Group.

Nisbett, R. E. (2003). *The geography of thought: How Asians and Westerners think differently . . . and why.* New York, NY: Free Press.

Osland, J. S., & Bird, A. (2000). Beyond sophisticated stereotyping: Cultural sensemaking in context. *Academy of Management Executive, 14*(1), 65–79.

Osland, J. S., Bird, A., & Gundersen, A. (2007, August). *Trigger events in intercultural sensemaking.* Presented at a meeting of the Academy of Management, Philadelphia, PA.

Oxford, R. L., & Anderson, N. J. (1995, October). A cross-cultural view of learning styles. *Language Teaching, 28,* 201–215.

Paige, R. M. (1993). Trainer competencies for international and intercultural programs. In R. M. Paige (Ed.), *Education for the intercultural experience* (pp. 169–200). Yarmouth, ME: Intercultural Press.

Paige, R. M., & Goode, M. L. (2009). Cultural mentoring: International education professionals and the development of intercultural competence. In D. K. Deardorff (Ed.), *The SAGE handbook of intercultural competence* (pp. 333–349). Thousand Oaks, CA: Sage.

Pettigrew, T. F. (2008). Future directions for intergroup contact theory and research. *International Journal of Intercultural Relations, 32*(3), 182–199.

Pusch, M. D. (2004). Intercultural training in historical perspective. In D. Landis, J. M. Bennett, & M. J. Bennett (Eds.), *Handbook of intercultural training* (3rd ed., pp. 13–36). Thousand Oaks, CA: Sage.

Sanford, N. (1966). *Self and society: Social change and individual development.* New York, NY: Atherton Press.

Smith, M. K. (2001). David A. Kolb on experiential learning. *The encyclopedia of informal education.* Retrieved from http://www.infed.org/b-explrn.htm

Ting-Toomey, S. (1999). *Communicating across cultures.* New York, NY: Guilford.

Vande Berg, M., Connor-Linton, J., & Paige, R. M. (2009). The Georgetown Consortium Project: Intervening in student learning abroad. *Frontiers: The Interdisciplinary Journal of Study Abroad, 18,* 1–75.

Wlodkowski, R. (2008). *Enhancing adult motivation to learn* (3rd ed.). San Francisco, CA: Jossey-Bass.

Yamazaki, Y. (2005). Learning styles and typologies of cultural differences: A theoretical and empirical comparison. *International Journal of Intercultural Relations, 29*(5), 521–548.

Yershova, Y., DeJaeghere, J., & Mestenhauser, J. (2000). Thinking not as usual: Adding the intercultural perspective. *Journal of Studies in International Education, 4*(1), 39–78.

CHAPTER 3

HOW TO DESIGN AND ASSESS AN INTERCULTURAL LEARNING EXPERIENCE

Jeanine Gregersen-Hermans and Margaret D. Pusch

This chapter focuses on the design and assessment of developing intercultural competence and offers some insights and practical guidelines based on our experience and grounded in the literature on developing intercultural competence and curriculum design.

A STEPWISE APPROACH TO DEVELOPING INTERCULTURAL COMPETENCE

Developing intercultural competence can be compared to learning to ride a bicycle, a complex activity that usually needs instruction and time before it's mastered (see Box 3.1).

Like learning to ride a bicycle, building cultural competence requires knowledge, skills, motivation to learn, and time for guided practice. Anyone involved in the design and assessment of an effective cultural competence learning experience therefore needs to take this into consideration. This chapter provides

- key principles and steps to design and assess a cultural competence building experience,
- insight into the underlying learning models for developing intercultural competence,
- suggestions on how to build a learning environment that invites participants to actively engage in the training program, and

- a checklist for the flawless organization of a training program.

WHAT IS INTERCULTURAL COMPETENCE ANYWAY?

Over five decades of scholarly work on definitions of intercultural competence have been produced. To create a more rigorous knowledge base for the definition of intercultural competence, Deardorff (2006) developed a model of intercultural competence that stresses the lifelong process of intercultural competence development. According to this research-based model, intercultural competence refers to behaving and communicating effectively and appropriately in cross-cultural situations to achieve one's goals to some degree (see the model for intercultural competence p. 29). Based on this and other definitions, three key themes suggest that intercultural competence

- requires a combination of specific knowledge, skills, and attitudes that lead to successful interactions;
- is developmental in nature (Bennett, 1998), which means individuals and organizations may progress from a more ethnocentric worldview toward a more global mind-set; and

---

BOX 3.1　Safely Learning to Ride a Bicycle

Person X has read a book about bicycles and bicycle riding. Can he or she now ride a bike?
No. Although X has acquired knowledge about bikes, how they are constructed, how they operate, and what the traffic rules are, he or she most likely will not be able to ride a bike based on that information.

We go out to a parking lot and instruct X how to operate the bike: how to get started, how to speed up, steer, and stop. Is it now safe for X to go out into the road?
No. Although X successfully developed the skills to ride a bike, he or she needs to apply the traffic rules in a real-life situation. Even though X knows the rules and is able to ride a bike, the next step is to master the complexity of traffic interaction. It is about effectively communicating one's own intentions, understanding the intentions of other participants in traffic, and making split-second and continuous implicit decisions on how to interact. Practice in a real-life context is needed to develop the routine to safely ride in traffic.

Suppose X has learned to ride a bicycle in Amsterdam. Will he or she be able to ride a bike in a city like Jakarta?
Probably not. Even though X can operate a bike and is capable of biking safely in a Dutch situation, the traffic rules—or the rules of engagement—might be different in a city like Jakarta or applied in a different way. Additionally, implicit assumptions about the intentions of others and vice versa might be invalid in this new situation. To manage the traffic in Jakarta, a willingness to understand and learn how traffic operates in this new context is required.

- requires a process of learning. To progress in their ability to handle intercultural incidents, participants need to go through several cycles of learning that include actual experience, reflection, conceptualization, and experimentation (Kolb, 1984). Figure 3.1 shows the process for developing intercultural competence.

These three premises should be embedded in the construction of the design and the sequencing of intercultural learning activities. Individual activities, or loosely linked activities, will not necessarily, and certainly not automatically, lead to greater intercultural competence per se. Experiences generated through the experimental elements in a training session, for example, need to be contextualized by a discussion of the related theoretical concepts, reflection on participants' own values and beliefs, and by adequate and well-timed feedback of a facilitator (Graff, 2004).

Designing an effective learning experience is therefore about selecting and sequencing modules or elements in a training program that jointly are expected to fulfill the objectives of that program or the learning experience. These objectives must be estab-lished based on the needs of the participants as they relate to their intercultural competence development and assessed to monitor whether participants have in fact achieved the learning objectives.

DESIGNING AN EFFECTIVE INTERCULTURAL LEARNING EXPERIENCE

What are the key framing principles for the effective design of the training process? Five principles you may want to consider are the following:

1. Meet the participants where they are.
2. Clarify specific outcomes of the program.
3. Create an appropriate learning environment.
4. Evaluate and assess the program and the learning outcomes.
5. Create a flawlessly organized experience.

Participant needs should always be at the center of the design of an intercultural learning experience. Participants determine to a large extent what they want to learn or which competences they need to develop. It might well be that in the course of a session these learning needs change because of increased

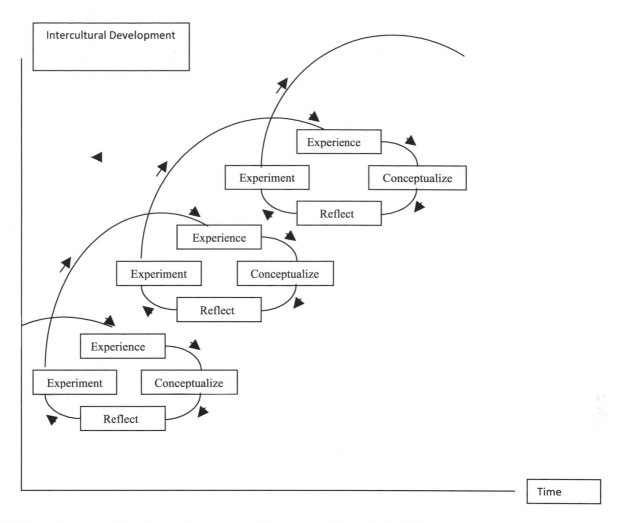

FIGURE 3.1   Process of Developing Intercultural Competence Through the Full Cycles of Learning

understanding and intercultural awareness. The reverse may also happen: the learning outcomes might have to be reformulated in terms of the level of challenge a group of participants can absorb. This demands flexibility in the design as well as points to the necessity of monitoring the learning experience throughout the training session and adapting the actual training design accordingly. Figure 3.2 reflects this dynamic process of designing an intercultural competence building experience.

Key Principle 1: Meet the Participants Where They Are

The process for developing intercultural competence aims at moving participants to a higher level of intercultural competence. The first step in designing a meaningful learning experience is the systematic exploration of the prior experiences of participants, their

perceived learning needs, and their current level of intercultural competence. Additionally it is important to determine how much challenge they can absorb, how much support they may need in those challenge areas, and how much time they have available for the training process.

Initial Perceived Learning Needs

An initial step in exploring the learning needs is to understand what type of change is envisioned, why, and by whom. Motives and expectations of organizations to engage in intercultural competence development programs may differ from the motives and learning goals of intended prospective participants. Examples of initial perceived learning needs are shown in Box 3.2.

The focus and actual content of the training program are based on three key areas: exploration of the learning needs, the time frame for the program, and

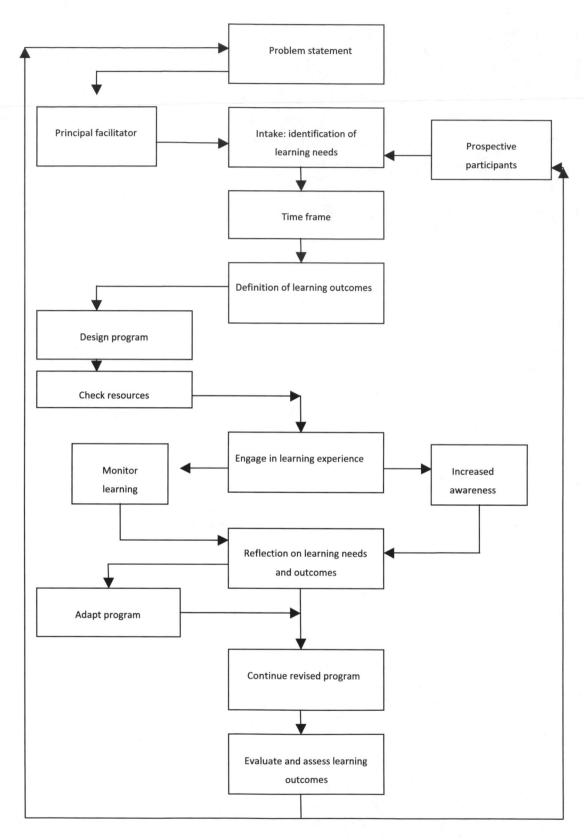

FIGURE 3.2 The Dynamic Process of Designing an Intercultural Competence Building Experience
Note. Adapted from "Cross-Cultural Training" by M. D. Pusch, 1994, in G. Althen (Ed.), *Learning Across Cultures*, Washington, DC: National Association of Foreign Student Advisors. Copyright 1994 by National Association of Foreign Student Advisors. Adapted with permission.

BOX 3.2   Examples of Problem Statements and Questions

- I would like information on adaptation or culture shock.
- How do I handle a conflict in the workplace in which culture plays a role?
- How do I advise international students?
- How do I negotiate with Indian business partners?
- How can culturally different families live together in my neighborhood?
- I have relocated to another country, what do I need to know?

---

the expected learning outcomes. It is important to agree in advance that the final training design necessarily has to result from this initial exploration with prospective participants, and even that the program may be subject to change depending on the learning process of the participants. Given that a key goal of a learning experience is individual change, it is wise to discuss how the organization or employer on return intends to absorb and further facilitate the change in the participants. Too often former participants tell us that although they have personally benefited from the program, it turned out to be difficult to implement their newly gained insights and competences since it was business as usual when they returned to their organization. It can therefore be useful to explore participants' needs in relationship to their home or work environment and the degree of openness to change in that environment. One need to be addressed in the program may well be how to successfully apply what is learned. Thus, new insights and learning may be identified as they occur, and application should be immediately considered.

Identification of Actual Learning Needs

The actual process of design starts with the intake of prospective participants. Ideally this intake should take place well in advance of the actual start of the training program, often in the form of individual sessions, needs surveys, or through a focus group of those representing participant needs, perspectives, and experiences. It might not be possible to meet prospective participants face to face for an intake. Alternatives like phone or Skype calls function very well and are usually appreciated by participants. It might be useful to ask prospective participants before the program to submit in writing their perceived learning needs and one or more intercultural incidents or difficult situations they would like to explore during training. This helps a facilitator

- gain insight into the personal and professional context of the participants, their cultural background, and what is relevant to them;
- establish an initial impression about the level of cultural awareness of participants and their ability to handle ambiguous situations;
- learn about the concerns participants might have toward intercultural exposure and to the program itself; and
- alleviate unrealistic expectations on the focus of the program, manage feasible outcomes of the program, and rephrase learning needs in terms of the original perceived learning needs and its time frame.

Intake should be considered essential and should be budgeted for accordingly. Some examples of questions for focus groups appear in Box 3.3.

Using Assessment Instruments as Part of the Intake Process

If time and resources allow, specific tools can be used to assess prospective participants on their level of intercultural competence and their learning styles. Several resources on assessment of intercultural competence and learning styles can be found in Paige (2004). Box 3.4 contains an overview of the various categories with questionnaires and test instruments that can be useful for preprogram assessment. The websites represent a number of free resources. For a multilingual group of participants, language testing is advisable to establish that all participants meet the requirement of actively interacting in the language of instruction.

When Intake Is Not Possible

In case a personal and in-depth intake is not possible before the start of a program, it is advisable to establish a common foundation with and among the participants about their perceived learning needs and

---

BOX 3.3   Examples of Questions for Focus Groups

- How many cultures are present in your environment? What cultures are represented?
- What are current examples of intercultural misunderstanding or conflict?
- What do you think can be improved in your situation?
- What is prevented or blocking that improvement?
- What do you expect to achieve in this training?
- What can you bring to the group?
- What are you looking forward to in this training?
- What makes you apprehensive?

BOX 3.4   Categories of Questionnaires and Test Instruments

- Intercultural competence, worldview, and values: Intercultural Development Inventory or Intercultural Readiness Check
- Learning styles: Learning Style Inventory or Productivity Environment Preference
- Need for structure: Paragraph Completion Method, Canadian Organizational Behavior questionnaire (Par. 3.5.)
- Perceptual modality: Perceptual Modality Preference Survey
- Language: IELTS (English), Goethe (German), or Delphi (French)

Note. From http://www.intercultural.org, http://www.learningfromexperience.com, http://www.mcgrawhill.ca, http://www.learningstyles.org, http://www.bulats.org.
See also *Cross-cultural communication: A trainer's manual*, by F. R. Oomkes and R. H. Thomas, 1992, Aldershot, UK: Gower.

---

relate these to the focus and the learning outcomes of the program during the first part of the session. This can be done by exploring some of the questions in Box 3.3 in pairs of participants and then in a larger group. Alternatively, a tool like VisualsSpeak (www .visualsspeak.com) can be used in which participants are asked to select pictures that represent their problem statement or learning need. Such an exercise depends less on immediate verbal skills and tends to reach beyond surface responses.

Level of Challenge in Program Design
The data collected on the participants during the intake help determine the level of challenge of the program. How much challenge is needed to bring participants out of their comfort zone and positively promote learning? According to Bandura's (1977) social learning theory, individuals are more likely to engage in certain behaviors when they believe they are capable of executing those behaviors successfully. By determining the entry level of participants and subsequently staging the learning process in doable activities and

steps, participants will be motivated to engage in different responses and new behavior and gain confidence in handling ambiguous intercultural situations. Two factors contribute to the level of challenge:

- the assessed or assumed level of intercultural competence, and
- familiarity with interactive and experiential learning settings.

Figure 3.3 illustrates this relationship. Defensive responses to the learning experience may occur when the level of challenge of the learning activities does not match the absorption capacity of the participants.

When selecting interactive and experiential learning activities, the facilitator should be aware of the cultural background of participants. Interactive and experiential methodologies are not common to every educational culture and might present high levels of challenge to participants, even when the level of intercultural competence is relatively high. Interactive methodologies therefore need careful introduction. It

Familiarity interactive and experiential design

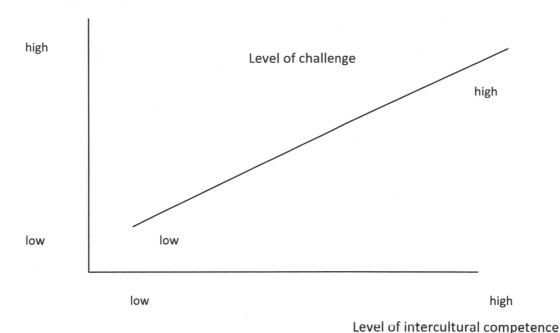

FIGURE 3.3   Level of Challenge in Program Design

is our experience that working in pairs or in homogenous subgroups helps participants actively engage in an experimental or explorative learning process.

Low challenge should not be confused with low involvement (Brislin, 1989). In our experience, even learning activities that demand low levels of visible involvement can lead to strong emotional responses, active participation, and transformative learning experiences. Exercises such as the Describe Analyze Evaluate (DAE) framework (pp. 53–57) or Observe, State, Explore, Evaluate (OSEE) tool (pp. 58–60), through which participants can observe ambiguous cultural situations, attribute meaning, and explore alternative ways to view these situations, are often low-challenge. Group discussions, especially when participants are not familiar or comfortable with interactive discussions in a classroom, often provide medium challenge. The most challenging exercises tend to be related to self-disclosure, role playing, and problem solving or conflict management in an intercultural setting. The activities in this book indicate the level of challenge, and it is important to match that challenge level with the participants.

It is rare to work with groups of participants who are at similar levels of intercultural competence development as well as similar degrees of comfort with interactive and experiential training design. More re-

alistically, there is often a risk of participants' disconnecting from the learning experience because they feel threatened and exposed or because they are bored. To address that risk, it is important to

1. Balance the design regarding the level of challenge.
2. Use a variety of activities to address the different challenge levels.
3. Acknowledge participants' experiences and knowledge when engaging in the learning experience—for example, invite more experienced participants to act as helpers in an exercise.

Time Frame

Before the learning goals are established in more detail, it is important to consider the time frame for a program. The development of intercultural competence is complex because of its multidimensional nature and therefore is a lengthy and even lifelong process. Certain knowledge components like understanding specific cultural practices might be developed within relatively short time spans. However, when it comes to changes in worldview, attitudes, beliefs, and the ability to apply new insights and skills to actual situations, the design of a training program will need to be longer or should be extended over several sessions. This understanding often conflicts with the actual available time that can vary between half a day to a maximum of five days for professionals, and educational programs that range from one week to a full semester.

A realistic reflection on the time frame is an essential part of the exploration of the intake of participants. For example, discussing the time frame with participants helps manage expectations and sensitizes the sending organization and the participants to the complex nature of intercultural competence development. It is important participants recognize that interacting successfully with those from different backgrounds involves more than discussing a list of dos and don'ts or memorizing facts about a country or culture. We usually also address the time frame in the introduction of a session. A possible dialogue in Box 3.5 is an example and summarizes how we have addressed the issue over the years.

The time available sets limits on the possible realistic outcomes and demands restraint in program design when time is short. This means that facilitators need to resist the urge to include too many activities in the design, even if those activities are valuable learning experiences. Even with intensive programs that last between three to five days it might only be possible to just begin a process of attitudinal or behavioral change that must be continued by the individual participants or their sending organization.

In summary, to meet participants where they are, it's essential to

1. Identify the issue you are trying to solve or needs you are trying to meet through an exploration of the perceived learning needs.
2. Conduct preprogram intake (and possible assessment) to identify the needs, capacities, and learning styles of the participants.
3. Establish the right level of challenge for participants.
4. Recognize and honor the constraints time limits will have on a program's design.

Key Principle 2: Clarify Specific Outcomes of the Program

Clear and specific learning outcomes attuned to the needs of participants are key in guiding an effective learning process. Specific learning outcomes not only help determine which activities are selected (com-

---

BOX 3.5   Dialogue Addressing the Time Frame

Facilitator: "Can one become interculturally competent in one day?"

Participants: "Probably not"

Facilitator: "The good news related to this question is that intercultural competence actually can be developed. The other good news is that we hope to start a process in this program aiming at a deeper understanding of culturally different others. We hope the program will inspire you to continue this learning process after the program.

Participants: "What is the bad news?"

Facilitator: "Once you are committed on this journey, it will last a life time."

---

bined with other factors already discussed) but help focus the learning, set participants' expectations, and help motivate participants to engage in the learning cycle described in Figure 3.1.

Clear and Doable Learning Outcomes

The intake of the participants has set the stage to develop the learning outcomes. A helpful tool for clear learning outcomes is the acronym SMART, which forms a guideline for the most important criteria for clear and doable learning outcomes (see Box 3.6). The S is for *specific*, which refers to concrete behavior that is observable and *measurable* (M). This implies that a learning goal is always formulated in terms of its outcomes. Specific and measurable learning outcomes are an essential input for evaluation and assessment.

To formulate learning outcomes in a smart way, use phrases such as, "On completion of the program,

---

BOX 3.6   Guideline for SMART Learning Outcomes

S—specific
M—measurable
A—acceptable
R—realistic
T—time

participants can describe" or "can analyze," or participants "are aware" or "appreciate," or "participants are able to apply." When developing learning outcomes, the learning needs as given by the participants are transformed into concrete and specific behavior. This transformation should be carefully checked with participants to be sure it is *acceptable* (*A*). Do the participants recognize the learning outcomes as their own, do they accept them as something they are motivated to engage in, and are they comfortable with the formulated learning outcomes as something they think or expect they can achieve? Facilitators should be aware of the fact that a lack of confidence in participants to actually perform the new behavior may negatively affect their willingness to change. (See also Box 3.7, which illustrates a participant's possible internal dialogue.) In the program design this concern can be met by attuning the level of challenge with various tasks and activities. For instance, a small-group discussion (lower challenge) on how to handle a specific intercultural incident may be more acceptable to participants than engaging in role playing (higher challenge).

Learning outcomes need to be *realistic* (*R*), not only from the perspective of a facilitator or a program designer or given a certain *time* (*T*) frame, but from the perspective of a participant as well.

Box 3.8 shows one example of specific and measurable learning outcomes for the perceived learning need: *I would like information on adaptation or culture shock* (see Box 3.2). The perceived learning need is reformulated in terms of cognitive (knowledge), affective (attitude), and behavioral (skills) learning outcomes. The learning outcomes in this example are organized according to the classification of learning outcomes as developed by Krathwohl (2002) for the cognitive and affective domain, and by Simpson (1972) for the behavioral domain. These classification systems are useful tools to help create a progression in learning outcomes that match the ability and learning needs of participants.

Although the learning outcomes in Box 3.8 are formulated as a linear process, other factors determine the sequencing of learning activities in the actual design, such as the previous experience of participants, their level of knowledge, their learning styles, and their level of intercultural competence. For example, when a group of participants is rich in experience but poor in theory, the facilitator can use the participants' previous experience to demonstrate the theory. In such a situation exploring the participants' prior

---

> **BOX 3.7   Participant's Possible Internal Dialogue Addressing Learning Outcomes**
>
> "Is this about me?"
> "Can I do this?"
> "Do I feel comfortable with it?

---

knowledge and experience first is helpful to motivate participants to engage in the theory or to experiment with new behavior. Often participants ask why the theory is important. For us, understanding the theory is a necessary step to distance oneself from the immediate experience and to create the possibility to consider different or other behavior.

Learning Outcomes in the Context the Level of Intercultural Sensitivity

As indicated in Figure 3.2, the design of a program is a dynamic process in which the facilitators act as an art director or a stage manager and jointly create the learning process with the participants. Developing and following up on the learning outcomes is an essential element of this dynamic process. From this perspective, well-defined learning outcomes also function as a road map for the facilitator during the program to monitor the learning process of the participants and the interaction between the facilitators and the participants in terms of content but also in terms of comfort (see Box 3.9).

Often when intercultural competence building programs do not succeed, it is at least partly because of mismatches between the actual level of intercultural competence and the level of competence required for successful completion of the tasks and activities (Hammer 2008). This highlights the importance of first learning about the participants' level of intercultural competence (through intake and pre-assessment, as discussed previously) and attuning learning outcomes to these actual levels. Hammer's developmental model of intercultural competence (adapted from Bennett, 1998) offers a framework for establishing realistic and feasible learning outcomes. In Box 3.10 the various phases of intercultural competence and the developmental conflict typical for the phases are summarized. We talk about a developmental conflict when an individual experiences tension or incongruence because his or her own behavior doesn't lead to the expected responses in others. The knowledge categories, attribution processes,

---

BOX 3.8   Specific and Measurable Learning Outcomes for Information on Adaptation or Culture Shock

Stated learning need   Information on adaptation or culture shock

---

Possible learning outcomes

Cognitive   Participants
- are able to describe and understand culture shock in terms of the latest theory on culture shock and related phenomena such as culture surprise or culture fatigue;
- are able to classify and interpret behavior as possible symptoms and signs of culture shock;
- can analyze how the processes of perception and attribution are related to culture shock and are able to attribute the experienced stress to explicit or implicit value differences;
- are able to differentiate between adaptation, assimilation, isolation, or disorientation as a possible outcome of culture shock and evaluate these possible outcomes as more or less helpful for coping with unfamiliar or uncertain situations; and
- are able to design and produce effective strategies for coping with culture shock across unfamiliar or uncertain situations for themselves or others.

Affective   Participants
- are aware of signs and symptoms of culture shock in themselves;
- are able to connect the own earlier experience of transition to the theory related to culture shock;
- are motivated to reflect on their own process of transition and share their experiences with others;
- are able to compare different value sets and attribute their stress reaction to an explicit or implicit confrontation with value differences; and
- internalize the evaluation of culture shock as a normal reaction to an abnormal situation, which to a greater or lesser extent happens to others as well when placed in an unfamiliar situation.

Behavioral   Participants
- can imitate behavioral strategies for coping with culture shock of others,
- can experiment with and practice different coping behaviors in unfamiliar or uncertain situations, and
- are able to effectively reduce the stress in themselves using appropriate coping mechanisms that lead to reduction of anxiety and uncertainty or helping others.

---

and coping mechanisms don't seem to work as efficiently as before, thus leading to anxiety and uncertainty. Working through a developmental conflict according to the learning process described in Figure 3.1 will increase the awareness of the relative validity of one's own values and norms and the ability to accommodate cultural difference in the construction

---

BOX 3.9   Monitoring the Learning Process

Facilitator's control questions:
   Are we still on the same wavelength?
   Are we in scope of the learning outcomes?
   Is the level of challenge balanced enough?

BOX 3.10   Learning Outcomes Based on the Adapted Developmental Model for Intercultural Sensitivity

Entrance Level	Developmental Conflict	Learning Outcome for Participants
Denial	Lack of awareness of diversity	• Are aware of cultural differences • Are curious and appreciate cultural differences • Can suspend judgment when encountering culturally ambiguous situations • Are motivated to explore and understand the situation first
Polarization (including reversal)	Ethnocentric attitude toward diversity	• Can describe differences and commonalities between themselves and culturally different others • Are able to make cultural generalizations (instead of stereotyping) • Can reflect on the underlying values of others and oneself • Can describe other possible worldviews and label these as similar solutions to common problems
Minimization	Assumption of similarity	• Are able to differentiate between similarity and equivalence • Accept that there exist no guiding underlying principles that are valid in all cultures • Accept that the basic values and beliefs of other cultures include both differences and commonalities from their own culture • Attribute causes for behavior to underlying value differences and worldviews, but accepts variations are possible and to be expected
Acceptance	Paralyzing equifinality	• Experience other worldviews as viable solutions to similar problems • Suspend the primary behavioral responses, that often are enacted unconsciously • Have developed additional forms of behavior that may feel counter intuitive at first and outside their own comfort zone but have become more natural • Are able to select and implement behavior that is effective and appropriate in a specific cultural context
Adaptation	Creating inclusiveness	• Have developed an identity based on the awareness of the self as a cultural being and the in-depth understanding of the multicultural world • Create mindful and effective behavior and communication styles appropriate to a specific cultural different context • Stimulate positive intercultural dialogue and effectively mediate in case of intercultural conflicts • Take responsible and ethical decisions in uncertain situations aiming at constructively including and reconciling the various cultural perspectives involved

---

BOX 3.11   Response Dilemma

The unconscious primary response of a female social worker is to shake hands as a formal and respectful way of greeting her clients. How should she respond when an older male client puts his hand to his chest when they meet?

---

of daily reality. The conflict is labeled developmental, because resolving or reconciling the conflict will lead to the next level of intercultural competence. The following example may clarify this: A former participant in acceptance explained she felt caught in the middle when confronted with the dilemma described in Box 3.11.

She was well aware of and accepted the fact that the older man intended to signal respect through a different way of greeting. This situation describes the dilemma on how to respond in a way that is mindful of the older male client and feels comfortable to the former participant as well. She felt stuck and unsure on how to resolve this dilemma.

When the appropriate psychological development has not fully taken place, the individual is not yet capable of responding effectively and appropriately toward the older man and toward herself. A behavioral paralysis may occur. Reconciliation became possible when the former participant reflected on the question of what the actual purpose of a respectful greeting was and how trust could be achieved otherwise. In Box 3.10 possible learning outcomes for each stage are formulated that participants need to achieve to progress to the next level of intercultural sensitivity.

In this section we extensively have dealt with developing learning outcomes. Concrete and doable learning outcomes help create a meaningful learning experience that is relevant to the participants in their daily functioning and that match their expectation and previous learning experience. They form the cornerstone of an effective training program and provide a road map when conducting the program.

Key Principle 3: Create an Appropriate Learning Environment

When the learning outcomes are clarified, the main focus and the general content of the program are set. The next step is to actually design the program in detail. Here the key challenge is to create a learning environment that enables and facilitates the learning process and change in the participants. Two factors are critical for an effective learning environment:

- trust and rapport among participants and the facilitators, and
- perceived relevance in terms of actual content, learning activities, and the level of challenge.

These factors determine whether participants are motivated to stay engaged in the learning process. The organization of the interaction between the content of the program, the activities of the participants, and the activities of the facilitators include

- attention to development of trust and rapport,
- decisions on the selection of the learning materials and learning activities, and
- decisions on the sequencing of learning activities.

Attention to Development of Trust and Rapport

Participants are asked to critically reflect on their own values, norms, and behavior and share their experiences and anxieties with others. This demands high levels of trust. Even when participants know each other—or just because of this—it is important to allow for building trust and rapport among the participants and with the facilitators. For this reason learning activities planned early in the program aim at getting to know each other through joint exploration of the learning outcomes and connecting the learning outcomes to the activities in the program. The joint exploration gives participants the opportunity to familiarize themselves with the other participants and get used to their communication styles and accents. Identification with other participants and the facilitators is important. Participants need to feel they understand the other participants and feel understood, that they can gain from the program, and they have something to offer as well. To make participants comfortable in the group, facilitators need to give sufficient attention and positive feedback to each participant individually.

As an example, a discussion on the process and ways of interacting in the group is helpful for developing trust and usually highly appreciated by participants. Box 3.12 shows an example of a possible dialogue between the facilitators and the participants

---

BOX 3.12   Possible Dialogue Addressing Flop and Go Factors

Facilitator: What will make this program flop?

Participants: Too much/too little lecturing, participants taking up too much space, not sticking to the time schedule, not concrete enough, not relevant for daily life, not sticking to the program, lack of flexibility, no sharing, interruption of speech, lack of confidentiality

Facilitator: What will make this program a success?

Participants: Variation in activities, interaction and sharing between participants, challenging content, something new, concrete advice and tips, applicable to one's context, respect for each other, willingness to consider alternatives, confidentiality

Facilitator: Who do you think is responsible to make this program a success?

Participants: All of us

---

that focuses on factors that will make the program flop and factors that will make it go well. Based on the items participants mention, a so-called flop and go chart functions as jointly agreed-upon ground rules for the focus of the learning experience and helps to monitor how participants interact with each other. Facilitators can also use this to hold participants accountable for their behavior during training.

Explicitly discussing these ground rules is a good way for each group of participants to develop trust and rapport. The facilitator makes sure these ground rules set the tone for positive intercultural dialogue and help keep a focus on the learning outcomes. The design should allow sufficient time for this initial part. During the program, facilitators and participants can refer to the ground rules to check if the process still fits the learning needs of participants or if adjustment or refocusing is necessary.

One of the pitfalls in maintaining trust and rapport is the management of time during a program. Since it is difficult beforehand to exactly determine how the learning process will evolve and how participants will react in certain learning situations, the time schedule needs to be flexible enough for on-the-spot adjustments. Avoid detailed time schedules for a program. Sticking to a time schedule too rigidly or, alternatively, running out of time will dissatisfy participants and negatively affect the credibility of the facilitators. Our golden tip is that time schedules only give the topics, starting and end times, and break times so there is a general schedule, especially for those participants who really desire a schedule. That guarantees we never run out of time, which keeps the participants satisfied.

Selection and Organization of the Learning Material and Learning Activities

Relevance of the learning material and activities in the eyes of participants is a critical success factor in any program. The learning material has to present new or additional perspectives on the participants' prior experience and knowledge that is perceived as valid and creates new ideas on how to interact more effectively and satisfactorily across cultures or in culturally ambiguous situations. Usually the learning material is organized from simple to complex, from known material to new input, and from concrete to abstract. First the key concepts on a certain topic are introduced, followed by the principles and mechanism explaining how the concepts are related and how they work. Next, the theory that explains why the principles and mechanism function as they do is discussed along with limitative conditions. The selection of the learning activities involves decisions on what participants are expected to know and do with the content (learning outcomes). Depending on the choice of teaching methodologies, participants, for instance, are supposed to listen, discuss, share, reflect, or experiment. Learning activities can be undertaken individually, in syndicate groups, or in plenary sessions. Activities can be planned during the session or program or as homework assignments outside training time. The methodologies used in the program preferably vary, on the one hand they are based on the various learning styles of participants, while on the other hand they are related to the intended outcomes of a certain activity. The program activities should be balanced in the level of challenge. Participants usually like to interact with each other but not all the time. In our programs we also use the discussion on learning outcomes to explain why certain methodologies are chosen. This enhances effectiveness and the motivation of participants to actively participate. Variation in methodology will keep participants and facilitators engaged and expand their attention span.

The Sequencing of the Learning Activities

To allow participants to digest the materials that are presented or the experiences that have been created, it is important for each learning outcome to include the full cycle of learning (see Figure 3.1) in the design. This element of the design can best be explained to participants by using the analogy of breathing. Essentially, breathing is a process of inhaling alternated with exhaling. After taking in new information and experiences participants need time to exhale, reflect, and integrate the new input within the existing cognitive, affective, or behavioral frameworks. As a facilitator, it is also important for you to include sufficient time for the debriefing of any activity, since this is often where crucial learning occurs. Allow twice as much time for debriefing as you allow for the activity itself. Follow strands of learning beyond a simple statement. That is, when someone says, "I just realized X, you might ask, "What made X apparent? How can you apply this to a real-life situation?"

Box 3.13 provides an example of a learning activity we designed exactly for this purpose, referred to as Personal Reflection Journal. After each program element, participants are asked to individually answer three questions that help them reflect on the program element and integrate what they have learned into their existing knowledge as well as prepare them to use what they have learned in their personal or work situation.

Often the process of exhaling takes place during the informal parts of a program—breaks, meals, or social events organized in conjunction with the program. Evaluations of participants even tend to suggest that informal exhaling is the most effective and rewarding part of a program. Therefore, the content and the methodologies used in the program need to be provoking enough to make participants talk about it during the breaks. Second, the sequencing of the learning activities needs to create a flow between taking in and processing the input.

The closing part of a program focuses on synthesis and on completing the full cycle of learning. The objective is to tie the knots together and make the *transfer* from what is learned and experienced during the program to the daily life of the participants. Often this is confused with evaluation. However, the closing is an essential part of the learning experience. A possible activity for bringing everything together is to ask participants to make an action plan for one doable change they would like to implement immediately after return to their daily work or environment based on their notes in their Personal Reflection Journal.

Checklist for Program Design

The checklist in Box 3.14 summarizes the key issues that need attention when designing a program.

Key Principle 4: Evaluate and Assess the Program and the Learning Outcomes

Evaluation and assessment complete the design of a program. Pusch (1994) lists a number of questions that should be considered when planning the evaluation and assessment (see Box 3.15).

The question for whom the evaluation or assessment is done raises an important issue. Results or data from any type of individual assessment have to be discussed with the individual participant first, especially in providing feedback to the participant on his or her own intercultural competence development. It is for the participant to decide what will happen with the results and if he or she agrees to share the results with others, including the sending organization. Confidentiality is a necessary requirement and has to be agreed upon in advance with all parties involved. How the findings are interpreted and used requires the joint decision of participants and facilitators.

BOX 3.13   Personal Reflection Journal

Training module title:

- What was the key content of the module?
- What have I learned? (What are the key insights or take-aways for me?)
- Why is this learning important?
- As a result of this learning, I will take the following action steps in my work or home situation:

BOX 3.14   Checklist for Program Design

- Is the content relevant in terms of agreed-upon learning outcomes?
- Are the learning activities reflecting the full cycle of learning for each intended outcome?
- Are the learning activities relevant for participants and attuned to the level of challenge they can handle?
- Are activities included that help develop and keep trust and rapport among participants and with the facilitators?
- Is the sequencing of the learning activities balanced in terms of level of challenge for participants?
- Is sufficient time allowed for the debriefing of activities and transfer to the home or workplace?

Evaluation of the Program

Areas to consider in the evaluation of a program include

1. The clarity of learning outcomes to all participants
2. The relevance and effectiveness of learning activities and the chosen methodologies to achieve the learning outcomes
3. If the program was conducted well (participant satisfaction)

When planning the evaluation of a program, it is important to keep the focus on the stated goals and outcomes and to be aware of a culture of critiquing that participants sometimes associate with evaluation.

For example, the atmosphere and the willingness to contribute to giving feedback changed positively when we started to ask for compliments on what the group had achieved.

Assessment of Development

Assessment primarily focuses on the question of if and to what extent the projected learning outcomes have been achieved. The assessment of learning outcomes needs to be aligned with the preprogram assessment of the intake and so must be considered in the beginning stages, not as an afterthought at the end of the process. Decisions on the use of instruments that measure levels of intercultural competence development have to be taken before the intake and are therefore part of the initial exploration of the problem statement

---

BOX 3.15   Questions to Consider When Planning the Evaluation and Assessment

- Who does the evaluation or assessment?
- For whom is it done?
- When is it done?
- What is to be measured?
- How is the measurement to be done?
- What is the criteria for measurement (based on what)?
- What is evidence that the results have been achieved?
- What are the optimal assessment instruments/methods to obtain the evidence that results have been achieved?
- How feasible and manageable are the logistics of the assessment instruments/methods selected?
- What is an appropriate format for the findings?
- How are the findings interpreted, used, and communicated?

Note. Adapted from "Cross-Cultural Training" by M. D. Pusch, 1994, in G. Althen (Ed.), *Learning Across Cultures*, Washington, DC: National Association of Foreign Student Advisors. Copyright 1994 by National Association of Foreign Student Advisors. Adapted with permission. Also based on "Matter of Logic," by D. K. Deardorff, 2005, *International Educator*, May–June, pp. 26–31.

and the scope of the program with the sending organizations. In addition to the quantitative measures, the use of qualitative approaches can create insight into the learning that occurred and provide a more complete picture of participants' learning. Some examples of qualitative approaches appear in Box 3.16.

For short-term intensive programs specifically, substantial development of intercultural competence should not immediately be expected. Often the experiences and insights gained in a program need to be processed and contextualized in daily life for learning to become apparent. Participants in retrospect commented that they changed because of the program and maybe not directly during the program. Longer-term programs or programs that include several separate sessions over an extended period of time offer the opportunity to assess the development of intercultural competence on a more continuous basis, thus not only providing feedback on the design of the program. Reflection on their own development makes participants focus on the challenge at hand and motivates them to take the next steps. When assessment is used as an inclusive and integrated part of the learning, it enhances the self-efficacy of participants and stimulates learning. For most training programs that focus on the development of intercultural competence, assessments that lead to pass or fail decisions are not applicable, desired, or appropriate. Further, research has shown that a multimethod, multiperspective assessment approach is needed to most accurately assess an individual's intercultural competence development (Deardorff, 2009).

In case the program is part of a study or research project on developing intercultural competence, additional requirements have to be included in the design of the assessment to ensure reliability and validity. Discussion of these additional requirements, however, falls outside the scope of this chapter.

Key Principle 5: Create a Flawlessly Organized Experience

The learning process must be supported by a flawless organization of the program. Glitches in organizational support lead to dissatisfaction and hinder learning, sometimes substantially. We know that skillful improvisation is part of being a facilitator. However, organizational support arranged beforehand will help you perform better in your role. Items to mention are the physical environment and facilities, the composition of the group, the facilitators, and communication with participants.

Physical Environment and Facilities

An effective learning environment needs to offer space for formal and informal learning. Participants appreciate and benefit from sharing experiences with other participants inside and outside the classroom and need the space and informal time to connect in a program schedule to do so. As part of this, it's important participants feel comfortable and at home in their physical environment.

Classroom size and room setup should allow for spatial intimacy and different teaching modalities that demand various ways of involving participants. Listening to a lecture or watching a video and taking notes at the same time require a different type of participant involvement than working in small groups or engaging in role playing that demonstrates the impact of personal space on an interaction. Box 3.17 provides an example of a checklist that can be used

---

BOX 3.16   Examples of Qualitative Approaches to Assessment

Essay writing related to

- knowledge of the topic,
- perceptions and attitudes toward diversity,
- development of action plans for changes to make on return to daily life and why.

Observation of participants' demonstration of the newly acquired competences in

- assessment interviews,
- simulation games and case studies, and
- real-life situations.

Box 3.17   Checklist for the Organization of the Program

Item	Remarks	Check
Plenary room	Enough space to include tables and chairs (all moveable) and plenary interactive activities	
Breakout rooms	Accommodate syndicate groups of up to five or six participants	
Informal space	Lounge area outside the plenary room, space for refreshments	
Physical environment	Daylight, fresh air, acoustics, privacy, facilities for disabled participants	
Technical equipment	Audiovisual equipment, computer, Internet connection, translation facilities (if applicable), copying (all tested beforehand)	
Technical assistance	Friendly relations, on hand and easily accessible	
Work material	Study guide, workbook, instruments, certificates (if applicable)	
Preprogram communication	Welcome letter, detailed program, participant list, preprogram assignments, special requests, location, travel instructions	
Other materials	Papers, flipcharts, pencils, markers, scissors, tape, and various props the learning activities demand	
Refreshments	Water, dietary requirements, fruit, or typical foods	

for optimal design and organization of the learning environment.

Composition of the Group

The composition of the group forms a part of the learning environment. Relevant characteristics are group size, gender, age distribution, cultural background, level of experience, and seniority. As sharing and learning from each other is important to most participants, the group needs to be diverse enough to allow for differences in perspectives and experience and at the same time homogenous enough for participants to be able to identify with the other participants. It might not always be possible to influence group composition. However, paying attention to the impact of the group composition on the group dynamics is part of the facilitator's role.

Preprogram Communication With Participants

A welcome letter to participants should be sent before the start of the program along with information on the program, the list of participants, locations, accommodations (if applicable), and travel instructions. Usually we also ask participants to notify us in advance of any medical, dietary, or other requirements we need to be aware of.

A participant study guide should include working materials, teaching methodologies, workload, preprogram assignments, and modes of assessment if applicable. A bibliography and the biographies of facilitators are usually included in the packet as well.

Facilitators

The second chapter of this book discusses the role of the facilitator in depth. Now that we have addressed facilitation design, it is worth briefly revisiting the role of the facilitator. We compared the facilitator to an art director or stage manager, a role that can best be described as leading from behind. The participants are at the center stage of the program. The facilitator guides the learning process based on proven expertise in the field of intercultural communication and competence and the ability to manage learning and group processes. Berardo's Wheel of Intercultural Skills tool (see p. 355) can help individuals to identify, map, and build the types of content and process skills needed for this type of work. Basically you have to be able to work at three levels at the same time. First, as a facilitator you introduce the learning materials and lead the discussion on the content. A facilitator must be able to spontaneously add or relate to other content and refer participants to further reading and resources, which requires a substantial base of formal and informal experience to draw from. Second, the facilitator is a process manager, meaning he or she guides the learning process of the individual participants and the interaction that takes place in the group. How does the discussion develop in terms of group dynamics and learning of participants? What angles should be followed up and how? The discussion on the content usually is explicit; processes and dynamics that take place in the group or in an individual participant are more difficult to observe. A facilitator needs the ability not only to observe these processes and dynamics correctly but also to respond appropriately. Observations therefore always need to be checked first. We once had a participant who did not actively engage in the discussion. During a break, we asked that participant if the program was interesting enough. It turned out the participant was quite involved internally with a lot of mental work, which took all the participant's energy and focus. Third, as a facilitator you have to monitor organizational support and make adjustments as the program proceeds. Once we had to decide to move a whole group from a university location to a conference hotel in one hour. The university location was excellent until the students of that university took a one-hour break, and the noise level made any discussion in the group impossible.

Facilitating a group is complex. Regular reflection on one's own performance and on one's own strengths and weaknesses is advised. Working with cofacilitators or engaging in peer reviews offers the opportunity for reflection.

CONCLUDING REMARKS

In this chapter we provide a number of insights and experiences we have accumulated over the years in developing meaningful intercultural learning sessions for a multitude of participants from a wide variety of cultures and backgrounds. This chapter offers some practical guidelines for teachers and professionals in the development of meaningful intercultural competence building experiences.

An effective training program for intercultural learning should be grounded in theory and designed to transfer insights and theories to the specific context and learning needs of the participants. Participants' objectives are primarily based on their own specific contexts in the here and now in relating effectively and satisfactorily to culturally different others. Even when groups of participants are relatively similar and express similar needs, tailoring a successful program design specifically for each group is an essential element in the preparation of a facilitator. Experienced facilitators will recognize that a training design tends to run stale when it is taken off the shelf one time too many. Because of its dynamic character, an intercultural training program is a learning lab in situ that evolves as the learning experience is re-created each session in interaction with the experiences and reflections of a unique group of participants. The learning activities in this book, then, will obviously need to be adapted to specific situations and placed within the context of a broader training program.

We realize that a number of earlier publications include a wealth of additional insights and resources that are valuable and provide a more in-depth treatment of the topics we discuss in this chapter (e.g., Gudykunst, Guzley, & Hammer, 1996; Kohls & Knight, 1994; Landis, Bennett, & Bennett, 2004; Seeley, 1996; Singelis, 1998; Pedersen, 2002). Littrell and Salas (2005), for instance, provide a review of best practices and guidelines for cross-cultural training. Further reading therefore is highly recommended. If this chapter motivates you to do additional reading, we have achieved more than we intended.

REFERENCES

Bandura, A. (1977). *Social learning theory*. New York, NY: General Learning Press.

Bennett, M. (1998). *Basic concepts of intercultural communication*. Yarmouth, ME: Intercultural Press.

Brislin, R. W. (1989). Intercultural communication training. In M. K. Asante & W. B. Gudykunst (Eds.), *Handbook of international and intercultural communication* (pp. 441–457). Newbury Park, CA: Sage.

Deardorff, D. K. (2005). Matter of Logic. *International Educator* (May–June, pp. 26–31). New York: NAFSA.

Deardorff, D. K. (2006). Identification and assessment of intercultural competence as a student outcome of internationalization. *Journal of Studies in International Education, 10*(3), 241–266.

Deardorff, D. K. (Ed.). (2009). *The SAGE handbook of intercultural competence.* Thousand Oaks, CA: Sage.

Graff, A. (2004). Assessing intercultural training designs. *Journal of European Industrial Training, 28*(2–3–4), 199.

Gudykunst, W. B., Guzley, R., & Hammer, M. R. (1996). Designing intercultural training. In D. Landis & R. B. Bhagat (Eds.), *Handbook of intercultural training* (2nd ed., pp. 61–80). Thousand Oaks, CA: Sage.

Hammer, M. R. (2008). The intercultural development inventory (IDI): An approach for assessing and building intercultural competence. In M. A. Moodian (Ed.), *Contemporary leadership and intercultural competence: Understanding and utilizing cultural diversity to build successful organizations* (pp. 245–261). Thousand Oaks, CA: Sage.

Kohls, L. R., & Knight, J. M. *(1994)*. Developing intercultural awareness: A cross-cultural training handbook (2nd ed.). Yarmouth, ME: Intercultural Press.

Kolb, D. A. (1984). *Experiential learning: Experience as the source of learning and development.* Englewood Cliffs, NJ: Prentice Hall.

Krathwohl, D. (2002). A revision of Bloom's taxonomy: An overview. *Theory into Practice, 41*(4), 212–218.

Landis, D., Bennett, J. M., & Bennett, M. J. (Eds.). (2004). *Handbook of intercultural training* (3rd ed.). Thousand Oaks, CA: Sage.

Littrell, L. N., & Salas, E. (2005). A review of cross-cultural training: Best practices, guidelines, and research needs. *Human Resource Development Review, 4*, 305–334.

Oomkes, F. R., & Thomas R. H. (1992). *Cross-cultural communication: A trainer's manual.* Aldershot, UK: Gower.

Paige, M. (2004). Instrumentation in intercultural training. In D. Landis, J. M. Bennett, & M. J. Bennett (Eds.), *Handbook of intercultural training* (3rd ed., pp. 8–128). Thousand Oaks, CA: Sage.

Pedersen, P. (2000). *A handbook for developing multicultural awareness* (3rd ed.). Alexandria, VA: American Counseling Association.

Pusch, M. D. (1994). Cross-cultural training. In G. Althen (Ed.), *Learning across cultures* (pp. 109–144). Washington, DC: NAFSA, Association of International Educators.

Seelye, H. N. (Ed.). (1996). *Experiential activities for intercultural learning* (Vol. 1). Yarmouth, ME: Intercultural Press.

Simpson, E. J. (1972). *The classification of educational objectives in the psychomotor domain.* Washington, DC: Gryphon House.

Singelis, T. (Ed.). (1998). *Teaching about culture, ethnicity & diversity: Exercises and planned activities.* Newbury Park, CA: Sage.

ACTIVITIES

SECTION 1

Introduce Core Concepts

1. FRAMEWORK: INTERCULTURAL COMPETENCE MODEL

Darla K. Deardorff

This is the first research-based framework of intercultural competence reflecting the consensus of leading intercultural experts that can be used to guide the structure of intercultural training, curriculum, and assessment, as well as help individual learners map their own intercultural competence. (See Figure S1.1.)

Key Focus

Introduce core concepts

Objectives

As a result of working with this model, participants will

- understand components of intercultural competence,
- reflect on their own intercultural competence development,
- develop their own specific intercultural outcomes, and
- map their own intercultural competence development.

Appropriate Audience

Adults

Level of Challenge

Medium

Summary Description

Successful intercultural interactions are often a primary goal of intercultural training. So what does it mean to interact successfully with those from different cultures? This is the key question underlying the concept of intercultural competence and the focus of the doctoral research that led to the development of this intercultural competence framework. The process model of intercultural competence can be used by trainers in designing their training curriculum and by participants in mapping their own intercultural competence development. The five components are

- *Attitudes:* respect, openness, curiosity, and discovery. Openness and curiosity imply a willingness to risk and to move beyond one's comfort zone. In communicating respect to others, it is important to demonstrate that others are valued. These attitudes are foundational to the further development of knowledge and skills needed for intercultural competence.
- *Knowledge:* cultural self-awareness (meaning the way one's culture has influenced one's

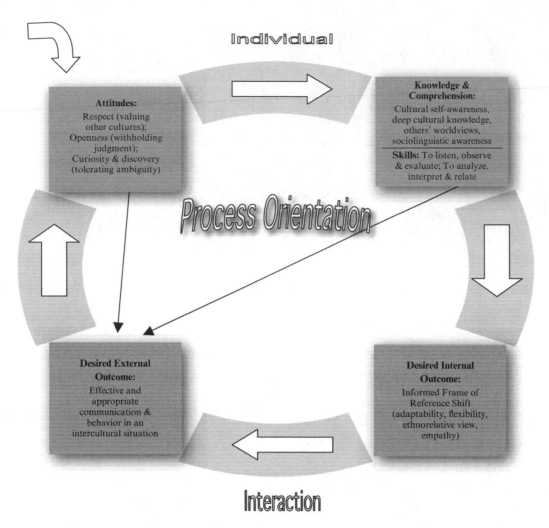

FIGURE S1.1   Process Model of Intercultural Competence

Note. From "Identification and assessment of intercultural competence as a student outcome of internationalization," by D. K. Deardorff, 2006, *Journal of Studies in International Education, 10*(3), 241–266; 2009a.

identity and worldview), culture-specific knowledge, deep cultural knowledge including understanding other worldviews, and sociolinguistic awareness. The one element agreed upon by all the intercultural scholars is the importance of understanding the world from others' perspectives.

- *Skills:* observation, listening, evaluating, analyzing, interpreting, and relating.
- *Internal outcomes:* These attitudes, knowledge, and skills ideally lead to an internal outcome that consists of flexibility, adaptability, an ethnorelative perspective, and empathy. These are aspects that occur within the individual as a result of the acquired attitudes, knowledge, and skills necessary for intercultural compe-

tence. At this point, individuals are able to see from others' perspectives and to respond to them according to the way the other person desires to be treated. Individuals may reach this outcome in varying degrees of success.

- *External outcomes:* The summation of the attitudes, knowledge, and skills, as well as the internal outcomes are demonstrated through the behavior and communication of the individual, which become the visible outcomes of intercultural competence experienced by others. This then becomes the agreed-upon definition of the intercultural scholars, that intercultural competence is the *effective* and *appropriate* behavior and communication in intercultural situations. However, it is important to understand that this definition is predicated on the elements highlighted here.

These five elements can be visualized through the process model of intercultural competence, thereby providing a framework, or map, to further guide efforts in developing intercultural competence.

Key Talking Points

- Intercultural competence unfortunately does not just happen for most; instead, it must be intentionally addressed. Having a framework of intercultural competence such as this one can help guide individuals in mapping their own development toward intercultural competence.
- Competence in general is defined as knowledge, skills, and attitudes. Over five decades of work exist on intercultural competence in the United States. (See Chapter 3 for further discussion.) This is the first grounded research-based framework, and it details the specific elements in those competence areas agreed upon by leading intercultural experts.
- This framework illustrates that intercultural competence is a *process*—lifelong—and there is no one point at which an individual becomes completely interculturally competent. Thus, it is important to pay as much attention to the development process of how one acquires the necessary knowledge, skills, and attitudes as to the actual aspects of intercultural competence. Critical reflection becomes a powerful tool in the process of intercultural competence development. The self-evaluation tool (Handout S1.1) can be used by participants for self-reflection. Further, a one-time training program is not sufficient for intercultural competence development.
- Intercultural competence doesn't happen in a vacuum, so it is important to be aware of the context in which this competence is occurring, and in particular in the interaction itself, as noted in the framework.
- Attitudes are at the foundation of intercultural competence development, noted by the arrow in the upper left box of the process model of intercultural competence (Figure S1.1) as the starting point. Without openness, respect (which manifests itself differently according to

the cultural context), and curiosity, it is very difficult to pursue knowledge or skills that are essential to intercultural competence development. One way to move individuals toward these attitudes is by challenging their assumptions. The Observe, State, Explore, Evaluate (OSEE) tool (see p. 58) is another way to do that.

- This framework illustrates that it is possible for an individual to have the requisite attitudes and be minimally effective and appropriate in behavior and communication even without further knowledge or skills. Adding the necessary knowledge and skills may ensure that an individual can be more effective and appropriate in his or her intercultural interactions. With the added flexibility, adaptability, and empathy, one can be even more effective and appropriate in intercultural interactions.
- What we see and experience with intercultural competence are the external outcomes: behavior and communication that is effective and appropriate. It is important to stress the implications of *effective* and *appropriate* behavior and communication: Effectiveness can be determined by the individual, while the appropriateness can only be determined by the other person, with appropriateness being directly related to cultural sensitivity.
- Note that the only item agreed upon by all experts in this study is found in the knowledge component—understanding others' worldviews and being able to see from other perspectives.
- The components in this framework were agreed upon by leading intercultural experts as absolutely essential to intercultural competence; however, intercultural competence is not limited to only what is found in this framework. This leads to questions such as, What is missing in this framework? What elements could be added for a particular context?
- While this is primarily a U.S.-centric framework of intercultural competence, it is being used by organizations and institutions around the world, and those from other cultures have also found this framework useful within non-U.S. contexts. That being said, it's interesting to explore what intercultural competence looks like from non-U.S. and non-Western

perspectives. (Some answers can be found in Deardorff, 2009a.)

- It is difficult for any model or framework to capture reality, so there are obvious limitations; end by noting that intercultural competence is quite complex, which is why it takes a lifetime to develop.

Suggested Uses

Use the following model in coaching or training situations to help participants understand more about their own intercultural competence development:

1. Start off by asking participants for their definition of intercultural competence (or ask, "What's necessary to be successful in interactions with those from different backgrounds?") before discussing this framework. Start from their own definitions before sharing this research-based definition and framework.

2. Introduce the model by distributing handouts of the model to each participant (see Figure S1.1 on page 46), and then highlight the various components using the summary and talking points.

3. Ask participants to circle two to three key elements they feel are most important in their particular context. Encourage participants to write down specific learning outcomes based on those elements using the SMART format (see Chapter 3, pp. 30–31). Participants could even develop a learning contract (Knowles, 1975) based on those outcomes in which they include the following: outcomes, how they will reach those outcomes, and evidence they have achieved those outcomes.

4. Use the self-reflection tool based on the process model of intercultural competence (Deardorff, 2009a) found in Handout S1.1. as a way for participants to engage in reflection on their own intercultural competence levels. In coaching situations, focus on the items rated lower by participants and help them develop a learning contract for those items. Participants can also use this reflection tool to help map areas of intercultural competence development where they feel they need more focus.

Facilitation Tips and Suggestions

- While the information here is sufficient to use the framework with participants, it is recommended to first read Deardorff (2006) for a more thorough background on the framework itself so that the facilitator can be even more knowledgeable about the framework when presenting and using it in coaching and training situations.

- It is best to do more than just present the model; participants need to apply it in some way, whether through discussion, or by using the self-reflection worksheet, and so on.

- This framework can be used to structure the training curriculum so that intercultural development efforts can be included in a more comprehensive, integrated approach instead of through random, ad hoc approaches that may occur in intercultural training.

- It is recommended to use this framework in conjunction with other intercultural frameworks, such as Milton Bennett's (1993) developmental model of intercultural sensitivity, in which this framework enhances the latter stages of that model by providing a more in-depth understanding of the specific elements of intercultural competence.

- This can work with older teenagers as well as adults, especially teenagers who are already abroad.

- Reflection questions (Handout S1.2) based on this framework are also available for trainers and teachers to use in reflecting upon their own skills in a classroom (Deardorff, 2011).

- If questions come up about assessment, respond by saying that based on research, assessing intercultural competence requires a multimeasure, multiperspective approach. One tool is not sufficient for assessing the complexities of intercultural competence. For more on assessing intercultural competence, see Deardorff (2009b).

- Another version of this model, known as the pyramid model of intercultural competence (Deardorff, 2006, 2009a), could also be used. Some audiences relate better to this more linear framework, and it's also easier to read the actual elements in the model (same elements, just a different way of visualizing them). When using the pyramid model, it is important to stress that there is no point at which we become interculturally competent since this is a lifelong process of development and it's not obvious in the more linear model.

About This Framework

This framework was developed from the research for my doctoral dissertation (Deardorff, 2004). The most basic question underlying this dissertation—What is necessary to get along together?—was motivated by my own faith beliefs, namely those involving peace making. Academically, this dissertation was written through an assessment lens: If we are going to assess intercultural competence, we must first define this concept much more clearly than has been done in the past.

REFERENCES

Bennett, M. (1993). Towards a developmental model of intercultural sensitivity. In R. M. Paige (Ed.), *Education for the intercultural experience* (pp. 21–71). Yarmouth, ME: Intercultural Press.

Deardorff, D. K. (2004). *The identification and assessment of intercultural competence as a student outcome of internationalization in higher education in the United States* (Unpublished doctoral dissertation). North Carolina State University, Raleigh.

Deardorff, D. K. (2006). Identification and assessment of intercultural competence as a student outcome of internationalization. *Journal of Studies in International Education, 10*(3), 241–266.

Deardorff, D. K. (2008). Intercultural competence: A definition, model and implications for education abroad. In V. Savicki (Ed.), *Developing intercultural competence and transformation: Theory, research, and application in international education* (pp. 32–52). Sterling, VA: Stylus.

Deardorff, D. K. (Ed.). (2009a). *The SAGE handbook of intercultural competence*. Thousand Oaks, CA: Sage.

Deardorff, D. K. (2009b). Implementing intercultural competence assessment. In D. K. Deardorff (Ed.), *The SAGE handbook of intercultural competence* (pp. 477–491). Thousand Oaks, CA: Sage.

Deardorff, D. K. (2011). Exploring a framework for interculturally competent teaching in diverse classrooms. In M. Magnan, M. Soderqvist, H. G. Van Liempd, & F. Wittman (Eds.), *Internationalisation of European Higher Education Handbook*. Berlin, Germany: Raabe Academic Publishers.

Knowles, M. S. (1975). *Self-directed learning: A guide for learners and teachers*. Englewood Cliffs, NJ: Prentice Hall.

 HANDOUT S1.1

INTERCULTURAL COMPETENCE: SELF-REFLECTION

PART ONE. The items listed below are invaluable in developing intercultural competence and in interacting effectively and appropriately with people from other cultures. Please rate yourself on the following:

5 = very high   4 = high   3 = average   2 = below average   1 = poor

	5	4	3	2	1
1. Respect (valuing other cultures)	5	4	3	2	1
2. Openness (to intercultural learning and to people from other cultures)	5	4	3	2	1
3. Tolerance for ambiguity	5	4	3	2	1
4. Flexibility (in using appropriate communication styles and behaviors, in intercultural situations)	5	4	3	2	1
5. Curiosity and discovery	5	4	3	2	1
6. Withholding judgment	5	4	3	2	1
7. Cultural self-awareness/understanding	5	4	3	2	1
8. Understanding others' worldviews	5	4	3	2	1
9. Culture-specific knowledge	5	4	3	2	1
10. Sociolinguistic awareness (awareness of using other languages in social contexts)	5	4	3	2	1
11. Skills to listen, observe, and interpret	5	4	3	2	1
12. Skills to analyze, evaluate, and relate	5	4	3	2	1
13. Empathy (do unto others as you would have others do unto you)	5	4	3	2	1
14. Adaptability (to different communication styles/behaviors, to new cultural environments)	5	4	3	2	1
15. Communication Skills (appropriate and effective communication in intercultural settings)	5	4	3	2	1

PART TWO. Reflect on situations requiring intercultural competence—what helped make you more appropriate and effective in your interactions? Now reflect on how you can continue to develop your intercultural competence, especially areas you rated as lower.

Note. Based on intercultural competence models developed by Deardorff, 2004, "Identification and Assessment of Intercultural Competence as a Student Outcome of Internationalization," by D. K. Deardorff, 2006, *Journal of Studies in International Education, 10*(3), 241–266.

 HANDOUT S1.2

INTERCULTURALLY COMPETENT TEACHING—REFLECTION QUESTIONS

The following reflection questions can be used by teachers in continuing to develop their own intercultural competence.

Attitudes
- How truly open am I to those from different cultural, socioeconomic, and religious backgrounds?
- Do I make quick assumptions about a student? Do I prejudge learners or situations or do I withhold judgment while I explore the multifacets of the situation?
- Do I measure a student's behavior based on my own culturally conditioned expectations or do I try to understand a student's behavior based on his or her own culturally conditioned background?
- Do I value those from different backgrounds? How do I demonstrate that I value others, even when I may disagree with their beliefs and opinions?
- Am I eager to learn about different cultures and, specifically, am I eager to learn about my learners' backgrounds and experiences? Do I make an effort to learn more?

Knowledge
- Can I describe my own cultural conditioning? For example, what cultural values affect how I behave and communicate with others? What are some of my core beliefs and how have they been culturally influenced?
- How would I describe my worldview?
- How would I describe some of learners' worldviews? How might these differ from the ways in which I see the world?
- How much do I know about my learners' cultural backgrounds? What information am I missing and how can I get that information?
- How can I incorporate my learners' worldviews into my course materials?
- What worldviews are demonstrated through the course materials I currently use? How can I enhance those materials so that other worldviews are represented?

Skills
- How much do I really listen to my learners?
- Do I engage in active observation in my classroom, paying attention to subtle nuances and dynamics among my learners? In my interactions with my learners?
- Do I engage in active reflection of my teaching practice and of my interactions with those from different cultural backgrounds? Do I not only seek to understand why something occurred but what lessons I learned from the situation?
- Do I know how to evaluate interactions and situations through an intercultural lens, seeking to understand underlying cultural explanations for what occurred?

Internal Outcomes (adaptability, flexibility, etc.)
- Do I know how learners want to be treated or do I assume they want to be treated by my cultural standards?
- Am I able to adapt my behavior and communication style to accommodate learners from different culturally conditioned communication styles?

- Am I able to be flexible in responding to learners' learning needs, seeking to understand those needs from their cultural perspectives?
- Can I easily view knowledge, cultural artifacts, or a situation or issue from multiple perspectives?

External outcomes (communication, behavior)
- How culturally appropriate have I been in my interactions with my learners? In my teaching? How would my learners answer this question?
- Was I able to meet my goals in an appropriate and effective manner?
- What could I do differently in the future to be more appropriate and effective in my communication and behavior, both in interpersonal interactions and in my teaching?

General Reflection Questions
In reflecting on how teachers can help develop learners' intercultural competence, the following questions arise:

- How can teachers specifically incorporate learners' cultural perspectives into the course?
- How can teachers allow space for learners to reflect on their own intercultural competence development?
- What role can teachers play in mentoring learners in this development?
- What role can others in the broader community play in developing learners' intercultural competence?
- What role can technology play in learners' development of knowledge and skills in relating to those from different backgrounds?
- How can teachers help learners demonstrate respect (in culturally appropriate ways) and openness to other ways of viewing the world?
- How can learners work together effectively and appropriately in small groups during the course?
- How can teachers move beyond objective culture in the classroom to pushing learners to learn more about subjective culture, which affects the ways in which learners actually interact with others?
- How can teachers help learners develop an intercultural lens through which to view the world and to think interculturally?

Note. Based on the Deardorff intercultural competence models, 2006, 2009; *The SAGE Handbook of Intercultural Competence*, by D. K. Deardorff, Ed., 2009, Thousand Oaks, CA: Sage; "Identification and Assessment of Intercultural Competence as a Student Outcome of Internationalization," by D. K. Deardorff, 2006, *Journal of Studies in International Education*, 10(3), 241–266. Copyright 2006 by D. K. Deardorff. Deardorff, D. K. (2011). Exploring a framework for interculturally competent teaching in diverse classrooms." In M. Magnan, M. Soderqvist, H. G. Van Liempd, and F. Wittman (Eds.) *Internationalisation of European Higher Education Handbook*. Berlin, Germany: Raabe Academic Publishers.

2. FRAMEWORK:
DESCRIBE-ANALYZE-EVALUATE (DAE)

Kyoung-Ah Nam

This model (see Table S1.1) is an alternative to what may be the most widely used intercultural exercise: describe, interpret, evaluate (DIE). DIE asks people to observe an unusual object or a photograph of an unfamiliar scene, and then describe what they see, interpret possible meanings, and finally evaluate by giving their value judgments. While the DIE exercise has been a favorite in intercultural communication, the ambiguity between interpretation and evaluation and the negative association of the word *die* in English have been a problem. This model proposes a DAE version using a significant Korean word, 대, DAE (in phonetics [dæ]), as a more positive and constructive acronym (Nam & Condon, 2010).

Key Focus

Introduce core concepts

Type of Activity

Framework

Objectives

As a result of working with this model, participants will

- discern between what can be said objectively, what can be said in the realm of inference or speculation, and what may be expressed as value judgment and personal opinion;
- foster self-awareness of personal and cultural assumptions; and
- learn to appreciate cognitive complexity and the importance of frame shifting when encountering the unfamiliar.

Appropriate Audience

All learners

Level of Challenge

Medium

Summary Description

As an acronym for the model, DAE is an alternative of DIE. By adapting DIE to DAE, *analyze* raises fewer questions than *interpret*. It is clearer to ask participants to interpret and analyze (objectivity) than interpret (subjective judgment). In addition to avoiding the negative association of the DIE acronym, the choice of a word from a language other than English with significant intercultural meanings may provide additional value.

The DAE model is an engaging way to bring out several themes important in communication generally and intercultural relations specifically. We often respond to people or situations unfamiliar to us with our most subjective evaluations, projecting our judgments onto what we think we see (or hear or feel or otherwise perceive). In other words, our implicit response is often to evaluate—using words such as beautiful, exotic, impersonal, friendly, strange, and so on.

This model encourages reversing the usual order of response, withholding one's first reactions, and in the process becoming more aware of how easily and unconsciously one may trespass into the realm of speculation and judgment, and how difficult it can be to limit one's comments to what can be described directly. The process suggested by this model is a critical step in cultural competence building, since these three kinds of observations (describe, analyze, evaluate) are often not distinguished, and people react and speak from personal and cultural perspectives as if they were describing some objective truth.

This simplest of models helps to foster a more thoughtful, sensitive, and exploratory atmosphere for serious discussions of more complex intercultural topics. It invites greater attentiveness to what is presented and thus encourages people to observe things they had

Table S1.1   The DAE Model

DAE		Process	Examples	Standards for Agreement
Level 1: Describe	• What happened? • What was said? • What did you see? • Statements about what appears to be "objectively" out there	What I see	"This is a plastic cup."	General agreement
Level 2: Analyze	• How do these observations fit together, and what else must be assumed to make sense of them? • Try to think of at least three different analyses/interpretations • "This might mean that . . ."	What helps explain what I see?	"Plastic cups are made from oil."	Alternative explanations possible
Level 3: Evaluate	• What positive or negative feelings do you have? (My gut reaction) • My reasoned judgment (any feelings of resistance when I tried to do D and A, but if you ask how I feel, if you ask my opinion . . .) • "Here's how I feel about that!"	What I feel about what I see	"Plastic cups are wasteful."	No one else has to agree

not immediately noticed, and to be more aware of what they do not realize. Thus through this model, a kind of modesty through self-awareness as well as objectivity may be encouraged.

The broader purpose of the model, of course, is to guide people toward greater discernment when encountering the unfamiliar, including mindfully withholding judgment. In some ways, this is an abnormal act, as it appears our reactions can be judgmental even before we consciously realize what provokes that reaction.

Key Talking Points

One way to explain the components of DAE is to pose three questions and indicate standards for agreement:

> Description: What is going on? (general agreement)
> Analysis: Why is it happening? (alternative explanations possible)
> Evaluation: How do I feel about it? (no one else to agree)

(Or if showing someone a photo of that person) How do I think she or he feels?

Background of DAE

The Korean word 대 (DAE [dæ]) is a significant and one of the most widely used words in Korea (see Handout S1.3). As shown in the following, it carries several meanings that reflect the values of this exercise: counter to our instincts; serious; and a foundation (*Si-Sa Elite Korean-English Dictionary*, 1996, p. 394):

1. 대 (dae; 對 in Chinese): "the opposite, anti, against"
2. 대 (dae; 大 in Chinese): "great," "prominent," "serious"
3. 대 (dae; 臺 in Chinese): "support, foundation"[1]

The first meaning of 대—the opposite, anti, against, or to go against our habits or instinct—is at the core of the DAE exercise. When facing something unfamiliar or different from our own cultural and social values, we unconsciously tend to immediately judge and evaluate rather than reflect on what we see or what actually happened. In addition, 대 can also mean "great," "important," "prominent," and "serious." The process of first describing and analyzing before evaluating is important to understand one's own cultural biases and to better appreciate different aspects and values of other cultures. It is a mindful perspective when encountering the unfamiliar. 대 also means "foundation" in Korean. The ability to be able to describe and objectively analyze before making any judgment or evaluation is part of the foundation in the field of intercultural communication, and underlies many of the capabilities of those who work professionally across cultures.

Use of DAE Model

The DAE model can be used with the same goals and in the same situations as the more traditional DIE model.

In its most frequently used form, as developed by Bennett, Bennett, and Stillings (1977), participants are presented with an unusual object, photograph, or other stimulus to use as the basis to apply the DAE model. Then, often working in smaller groups, people are asked to describe, as objectively as possible, what they see, avoiding guesses or value judgments. For many this is a surprisingly difficult task. If the stimulus item is a photograph, for example, observers often find it hard to distinguish what the picture represents from the meanings that those viewing the photo infer.

For example, if shown a picture of a student in a classroom putting her feet on the empty desk in front of her, some may say they see a student who is relaxing, while others may say that they see a student who is rude, and someone else may see behavior that is absolutely unacceptable in a classroom. Generally, people find it most challenging to restrict their first comments to those that can be considered objective, limited to the visual information presented. The next task, analyze or make educated guesses, is somewhat easier since one has more freedom to imagine contexts in which many analyses and explanations might be plausible. Here is where first reactions that were not purely descriptive may now be appropriate. The last task, to express their evaluations, is the easiest of all, as there may be an even wider range of judgments offered depending upon, in this case, one's expectations of appropriate behavior in the classroom.

Used in this way, the DAE model can be employed in a variety of teaching, training, and coaching settings:

- After following the conventional procedure in the model, participants may then talk about their feelings, memories, and stories that they connect with what was just discussed by the classmates. As a result, the model moves beyond one that emphasizes careful observation, critical thinking, and suspension of judgment. It provides one of those teachable moments when the learning links the objective and the affective, the content and relationship meanings, which in turn may also lead to increased respect and understanding among the participants themselves.

- In ethnographic fieldwork, to increase students' sensitivity to visual detail and complexity, requiring students to continue to describe before moving to analysis and judgments (including aesthetic and rhetorical effectiveness), the DAE model sharpens the students' abilities as photographers and critics.

- In training before departure for another country and assessment of the impact of the experience abroad, photographs of social situations in the host society, especially of potential challenges, may be presented. The DAE serves to sharpen the perception, clarify possible explanations for what one sees in the photo, and encourage suspension of judgments. Upon return, the sojourners may be expected to notice even more detail in such photos, suggest more thoughtful analyses, and evoke fresh and perhaps more positive evaluations.

Key Insights and Learnings

- *Maintaining objectivity.* We easily project what is inside us onto what can be observed outside us. Our inferences and feelings easily become expressed as if they were objective descriptions and facts, especially when we talk about the unfamiliar.

- *Cultivating self-awareness.* Judgments often reveal more about the person making a judgment and the cultural meanings the person has internalized than about the image or other physical stimuli that evokes the judgment.

This theme is one that people come to recognize through their discussions of the process and includes stereotypes that exist only in the mind of the observer and not in what is objectively presented.

- *Avoiding misunderstandings.* Every day we talk about our feelings and speculations about others as if they were statements of fact; if we do this in our own family, imagine how much we make these mistakes when we talk about people from culturally different backgrounds including gender, generation, religion, geographical location, sexual orientation, race and ethnicity, and so on. There is a danger of presenting things as fact or description that may actually arise from personal, cultural, and often historic power relationships. History, descriptions of a culture, and other such categories may be questioned as presenting a description, which is a disguised evaluation.

- *Frame-shifting.* Learn and realize the importance of frame-shifting when encountering unfamiliar people, situations, objects, and such. Participants learn how surprisingly difficult it is to hold their subjective judgment until objective description and analysis have been considered; however, they also find how this suspension of judgment can better enable them to comprehend and work effectively in different environments.

Facilitation Tips and Suggestions

This is not about new information but about moving beyond personal and cultural assumptions we as humans make. Therefore, this simple model often requires more time than one would think to debrief. Even one sentence may have to be discussed from various perspectives before people realize that what they thought was actually about descriptions of

their own feelings rather than descriptions of the facts.

About This Framework

The DIE exercise, developed in the 1970s by Bennett, Bennett, and Stillings (1977), was derived from general semantics exercises in the speech discipline decades before intercultural communication emerged as a field in itself. It was originally created by Janet M. Bennett and Milton Bennett for use in intercultural communication workshops at the University of Minnesota.

Special thanks to John Condon (1967). The DAE model was developed based on our coauthored article (Nam & Condon, 2010). I was inspired, encouraged, and guided by him throughout the development process. This model would not have been completed without his support and inspiration.

NOTE

1. Before the phonetic writing system for the Korean language (Han Gul) was invented in the 15th century by King Sejong in the Chosun Dynasty, Korean people spoke Korean, but Chinese characters were used for writing. For this reason, some Korean vocabulary reflects Chinese influence and Chinese characters remain in limited use for word clarification in modern Korean.

REFERENCES

Bennett, J. M., Bennett, M. J., & Stillings, K. (1977). *Intercultural communication workshop facilitator's manual.* Portland, OR: Portland State University.

Condon, J. (1967). *Semantics and communication.* New York, NY: Macmillan.

Nam, K-A, & Condon, J. (2010). The D.I.E. is cast: The continuing evolution of intercultural communication's favorite classroom exercise. *International Journal of Intercultural Relations, 34*(1), 81–87.

 HANDOUT S1.3

DIFFERENT MEANINGS OF DAE (대) IN KOREAN

DAE (대) in the Korean language carries at least 20 different meanings (*Si-Sa Elite Korean-English dictionary*, 1996)

대: 1) a bamboo (flexibility)
대 (對 in Chinese):*
       2) the opposite; anti; against
       3) a pair; a counterpart; a parallel; a couple
       4) versus; against; between; toward; to

대 (大 in Chinese):
       5) great (scholar); prominent (writer)
       6) serious (matter); grave (question)
       7) largeness; bigness; greatness; large size
       8) heavy (loss); severe (storm)

대 (臺 in Chinese):
       9) a support; foundation; stand; a rest; a pedestal; a base; a rack
      10) a level; a mark
      11) a unit of counting automobiles, machines, and so forth
      12) a zone; a region (e.g., a tropical zone)
대: 13) a stalk; a stem; a pipe; a holder
      14) spirit; mettle; backbone; pluck; courage
      15) a smoke; a puff
      16) a blow; a stroke; a punch; a hit
      17) a shot; an injection

대 (代 in Chinese):
      18) a generation; an age (in his 20s); an era
      19) a price; a charge; a rate; a fee

대 (隊 in Chinese):
      20) a party; a company; a body (of troops); a corps

Note: The phonetic writing system for the Korean language (Han Gul) was invented in the 15th century by King Sejong in the Chosun Dynasty. Before then, Korean was a spoken language but Chinese characters were used for writing. Based on this historical background, some Korean vocabulary has Chinese roots, and the Chinese characters remain in limited use for word clarification in modern Korean.

Reproduced from: Kyoung-Ah Nam, "Framework: Describe-Analyze-Evaluate (DAE)," in *Building Cultural Competence: Innovative Activities and Models,* eds. K. Berardo and D. K. Deardorff (Sterling, VA: Stylus, 2012), 53–57.

3. FRAMEWORK: OBSERVE, STATE, EXPLORE, EVALUATE (OSEE) TOOL

Darla K. Deardorff

This tool is inspired by the scientific method and provides a practical process for moving beyond assumptions.

O—observe (and listen to) what is happening

S—state objectively what is happening

E—explore different explanations for what is happening

E—evaluate which explanation(s) is the most likely one(s)

(Deardorff & Deardorff, 2000; Deardorff, 2008)

Key Focus

Introduce core concepts

Objectives

As a result of working with this model, participants will

- understand the process for moving beyond assumptions and
- use the tool to reflect more objectively on a cross-cultural situation.

Appropriate Audience

Adults

Level of Challenge

Medium

Summary Description

Making assumptions is an inherent part of the human experience. In developing intercultural competence, it is important to develop skills for moving beyond assumptions. OSEE starts with the basics of observation, and listening—of really being aware of what is occurring in intercultural situations, since this is an essential skill in intercultural competence development and a key starting point. The next step is to state as objectively as possible what is happening. This is much more difficult than it sounds, and a variety of activities can be used to help students practice the development of objective statements, including viewing brief film clips and writing about them. The next step, exploring different explanations, addresses the need to see from others' perspectives. It also allows one to begin to move beyond initial assumptions that may have been made inadvertently. Different explanations could include personal and cultural explanations, the latter of which necessitates the need to know culture-specific information. The last step, evaluation, is the most difficult, since it is often challenging to know which explanation(s) is the most likely one for the situation that is occurring. There are a number of different ways to evaluate the likely explanations, including collecting further information through conversations with others and asking questions. When these steps are followed, one is able to move beyond assumptions and view behaviors more objectively, thus achieving a measure of intercultural competence.

Key Talking Points

- Making assumptions is an inherent part of the human experience. In developing intercultural competence, it is important to develop skills for moving beyond assumptions.
- This tool provides a practical way in which individuals can respond more objectively in intercultural situations.
- Emphasize that it is important to first observe and listen carefully in situations—these are key intercultural competence skills.
- Objectively stating what is happening can sometimes be difficult to do (without letting our judgment enter in).
- In exploring possible explanations for what is happening, a cultural explanation could just

be one explanation; there could be a combination of explanations including physical, environmental, or personal explanations.

- When evaluating explanations (often the most difficult step to do), possibilities could include asking a cultural guide, seeking information through culture-specific books, or talking with the person directly, depending on the context.
- Using OSEE helps participants begin to move beyond cultural assumptions and learn a fundamental lesson in cross-cultural understanding, that of discovering the rationale underlying others' behavior, given that most people behave rationally (Storti, 1994).

Suggested Uses

Use this tool when focusing on intercultural competence development. For example, this can be used in conjunction with the process model of intercultural competence (Deardorff, 2006; also see Figure S1.1, on page 46) as a way to go into more depth on the specific skills highlighted in that model. The OSEE tool can be applied to film clips, critical incidents, photos (such as those from *National Geographic*) or with examples such as the following:

1. A student calls her instructor *Teacher*. The teacher gets quite upset, and says, "Stop calling me Teacher; my name is Ms. Smith. Please call me Ms. Smith."
2. Two people of the same sex hold hands.
3. A person slurps when eating.
4. A person does not make eye contact.

Facilitation Tips and Suggestions

- One way to introduce the OSEE tool is to have participants fill in the blanks on the worksheet in Handout S1.4. Ensure participants brainstorm various explanations before moving to the evaluation—this helps establish the relativity of interpreting different behaviors. For example, possible explanations

for someone's not making eye contact could include the following:

- ○ The person is shy.
- ○ The person is trying to hide something.
- ○ The person doesn't want to be called on or singled out.
- ○ The person is blind.
- ○ The person considers it impolite to make direct eye contact.

- Participants can practice applying the OSEE tool through discussion or through a writing assignment, depending on the context.
- Note that the tool is pronounced O-SEE and not spelled out (O-S-E-E).

About This Framework

This tool was developed through conversations with my husband, who is a physicist, in an attempt to apply the scientific method to intercultural situations. It follows the scientific method, which begins with making an observation.

REFERENCES

Deardorff, D. K. (2006). Identification and assessment of intercultural competence as a student outcome of internationalization. *Journal of Studies in International Education, 10*(3), 241–266.

Deardorff, D. K. (2008). "Intercultural Competence: A Definition, Model and Implications for Education Abroad." In Victor Savicki (Ed.), *Developing intercultural competence and transformation: Theory, research, and application in international education,* (pp. 32–52). Sterling, VA: Stylus.

Deardorff, D. K., & Deardorff, D. L. (2000). *Diversity awareness and training: Tools for cultural awareness.* Presentation made at North Carolina State University, Raleigh.

Storti, C. (1994). *Cross-cultural dialogues: 74 brief encounters with cultural difference.* Yarmouth, ME: Intercultural Press.

 HANDOUT S1.4

MOVING BEYOND ASSUMPTIONS: THE OSEE TOOL

O - _____ what is happening

S - _____ what is happening objectively

E - *EXPLORE* _____ for what is happening

E - _____ the explanations

Note: Adapted from Deardorff, D. K., & Deardorff, D. L. (2000). *Diversity awareness and training: Tools for cultural awareness*. Presentation made at North Carolina State University, Raleigh.

4. FOUR ANALOGIES

Kate Berardo

Through the four analogies of an onion, iceberg, fish in water, and lenses, participants quickly and effectively learn how to think about culture, helping them to think creatively about what it means to work across cultural boundaries. This simple exercise serves as a more creative and high-context way of introducing and defining culture and establishes an interactive tone for a training session.

Key Focus

Introduce core concepts

Type of Activity

Icebreaker

Objectives

As a result of this activity, participants will learn to
* describe culture and its influence on us in a creative, multidimensional way, and
* work sensibly and sensitively with concepts of culture.

Appropriate Audience

Adults, teenagers, children

Level of Challenge

Low

Group Size

1 to 100 plus people

Time

20 minutes

Materials

Handouts

Preparation

Distribute the photos around the room (for example, if people are at tables, place one photo on each table; see Handouts S1.5, S.1.6, S1.7, and S1.8). Ideally, this can be done in advance, either before the start of the program or during a break, depending on when you are doing this exercise.

Activity Setup

Introduce the activity, for example: "In front of you you will find a picture, either of an onion, an iceberg, a fish in water, or lenses. All of these are analogies for understanding culture. For the next two minutes, I would like you to discuss with the people at your tables the following questions" (show these questions on a flipchart or PowerPoint slide):

* What is the similarity between the object in front of you and culture?
* What insight does this give you about how to work effectively across cultures?

Managing the Activity

Give people two minutes to discuss the questions related to the analogies. Most of the time people are self-sufficient; however, at least initially, it may be useful to circulate to check if there are any questions.

Debriefing the Activity

Show each image in the handouts on a main slide (or ask the group at the table with the corresponding image to hold it up), and ask one person to summarize the group's discussion. Supplement the group's interpretation with the following:

Onion

- Like an onion, people are shaped by many layers of culture: national culture, regional culture, organizational culture, and many other types of culture (gender, religion, family, etc.).
- Often, we may catch ourselves thinking about someone as only one layer, for example, a French person or a woman. We then typically get stuck in divisive language: *us* and *them*. When we think of or see only one layer of an individual, we are not seeing that person for the complex individual he or she is and what he or she brings to a situation. We want to be recognized as being complex individuals shaped by a number of layers, and we need to do the same for others.

Iceberg

- When we think of a culture, we often tend to think of the tip of the iceberg elements (food, dress, national symbols such as famous buildings, a nation's flag, etc.), yet the majority of culture is hidden from view and is represented by deeper elements of culture, such as ideas about what is right and wrong and fundamental beliefs.
- The deeper the element of a culture's iceberg you experience, the harder it is to adapt or shift. We can often adapt more easily to the local customs of dress or food, or adopt another culture's way of doing, such as how to pass out business cards, but when asked to switch how we think about something, or when our worldview is different from someone else's, it becomes more challenging.
- The goal of learning about cultures is to continue to probe the depths of an iceberg to seek to understand the drivers behind the actions and behaviors of another.

Fish in Water

- Like water to a fish, the influence of our own culture is often invisible to us: It is simply what we know and what we depend on for survival.
- It is not until we become a fish out of water that we may realize our dependency on our own cultural environments or be able to see clearly what the water was that we lived in.
- Often the first step in working across cultures is to discover your own ocean and understand your own cultural influences.

Lenses

- Refer to the quote attributed to French-Cuban writer Anaïs Nin: "We don't see things as they are; we see them as we are." Note that culture is a system for making meaning of things, and as a result, we all wear cultural lenses or filters when we interpret a situation. This may lead to different concepts about everything, from what makes a good meeting to the role of a teacher or leader.
- Highlight that the goal of working across cultures is to recognize our own lenses or cultural filter we are wearing in any situation and learn to put on the lenses of someone from a different cultural background.

Encourage people to remember these analogies as you start to work with the topic of culture throughout the day. Recall the objectives of your session and then make the transition to the next activity in your program.

Key Insights and Learnings

Aside from these key messages, this exercise also demonstrates there are many interpretations when we are looking at the same thing—even these images. When facilitating this exercise it is important not to suggest that other people's interpretations are wrong. The more you can build on the interpretations others offer with the insights and learnings in the preceding sections, the better.

Variations

Variation 1: When the group size is big (e.g., in an auditorium setting), you can still use this icebreaker by showing the four images on one slide, dividing up the room into four groups each focused on one image, and ask individuals to pair off to discuss the answer to each question.

Variation 2: Begin by asking people to create their own analogies for culture (either drawing them or describing them, working alone or in small groups) and then build on their answers with these four analogies.

Variation 3: Make this an icebreaker introduction by creating name tags for participants with an image of one of the four analogies. Instruct people to find another person (or form small groups, depending on the group size) with the same image and introduce themselves. If you can't print the images on the name tags, simply put a number on a name tag, and once people have formed pairs or small groups, assign a picture to each number. Then have the pair or small group discuss the image. When you reconvene as a group, have people introduce their partners and say what they discussed about their image. That way, you will be introducing the participants and the topic of the session (culture) simultaneously.

Variation 4: Apply this same process by using other analogies for culture (software, kaleidoscope, pyramid, mirror, garden, tree, or house) and their images. You could also put pictures on the table, even others (from magazines, Internet, and so on), and ask participants to select an image they feel represents culture and then invite them to tell the group how the image they selected is an analogy to culture. The goal here is to create a multidimensional view of what culture is, rather than giving a dry definition of the term. Choose a set of analogies that effectively highlights some of the key messages you want to convey about culture or that tie to your objectives for the larger session. The following are examples of other analogies and some of the key lessons.

House

* Culture, like a house, is a refuge and a place of comfort. When interacting across cultures, it is important people understand there will be some discomfort in moving beyond the house.
* Clear boundaries delineate the inside of the house from the rest of the world. Likewise, culture often determines who is part of our group (the *in* group) and who is not part of our group and not like us (the *out* group). This is one of the realities of the human experience. In crossing cultures, it is important to pay attention to how we respond to those who are not like us.

Tree

* Culture, like a tree, has deep roots and it is important to understand historical contexts of cultures.
* Likewise, there are different variations (branches of the tree) in a culture but they

come from the same roots. Thus, when we talk about a culture, it's important to remember it is not monolithic and static but is changing, growing, and contains many variations.

Variation 5: To involve more of the five senses in the process, give each participant a blank sheet of paper and ask him or her to fold the paper in half and then in half again, so that the sheet has four quarters or squares. Have participants unfold the paper (the folding simply helps participants see four quadrants on the paper), and ask them to start in the top left-hand quarter and draw one of the images. For example, tell them, "Draw a house." Give them a minute or so, and then ask them to go to another square (it doesn't matter which one), and draw another one of the images until they have drawn one of the images on each quadrant of the paper. (For the purposes of this variation, it is best to save the iceberg as the last image that participants draw.) Ask them what these four drawings have in common with each other. Tell them these are all analogies for culture. Now have participants write a few brief words or phrases next to each picture on the commonalities they see between the pictures and culture. Then have them discuss what they've written and see if each pair or small group can develop its own definition of culture, which is then revealed to the rest of the group. This entire process takes about 20 minutes, depending on the size of the group.

Facilitation Tips and Suggestions

* Start with the images of the onion or the iceberg, as these two tend to be more quickly grasped by groups and may already be familiar with them. The lenses and the fish in water are sometimes more challenging, so it creates a nice build to end with these two pictures. (Note too that you should do the opposite if you use Variation 5: Have participants draw the iceberg or onion last so they don't guess the point of the activity in advance.)
* When you have more time, use examples to bring each analogy to life. For example, if you are focusing on a particular culture, use that to discuss what might be the tip-of-the-iceberg elements of that culture. Then give a few examples of deeper, hidden elements of the culture as a preview of what lies ahead in

the session. For the lenses, choose a simple situation, like someone being late for a meeting, and demonstrate how there could be multiple ways to view or interpret this situation. These types of examples help create interest and intrigue for the rest of the session.

- As an alternative or additional question, you can also ask: What is the connection between this analogy and our goals for today? This can be an effective way to frame and speak about the goals and agenda for a larger training program. For example, if your session is focused on the values of a specific culture, tell them that today will be largely spent in the depths of the iceberg rather than on the tip, like customs and dress. As you explore some of the values of the culture of focus, you will continually ask the group to really step into the shoes of individuals from this culture, to effectively put on their lenses and seek to see reality as they may conceive it. A clear connection can generally be drawn for most cultural awareness and culture-specific programs and some of the key messages of these analogies.

- You can also start a tool kit of strategies for working across cultures through this exercise. For example, for the onion, you might write, "People are complex: respect and seek to peel the layers of the onion." Write down one such key insight for each picture on a flipchart so there are four key lessons stemming from this activity. Continue to add to this tool kit throughout the day, and then dis-

tribute an electronic version of the tool kit of insights as a take-away after the session.

- This activity creates a common language that can be referred to throughout the rest of the session. For example, when someone gets caught seeing a situation from only one perspective, encourage that person to take off his or her lenses and put on the lenses of the other individual. When having people profile themselves along cultural dimensions, frame the profile as a chance for people to discover their own fishbowls and discuss the implications of their preferences in working across cultures.

About This Exercise

I began experimenting with more creative and effective ways of introducing culture in 2005 that built on tried and trusted approaches in our field. Over the years, I have played with different combinations of analogies and metaphors with group sizes from one to hundreds. I ultimately settled on the four analogies here and have used this exercise with individuals from over 30 cultures in a variety of industries and at all skill levels. I find this simple alternative approach to defining *culture* effective: It creates a higher-context understanding of culture and draws out insights quickly about culture. Moreover, participants typically value being included from the beginning in adding their insights and perspectives about culture. Thanks also to Darla K. Deardorff and her colleague Suzanne Gulledge, who provided Variation 5 and the house and tree examples, which they used in a joint course at the University of North Carolina at Chapel Hill.

 HANDOUT S1.5

ONION

 HANDOUT S1.6

ICEBERG

 HANDOUT S1.7

FISH IN WATER

 HANDOUT S1.8

LENSES

5. GO BANANAS!

Kimberly Pineda

By exploring different ways to peel a banana, individuals are reminded there are many right ways to do things across cultures.

Key Focus

Introduce core concepts

Type of Activity

Icebreaker

Objectives

As a result of this activity participants will

- recognize they have automatic ways of doing things they do not think about, and
- recognize the power of diversity and appreciate that there is more than one valid way to accomplish something.

Appropriate Audience

Adults, teenagers, children

Level of Challenge

Low

Group Size

6 to 75 people

Time

20 minutes

Materials

Bananas

Activity Setup

1. Ask participants to form groups of 2, 3, or 4.
2. Give a banana to each participant in the group or one banana per group.
3. Ask participants not to peel the banana until they are asked to.
4. Tell them each group has three minutes to create clear instructions on how to peel a banana.

Managing the Activity

1. Once the groups have completed their initial exploration, have one group share its instructions.
2. As the group makes its presentation, use a banana as a visual aid. For example, if a participant says, "Peel back the top," hold up the stem and ask which end they are calling the top. This type of clarification helps demonstrate the relativity of terms. Do not actually peel the banana yet, just imitate the actions.
3. Ask if any other groups found other ways of peeling a banana. If so, have them demonstrate how they would peel a banana.
4. Note the similarities and differences and summarize how most people in the room peel a banana: "With the exception of a couple who use knives, most participants open their banana . . ."
5. If all common ways of peeling a banana have been offered, move on to the debriefing questions.
6. If not, proceed with the following instructions (adjust as appropriate):

   - "Let me offer you another set of instructions for how to peel a banana."

   - "This time, you may actually peel the banana."

- "Hold the banana with the stem down, like this" (demonstrate).

- "Grab the tip of the banana and split it with your fingernail."

- "Pull the skin of the banana back and enjoy."

7. Make a mental note of people's reactions (e.g., laughter, looks of confusion, disagreement).
8. Tell them that everyone has just peeled his or her banana according to the common practice in, for example, much of Central America and certain African countries.

Debriefing the Activity

As a group, discuss the following questions:

- Were any instructions for peeling a banana wrong?
- What are the advantages and disadvantages to these different ways of peeling a banana?
- How did you react when you encountered a different way of peeling a banana? (At this point, share your own observations of the reactions you noted from people in general.)
- How many of you have previously sat around discussing how you peeled a banana?
- How did you learn to peel a banana?
- What does this simple exercise teach us about what we can learn from others with diverse perspectives?
- Do you imagine there are other things each of us do automatically without thinking about it?
- In your environment, what's the equivalent of peeling a banana, where individuals may have different perspectives on how to do something? (For business people, for example, explore topics such as how to conduct a successful meeting or what to do to be effective as a leader. For students, you might discuss expectations for student-teacher relationships or how to write a paper.)

End the activity by synthesizing the themes resulting from the discussion. Tell the following story if relevant:

One day, while a colleague of mine was in El Salvador visiting in-laws, her 12-year-old twin brothers-in-law

were laughing at her. Nervous, she asked them what was so funny, and they asked her why she was eating a banana upside down. Quite confident that she knew the right way to eat a banana, she challenged the boys saying that she had several more years of experience eating bananas than they did. (Act out the next lines with a banana.) At that, each of them grabbed a banana, turned it upside down, and peeled from the base. "See," they said, "If you open it from this side you can use the stem as a handle, the top piece won't get all mushy, and you won't have to deal with the strings!'"

This small story is a simple reminder of two important insights about working across cultures. First, it reminds us that when working across cultures, there are many different right ways to do things, and our way is rarely the only good way. Second, it shows us how we tend to assume that others do things the same way we do, and highlights the need to make explicit some of your basic expectations when interacting with others across cultures.

Key Insights and Learnings

- We have automatic ways of doing things that we don't question and assume to be right.
- There are different ways to reach the same outcome.
- Things can be learned from diverse perspectives.
- Even though individual differences exist, cultural generalizations can be made.
- Seeing some contrasting ideas helps individuals recognize automatic assumptions.

Facilitation Tips and Suggestions

- If you are going to demonstrate peeling a banana in a way that is unfamiliar to you, practice a couple of times on your own before using this activity.
- For easiest peeling, use bananas that are no longer green.

About This Exercise

This activity was inspired by an interaction with my brothers-in-law in El Salvador in 2001. I was impressed by the incident, and when I returned home,

I began sharing my new-found knowledge with family and friends. Their reactions inspired me to create a training activity. Since then I have used this ice-breaker with a wide variety of groups in the United States, ranging from health care to business to government to all levels of education. The groups had from 5 to 125 people, and the feedback has always been positive. Many times people have told me, "I took one of your trainings and think about it every time I peel a banana."

6. YES/NO

Darla K. Deardorff

This quick activity helps introduce the concept of cultural conditioning.

Key Focus

Introduce core concepts

Type of Activity

Icebreaker

Objectives

As a result of this activity, participants will gain an awareness of cultural conditioning.

Appropriate Audience

Adults, teenagers, children

Level of Challenge

Low

Group Size

2 to 300 plus people

Time

10 minutes

Materials

None

Activity Setup

Have participants pair up.

Managing the Activity

1. Have participants take turns asking each other yes/no questions, either about the other person or have them play Twenty Questions to guess an object. In Twenty Questions, one person asks up to 20 yes/no questions in an attempt to guess which object (usually an object in the room) the other person is thinking about who nods or shakes his or her head when answering *yes* or *no*. Have this go on for about one minute or less. They should go back and forth as quickly as possible when asking and responding to questions.

2. Then have them continue to ask yes/no questions, but this time tell the respondents they need to move their head in the opposite way. For example, if the person had been nodding when saying *yes*, the person would shake his or her head side-to-side when saying *yes*. Have this go on for another minute.

Debriefing the Activity

This activity helps persons understand cultural conditioning. In this debriefing, have the group discuss the following:

- What happened?
- What did you notice about the second round?
- How did you feel about using a different nonverbal method to mean *yes* or *no* in the second round? How did you feel about seeing the nonverbal communication in your partner?
- What happens when nonverbal communication contradicts verbal communication?
- What is the impact of one's cultural conditioning in interacting with others?
- As you reflect on this activity, what are some of the things you can take away?

Key Insights and Learnings

- Culture determines even certain basics like nodding and shaking our heads. Our cultural conditioning plays a key role in our intercultural interactions.
- Our cultural conditioning feels natural and normal; when asked to do something contrary to our cultural conditioning, it can feel unnatural and may mean we now need to consciously think about what we're doing.
- We may encounter dissonance between verbal and nonverbal communication in other cultures.
- When we're asked to do something outside our cultural conditioning, it may not be easy for us.

Variation

This can also be used as an introduction activity to interview the other person using yes/no questions and then have participants report on what they learned about their interviewee.

Facilitation Tips and Suggestions

- This activity is very quick and can be used to introduce the concept of cultural conditioning.
- Be sure to emphasize the importance of engaging in the nonverbal head movements as well as saying *yes* or *no*.
- Instruct participants to do this as quickly as possible and try to get in as many questions as possible in the allotted time (which can be shortened to 30 seconds, if desired).

About This Exercise

In thinking about cultural conditioning and the role it plays in communication, I developed this activity as a quick and simple way to help participants understand the power of cultural conditioning through something as basic as saying *yes* or *no* and using nonverbal methods. I have also found it to be a fun way for participants to get to know each other.

7. POINT AND NAME

Darla K. Deardorff

This activity helps introduce the concept of cultural conditioning.

Key Focus

Introduce core concepts

Type of Activity

Icebreaker

Objectives

As a result of this activity, participants will gain an awareness of cultural conditioning.

Appropriate Audience

Adults, teenagers, children

Level of Challenge

Low

Group Size

15 to 300 plus people

Time

10 to 15 minutes

Materials

None

Activity Setup

Ask participants to walk around the room and point and name (loudly) the objects they see. For example, "Chair!" or "Window!" in their first language. Make sure the instructions are clear, and start the exercise.

Managing the Activity

- Allow 20–30 seconds for this first round.
- Then call the group together and ask them to do the same again, except this time, give different names to the objects they see. Demonstrate this by pointing to a chair and calling it "Banana!" and then pointing to a window and calling it "Dog!"
- Say "Go," and observe as the group walks around and names objects in a new way. Allow 30–40 seconds for this round.

Debriefing the Activity

This activity helps people understand cultural conditioning. In this debriefing, discuss the following:

- What happened?
- Which round was easier? Which round required more thought? Why is that?
- How did you feel about giving different names to objects in the second round?
- What did you observe about the second round? What patterns emerged?
- What strategies did you use in naming objects in the second round? What strategies did you hear others using?
- How did others influence your strategies?
- Why do you think I had you do this simple exercise?
- What is the influence of our own culture on how we make sense of the world around us?
- As you reflect on this activity, what are some things you can take away?

Key Insights and Learnings

- Being aware of the extent of culture's influence on how we see the world is very important.
- Having to do something contrary to the way we've been culturally conditioned can create some challenge for us.
- It's natural for humans to want to categorize.
- Strategies we adopt may be influenced by those around us, especially those from our same cultural group.
- It's okay to go beyond how we normally see the world and how we've been conditioned to see the world. Our cultural conditioning may actually limit us and inhibit creativity to different possibilities.
- When we're asked to do something outside our cultural conditioning, it may not be easy for us.

Variation

If there are enough speakers of second languages in the room, you can ask participants to do a third round naming objects using a second language. In the debriefing you can ask how that felt compared to naming objects in one's first language and discuss the role of language in cultural conditioning.

Facilitation Tips and Suggestions

- Encourage participants to be enthusiastic about naming objects, pointing and naming them loudly and with excitement so that others can also hear what's being said as they walk around. This also provides a good way to energize the group.
- With the second round, a common strategy is to use categories such as fruits, animals, and so on since that helps make it easier for participants, and they don't have to think as much about giving something a different name.
- If children and adults are involved in the activity, ask how each group named the objects. Often, children see more creative possibilities (such as calling a chair *a house*).
- This activity works especially well in larger groups of 30 or more.
- Be sensitive to participants who may not all have the same first language. For example, don't assume English is the first language for everyone.

About This Exercise

I saw Patti Digh lead this activity at a Society for Intercultural Education Training and Research-USA conference and decided to adapt it to use as a quick way to specifically illustrate cultural conditioning. I have found it to be a fun, energizing activity in introducing the concept of how ingrained culture is in each of us and how even renaming items can be a bit challenging.

8. MEETING ON THE CONGO

Merry Merryfield

This activity teaches the need to understand the power of perspectives and worldviews as a key part of intercultural competence development.

Key Focus

Introduce core concepts

Type of Activity

Icebreaker

Objectives

As a result of this activity, participants will

- learn the meaning of perspective consciousness,
- compare conflicting points of view, and
- analyze the benefits of multiple perspectives.

Appropriate Audience

Adults, teenagers

Level of Challenge

Medium

Group Size

15 to 30 people

Time

30 minutes

Materials

Handouts

Preparation

- Duplicate the handouts.
- Arrange the room so you can give half the class one handout and the other half the other handout without their knowing there are two handouts.

Activity Setup

Introduce the concepts of perspective consciousness and multiple perspectives by exploring examples in participants' own lives or the local community where there may be multiple sides to the same story. Have them explain how a person's perspective might influence the way he or she makes meaning of an event. Help them break down the terms, asking,

- What is consciousness?
- Can you think of ways in which you and your friends or family might have multiple or conflicting perspectives about something going on this month?

Then have them apply what perspective consciousness might mean as they enter or study another culture. Tell them you want them to practice identifying people's perspectives.

Managing the Activity

- Next, give half the group the handout "That Was No Brother" (see Handout S1.9), and give the other half "That Was No Welcome" (see Handout S1.10), but don't let them know there are two different handouts. Ask them to read the handouts and circle words that identify the narrator's perspective.
- Then ask some people who read the African perspective, "That Was No Brother," what

happened on the Congo River? What are some words that tell us the perspective of the narrator? Then ask some people who read the other perspective, "That Was No Welcome," the same questions.

- When they get into questions or disagreement, let them discuss the readings for a few minutes before letting them guess (or some may figure it out quickly) why their understanding of what happened is different.
- Finally, give each participant the other handout to read.

Debriefing the Activity

After participants have read both handouts, ask them the following:

- Why do we have two different written accounts of the same event?
- What do these two readings mean for our study of history or culture or current events?
- Is one reading correct and the other wrong?
- If we want to understand African history, why would we benefit from understanding both points of view?

As you end the class discussion, ask participants about the implications of people developing perspective consciousness:

- What effect would such skills have on our everyday lives?
- Are there negative as well as positive effects?

Key Insights and Learnings

- There may be several different interpretations of events and issues based on people's cultural lenses, their experiences, and the contexts of time or space.
- By examining more than one perspective we are more likely to understand the event or issue and ensuing conflicts.
- The views of people who are oppressed or in a minority often are underrepresented in mainstream texts.

Variations

Variation 1. You can apply this process to any important event or issue such as the Crusades or local changes

(refugees coming into a community) to recent events in the Middle East.

Variation 2. This exercise can also create a safe entry to discussing a key event or conflict that might exist in a group or between two groups. Follow this more general exercise on switching perspective by having the group explore in a facilitated discussion the perspectives that exist around a real issue the group is facing.

Facilitation Tips and Suggestions

- The Meeting on the Congo activity is ideal for helping participants develop their consciousness and respect for multiple perspectives so they do not assume that everyone sees or interprets an event the same way they do. Therefore it would be useful when they are facing something that profoundly affects people's lives, from a marriage or a funeral to a political protest or the advent of a transnational company offering hundreds of jobs.
- The activity can also be used after a participant makes a faux pas in assuming people in another culture think the same way he or she does and then does not recognize the problems such assumptions can create (for example, assuming teachers in China support the prodemocracy protestors in Syria, and acting from that assumption during a visit to a school there).
- The first critical part of the activity is that people should not know two primary sources are being discussed. Second, participants must have time to read the second primary source so they can see how differently the narrators processed what was happening around them. Each rationale was the result of the narrator's own historical and cultural context.
- This activity works well for U.S. Americans and Europeans and especially well for U.S. Americans or Europeans who are going to be interacting with people from Africa. Choose different primary sources (ones related to the country or continent) if the participants are going to Asia or Latin America.

About This Exercise

An earlier version of this lesson was published in *Lessons From Africa*, which I edited in 1989 (Bloomington: Indiana University). I have found it works well with people who have been grounded in one worldview their whole life and are going overseas or working with people from other cultures in their own community. I have used it in seven countries, with middle and high school students as well as with adults, in classes, at orientations, and at professional conferences.

REFERENCES

Merryfield, M. M. (Ed.). (1989). *Lessons From Africa.* Bloomington: Indiana University, Social Studies Development Center.

Schiffers. H. (1957). *The quest for Africa.* New York, NY: Putnam & Sons.

Stanley, H. M. (1885). *Through the dark continent* (Vol. 2). New York, NY: Harper & Row.

 HANDOUT S1.9

THAT WAS NO BROTHER

In this story, King Mojimbo, who lived along the Congo River, tells how his people welcomed the first White man they had ever seen. He told this story to a Catholic priest.

When we heard that the man with white skin was traveling down the river, we were open-mouthed with surprise. We stood still. All night long the drums told the strange news—a man with white skin! If he has white skin he must be from the river kingdom. He is one of our brothers who was drowned in the river. All life comes from the water, and in the water he has found life. Now he is coming back to us. He is coming home.

We will prepare a feast, I ordered. We will go meet our brother and bring him into the village with rejoicing!

We will put on our ceremonial dress. We got the great canoes. We listened for the gong which would tell us that our brother has arrived on the river.

Now he enters the river! We swept forward, my canoe leading, the others following, with songs of joy and dancing, to meet the first white man our eyes had ever seen and to honor him.

But as we came near his canoe there were loud sounds, bang! bang! bang! And fire sticks spit bits of iron at us. We were frightened. Our mouths hung wide open and we could not shut them. Things as we had never seen, never heard of, never dreamed of—were they the work of evil spirits?

Several of my men fell into the water. Why? Did they fly to safety? No, for others fell down in the canoes. Some screamed terribly. Others were silent. They were dead and blood flowed from little holes in the bodies.

"War, war, this is war," I yelled. "Go back!"

The canoes sped back to our village with all the strength we could give to our arms. They followed us.

That was no brother! That was the worst enemy our country had ever seen.

Note. Remarks of King Mojimba, as told to Father Joseph Fraessle. Reprinted in *The Quest for Africa*, pp. 196–197, by H. Schiffers, 1957, New York, NY: Putnam & Sons.

Reproduced from: Merry Merryfield, "Meeting on the Congo," in *Building Cultural Competence: Innovative Activities and Models,* eds. K. Berardo and D. K. Deardorff (Sterling, VA: Stylus, 2012), 76–80.

 HANDOUT S1.10

THAT WAS NO WELCOME

Henry Stanley was the first White man to travel the entire Congo River. He was a newspaperman and wrote a book about his travels. In this story he recounts how he was met by some Africans while traveling the Congo over 100 years ago.

About 8am we saw a marketplace where there were many small canoes. The men got into them and circled all around us. We stayed still a long time, but they became bolder and began to throw their wooden spears whenever anyone cried "mutt" (the word for sticks). We shot our guns a few times which made them leave. Drums then awakened the whole country and horns blew deafening blasts. Some canoes boldly followed us.

At 2pm we came upon a very large stream. There we saw a greet fleet of canoes. The men in the canoes stood up and gave a loud shout when they saw us and blew their horns louder than ever. Looking upstream we saw a sight that sent blood tingling through every nerve and fiber of our bodies: a fleet of gigantic canoes bearing down on us, which was bigger in size and numbers than anything we had seen. . . . There were 54 of them!

A monster canoe led the way. In the bow were ten young warriors, their heads gay with red feathers; at the stern, eight men with long paddles, whose tops were decorated with ivory balls, guided the monster vessel. The crashing sound of drums and horns and the thrilling chant of 2000 human throats did not help calm our nerves.

I said to them "Boys, be firm as iron; wait till you see the first spear, then take good aim. Don't think of running away because only your guns can save you."

The monster canoe aimed straight for my boat as though it would run us down, but when it was 50 yards away it swerved to the side. When it was nearly opposite us the warriors threw their spears. Every sound was lost in the ripping cracking gunfire. We were angry now.

It was a murderous world and we felt for the first time that we hated the filthy people in it. We followed them upstream until we saw their villages. We hunted them in the woods until we finally stopped.

Note. From *Through the Dark Continent,* Vol. 2, pp. 268–275, 1885, by H. M. Stanley, New York, NY: Harper & Row.

SECTION 2

Understand Differences

9. THE FORM

Darla K. Deardorff

This mini-simulation provides participants with a brief experience of difference.

Key Focus

Understand differences

Type of Activity

Icebreaker

Objectives

As a result of this activity, participants will

- briefly experience dissonance and discomfort,
- gain an awareness of cultural difference, and
- begin to develop strategies for dealing with difference.

Appropriate Audience

Adults, teenagers

Level of Challenge

Low

Group Size

2 to 50 people

Time

15 minutes

Materials

- Handout (one per person)
- Pencils or pens

Preparation

Make copies of The Form (see Handout S2.1), one per participant.

Activity Setup

1. Tell participants that before you can continue with the training, you have a form you need them to complete.
2. Distribute The Form.
3. Tell participants they have two minutes to complete this form starting right then: "Go!"

Managing the Activity

1. Regularly remind participants of the amount of time left: "90 seconds, 1 minute, 30 seconds, 20 seconds, 10 seconds, 5 seconds, stop."

2. Ask how many of them have completed the form. Tell them you won't be collecting it, but you will discuss this some more together.

Debriefing the Activity

People experience discomfort in this activity. In the debriefing, discuss the following:

1. What one word describes how you felt during this activity, especially in the very beginning?
2. Why do you think the facilitator kept calling out the time? How important is time in some cultures? (Note that some cultures are more time-oriented, or monochronic, which is what the adherence to time represents.)
3. What strategies did you use to try to complete this form?
4. Were there items on it that did or did not make sense to you? Now let's talk about the questions on this form and how those relate to culture and cultural difference (You may pick and choose which ones to discuss based on participant response/context.):

   • Any surprises? Any questions you didn't understand?
   • What is the importance of family name to culture? Of hometown? (For example, family name may be more important in collective cultures, and hometown may be difficult to determine in more mobile cultures.)
   • What does your favorite shoe have to do with culture? (This alludes to materialism in some cultures, whereas in other cultures, some may not have the luxury of having multiple pairs of shoes.)
   • What about the 5th cousin? Could you answer that? (In some more group-oriented cultures, it may be possible to actually name a 5th cousin, while those from more individualistic cultures may find it more challenging.) Another question that also relates to this underlying cultural value is the one about the number of people in your family. How many did you put? (In more individualistic cultures, the number may be smaller.)
   • What about the European-style of writing a date, or your age in Korean? (Even

something like date or age can be written differently in other cultures. In Korea your age starts before you are born, so newborns are considered to be one year old.)
   • What is Geburtstag? (German for *birthday*.)
   • What about your zodiac sign or blood type? (Those are ways to determine the kind of person you may be. In Japan, for example, people may ask you what your blood type is.)
   • What about occupation? (One's work position can be really important in some cultures such as in the United States where a very common question is "What do you do?")
   • What about your supervisor's name? Did you write the first name? First and last name? Only last name? Anything else? (This may depend on the level of formality and hierarchy in different cultures.)
   • How does this relate to the experience of working across cultures? What strategies could you use in real-life cross-cultural situations? What are real-life equivalents of The Form?
   • How many of you have experienced a time when you didn't understand or know what was going on? What was that like for you?
   • How do you think others feel when they go into another culture?
   • What does this tell us about what is important to remember and do when we work across cultures?
   • As you reflect on this activity, what can you take away from this activity that you can use in your context?

Key Insights and Learnings

• Being aware of cultural difference is quite important, especially how apparent commonalities like age may have different conceptions in other cultures.
• What we think of as normal may only be cultural. For example, reading left to right, as in The Form didn't work.
• Not knowing and understanding can be quite an uncomfortable experience for anyone. It is important to remember how others may feel going into situations where they are unfamiliar with the cultural rules or norms.

- Strategies for dealing with cultural difference can be useful when confronted with discomfort (see DAE, pp. 53–57; or OSEE, pp. 58–60).

Variations

Variation 1. When time is limited, have people complete the exercise and debrief them without going into the cultural aspects of each question.

Variation 2. Before debriefing, ask people to write at the bottom of The Form everything they were thinking or feeling while they were doing this exercise. This allows people to reflect on what was going on for them before you start the discussion. Then ask people to call out their feelings and build a list of words like *frustrating, confused, pressured, fun.* When you end the debriefing, read the list of reactions out loud and tell your group that many of the same types of reactions occur when people move across cultures or work across cultures on an ongoing basis. Use this to segue into a discussion around what helps to think or do to manage some of these reactions when interacting across cultures.

Facilitation Tips and Suggestions

- Be prepared for confusion and frustration on the part of participants, especially initially.
- Some participants will quickly turn the paper over and hold it up to the light to read it, which is fine; you can discuss this during the debriefing.
- This activity works well as an initial way to engage participants in a mini-simulation, especially if time does not permit a longer, full simulation.
- It's very important to distribute The Form immediately before the activity. Do not distribute it in advance. Participants are not

supposed to have much time to look at it before you tell them to begin.
- You may want to end with a discussion about stereotypes and generalizations, especially if you are going into more culture-specific training. (For example, *stereotype* is usually fixed, applied to everyone in a group and based on limited information, while *generalization* is more fluid, not applied to everyone in a particular group, and is based on patterns found in a particular group that are often determined through research, and not everyone fits the patterns.)
- This works well with groups of 50 or less because the handout is necessary: It's difficult to distribute this quickly in larger groups and it should not be distributed in advance.
- This works well in groups that have not had much experience with other cultures. If participants already have significant experience with other cultures, this exercise would not be very effective.

About This Exercise

I adapted this activity from "The Form" by Kohls & Knight (1994). I wrote my own questions that address some parts of cultural difference specifically and developed a fuller approach to debriefing the activity. I've found it to be an effective mini-simulation and a great way to introduce cultural difference, and it's worked well with different ages and groups, from business to education.

REFERENCE

Kohls, L. R., & Knight, J. (1994). *Developing intercultural awareness: A cross-cultural training handbook* (2nd ed.). Yarmouth, ME: Intercultural Press.

 HANDOUT S2.1

THE FORM

10. Your Family Name: _____

9. Your Occupation: _____

8. Today's date, European-style: _____

7. Your age in Korea: _____

6. Your blood type: _____

5.5 Your favorite shoe: ____

5.2 Your hometown: _____

5. Name of a 5th cousin on your mother's side: _____

4. What is your zodiac sign? _____

3. How many people in your family? _____

2. Number of days until your Geburtstag: _____

1. Your supervisor's name: _____

Note: Developed by D. K. Deardorff.

10. Your Family Name: _____

 9. Your Occupation: _____

 8. Today's date, European-style: _____ _

 7. Your age in Korea: _____

 6. Your blood type: _____

5.5 Your favorite shoe: _____

5.2 Your hometown:_____

5. Name of a 5th cousin on your mother's side: _____

4. What is your zodiac sign? _____

3. How many people in your family? _____

2. Number of days until your Geburtstag: _____

1. Your supervisor's name: _____

Note: Use as reference only—not to be distributed. Developed by D. K. Deardorff.

10. THE GREAT GAME OF POWER

Stephanie Pollack

Participants one at a time arrange the objects in the room so that one chair becomes the most powerful object in relation to the other chairs, a table, and a bottle. Any of the objects can be moved, but none of them can be removed altogether from the space. A number of variations are created, allowing each person who so desires the opportunity to rearrange the objects. Each variation on why or why not the chosen chair has the most power is discussed. There is no right answer; it is about the conversation, which highlights various views of power and how relative they are to cultural context.

Key Focus

Understand differences

Type of Activity

Exercise

Objectives

As a result of the activity, participants will

- become aware of how power varies depending on culture, context, perspective, and belief systems, and
- increase their understanding of how power influences any and every situation.

Appropriate Audience

Adults, teenagers

Level of Challenge

Medium

Group Size

12 to 50 people

Time

30 to 60 minutes

Materials

- Table
- Six chairs
- An opaque bottle
- Handout

Preparation

The most productive room setup is having participants form a curve or a U shape, and placing the table, chairs, and bottle near the opening of the U.

Activity Setup

1. Explain to the group there is one objective to this activity: to rearrange the furniture so that one chair has the most amount of power. Let participants determine what that means to them, rather than giving a definition of *power*.
2. Ask participants to come up one at a time and arrange the objects to make one chair the most powerful. Any of the objects can be moved, but none of the objects can be removed. Invite the first volunteer to rearrange the furniture. Ask the volunteer not to speak during the next portion of the exercise.

Managing the Activity

1. After the arrangement is made, thank the volunteer and ask him or her to remain silent as the group discusses the result. Ask the group the following questions:

   - Which chair do you think has the most amount of power?

- What makes you say that?
- Does anyone see anything different?

2. When the discussion is complete, ask the volunteer to explain his or her thoughts behind the arrangement. Discuss as necessary. Thank everyone.
3. Ask the next volunteer to rearrange the furniture, and repeat the process.
4. After two arrangements, add the following questions to the discussion:

   - What real life situation does this remind you of?
   - What other real life situations could this be?

5. Run through a number of variations, if possible allowing each person who desires the opportunity to rearrange the objects.

Debriefing the Activity

- This activity is all about the discussions that occur after each person completes an arrangement, so debriefing occurs continually throughout the session. Where the conversation goes is up to the facilitator. If the session concerns something specific, like leadership and cultural conflict, the discussion can be focused there. If the session is more general, let the discussion go wherever the participants take it.
- Seeing the participants' rearrangements of the furniture will reveal a lot about their context and belief systems, which can inform the facilitation. Discuss power in terms of its highly contextual nature and continually point out that there are different (not necessarily bad or good) viewpoints of power.
- This activity can reveal large and small issues about anything imaginable (and unimaginable). In one session, numerous topics and situations will be raised by the group, such as organizational hierarchy, styles of leadership, teamwork, internal organizational politics, interpersonal relations, family dynamics, world politics, war, current events, immigration, airport screenings, schooling, systems and processes of every sort, and so on. (This activity is never boring or repetitive to facilitate.) What is revealed in the arrangements and ensuing discussion can be more substantive in a shorter time than seems possible.

- Reminder: There is no right answer; it is about the conversation.
- A short general debriefing of the entire activity can be conducted once all arrangements are complete. Since the majority of the learnings and insights occur during the debriefing of each individual arrangement, it is best to conduct a quick debriefing following the typical process by asking the following:

   - What happened?
   - How did it make you feel?
   - What did it make you think?
   - What did you learn?
   - How can you apply what you learned?

Key Insights and Learnings

Through this process and debriefing, participants usually learn that

- power is relative to context;
- power can be perceived, understood, and acknowledged in countless ways;
- some types of power can have negative consequences, while others can be positively empowering;
- systems can go awry, and it is up to the people involved in the systems to do something to fix them;
- there are multiple ways to view the exact same thing;
- prior life experience determines how something is viewed;
- everyone is a teacher and learner;
- people's brains work in a million different ways and are constantly surprising, especially when it comes to intercultural communication and power;
- one has more power than he or she thought.

Variations

Variation 1. After numerous arrangements have been discussed, which takes about three fourths of the time allotted for the activity, introduce a new element: Ask one participant to place himself or herself in the most powerful position without moving anything. Once someone is in place, other players can enter the space and try to place themselves in an even more powerful position and take away the power the first person established.

Variation 2. Use a transparent bottle partially filled with water. This can shift the focus of the activity to being more environmental and resource-oriented if the water in the bottle represents a precious resource (water, money, etc.). Potential learnings can include a heightened understanding that different cultures view resources differently, the questioning of the individual or collective nature of resources, and that resources equal wealth, which equals power.

Facilitation Tips and Suggestions

- The chairs should be the easily stackable kind without wheels.
- The table should not be too large or too heavy to be moved by one person (including turning it on its side or upside down).
- Be prepared and warn the client organization, as well as the participants, about the possibility of furniture falling. (Using a prized, handmade teak table is not the best idea.)
- Practice this exercise with friends or colleagues first, and practice a lot. While this is a simple process, guiding it is anything but simple. The weight of the activity is on the facilitator, and it can fail if it is not guided correctly. You must ask endless questions and be able to choose the exact right question at the right time. Having staged The Great Game of Power for over 10 years, I still have much more to learn. It is amazing how complex the debriefing is after each arrangement, and how much the size and shape of the furniture changes the participants' contributions. Determining how to match intercultural communication or leadership theories with the myriad of quick furniture arrangements that appear is challenging, as is knowing when to focus on a huge piece of personal information someone surprisingly reveals and how far to take the discussion.
- Partway through the activity, or when a particularly interesting arrangement is before the group, ask the participants to change seats. Their location in the room can alter their perspective and, therefore, their interpretation of the arrangement.
- If someone says, "If X were just a little different" (meaning if the bottle were in a different place, or one chair in a different space), ask the person to actually make the change, with the permission of the original arranger first.
- Where the conversation leads is up to the facilitator. When participants come up with ideas for what the arrangements look like in real life, if that particular subject is relevant, ask more questions about it; if it is not appropriate for it to become the focus of conversation, steer away from it.
- Since the activity can bring up large, looming power-related issues, be prepared. It may become necessary to either discuss the elephant in the room or gracefully dance around it.
- Ask participants to use the DAE model (see pp. 53–57) when talking about the arrangements, if the group is familiar with that model. For a theoretical discussion, distribute definitions of types of power, cultural styles of leadership, and so on.

Note on Title Language

The choice of words for a title is crucial. Having facilitated The Great Game of Power dozens of times over the past decade with groups of 10 to 160, I've continually changed the title to frame the learnings appropriately. Here are a few examples of titles that have been used and their impact:

- Theatre Games. With adolescent girls. Learnings include a new understanding of how different families are structured, the power of girls in school systems, boy-girl relationships, and peer pressure.)
- Leadership and Power. Native American college students, museum staff, experiential educators. Learnings include a new understanding of educational administration systems, the positive power possessed by any one student, Native American and mainstream population perceptions of power and culture, and how teachers can successfully navigate the power held by school principals.
- Building Community in Your Classroom. Teachers and professors. Learnings include a new understanding of how to physically set up a classroom to achieve desired results, how the inherent power in the teacher/professor role can be positively used or abused,

how to break up powerful student cliques, and how to support individual students.

- Empathy. Tolerance building for youths in Gaza. Learnings include a new understanding of where each person was coming from culturally and religiously, political decision making, and how to support one another.
- The Great Game of Power. This creates the most mystery. Learnings include a new understanding of anything and everything; the conversations purposefully go in 101 different directions.

Choose wisely.

About This Exercise

This exercise was adapted from Boal (1992). See the additional background on Boal and this activity in Handout S2.2. I became aware of Theatre of the Oppressed in general, and this activity in particular, when I attended my first Pedagogy and Theatre of the Oppressed conference in 1998. I began using this activity with university students within weeks of experiencing it myself, and was amazed with the breadth and depth of the conversations it inspired. I have used it all over the world with various populations for numerous purposes, and am continually adapting it depending on the group, the context, the physical space, and the desired outcomes. It remains one of my all-time favorite exercises because it has an inherent complexity that keeps me completely engaged as a facilitator, every single person always learns something, and people talk about it in great detail long after the exercise is over, hours, days, months, and years later.

REFERENCES

Boal, A. (1992). *Games for actors and non-actors.* London, UK: Routledge.

Freire, P. (1970). *Pedagogy of the Oppressed.* New York: Herder and Herder.

Schutzman, M., & Cohen-Cruz, J. (1994). *Playing Boal: Theatre, therapy, activism.* New York, NY: Routledge.

 HANDOUT S2.2

ADDITIONAL INFORMATION OF THE GREAT GAME OF POWER

What Is Theatre of the Oppressed (TO)?

TO is an arsenal of theatre exercises for nontheatre people that supports the mutual exploration of a topic in an experiential, interactive, team building, nonthreatening way. Augusto Boal created TO in the early 1970s based on Paolo Freire's *Pedagogy of the Oppressed* (1970) which explores libratory education. While TO was originally conceived specifically to explore issues of oppression by having the oppressed people come up with their own solutions, it can be successfully employed in both training and education settings to address a variety of topics. In addition to the original processes and activities of Forum Theatre (with words), Image Theatre (without words), and Invisible Theatre (imagine *Punk'd* or *Borat* with a purely social education mission), Boal has also created Legislative Theatre for use in politics (he was a *vereador*, member of Parliament's Legislative Chamber for Rio de Janeiro in the 1990s) and the Rainbow of Desire for use in therapy. Boal has developed a worldwide following (ptoweb.org, http://theatreoftheoppressed.org). And rightly so; the techniques are incredible.

More About Theatre of the Oppressed

Augusto Boal is an internationally renowned Brazilian director and political activist who created his groundbreaking theatre techniques based on Paulo Freire's *Pedagogy of the Oppressed* (1970). As Boal (1992) states: "Each exercise, game and technique, while having specific objectives of its own, in itself contains the totality of the process. There is a built-in and continuous interplay between the exercises, games and techniques of all the forms of the *Theatre of the Oppressed*" (p. 164). Boal continues: "The objective is to encourage autonomous activity, to set a process in motion, to stimulate transformative creativity, to change spectators into protagonists. And it is for precisely these reasons that the Theatre of the Oppressed should be the initiator of changes the culmination of which is not the aesthetic phenomenon but real life" (p. 245).

Forum Theatre is a technique that "begins with the enactment of a scene in which a protagonist tries, unsuccessfully, to overcome an oppression relevant to that particular audience. The joker (Boal's version of a facilitator) then invites the spectators to replace the protagonist at any point in the scene that they can imagine an alternative action that could lead to a solution. The scene is replayed numerous times with different interventions. This results in a dialog about the oppression, an examination of alternatives, and a 're-hearsal' for real situations" (Schutzman & Cohen-Cruz, 1994, p. 236).

Invisible Theatre is "a rehearsed sequence of events that is enacted in a public, non-theatrical space, capturing the attention of people who do not know they are watching a planned performance. It is at once theatre and real life, for although rehearsed, it happens in real time and space and the 'actors' must take responsibility for the consequences of the 'show.' The goal is to bring attention to a social problem for the purpose of stimulating public dialog" (Schutzman & Cohen-Cruz, 1994, p. 237).

In Image Theatre participants literally sculpt each other's bodies (in various ways) as clay into images. It is designed to "uncover essential truths about societies and cultures without resort to spoken language. . . . the frozen image is simply the starting point for or prelude to the action. At its simplest, the idea underlying this is that 'a picture paints a thousand words'; that our over-reliance on words can confuse or obfuscate central issues, rather than simplifying them; that images can be closer to our true feelings, even our subconscious feelings, than words, since the process of 'thinking with our hands' can short-circuit the censorship of the brain, the 'cops in the head' placed there by society or personal experience" (Boal, 1992, p. xxiii).

11. STRANGE SITUATIONS

Lothar Katz

This activity explores the personal discomfort and potential conflict inherent to cross-cultural interactions in a lighthearted manner. It encourages participants to question their assumptions and explore those of others, rather than jumping to conclusions too quickly. At the same time, it serves as a great icebreaker at the beginning of a session.

Key Focus

Understand differences

Type of Activity

Exercise

Objectives

As a result of this activity, participants will

- realize how cultural differences can cause misunderstandings,
- experience the discomfort of dealing with a foreign culture, and
- gain interest in learning more about cultural differences.

Appropriate Audience

Adults

Level of Challenge

Low

Group Size

6 to 30 people (can become difficult to manage with larger groups)

Time

30 to 60 minutes

Materials

- Projection screen or handouts
- A flipchart for each team of 4 to 6 participants (optional)

Activity Setup

1. Split the audience into teams of about 4 to 6 participants each.
2. Tell the participants that the purpose of this activity is to test their team creativity. Next, ask participants who are familiar with the test to please remain passive and not give others the right answer, allowing them to experience the test for themselves.

Managing the Activity

1. Show or distribute the first handout (see Handout S2.3), and read each line aloud. If shown as a screen presentation, it is more effective if the text is displayed and read line by line.
2. Tell the teams they have five minutes to decide on a strategy of how to get out of the dangerous situation. If flip charts are available, ask all teams to assign one member to write down key elements of the team's strategy on its flip chart.
3. Have each team work on its strategy/solution for up to five minutes.
4. When the five minutes are up, ask each team to present or explain its solution.
5. After all teams have presented their solutions, or when the first team says "Carousel," confirm the correct answer by

showing the contents of the second handout (see Handout S2.4) or simply telling them the answer. This usually triggers reactions ranging from laughter to participants' rolling their eyes or looking embarrassed.

6. Ask the group what made it so difficult for them to identify the correct answer, when it now seems so logical. If needed, guide the group toward the observation that an important piece of information was missing that caused the teams to make assumptions instead.

7. Apologize to the groups for setting them up and promise that this weird exercise will soon make more sense to them.

8. Tell the participants there is another scenario where they are again asked to identify what is going on. Show them the third handout (see Handout S2.5) and read it to them line by line.

9. This time, tell the group they are all going to figure it out collectively. Then ask them, "What is going on here?" This question will either meet with complete silence or lead to a few observations.

10. When the group seems ready to give up, give them the right answer: "You are a Japanese first-time visitor to (name the place or nearest city where the session is being held)." This answer most likely will make little or no sense to any of the group members.

11. Explain line-by-line what happened, while keeping the third handout on the screen or in participants' hands. It is important to start by saying, "Imagine that you are the Japanese visitor" before giving the following explanations:

- The waitress offers you the soup of the day. You say, "That sounds very good." She brings you the soup. You laugh. Explanation: You, the Japanese person, did not want soup. However, it would be impolite in your culture to say so, so instead you said that it sounds very good. When the waitress brings the soup you did not order, you laugh to conceal your embarrassment, as some Japanese might do in such a situation.
- After you have finished your main course and asked for the check, the waitress

brings it, together with four sweets. You wonder why she is so rude. Explanation: In Japan, giving someone four of anything is a serious faux pas. The Japanese word for *four* sounds like the word for *death*. You give four items of anything only to an enemy, as doing so is usually interpreted as wishing for the other person's death.

- You pay and get ready to leave. The waitress gives you a hostile stare. You are concerned she does not like you but are not sure why. Explanation: In Japan tipping is uncommon and may even be perceived as offensive. You, the Japanese visitor, did not leave a tip, which is why you got the hostile stare from the waitress, who expected to get one.

Debriefing the Activity

The primary objective of this debriefing is to lead all participants to the conclusion that the carousel and Japanese visitor scenarios have much in common, and that the confusion participants experienced (or watched others experience) in the carousel setting is similar to what the foreign visitor in the other scenario may have been experiencing when visiting another country. Once this objective has been met, the group is likely ready for and eager to enter a deeper exploration of cross-cultural challenges.

1. Begin the debriefing by asking the group whether the Japanese visitor scenario makes sense to them, although most or all of them were unable to figure out what was going on. After several participants confirm this, ask which analogies participants see between the carousel exercise and the Japanese visitor scenario.

2. Repeat or record on a flip chart important comments, such as,

- an important fact that was not known or not communicated,
- we, the Japanese visitor, and the waitress made assumptions that weren't correct, and
- the communication didn't work.

3. Ask the participants how they felt when they saw the answer to the carousel scenario, and repeat or record comments, such as,

- I was confused.
- I knew that something just didn't make sense but couldn't figure out what it was.
- I felt betrayed.
- I got angry.

4. Ask the group to imagine how the players in the Japanese visitor scenario must have felt in the situation. Answers will probably be similar to those given in 3. If necessary, the facilitator may have to ask additional questions to guide the group to that conclusion, such as, "Do you believe the way the waitress and the Japanese visitor felt is similar to how you felt in the carousel exercise?"

   - Summarize the group's findings, emphasizing that the two scenarios are similar in that they were highly confusing initially but made sense once important information was available, and that significant frustration was generated from both of them. Next, say, "What you just experienced is some of the frustration everybody experiences at some point when working with others from different cultures."

5. Other debriefing questions that can be used with the entire group at the end of the session are:

   - What surprises occurred for you in this activity?
   - What situations have you been in that involved a cultural conflict, frustration, or misunderstanding? What happened and what did you learn as a result?
   - What are some important lessons to remember in working through cross-cultural conflict?
   - What can you take from this activity and apply in other situations in the future?

Key Insights and Learnings

Participants frequently report insights such as the following:

- Not knowing enough about the situation or the people involved meant I totally misinterpreted what was happening.

- Different cultures sometimes interpret the same behaviors in very different ways. This can be very frustrating.
- I need to be careful not to rely on assumptions and try instead to understand what is really going on.
- It is important for me to know something about the cultural values and practices of the person or people with whom I am dealing.

Depending on the focus of the rest of your session, you can use the responses that were summarized or recorded on the flip chart to start a discussion about any of the following:

- Dealing with unknown cultures can be discomforting. For instance, ask, "Has anyone here had a similar experience when you were traveling abroad or dealing with a foreigner?"
- Cultural differences frequently lead to misunderstandings and cultural conflict. For example, lead with this: "As we saw in the Japanese visitor situation, misunderstandings happen easily when communicating across cultures. Can any of you think of a misunderstanding you experienced when you were traveling abroad or dealing with a foreigner?"
- It is important to understand cultural differences, since that gives the involved parties a chance to avoid such misunderstandings.
- One must refrain from making assumptions and instead try to find out about the motivation of others to understand why they behave the way they do. For example, ask this: "We have found out that assumptions can lead to wrong conclusions and may cause you to do the wrong thing, although you mean well. Can any of you think of a situation you experienced when you were traveling abroad or dealing with a foreigner and you made an assumption that turned out to be incorrect?"

Variation

If many of the participants are or might be familiar with Japan's culture, the activity can easily be adjusted to a similar dinner setting with a member of another culture in the role of the visitor. For instance, a U.S. visitor might

- ask for a glass of water and then be irritated because it comes without ice and is on the restaurant bill (in the United States, it is customary in most restaurants, even upscale ones, for water to be served with lots of ice and free of charge);
- wait a long time until asking for the check (in the United States, the check usually arrives automatically without having to ask); and
- give a much larger tip than the server expected (tips of 15% to 20% are customary in the United States).

Facilitation Tips and Suggestions

- This activity is suitable for audiences in most industries and cultural groups.
- When introducing the carousel team exercise, make the situation sound as dangerous as possible. For example, using your hands to stress the enormous size of the fire truck and the horse, as well as the low altitude of the helicopter, is helpful. It is important to convey a sense of discomfort and potential danger, so use voice inflection and gestures as needed to achieve that.
- It can actually be helpful to get the audience slightly irritated, even angry, with the facilitator during the carousel exercise. When participants figure out later, usually during the debriefing, why they were set up, that anger often stimulates self-reflection: "I was angry at the instructor when in reality I should have been angry at myself for making misplaced assumptions." It is very important to make the apology in an honest and sincere fashion. If some group members are still irritated with having been set up, ask the group during the debriefing how they now feel about having been misled in the carousel scenario, assure them that these feelings are completely valid, and apologize again.
- The carousel exercise should be stopped after five minutes and may take even less time than that. Once some of the teams are finished and their members start looking distracted or

bored, it is okay for the facilitator to cut the exercise short and ask each team to present its solution or the current state of team members' discussion.

- Teams rarely figure out the carousel exercise. Typical proposed solutions include rational approaches, such as brake slowly and carefully, or wild ideas such as use the eject seat function of your James Bond car. Occasionally, a team might guess the right answer. To prevent this from adversely affecting the learning effect for others, do the following: While the teams are working on their strategy/solution, walk around the room to get a sneak preview of each team's ideas. If you notice that one or more teams came up with the correct answer, ask them quietly not to share their solution with others. Teams with the correct answer are called last during the team debriefing, so be sure to have the other teams give their answers first. That way, these team members experience the confusion that others may have with the situation before they get to proudly present their solution. Praise them for figuring it all out.
- In the Japanese visitor scenario it is unlikely that someone in the audience develops a plausible answer, unless some of the participants are familiar with the Japanese culture and see the connection with the story. If someone thinks he or she can explain the whole scenario, ask that person to do so and help with comments should the participant not be able to move forward on an explanation.

About This Exercise

The carousel riddle was taken from an e-mail that was forwarded to me by a friend many years ago. It was slightly modified for the purpose of this activity. The story with the Japanese visitor is fictional and is based on my own experience working in Japan and with Japanese visitors.

I have used this exercise with many different audiences and always found it to be highly engaging and triggering very productive group conversations.

 HANDOUT S2.3

CHALLENGING SITUATION

A Challenging Situation …

➢ You are in a car that's moving at a constant speed.

➢ To your left is a steep downward slope. To your right, a large fire truck moves at the same speed as yours.

➢ Directly ahead of you is a helicopter flying less than two feet off the ground. You can't seem to get around it.

➢ Suddenly, you notice a rider on a large horse behind your car. He's keeping pace and seems alarmingly close.

How will you get out of this situation without hurting yourself or someone else?

As a table team, please spend 5 minutes to decide what you will do and write down your plan on your flipchart

---

Reproduced from: Lothar Katz, "Strange Situations," in *Building Cultural Competence: Innovative Activities and Models,* eds. K. Berardo and D. K. Deardorff (Sterling, VA: Stylus, 2012), 91–97.

HANDOUT S2.4

A CHALLENGING SITUATION

A Challenging Situation …

> ➤ You are in a car that's moving at a constant speed.

> ➤ To your left is a steep downward slope. To your right, a large fire truck moves at the same speed as yours.

> ➤ Directly ahead of you is a helicopter flying less than two feet off the ground. You can't seem to get around it.

> ➤ Suddenly, you notice a rider on a large horse behind your car. He's keeping pace and seems alarmingly close.

How will you get out of this situation without hurting yourself or someone else?

Carefully step off the carousel and run back to your Mom!

Reproduced from: Lothar Katz, "Strange Situations," in *Building Cultural Competence: Innovative Activities and Models,* eds. K. Berardo and D. K. Deardorff (Sterling, VA: Stylus, 2012), 91–97.

 HANDOUT S2.5

ANOTHER STRANGE SITUATION

Another Strange Situation ...

➢ You are going out for dinner, alone in _____,
a city you're visiting for the first time.

➢ The waitress offers the soup of the day. You say "That
sounds very good." She brings you the soup. You laugh.

➢ After you have finished your main course and asked for
the check, the waitress brings it, together with four
sweets. You wonder why she is so rude.

➢ You pay and get ready to leave. The waitress gives you
a hostile stare. You are convinced that she hates you.

Reproduced from: Lothar Katz, "Strange Situations," in *Building Cultural Competence: Innovative Activities and Models,* eds. K. Berardo and D. K. Deardorff (Sterling, VA: Stylus, 2012), 91–97.

12. NARRATIVE INSIGHTS

Lily A. Arasaratnam

The short story becomes an interactive learning instrument in this exercise where participants read and reflect on a short story that addresses race issues and stereotyping. Through fictional interviews with characters, they discuss the issues addressed in the story, hold meaningful dialogues, and build key cultural competency skills like perspective taking and empathy.

Key Focus

Understand differences

Type of Activity

Exercise

Objectives

As a result of this activity, participants will

- recognize the subtle ways intercultural concepts are interwoven into daily life,
- practice empathy to understand different perspectives, and
- practice thinking through the consequences of people's thoughts and actions in everyday situations.

Appropriate Audience

Adults, teenagers

Level of Challenge

Medium

Group Size

4 to 40. You can use this exercise for larger groups as well; simply divide the participants into groups of 4 to 5 for the discussion.

Time

40–65 minutes

Materials

Short story handout per person

Activity Setup

1. Divide the students into groups of 3 to 4 people.
2. Distribute a copy of the short story to each person.

Managing the Activity

1. Instruct students to read the story (see Handout S2.6) and briefly discuss it in their groups.
2. Ask them to choose one character from the story (they can be major or minor characters, named or unnamed; if unnamed character, the participants can give the character a name if they wish) whom they would interview. If there is more time, increase the number of characters.
3. Students decide on the questions they would ask the characters and write down the answers they believe the characters would give, so the full interview unfolds. The trajectory of the interviews must be true to the characters (based on the story). The purpose of the interview is to find out more about what the characters may have been thinking or feeling. Students should be given time to present their interviews at the end of the exercise. If time is short, allow each group to present one character.

Debriefing the Activity

Allow the discussion to flow freely. Where relevant, ask leading questions for the theoretical concepts you want to draw out. For example, in the short story, you can discuss the process of stereotyping, stereotype change (such as models of stereotype change), and so forth. At the end of the activity, talk about how real-life situations educate us every day, and ask the students what they learned from this exercise by trying to put themselves in the mind of the various characters.

Suggested discussion questions for "Nathan's Hero" are the following:

1. What can we learn about stereotypes from Nathan's story? Talk about the nature of generalizations and how we may make generalizations about a group of people based on specific experiences in our life.
2. Does the story illustrate stereotype change? For example, in Mr. Wall's experience with the White cop, the conversation model of stereotype change is demonstrated. The premise of this model is that stereotype change could occur as a result of one significant transformative event in such a way that one is converted to a different way of thinking.
3. Is this story realistic? If not, why not?
4. What parallels can you draw from Nathan's experience and yours?
5. Which character do you identify with the most, and why?

Key Insights and Learnings

Through this process and debriefing, participants usually learn that

- we should be alert to lessons we can glean from real-life examples,
- making stereotypical generalizations about a group of people based on individual experiences can be destructive (though that is how stereotypes are usually formed),
- it is helpful to put oneself in another's shoes to understand the other person's perspective (as demonstrated by the participants putting themselves in the shoes of the characters to interview them), and
- prejudice is self-perpetuating unless someone chooses to stop the cycle.

Variations

Variation 1. Ask each group of participants to write the interview for one character and then the rest of the groups get to evaluate the extent to which the group being evaluated has plausibly portrayed what the character would say. This can generate interesting discussions as well.

Variation 2. To make the exercise more interactive, have individuals play the characters and act out the interviews. In this case, the students should create a list of questions they would want to ask this character. Then the character can come to the front of the room and be asked questions by the different small groups.

Variation 3. If time permits, the participants can also be given the opportunity to rewrite the story with a different twist and explain the reason behind the changes and the concepts illustrated by the changes. For example, if the participants think that Nathan's change of heart in the end is unrealistic, then they may want to rewrite a scenario in which the process happens more gradually. Or perhaps they would want to write the story from the perspective of the Black student who makes eye contact with Nathan at the end of the story.

Facilitation Tips and Suggestions

Because this is an abstract activity, it is good to first prepare students by saying that you're going to ask them to do something abstract. Participants who are literal thinkers may not be amenable to the idea of interviewing a fictional character. Anticipate this and explain that an activity like this is an exercise in putting yourself in someone else's position and thinking through what that individual's thoughts and feelings would be. Explain that this process is helpful in intercultural communication (see Arasaratnam & Doerfel, 2005) because it helps you to try to understand the perspective of the other person.

The same learning process can be applied to a number of short stories. Short stories present an accessible way to communicate insights in a manner similar to how insights are learned from everyday events. Unlike critical incidents or case studies, the short story approach can be less clinical and more authentic to real-life experiences (Arasaratnam, 2011).

Consider writing your own short story to bring to life different learning objectives, or pull a short story from Arasaratnam's (2011) *Perception and Communication in Intercultural Spaces.* The book contains a chapter of short stories and character interviews that can be used as further resources.

About This Exercise

This exercise arose from an idea I had when I was working on *Perception and Communication in Intercultural Spaces*. I had noticed my students responded much more to stories I told in class than to the case study type of activities. When I told stories in the classroom (based on my experiences, for example), students asked more questions and seemed to relate to the ideas more personally. Having been raised in a predominantly oral culture where narratives play a major role in communicating moral and cultural values, I realized that narratives have a way of cutting through inhibitions and reaching people at a personal level especially when dealing with sensitive topics. This fact is well-established in literature, such as in situations of organ donation (Morgan, Movius, & Cody, 2009) and marriage therapy (Blanton & Vandergriff-Avery, 2001). Hence, instead of using case studies in my book, I wrote a chapter of short stories, at the end of which I interviewed the characters to draw out the points I wanted to communicate. When tested in the classroom and in training situations in Australia and New Zealand, this method proved to be highly effective among the participants in facilitating their ability to put themselves in someone else's position and think through the specifics of that person's experiences. The exercise works well with traditional-age students and mature participants.

REFERENCES

Arasaratnam, L. A. (2011). *Perception and communication in intercultural spaces.* Lanham, MD: University Press of America.

Arasaratnam, L. A., & Doerfel, M. L. (2005). Intercultural communication competence: Identifying key components from multicultural perspectives. *International Journal of Intercultural Relations, 29,* 137–163.

Blanton, P. W., & Vandergriff-Avery, M. (2001). Marital therapy and marital power: Constructing narratives of sharing relational and positional power. *Contemporary Family Therapy, 23*(3), 295–308.

Morgan, S. E., Movius, L., & Cody, M. J. (2009). The power of narratives: The effect of entertainment television organ donation storylines on attitudes, knowledge, and behaviors of donors and nondonors. *Journal of Communication, 59,* 135–151.

 HANDOUT S2.6

"NATHAN'S HERO" SHORT STORY

By Lily A. Arasaratnam

Nathan clenched and unclenched his fists because somehow that action seemed to prevent him from punching the young man standing in front of him, though he longed to do so. He was so furious that he could feel the rage boiling his blood and pounding down his veins. He took a few deep breaths before speaking.

"Get out of my way."

The guy's face broke into a slow humorless grin. "Whatever you say, white boy," he replied, half raised his hands in a gesture of mock surrender, and slowly backed away.

Nathan stormed passed him, not lingering to find out whether his self-control would have held out for much longer. He reached the benches by the side of the cafeteria and sat down, still shaking in rage. His Dad had always taught him that the best way to control one's anger is to first physically position one's self in a relaxed posture. He took a few more deep breaths. This exercise reminded him of his father; and tears of anger and deep sorrow stung his eyes. Everything was so wrong.

As he fought to control his temper, Nathan remembered the letter his mother got six months ago. She had read it and sat down with a dazed expression, holding it limply in one hand. When Nathan gently retrieved it and proceeded to read, the letter said:

Dear Mrs. Wilson,

We have finally concluded the investigation as per your request into your husband's presumed death four years ago. The results of our investigation reveal that your husband was killed while attempting to break up a violent street fight. As the fight happened to involve some highly connected members of the crime world, they had quickly disposed of his body and wiped all traces of his presence to avoid trouble, especially once they discovered that he was American. Though I have reported this matter to the Somalia officials, I doubt the murderer will be identified or arrested given the time that has elapsed since his death. It was by accident that I stumbled upon the truth, as I happened to question someone who used to live in the neighborhood where your husband had worked and recalled the tragic incident that led to his death. He was most reluctant to speak of it, but upon persistent questioning and the promise of discretion confirmed that the white man who was killed in their village was indeed your husband. Even though your husband's killer cannot be brought to justice, I hope this letter will at least bring closure to you and your family.

Sincerely,
R. J. Bingham

Nathan felt like someone had punched him in the stomach. After all these years, finally, there it was—the tiny ray of hope that his father might be alive, completely snuffed out. Mr. Bingham was one of his father's most trusted colleagues, and Nathan knew that unless he was absolutely sure he would not have sent that letter. When his father who was employed by a non-profit organization had accepted a covert diplomatic assignment to Somalia a little over four years ago, his mother was keen to go with him. But he had convinced her to stay in Chicago with Nathan, given Nathan was twelve at that time and very involved in sports and school activities and his father did not want to uproot him for six months. Nathan had always thought of his father as a superhero, one who dived in wherever there was trouble and solved it! His father

Reproduced from: Lily A. Arasaratnam, "Narrative Insights," in *Building Cultural Competence: Innovative Activities and Models*, eds. K. Berardo and D. K. Deardorff (Sterling, VA: Stylus, 2012), 98–103.

had taught him to be open-minded about different people, and always see the positive aspect in a situation. When they stopped hearing from his father for several weeks, his mother had tried to contact him through the official channels. It appeared he had somehow disappeared without a trace. Nathan's mother tried all means possible to find out what had happened to him, including attempting to go to Somalia herself in search of answers; but her parents and relatives had dissuaded her from following this course of action due to the political unrest in Somalia. As months turned to years, they feared the worst and then began to reluctantly accept the grim possibility that Ted Wilson was dead. When one of Nathan's father's colleagues, Bingham, accepted a position in East Africa years later, he had paid a visit to Nathan's home and promised his mother that he would attempt to find answers. And finally they had the answer for which they had waited.

Nathan could not fathom that this man who had dedicated his life to diplomacy and peace had been killed violently in a strange land by strange men who would never be brought to justice. He felt unspeakable anger toward the unknown Somalian man who had murdered his hero—and he felt worse for feeling such hatred, because he knew his hero wouldn't have approved of such feelings.

Nathan had walked past the group of black guys hanging out outside the cafeteria a hundred times. They often spoke loudly and laughed riotously as if they were having the time of their lives. They never paid attention to Nathan as he walked by them on his way home every day. It was as if he was invisible.

But everything changed when, after an exciting win over a rival team, the school quarter-back assaulted one of the cheerleaders in a drunken haze. The incident was particularly volatile because the cheerleader happened to be black—and the quarter-back was white. The whole school was abuzz with gossip, indignation, outrage, and racial tension.

Several fights had broken out between groups of white and black students. A few black students had cornered and harassed a white girl in retaliation for the incident with the cheerleader. Outraged, a few of the white players from the football team had beaten up a couple of black students on their way to the library late one night.

It was during this time that the group of black men who hung out by the cafeteria noticed Nathan as he walked by.

One of them called out loudly, "Yeah, that's it, hurry along white boy! This is a dangerous part of town for you."

Another one said, "You're not so tough when you're on your own, are you?"

Something about the guy's tone and attitude unleashed a flood of images in Nathan's mind about what his father's last moments must have been like as he intervened in a street fight. And boiling rage, as he had never known before, descended upon him.

Nathan was shaking in his rage, as he sat on the bench.

He didn't want to walk away. He didn't care that he was outnumbered. He didn't care that if he acted on his anger he'd end up adding fuel to the already volatile climate on campus. He just wanted to go back and punch every single one of those guys.

But just as he was about to act on his rage, he heard his name called.

"Nathan, do you have a moment?"

He looked up to see his Sociology teacher, Mr. Walls, walking toward him with his usual briefcase in one hand and cup of coffee in the other. He stopped in front of Nathan, his eyes on level with Nathan's as Nathan continued to stare at him from his seated position on the high bench.

"I found your essay on peace quite interesting," Mr. Walls said. "Batman as a metaphor for enforcing peace through taking justice into one's own hands?"

Nathan was in no mood to discuss his essay, but he didn't want to be rude to Mr. Walls as he was one of his favorite teachers.

"Sometimes the justice system doesn't work," Nathan said. "Sometimes the only way to enforce peace is to find and punish the lawbreakers yourself. But you have to do it justly. Like Batman and the other superhero figures. Their way of enforcing peace resonates with people. That's why these mythical characters have lasted generations of folklore."

"I saw those boys taunting you just now. According to your view of justice, what should you do?"

Nathan didn't want to admit to a teacher that he was contemplating getting into a fist fight, but he was too angry to self-monitor—and he trusted Mr. Walls. So he blurted out, "I want to go back there and have it out with them. If they think they're accomplishing something by standing there bullying people, then someone has to stand up to them."

"So where does it stop?" Mr. Walls asked in his quiet deep voice. "One thoughtless drunk student did something cruel and foolish. Others did more cruel and foolish things to try to make up for the first cruel and foolish act. Now the whole campus is a warzone. Where does it stop, Nathan?"

Nathan remained silent.

Mr. Walls sat down beside him on the bench. He gazed ahead, looking at the group of black men now eying the both of them from across the lawn. "You know, when I was young I lived in a project. Every time there was a robbery or any incident, the cops would come and round up any guys they found on the streets. It was as if every black guy they saw was a potential criminal. I was arrested at least five times before I turned sixteen. I remember being furious about the injustice of it all. I could say I even hated white people on sight. I felt they were either oppressors or enablers who knew nothing about me or the injustice I was being subjected to simply because of the color of my skin. I wanted to graffiti all of their preppy white neighborhoods!" He shook his head wistfully and laughed.

Nathan stared at him with wide eyes. He couldn't imagine the wise, gentle Mr. Walls as a street thug with a spray can. "Did you ever do it, Mr. Walls?" he asked.

"No," he smiled. His dark eyes focused on Nathan. "No I didn't, because one day I met a white cop who changed my life. I was walking home late at night and the cop car pulled up beside me. Here we go again, I thought. I braced myself for another arrest. But the cop rolled down his window and asked me, 'Do you know where Graham Street is? I'm new on patrol and a bit lost!' he grinned sheepishly. 'My partner went to get coffee on Graham Street and called me to pick him up but I kinda got turned around.' It was the weirdest thing. I had never had a cop talk to me like I was a human being. But here was this guy, asking me for directions like it was the most normal thing to do. I gave him directions. He thanked me and said, 'Be careful now. I hear this is a rough neighborhood. Are you okay walking by yourself?' And that was what did it. The way that cop spoke to me that day, not at all noticing my color, talking to me like he would to any other kid walking alone at night . . . not assuming I was up to no good just because I was black. He broke a pattern that day. And he broke something in me."

Mr. Walls paused and took in Nathan's somber expression. "Violence and hatred are self-perpetuating, Nathan. One wrong deed to correct another isn't going to bring about peace. Someone has to break the cycle. Someone has to choose that they're not going to contribute to hatred, no matter how much they've been wronged." He sipped the last of his coffee, hopped down from the bench, and picked up his briefcase. He turned his steady gaze once more to Nathan. "Even Batman may have ended up as a high school teacher if he hadn't decided to go after the criminals of Gotham City in retaliation for the ones who had once killed his parents." With that, he walked away.

It wasn't until Mr. Walls had become a tiny dot on the horizon that Nathan realized that his cheeks were wet with tears. He looked up as he heard voices coming by. It was the same group of black guys who had taunted him. One of them stared at Nathan, as if daring him to say something. Nathan held his gaze . . . and slowly nodded. Not a challenge, but a courtesy. He saw the expression in the guy's eyes change from a dare to confusion. Then his expression slowly became thoughtful as he continued walking by. Nathan caught him turning around to look at him again, as the group disappeared out of sight.

"Somebody has to choose to stop the cycle," Mr. Wall's words echoed in his head. Somehow they sounded like his Dad's.

13. WEB SAVVY: CULTURAL DIFFERENCES

Jeanne Feldman

This activity objectively examines cultural difference through the medium of Internet website design. Certain cultural tendencies actually manifest themselves physically in the way websites are structured and conceived.

Key Focus

Understand differences

Type of Activity

Case study

Objectives

As a result of this activity, participants will

- recognize cross-cultural communication differences,
- see one's own culture more clearly, and
- see the concrete effects of different cultural values representing the same organization or profession.

Appropriate Audience

Adults and university students

Level of Challenge

Medium

Group Size

6 to 20 people

Time

2 to 3 hours

Materials

- Handouts
- Access to Internet

Preparation

- Make copies of the article in sections.
- Ensure that computer/Internet access is available.

Activity Setup

Introduce the handout on cultural dimensions and web design as a framework (see Handout S2.7), and let the participants know they will be doing research online as a group, discussing their findings based on the article framework, and providing a summary of their discussions with the whole group.

Introducing the article can be done one of two ways:

1. Distribute different sections of the article to subgroups (one part per group). Have each group read its part of the article and then present the information to the entire group. Discuss the findings to make sure there is a consensus of understanding, and then distribute the debriefing website analysis questions (see Handout S2.8).
2. Simply distribute the article to each group and have each group discuss it to make sure group members understand it.

Managing the Activity

Regardless of how the initial article is introduced, follow these instructions for using the websites:

1. Each subgroup analyzes related websites (either two websites in the same profession/

industry from two different countries or two websites from the same international company in two different countries). The assignment is to answer the debriefing questions in Handout S2.8.

2. Each subgroup presents a summary of its discussion to the entire group.

3. Debrief the group on the overall activity, following the group summaries, using the questions in the following section. In addition, have a discussion on the validity or not of the cultural differences predicted in the article and the actual differences found on the websites.

Debriefing the Activity

1. What happened in this activity?
2. How did your responses/perspectives compare to others in your group?
3. What surprised you in this activity?
4. What cross-cultural lessons can be learned from this activity and why are those lessons important?

Key Insights and Learnings

Through this process and debriefing, participants usually learn that

- cultural differences do exist and can determine how we see the world,
- cultural differences can be seen visually,
- website design reveals cultural values, and
- there is no one correct way to see the world.

Variations

Variation 1. The exercise can be done by subgroups or by individual participants who then discuss it in pairs.

Variation 2. Instead of distributing the article in sections, just give the entire article to each group, which would eliminate some of the time needed to complete this activity.

Facilitation Tips and Suggestions

This exercise works particularly well with web-savvy groups as it allows them to work with a medium they are naturally familiar with to explore cultural themes.

- Allow participants to make discoveries on their own.
- Encourage group discussion, as there may be differences of opinion within the group.
- Adapt a list of websites you put on a handout (see Handout S2.8) to the needs/interests/backgrounds of the participants. For example, if you are working with human resources professionals, suggest they compare the recruiting pages on different companies' websites to look at how the same company may be marketed differently to appeal to professionals in different countries.
- Encourage participants to use technology to creatively present their findings, either by showing the websites and highlighting key differences or pulling screen shots of the websites into a presentation and pointing out the differences. When conducted in this way, this exercise can essentially become an overnight assignment if used with student groups to give them more time to prepare their presentations.
- The focus of this exercise is for participants to experience and to see visually what is usually described intellectually.

About This Exercise

I read Marcus and Gould's (2000) article and realized that students could see objective examples of cultural differences in a totally modern medium. After examining the website examples in the article, I realized concrete differences in the conception and design of websites revealed different ways of seeing the world and were consistent with the dimensions of culture in Hofstede's (2001) model (see Handout S2.7).

REFERENCES

Hofstede, G. (2001). *Culture's consequences: Comparing values, behaviors, institutions and organizations across nations*. Thousand Oaks, CA: Sage.

Marcus, M., & Gould, E. W. (2000, June). *Cultural dimensions and global web user interface design: What? So what? Now what?* Paper presented at the Sixth Conference on Human Factors and the Web, Austin, TX.

 HANDOUT S2.7

CULTURAL DIMENSIONS AND GLOBAL WEB USER-INTERFACE DESIGN: WHAT? SO WHAT? NOW WHAT?

Aaron Marcus and Emilie W. Gould

Abstract

This paper introduces dimensions of culture, as analyzed by Geert Hofstede in his classic study of cultures in organizations, and considers how they might affect user-interface designs. Examples from the web illustrate the cultural dimensions.

Introduction

Professional analysts and designers generally agree that well-designed user interfaces improve the performance and appeal of the web, helping to convert "tourists" or "browsers" to "residents" and "customers." The user-interface development process focuses attention on understanding users and acknowledging demographic diversity. But in a global economy, these differences may reflect worldwide cultures. Companies that want to do international business on the web should consider the impact of culture on the understanding and use of web-based communication, content, and tools.

A few simple questions illustrate the depth of the issues.

Consider your favorite website. How might this website be understood and used in New York, Paris, London, Beijing, New Delhi, or Tokyo, assuming that adequate verbal translation were accomplished? Might something in its metaphors, mental model, navigation, interaction, or appearance confuse, or even offend and alienate, a user?

Consider the order in which you prefer to find information. If you are planning a trip by train, do you want to see the schedule information first or read about the organization and assess its credibility? Different cultures look for different data to make decisions.

Hofstede's Dimensions of Culture

During 1978–83, the Dutch cultural anthropologist Geert Hofstede conducted detailed interviews with hundreds of IBM employees in 53 countries. Through standard statistical analysis of fairly large data sets, he was able to determine patterns of similarities and differences among the replies. From this data analysis, he formulated his theory that world cultures vary along consistent, fundamental dimensions. Since his subjects were limited to one multinational corporation's worldwide employees, and thus to one company culture, he ascribed their differences to the effects of their national cultures. (One weakness is that he maintained that each country has just one dominant culture.)

In the 1990s, Hofstede published a more accessible version of his research publication in *Cultures and Organizations: Software of the Mind* (1996). His focus was not on defining culture as a refinement of the mind (or "highly civilized" attitudes and behavior) but rather on highlighting essential patterns of thinking, feeling, and acting that are well established by late childhood. These cultural differences manifest themselves in a culture's choices of symbols, heroes/heroines, rituals, and values.

Hofstede identified five dimensions and rated 53 countries on indices for each dimension, normalized to values (usually) of 0 to 100. Three of his five dimensions of culture are the following:

- Power distance
- Collectivism versus individualism
- Uncertainty avoidance

Reproduced from: Jeanne Feldman, "Web Savvy: Cultural Differences," in *Building Cultural Competence: Innovative Activities and Models,* eds. K. Berardo and D. K. Deardorff (Sterling, VA: Stylus, 2012), 104–110.

Each of Hofstede's terms appears below with our explanation of implications for user-interface and web design, and illustrations of characteristic websites.

Power Distance

Power distance (PD) refers to the extent to which less powerful members expect and accept unequal power distribution within a culture.

Hofstede claims that high PD countries tend to have centralized political power and exhibit tall hierarchies in organizations with large differences in salary and status. Subordinates may view the "boss" as a benevolent dictator and are expected to do as they are told. Parents teach obedience, and expect respect. Teachers possess wisdom and are automatically esteemed. Inequalities are expected, and may even be desired.

Low PD countries tend to view subordinates and supervisors as closer together and more interchangeable, with flatter hierarchies in organizations and less difference in salaries and status. Parents and children, and teachers and students, may view themselves more as equals (but not necessarily as identical). Equality is expected and generally desired. There are some interesting correlations for power distance: low PD countries tend to have higher geographic latitude, smaller populations, and/or higher gross domestic product (GDP) per capita than high PD countries.

Hofstede notes that these differences are hundreds or even thousands of years old. He does not believe they will disappear quickly from traditional cultures, even with powerful global telecommunication systems. Recent research has shown that the dimensions have remained quite stable for the last twenty years.

Based on this definition, we believe power distance may influence the following aspects of user-interface and web design:

- Access to information: highly (high PD) versus less-highly (low PD) structured.
- Hierarchies in mental models: tall versus shallow.
- Emphasis on the social and moral order (e.g., nationalism or religion) and its symbols: significant/frequent versus minor/infrequent use.
- Focus on expertise, authority, experts, certifications, official stamps, or logos: strong versus weak.
- Prominence given to leaders versus citizens, customers, or employees.
- Importance of security and restrictions or barriers to access: explicit, enforced, frequent restrictions on users versus transparent, integrated, implicit freedom to roam.
- Social roles used to organize information (e.g., a managers' section obvious to all but sealed off from nonmanagers): frequent versus infrequent.

These PD differences can be illustrated on the web by examining university websites from two countries with very different PD indices. The Universiti Utara Malaysia (www.uum.edu.my) is located in Malaysia, a country with a PD index rating of 104, the highest in Hofstede's analysis.

The website from the Ichthus Hogeschool (www.inholland.nl) is located in the Netherlands, with a PD index rating of 38.

Note the differences in the two websites. (www.ISCOM.fr)

Individualism Versus Collectivism

Individualism in cultures implies loose ties; everyone is expected to look after one's self or immediate family but no one else. Collectivism implies that people are integrated from birth into strong, cohesive groups that protect them in exchange for unquestioning loyalty.

Hofstede found that individualistic cultures value personal time, freedom, challenge, and such extrinsic motivators as material rewards at work. In family relations, they value honesty/truth, talking things out, using guilt to achieve behavioral goals, and maintaining self-respect. Their societies and governments place individual social-economic interests over the group, maintain strong rights to privacy, nurture strong private opinions (expected from everyone), restrain the power of the state in the economy, emphasize the political power of voters, maintain strong freedom of the press, and profess the ideologies of self-actualization, self-realization, self-government, and freedom.

At work, collectivist cultures value training, physical conditions, skills, and the intrinsic rewards of mastery. In family relations, they value harmony more than honesty/truth (and silence more than speech), use shame to achieve behavioral goals, and strive to maintain face. Their societies and governments place collective social-economic interests over the individual, may invade private life and regulate opinions, favor laws and rights for groups over individuals, dominate the economy, control the press, and profess the ideologies of harmony, consensus, and equality.

Based on this definition, we believe individualism and collectivism may influence the following aspects of user-interface and web design:

- Motivation based on personal achievement: maximized (expect the extraordinary) for individualist cultures versus underplayed (in favor of group achievement) for collectivist cultures.
- Images of success: demonstrated through materialism and consumerism versus achievement of social-political agendas.
- Rhetorical style: controversial/argumentative speech and tolerance or encouragement of extreme claims versus official slogans and subdued hyperbole and controversy.
- Prominence given youth and action versus aged, experienced, wise leaders and states of being.
- Importance given individuals versus products shown by themselves or with groups.
- Underlying sense of social morality: emphasis on truth versus relationships.
- Emphasis on change: what is new and unique versus tradition and history.
- Willingness to provide personal information versus protection of personal data differentiating the individual from the group.

The effects of these differences can be illustrated on the web by examining national park websites from two countries with very different IC indices. The Glacier Bay National Park website (www.nps.gov/glba/evc.htm) is located in the USA, which has the highest IC index rating (91). The website from the National Parks of Costa Rica (www.costaricahomepages.com/places_to_go/national_parks) is located in a country with an IC index rating of 15.

Uncertainty Avoidance

People vary in the extent that they feel anxiety about uncertain or unknown matters, as opposed to the more universal feeling of fear caused by known or understood threats. Cultures vary in their avoidance of uncertainty, creating different rituals and having different values regarding formality, punctuality, legal-religious-social requirements, and tolerance for ambiguity.

Hofstede notes that cultures with high uncertainty avoidance (UA) tend to have high rates of suicide, alcoholism, and accidental deaths, and high numbers of prisoners per capita. Businesses may have more formal rules, require longer career commitments, and focus on tactical operations rather than strategy. These cultures tend to be expressive; people talk with their hands, raise their voices, and show emotions. People seem active, emotional, even aggressive; shun ambiguous situations; and expect structure in organizations, institutions, and relationships to help make events clearly interpretable and predictable. Teachers are expected to be experts who know the answers and may speak in cryptic language that excludes novices. In high-UA cultures, what is different may be viewed as a threat, and what is "dirty" (unconventional) is often equated with what is dangerous.

By contrast, low-UA cultures tend to have higher caffeine consumption, lower calorie intake, higher heart-disease death rates, and more chronic psychosis per capita. Businesses may be more informal and focus more on long-range strategic matters than day-to-day operations. These cultures tend to be less expressive and less openly anxious; people behave quietly without showing aggression or strong emotions (though their caffeine consumption may be intended to combat depression from their inability to express their feelings). People seem easy-going, even relaxed. Teachers may not know all the answers (or there may be more than one correct answer), run more open-ended classes, and are expected to speak in plain language. In these cultures, what is different may be viewed as simply curious, or perhaps ridiculous.

Based on this definition, we believe uncertainty avoidance may influence contrary aspects of user-interface and web design. High-UA cultures would emphasize the following:

- Simplicity, with clear metaphors, limited choices, and restricted amounts of data
- Attempts to reveal or forecast the results or implications of actions before users act
- Navigation schemes intended to prevent users from becoming lost
- Mental models and help systems that focus on reducing "user errors"
- Redundant cues (color, typography, sound, etc.) to reduce ambiguity

Low-UA cultures would emphasize the reverse:

- Complexity with maximal content and choices
- Acceptance (even encouragement) of wandering and risk, with a stigma on "overprotection"
- Less control of navigation; for example, links might open new windows leading away from the original location
- Mental models and help systems might focus on understanding underlying concepts rather than narrow tasks
- Coding of color, typography, and sound to maximize information (multiple links without redundant cueing)

Examples of UA differences can be illustrated on the web by examining airline websites from two countries with very different UA indices. The Sabena Airlines website (www.sabena.com) is located in Belgium, a country with a UA of 94, the highest of the cultures studied. This website shows a home page with very simple, clear imagery and limited choices.

The British Airways website (www.britishairways.com) from the United Kingdom (UA = 35) shows much more complexity of content and choices with popup windows, multiple types of interface controls, and "hidden" content that must be displayed by scrolling.

Conclusions

There is no escaping bias; all people develop cultural values based on their environment and early training as children. Not everyone in a society fits the cultural pattern precisely, but there is enough statistical regularity to identify trends and tendencies. These trends and tendencies should not be treated as defective or used to create negative stereotypes but recognized as different patterns of values and thought. In a multi-cultural world, it is necessary to cooperate to achieve practical goals without requiring everyone to think, act, and believe identically.

Aaron Marcus, president
Aaron Marcus and Associates, Inc.
E-mail: Aaron@AmandA.com
Web: www.Amanda.com

Emilie West Gould, adjunct
Lally School of Management
Rensselaer Polytechnic Institute (RPI)
E-mail: goulde@rpi.edu

 HANDOUT S2.8

QUESTIONS FOR WEBSITE ANALYSIS AND DISCUSSION

1. Describe the website—what images are used? What is the navigation? In your opinion, how formal or informal are the sites? Based on what? What is the balance between images and text? Is the design static or is there movement on the screen? Is the focus on hierarchy or on equality (how do you know?)? How do different group members describe the website in these terms?
2. What cultural values are promoted through the website, based on the Hofstede values outlined in this article? Is importance given to individuals or to groups? Is the site navigation simple or complex?
3. How is this website viewed in terms of your own cultural conditioning? What impresses you most about the website? How does this differ from others in your group? What could be attributed to these differences in responses?
4. What other cultural insights can you gain by reviewing this website?

Sample websites that can be used for analysis:

Holland
 Ichthus Hogeschool
 http://www.inholland.nl/
France
 L'Institut d'études politiques (Sciences Po)
 http://www.sciences-po.fr/portail/
 Ecole nationale d'administration (ENA)
 http://www.ena.fr/accueil.php
 Ecole Polytechnique
 http://www.polytechnique.fr/
 Institut supérieur de communication (ISCO)
 http://www.iscom.fr/pages/bienvenue/index.php
U.S.
 Harvard University
 http://www.harvard.edu/
 Yale University
 http://www.yale.edu/
 Stanford University
 http://www.stanford.edu/
 Duke University
 http://www.duke.edu/
 American University
 http://www.american.edu/index1.html
Companies:
 McDonald's U.S.
 http://www.mcdonalds.com/us/en/home.html
 McDonald's France
 http://www.mcdonalds.fr/
 Ikea U.S.
 http://www.ikea.com/us/en/
 Ikea France
 http://www.ikea.com/fr/fr/

14. CULTURE IN CURRENT EVENTS

Jennifer Evanuik

Through this case study approach, participants apply aspects of intercultural communication to real-life events. Best used as a culminating exercise at the end of an intercultural training session, this activity will engage participants in a discussion of intercultural aspects in a context that is familiar to them.

Key Focus

Understand differences

Type of Activity

Case study

Objectives

As a result of this activity, participants will be able to

- identify aspects of intercultural communication, such as direct versus indirect communication, in real-life current events;
- understand the unintended consequences of intercultural miscommunication; and
- identify the manifestation of values in real-life current events.

Appropriate Audience

Adults

Level of Challenge

Medium

Group Size

3 to 40 people

Time

20 minutes

Materials

One copy of the case study and one copy of the debriefing questions per participant

Preparation

- Look for a short international news item (i.e., case study; see Handout S2.9) in newspapers, magazines, or journals that highlights values or cultural traits that are different from those of the target audience, or that demonstrate instances of intercultural conflict. The facilitator should draw upon his or her own personal knowledge of current events and consider the academic or professional interests of the participants when searching for news items. For example, if participants are business professionals, consider looking for articles regarding an international marketing failure or the failed introduction of a company or product into a new culture. Search various online and print news sources including newspapers or magazines from different countries with varying perspectives (e.g., CNN, BBC, *New York Times, Time, Life, Le Monde, Christian Science Monitor*, etc.).
- When reviewing articles, look for an example of a misunderstanding, conflict, or failure to succeed in the international arena. Some articles may directly state the cultural difference(s), while other differences are inferred. The facilitator should decide which type would be most appropriate for his or her audience (see Handout S2.10).
- Identify key phrases as well as the conflicting values or cultural traits in the case study article for participants during the discussion. This step may require the facilitator to familiarize himself or herself with the culture(s)

involved in the case study to help fill in any gaps in the discussion.

- Print one copy of the article (with citation) and debriefing questions (see Handout S2.11) for each participant.

Activity Setup

This activity is most effective if it is preceded by an overview of intercultural communication and aspects of culture (e.g., values, perceptions, stereotypes, communication styles, proxemics, etc.). It can be used as a culminating exercise at the end of a training session to demonstrate how all these elements come together in real-world situations.

To set up this activity, briefly restate the topics that have been covered in the training session thus far. Tell the group this exercise is meant to provide an opportunity to apply what was learned in the training session to a real-life situation, as well as to witness how intercultural communication has an impact on everyday occurrences.

Managing the Activity

1. Distribute a relevant article you found in accordance with the guidelines under "Preparation" and the debriefing questions to each participant.
2. Ask the participants if, based on the headline, they are familiar with this particular situation. If so, ask for their opinion on it, such as, "What do you think about what happened?" as a casual discussion before starting the activity. This will help the facilitator gauge where the participants are coming from or if they have strong feelings or biases about the situation. This information may be useful during the debriefing.
3. Allow up to five minutes for participants to thoroughly read and analyze the article.
4. Ask participants to underline key phrases that reveal values, cultural traits, or sources of intercultural miscommunication.
5. If desired, encourage small-group discussion before debriefing the whole group.

Debriefing the Activity

- Ask the group to name the key phrases they underlined. Write these on a board, if desired.

- Then open a discussion with the following questions:
  - What value(s), communication style(s), or cultural trait(s) do these key phrases indicate?
  - What if this same situation occurred in your home culture? Would you expect to see the same reactions? Why or why not? (This question should prompt participants to compare and contrast the value[s], communication style[s], or cultural trait[s] of their home culture[s] to the culture[s] described in the article.)
  - How might someone from a different cultural background misinterpret or react to the situation described in this case study?
  - How does having an awareness of the cultural explanation behind this story change your outlook on the situation (assuming the case study is in contrast to the culture[s] of the participants)?
  - What are the broader insights and lessons that can be applied through this activity to other cross-cultural situations?

Key Insights and Learnings

Through this process and debriefing, participants usually learn that

- differences in communication styles or values can lead to undue misunderstandings;
- failures or conflicts in the business or political world always have a cultural subtext and can usually be explained, at least in part, by a misalignment of cultural perspectives;
- it is imperative for an individual to take time to deconstruct a situation and consider another's point of view before reacting to a situation; and
- the concepts taught in intercultural training sessions do not exist in a vacuum and are manifested in everyday life.

Variations

Variation 1. The exercise will work with one to three case studies. Depending on the time available and the size of the audience, choose the appropriate number of case studies to discuss.

Variation 2. Case studies may be discussed in smaller groups. Divide the audience into small groups (three to five participants each), and assign each group a different case study to analyze and present to the larger group.

Variation 3. If participants are able to do advance work, have them look for an example of a news article in advance and bring a copy of it with them. Make sure they understand the news article needs to reflect an underlying cross-cultural tension or issue. The articles can be shared in pairs so that copies are not needed for everyone. Then pairs can be grouped to debrief their discussions and learnings (i.e., two pairs in each group). Having participants bring articles with them ensures that they bring articles relevant to their situation. The risk is that the article they bring may not have a relevant underlying cultural issue to discuss, so it is best to be prepared with additional articles.

Facilitation Tips and Suggestions

- The success of this exercise rests on the facilitator's ability to identify case studies that will pique the interests of the audience. It is a living exercise that can and should be adapted as news evolves and as participant groups change. Additionally, potential case studies can be kept in an archive for future use.
- Depending on the particular article(s) being used, different aspects of intercultural conflict and communication may be discussed. Debriefing questions should target the specific content.
- Participants should already have a basic understanding of cultural concepts related to communication before completing the exercise. This exercise works well when administered toward the end of a program after concepts such as subjective/objective culture, individualism and collectivism, direct and indirect communication, verbal and nonverbal communication, and high/low context, values, stereotypes, and perception have been discussed. It then serves as a good overarching wrap-up activity that brings together many components that have been discussed previously.
- This exercise was originally designed for intercultural training for university students

about to embark on exchange programs. The participants largely came from engineering and science backgrounds. This exercise was effective because students from these fields generally do not already have a cultural vocabulary. The exercise allowed participants to see terms and concepts discussed in orientation (such as values, perception, stereotypes, and styles of communication) presented in concrete and current scenarios. For this reason, this exercise would be appropriate for participants from fields such as business or engineering with practical and relevant examples.

- This exercise is most effective with participants from a variety of cultural backgrounds.
- Well-known current events can be used as case studies so participants can learn how to see the cultural subtext in the world around them. For example, the 2010 Toyota recall scandal and the BP oil spill in the Gulf of Mexico are excellent examples of intercultural conflict because of different communication styles (e.g., direct versus indirect communication, the concept of saving face, the use of self-deprecating humor, detached versus emotional responses).
- If participants do not provide much discussion, the facilitator should suggest one or two of the predetermined themes to encourage further discussion. The facilitator may need to fill in the blanks if participants do not make the connections on their own.
- Because of the breadth of news stories available, this exercise could be conducted with participants from a variety of fields, such as health care, public policy, business, science, engineering, or architecture.

About This Exercise

Working in the international programs office at a university, one of my responsibilities is to develop intercultural communication training seminars for undergraduate students about to embark on international study programs. I typically use case studies as part of my seminars but found that scripted case studies did not resonate with my particular student population (largely from engineering and science). To make intercultural concepts seem relevant and tangible to my students, I began to look for examples of intercultural conflict or miscommunication in current events I knew my students would relate to. I found that many news stories from around the world could be analyzed through an intercultural lens. Linking the real world to intercultural theories was my main goal in developing this exercise. I have found that students are more engaged in these real-life case studies and consequently demonstrate a better understanding of the seminar material.

 HANDOUT S2.9

INTERCULTURAL COMMUNICATION IN CURRENT EVENTS:
CASE STUDIES

Take 5 minutes to read the article and complete the following tasks/questions:

1. Underline key phrases that reveal values, cultural traits, or sources of intercultural miscommunication.

2. What value(s), communication style(s), or cultural trait(s) do these key phrases indicate?

3. Would you expect to see this situation play out this way in the United States (or in your home culture)?

4. Why or why not?

5. How might someone from a different cultural background misinterpret or react to the situation described in this case study?

6. How does having an awareness of the cultural "explanation" behind this story change your outlook on the situation?

Reproduced from: Jennifer Evanuik, "Culture in Current Events," in *Building Cultural Competence: Innovative Activities and Models,* eds. K. Berardo and D. K. Deardorff (Sterling, VA: Stylus, 2012), 111–118.

📄 HANDOUT S2.10

SUGGESTED CASE STUDY ARTICLES

- Bolt, Kristen Millares. "Starbucks adjusts its formula in China." Seattle Post-Intelligencer.com. 16 June 2005. <http://www.seattlepi.com/default/article/Starbucks-adjusts-its-formula-in-China-1176089.php>

- Fowler, Geoffrey A. "Converting the masses: Starbucks in China." *Global Policy.org*. 17 July 2003. <http://www.globalpolicy.org/component/content/article/162/27615.html>

- Quinn, Ben. "British hear prejudice in US tone on BP oil spill." *Christian Science Monitor.com*. 4 June 2010. <http://www.csmonitor.com/World/Europe/2010/0604/British-hear-prejudice-in-US-tone-on-BP-oil-spill>

- Voigt, Kevin. "Toyoda in Washington: A clash of cultures?" *CNN.com*. 2 April 2010. <http://www.cnn.com/2010/BUSINESS/02/24/money.toyoda.culture.clash/index.html>

- Watkins, Michael. "I want to live like common people: BP and the great PR divide." *Harvard Business Review.org*. 18 June 2010. <http://blogs.hbr.org/watkins/2010/06/i_want_to_live_like_common_peo.html>

- Winterman, Denise. "BP's gift for the gaffe." *BBC.com*. 21 June 2010. <http://news.bbc.co.uk/2/hi/8744173.stm>

 HANDOUT S2.11

EXAMPLE OF THE ACTIVITY AND DEBRIEFING

Distribute the CNN article "Toyoda in Washington: A clash of cultures?" While distributing, casually ask participants if they remember this incident and what they thought about it. Allow 5 minutes for participants to thoroughly read the article. Ask them to underline or circle any key phrases that indicate a conflict, difference in values, perception, or communication styles. If participants are seated in groups, encourage small-group discussion before starting group debrief.

1. Underline key phrases that reveal values, cultural traits, or sources of intercultural miscommunication. Possible phrases from the article that could be circled are:

   "the company leadership responded in a very Japanese fashion"
   "decision-making process was painfully slow"
   "long silence"
   "hallmark of the Japanese culture of consensus building"
   "you don't see a lot of rapid response"
   "how Toyoda handles hostile questioning"
   "deferential Japanese press"
   "they are careful not to upset or annoy business leaders"
   "In the West . . . they are targets of aggressive media"
   "when in an apology mode . . . will be very humble"
   "you don't necessarily look people in the eye"
   "mistaken as weakness or perhaps trying to hide something"
   "Japanese language tends to be indirect"

2. What value(s), communication style(s), or cultural trait(s) do these key phrases indicate?
   The article references the fact that the Japanese tend to use an indirect communication style. This style is in direct contrast to the more direct style of Americans. The American media mistook Mr. Toyoda's indirectness as unwillingness to answer questions and to be forthcoming. The article also references the fact that he would not make eye contact. In Mr. Toyoda's culture, this is consistent with being apologetic. But, to Americans, this was again a sign that he was being evasive. Finally, the article mentions that Toyota took a longer time than Americans would expect to provide a response to the brake failures. While Americans interpreted this as indifference or weak leadership, the Japanese were taking time to build consensus on the most appropriate measures.

3. Would you expect to see this situation play out this way in the United States (or in your home culture)?
   No.

4. Why or why not?
   In the United States, we would expect the CEO of a company to respond quickly and emotionally to a negative situation. We would expect him/her to take full responsibility immediately, show compassion for those affected, and to demonstrate that they are working fastidiously on finding a solution. We are accustomed to quick responses during times of crises (and criticize those who "take too long to respond"). We associate leaders with people who are, in American terms, excellent public speakers (i.e., concise, emphatic, relatable, and direct).

Reproduced from: Jennifer Evanuik, "Culture in Current Events," in *Building Cultural Competence: Innovative Activities and Models,* eds. K. Berardo and D. K. Deardorff (Sterling, VA: Stylus, 2012), 111–118.

5. How might someone from a different cultural background misinterpret or react to the situation described in this case study?
   (This question is included in case the participants come from a variety of cultural backgrounds and have alternative interpretations of the situation aside from those discussed in number 4.)
   Alternative question for number 5: Would you expect this situation to play out differently in the culture where you will be studying/working? How?
   (Responses to this vary depending on how familiar the participants are with the culture[s] in which they are going to be living.)

6. How does having an awareness of the cultural "explanation" behind this story change your outlook on the situation?
   Yes; it makes one more empathetic to Mr. Toyoda's difficulty with dealing with the American press and Congress. It also helps one appreciate that in some cultures, it is most appropriate to take time to discuss and evaluate possible courses of action before speaking publicly. Finally, it serves as a reminder of the importance of dissecting an intercultural conflict objectively. As we covered in the "Perception" unit of this training session, there are always multiple ways to interpret a situation. Rather than immediately making a judgment based on your own cultural perspective, analyze the different elements of a situation first, trying to think of other possible interpretations (e.g., Ask yourself why the company may have taken what you would consider a "long time" to respond; Think about possible reasons why Mr. Toyoda did not want to make eye contact with his interviewers, etc.).

SECTION 3

Explore Cultural Values

15. LISTENING DEEPLY FOR VALUES

Kate Berardo

In this exercise, people share stories of intercultural challenges they have made while others listen deeply for the values held by the storytellers. This exercise demonstrates that people often bring to the surface and communicate the values that drive them, and shows that the real task is to learn how to listen to others and ourselves to discover these values.

Key Focus

Explore cultural values

Type of Activity

Exercise

Objectives

As a result of this activity, participants will learn to

- listen in a new way to themselves and others to hear the values people live by,
- explore the connection between our values and cultural identity, and
- engage in exploratory values-based conversations with others.

Appropriate Audience

Adults

Level of Challenge

High

Group Size

1 to 30 people

Time

60 to 90 minutes

Materials

Handouts

Preparation

Think through a story of an intercultural challenge you have experienced that you can share with the group. You should be able to give the details of this story in three to five minutes.

Activity Setup

This exercise has four main phases:

1. The introduction, which involves opening a discussion on values, explaining the purpose and process of the exercise, relating some of the assumptions behind the activity, and identifying what is needed to effectively listen deeply for values.
2. The demonstration in which you share a personal story of facing an intercultural challenge, and the group as a whole starts to explore the values that are being highlighted.
3. The pair practice in which pairs take turns describing challenging situations they have faced and exploring with others the values that they are sharing and hearing.
4. The debriefing in which the process of listening deeply for values is discussed and key insights and learnings drawn out.

Introduction: Open a discussion with the group about values by asking the following questions:

- If I were to ask you to identify your top values right now, how many of you could do this? (Usually few, if any, hands go up.) Why is it often hard to identify our core values? (This is quite challenging to do because we often hold many values, so identifying the top values is challenging, and more importantly, our values, though influencing many of our actions and beliefs, are rarely something we stop to articulate.)
- Why is understanding our own values and others' values important when working across cultures? (Point out that although we can often adopt different cultural practices quite easily—for example, change the way we exchange business cards and greetings—encountering different values and working across value differences is often at the heart of true intercultural challenges. Therefore, knowing one's own values—and listening to understand another person's values—are core components of being effective when working across cultures.)

Explain the purpose of the activity:

The next exercise is designed to help you identify some of your own core values and enable you to help others do the same. It is based on the belief that

- identifying and articulating our own values is often quite challenging;
- whether we realize it or not, we often give cues and clues about the values that are important to us when we speak;
- exploring our values with others can be a helpful way to understand what matters most to us; and
- if we train ourselves to listen deeply, we can learn a lot about the values that are important to us and to others.

Set the tone of the exercise and explain what you mean by listening deeply. Share the following quote from Senge, Ross, Smith, Roberts, & Kleiner (1994):

To listen fully means to pay close attention to what is being said beneath the words. You listen not only to the "music," but to the essence of the person speaking. You listen not only for what someone knows, but for what he or she is. Ears operate at the speed of sound, which is far slower than the speed of light the eyes take in. Generative listening is the art of developing deeper silences in yourself, so you can slow your mind's hearing to your ears' natural speed, and hear beneath the words to their meaning.

Tell them this will be the goal in terms of how we start listening to each other in the following exercise.

Managing the Activity

Demonstration:

1. To start, ask the group to listen deeply to what you are about to say, listening not just for the content, but for the values you may be expressing. Encourage the group to write down specific words and phrases they hear you say that may offer insights into the values you hold.
2. Tell a story of an intercultural challenge you have faced for roughly three to five minutes. (For example, I often tell my story of moving

to Japan alone and the challenges I faced when the apartment I arrived in had all kinds of problems. I wanted to respect the local customs for indirect communication styles and emphasize relationship building over tasks, but I also wanted an apartment that had heating, and I needed to find an effective way to communicate this to my manager, who had found the apartment for me. I tell the group about this dilemma, the decision I made ultimately, and also much of the thinking that went through my head at the time.)

3. At the end, ask the participants to offer their perspective on what they believe is important to you, based on the story you told. It is critically important that you stay open and curious to the perspectives of the others. If, for example, someone suggests that a value is important to you that you don't recognize, try to understand how that came through in the story. Your focus should be on modeling understanding others' perspectives and learning more about yourself with the observations others provide.

4. Conclude by summarizing what you have heard from the participants. Thank them for their observations. Then reflect with the group on the process that you just went through. Note that values run deep in us, and interaction with others on values requires sensitivity. Hold a general discussion around what enabled the group to have this type of deep conversation in an open fashion by asking:

   • What was it important for you, the listener, to do when you were sharing your observations from the story? For example, offer their observations of values as possibilities rather than certainties, be curious rather than critical. Use examples from the conversation that just took place to highlight what was most effective.

   • What is important for the storyteller to do when he or she hears these observations? For example, stay open, try to understand others' perspectives. Again, refer to the conversation that just took place to demonstrate these points. Encourage the group to explore the implications of what would have happened, for example, if you

had just rejected someone's observation rather than staying open to it.

   • For experienced and mature groups, it is often best to hold this discussion after people have shared their observations. That way, you can use real examples from the group of what worked well and what didn't. For less experienced groups, it may be helpful to introduce these suggestions for how to hold these conversations before people share their observations to guide the process.

5. Encourage people to remember these things when they have a chance to practice their own storytelling and deep listening.

Pair Practice:

1. Give people two to three minutes to think of a challenging intercultural situation they faced that they would like to tell the group about.

2. Have people pair up and give each person either a speaker (see Handout S3.1) or listener (see Handout S3.2) handout. Give people 20 to 30 minutes to have these conversations. If space allows, have people spread out and find a place where they can have more privacy for these conversations. Encourage people to monitor their own time to ensure each person gets a chance to talk and explore his or her values.

3. Pairs are best largely left alone and self-managed. Walk around at the start to ensure the task is clear and again at the end to encourage people to start wrapping-up and reconvening.

Debriefing the Activity

Welcome people back and explore together the exercise of sharing stories. This is often a powerful experience for people, so it is important to give ample time for people to talk about the experience itself before moving into more application-focused questions:

   • How was the experience? How did you feel during the experience? How do you feel now?

   • What was it like to share stories and explore values together? What was easy? What was challenging about it?

- What did you learn about each other and yourself through this process?
- What did you learn about the process of listening deeply for values? What helps? What makes it hard?
- How do your own values potentially influence what you hear and what you share as observations in this activity?
- What were the implications of asking people to talk about an important decision or challenging intercultural situations they have faced? What if we had chosen a different topic?
- How can you apply what you learned from this process to your work or life?

Key Insights and Learnings

- The values that drive people are often described as being beneath the surface and hard to see, yet people give us cues and clues about the values that are important to them constantly. It's a matter of listening for and checking our understanding of them.
- Exploring values with others can be a powerful process that brings people together and creates a deep sense of connection.
- It's important when having conversations with others on exploring values that we offer our observations only as possibilities and not as certainties.
- Offering our observations only as possibilities is especially important since our own values and beliefs can create a lens through which we view and interpret what we hear.
- When others share their observations of us, it's vital to understand and learn from their perspective as a means to better understand ourselves and how others may see us.
- Listening deeply for values is a technique and mind-set. We can train ourselves to listen in a slightly different way than we normally do: to listen behind the words and to listen to discover what is not being said. To do so, and to do so effectively, we need to be open, curious, fully present and nonjudgmental as we interact with others.
- If we choose to listen to others in this way, we can learn a lot about the potential motivations, needs, and beliefs of those we work

with and find more effective ways of working together.

Variations

Variation 1. Instead of framing the activity as focusing on listening deeply for values, start the activity by saying you would like to share a story and then launch directly into the story. Once completed, ask people for thoughts and reactions to your story. Then, offer the idea that the story you just told them actually gives them a lot of insight into what you value most. Read the quote from Senge et al. (1994). Tell them you will tell the story again and encourage them to listen this time behind the words to what the story says about what you value. Then continue the exercise as detailed previously. This variation can create a powerful ah-ha moment. Participants experience firsthand the impact of switching what they focus on in listening and the power of deep listening to uncover deep insights about others.

Variation 2. At the root of most important decisions and challenging intercultural situations is often a values-based challenge or negotiation, which makes both of these scenarios rich ones for the exercise. That said, many different types of stories and sharing can be used in this exercise and be effective in exploring values. For example, you can ask people to share stories that are more closely correlated with the themes and goals for a session, for example:

- For a global leadership session, ask about
  - a leader they admire and why,
  - when they first recognized they were a leader (or had leadership potential), or
  - the most challenging situation they have faced as a leader.

- For a global teams session, ask about
  - the best team they have been on, or
  - the worst experience they have ever had on a team.

When you create this more focused topic area, you will need to ensure you debrief the process of deep listening and the content that emerged from the stories. It is usually best to have people discuss the content of these stories first (e.g., what themes emerged from different stories about global teams), and then move the discussion to one about the process of deep listening for people's values.

Facilitation Tips and Suggestions

You have a lot of influence with the story you tell: it will set a tone and sometimes a pattern for the types of stories told by the rest of the group. Choose a story that is relevant to the group, creates the right level of disclosure for the culture and group, and models the type of stories you want others to share.

Trust in the participants to share stories that are relevant and important to them. If participants are struggling to think of an intercultural story, ask them to recall the last transition they faced (e.g., moving to a new house, going to a university, getting married, etc.). Even these types of stories will likely yield interesting information about the values that are important to that individual.

About This Exercise

I designed this activity to bring together several distinct yet related topics that are critical in working across cultures: identity work, constructive intercultural dialogues, and deep listening. I have found the process to be simple and highly constructive in creating powerful learning experiences.

REFERENCE

Senge, P., Ross, R., Smith, B., Roberts, C., & Kleiner, A. (1994). *The fifth discipline fieldbook: Strategies and tools for building a learning organization.* New York, NY: Doubleday/Currency.se

 HANDOUT S3.1

LISTENING DEEPLY FOR VALUES: SHARING STORIES

Speaker Instructions: Think of yourself as a storyteller. Share with your partner either

- One of the most challenging intercultural situations you have faced

    ○ *What happened?*
    ○ *Who was involved?*
    ○ *Why was the situation challenging?*
    ○ *How did the situation end?*

or

- An important transition in your life (e.g. marriage, moving, having kids)

    ○ *Describe the transition you faced.*
    ○ *What were you thinking and feeling during the transition?*
    ○ *Why did you ultimately decide to make this transition?*

    Be as vivid and descriptive as possible as you tell this story.
    Once you have told your story, your listening partner will say what she or he heard.
    Use your remaining time to have a conversation about your values and what is important to you. Aim to identify at least one or two values of core importance to you by the end of the discussion.

You have 10 minutes for this time as a speaker. At the end of this time, switch cards with your partner.

 HANDOUT S3.2

LISTENING DEEPLY FOR VALUES

Listener Instructions: Listen deeply to your partner and his or her story. You may ask questions during or after the story, letting your curiosity guide you. As you listen, notice what you are hearing from this individual from a values perspective (it may also be helpful to take notes). At the end of the conversation, offer your observations of what you heard and what values you seemed to hear this person expressing.

Offer these statements as possibilities rather than certainties, for example, "What I found interesting was that you said (specific words and/or phrase). It suggested to me that (value) is important to you."

Use the remaining time to share more of your observations and have a conversation about what values are important to the speaker. Help this individual to identify at least one or two values of core importance to him or her by the end of the discussion.

You have 10 minutes for this time as a listener. At the end of this time, switch roles and instruction sheets with your partner.

16. HUMAN VALUES CONTINUUM

Darla K. Deardorff

This activity gets participants physically involved in thinking about their responses to value statements and generates discussion among participants. This is a good way to introduce the cultural values framework (Hofstede, 2001). It is also a good way to gain a cultural profile of the group.

Key Focus

Explore cultural values

Type of Activity

Icebreaker

Objectives

As a result of this activity, participants will

- gain an awareness of cultural values framework and
- visually see differences, even among those from the same cultural group.

Appropriate Audience

Adults, teenagers

Level of Challenge

Medium

Group Size

4 to 50 people

Time

10 to 15 minutes

Materials

None

Activity Setup

Explain to participants that you will read a series of statements and ask them to move to the appropriate side of the room based on how they feel about the statement. Example: "'Life is what happens to me.' If you resonate with this statement, please move to the left side of the room. 'Life is what I make it.' If you resonate more with this statement, please move to the right side of the room. You may also find yourself somewhere in between. If you feel very strongly about the statement you should be standing against the wall."

Managing the Activity

1. Once people have moved to their positions, ask them to discuss their thoughts on these statements with their neighbors.
2. Then ask for volunteers to explain briefly why they're standing where they are on the continuum. Try to get volunteers from each side as well as someone from the middle to tell why they're standing where they are along this invisible continuum.
3. Repeat this process with at least two more sets of statements. Then ask participants to sit down, and say, "Now, let's discuss this further."

Examples of continuum value statements:

1. Life is what happens to me/Life is what I make it.
2. Competition brings out the best/Cooperation is the way to get things done.
3. Change is good/Tradition is important.
4. People should tell it like it is even if it hurts/ Maintaining harmony is important even if it means not telling the complete truth.
5. Group membership is essential for my success/I don't need to belong to a group to be successful.

Debriefing the Activity

This activity helps people understand cultural differences. As you debrief, discuss the following:

1. What was it like to place yourself along this continuum?
2. What stood out to you from this activity?
3. Based on these statements, what do you think some of the underlying cultural values might be?
4. Why is it important to understand underlying cultural values?
5. As you reflect on this activity, what are some things you can take away?

Key Insights and Learnings

- One of the ways cultures differ is in their underlying cultural values, which can be thought of as being on a continuum. The values are not right or wrong, just different.
- Underlying cultural values affect our behaviors and the behaviors we encounter in others. By seeking to understand those values, we can begin to understand others better.
- Not everyone from the same cultural group feels exactly the same way about underlying cultural values in that culture. Cultural values are about patterns found in different cultures, but not everyone from that culture will fit that pattern.

Variations

Variation 1. If space limitations prevent physical movement, you could read the statement sets and have participants write them down on either side of a sheet of paper, draw a horizontal line across the paper beneath the two statements, and then put an X on where they would place themselves on the continuum.

Variation 2. Write the statements on either side of a board or flip chart, draw a horizontal line beneath the two statements, then have participants write their name on the spot where they fall on the continuum, based on how they've been culturally conditioned to respond to the statements.

Facilitation Tips and Suggestions

- Participants can use the whole room (they don't all need to stand along one particular line).

- Emphasize that if participants feel 100% about a statement you've read, they need to be all the way up against the wall of the side of the room they have chosen for that particular statement. If not in 100% agreement, then they'd be somewhere in between.
- It's helpful to have participants discuss with each other why they're standing in a particular place on the continuum, so try to allow a few minutes for that discussion to happen before moving on to volunteer sharing.
- After about 3 sets of statements, participants are usually ready to move on to the next activity, so don't try to do too many statement sets.
- Choose the statement sets that work best in your context or develop your own based on the examples given here. Statements should be based on underlying cultural values.
- Be sensitive to those in the group who may have physical difficulties in participating in this activity.
- You can either have participants respond based on their cultural conditioning and how their culture expects them to respond to these statements, or you can have them respond based on their own personal opinion, but it's important to be clear about what you're asking them to do.
- It's important to have a room with space to move around in.

About This Exercise

I developed this activity as a physical way to involve participants in understanding cultural values frameworks. I found it to be a great way to introduce the values frameworks visually before we begin discussing them more in depth. Plus it seems to stimulate quite a bit of discussion throughout the activity.

REFERENCE

Hofstede, G. (2001). *Culture's consequences: Comparing values, behaviors, institutions, and organizations across nations* (2nd ed.). Thousand Oaks, CA: Sage.

17. VALUES WHEEL

Rita Wuebbeler

Participants build trust with and develop an understanding of each other by creating values wheels and sharing the values that are important to them at work.

Key Focus

Explore cultural values

Type of Activity

Exercise

Objectives

As a result of this activity, participants will

- become aware of the influence values have on behavior,
- better understand their own and others' values at work, and
- increase the level of trust in their fellow team members.

Appropriate Audience

Adults

Level of Challenge

Medium

Group Size

6 to 12 people

Time

20 to 30 minutes

Materials

- Handout or sheets of paper
- Pens
- An object that can serve as a talking piece

Activity Setup

1. Have participants sit in a circle.
2. Ask the group

   - What are values?
   - How do they show up?
   - How do they influence us in our personal lives? At work? (For students: At school?) On our team?
   - Are values in our personal lives different from those at work? If so, how do they differ and why?

3. Find ways to continue a gentle exploration of the topic. For example, show them a paragraph or a quote about values and the importance of being aware of one's values, such as the following:

   - "Your values are your current estimations of truth. They represent your answer to the question of how to live." Steve Pavlina
   - "We can tell our values by looking at our checkbook stubs." Gloria Steinem
   - "I have my values, and if you don't like them, well I've got some others." Mark Twain

4. Explain you will focus on values in the work environment in this activity.
5. Pass out the values wheel (see Handout S3.3), or simply ask each participant to draw a circle on their piece of paper and divide the circle into three sections (similar to a peace sign). Then ask them to write down their top

three work values on their values wheel. Ask them to provide an example of how their three top values show up in their work lives (for example, Honesty: Not holding back in difficult conversations but being open and direct). You can also adapt this to different groups. For example, ask students to write down their top three values and how this shows up in their group work.

6. Give them 10 minutes to complete the task.

Managing the Activity

1. Ask for a volunteer to share one of his or her values. Give the volunteer the talking piece.

2. When the first person is finished talking about one of his or her values and how it shows up in daily life, ask, "Does anyone have a similar value?" In 99% of the time, someone else will say, "I do." The second person might share a very similar value or might take the conversation into a slightly different direction.

3. Keep asking, "Who has something to add to this?" or "Whose value is connected in some way to this one?"

4. If there is no connection and nobody feels inclined to go next (which rarely, if ever, happens), ask "Who wants to share another value?"

5. Let the conversation take its course without interfering too much except for keeping it going when it stops and making sure the talking piece gets passed around.

6. After a short while, people tend to begin sharing their values quite openly and even asking each other clarifying questions.

7. The activity ends when everyone has shared their three values.

8. You can ask the participants to put their names on their values wheels and put them on the ground inside the group circle or put them on the wall as a visual reminder.

Debriefing the Activity

Debrief the exercise generally:

1. What did you notice in this activity?
2. What common understandings emerged?

3. Were there surprises, and if so, what were they?
4. What are some examples of behaviors related to the values that emerged?
5. Is it possible to develop a set of shared values despite our different backgrounds?

Facilitate a brief discussion on learnings from this exercise: What did you learn from this exercise about

- values,
- each other,
- the role of culture,
- working with each other,
- how hard or easy it was to list your top three values, and
- how this exercise influenced your view of your colleagues?

Key Insights and Learnings

- Our behaviors (and cultural preferences) are shaped by our values.
- It is important to know yourself and how your values influence you at work.
- There is value in understanding (and seeking to understand) the values that drive another person.
- Sharing what's important to us helps develop team trust and esprit de corps.
- Values are not right or wrong, they are just different.
- It can be challenging to clearly identify our most important values; it might take a conflict between our reality and our values for them to surface.

Variation

It is good for people to share and receive each other's values in an open and curious fashion. However, when there is tension or people in a group are facing challenges interacting with one another, it may also be important during the debriefing to ask such questions as the following:

1. What happens when one of your values is conflicted in some way (e.g., when you do not feel you can act, or others are not acting, according to your values)?

2. How is your value lived in other cultures (e.g., what does honesty look like in Japan)?

This discussion can draw out the following additional themes:

- the benefits and challenges of having shared and different values within a group,
- the need to negotiate value differences between people to work successfully together, and
- the importance of recognizing that the same value may be demonstrated at a behavioral level in different ways in different cultural contexts.

Facilitation Tips and Suggestions

- This exercise works best with a minimum of 4 to 6 people and a maximum of 10 to 12. For larger groups, have each person name one value rather than three.
- It is advisable to do this exercise once a certain trust level has been built among the participants, so don't do this exercise at the very beginning of a training program.
- It is recommended to sit in a circle, which helps with interaction and discussion.

About This Exercise

I used this simple and gentle activity during a team building workshop for a multicultural management team in which one of the major goals was for team members to get to know one another better. It can also be used with diverse teams to build trust among team members as well as with groups of people interested in reflecting on and deepening their understanding of their own and their counterparts' values and beliefs. My design of this activity (one could say, a simplified version) was inspired by the online cultural competence building tool Cultural Detective (www.culturaldetective.com), among others. The "Self-Discovery" tool from Cultural Detective by George Simons, Kate Berardo, and Dianne Hofner Saphiere offers a powerful way to explore this topic in a more complex way.

 HANDOUT S3.3

VALUES WHEEL

Instructions: Write down your top three work values on the values wheel. For each value, provide an example of how this value shows up in your work life. *Example:* Honesty: Not holding back in difficult conversations but being open and direct, even with the boss.

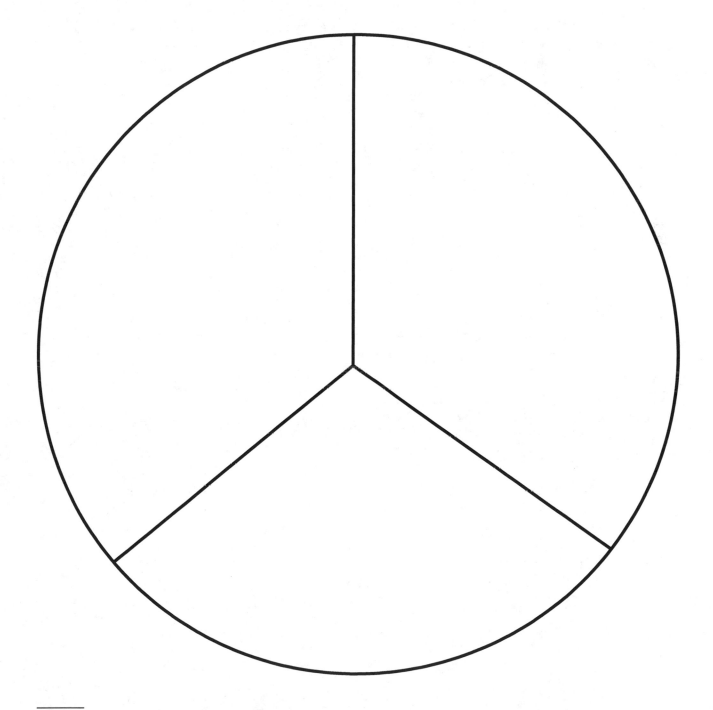

Reproduced from: Rita Wuebbeler, "Values Wheel," in *Building Cultural Competence: Innovative Activities and Models,* eds. K. Berardo and D. K. Deardorff (Sterling, VA: Stylus, 2012), 128–131.

18. VALUES AUCTION

Kristin Draheim

After participants share proverbs from their childhood and explore the values these proverbs represent, they engage in an auction to buy the values that are most important to them. This exercise quickly and creatively helps participants identify which values are most important to them and shows how emotionally charged our values often are to us.

Key Focus

Explore cultural values

Type of Activity

Exercise

Objectives

As a result of this activity, participants will

- become aware of their values,
- understand that values vary from culture to culture, and
- realize they have learned these values through their own language during their own socialization.

Appropriate Audience

Adults

Level of Challenge

Medium

Group Size

8 to 16 people

Time

90 minutes

Materials

- Gavel
- Two separate sheets of paper per person
- Index cards
- Pens
- Valutas

Preparation

Create bundles of 10,000 valutas for participants to use in the auction by printing the valuta currency sheet (see Handout S3.4), making copies, and cutting out the bills.

Activity Setup

1. Collect proverbs and sayings.
   Explain to the group that this exercise will help them understand what values are, what they mean to us, and how we learn cultural values, and that we'll achieve this through the exploration of proverbs. Ask participants to think of proverbs used in their home cultures they regard as important (5 to 10 minutes). The proverbs or sayings should really mean something to them, that is, they cause emotional resonance or have influenced them deeply because they are used by their parents or grandparents or because they are often used by the media in their home country. Have participants write down their two most important proverbs on two separate sheets of paper.
2. Present the proverbs and sayings and how they are used to the group.
   Have participants present their two proverbs one after another. Ask them to explain how, when, where, and how they are used in their home cultures (in other words, stress the difference between the literal meaning and the

figurative meaning of the proverb). Encourage individuals to say what the proverbs mean to them personally or to the people in their home country and why. Give the other participants the chance to ask questions. These proverbs can be posted on the wall or on a screen so other participants can see them.

3. Analyze the values.

Ask the group to think about which values are expressed in the proverbs; that is, what do the proverbs allude to, hint at, or tell one to do? Some proverbs express only one value. Other proverbs represent multiple values. This part of the exercise may be done in small groups to make it more effective. Sometimes the understanding of values differs between group members, based on members' own perspectives, experiences, and cultural conditioning. In this case, the person who brought up the proverb defines the value according to his or her understanding. For example, a value in the proverb "The early bird catches the worm" is punctuality; a value in the proverb "An apple a day keeps the doctor away" is health.

The values (e.g., love, friendship, honesty, modesty) are listed on a blackboard or flip chart so that all participants can see them. The list should contain about 25 to 30 values.

4. Ranking of values.

Ask each participant to rank the values according to their importance to him or her. These individual rankings will be used in the auction of values in which all participants have to purchase those values that are most important to them. Each participant is given 10,000 valutas that can be used in any amount to purchase the values in the auction. While the participants are ranking the values, write each value on a single card. Then auction off the values one by one.

Managing the Activity

For the auction, arrange chairs in rows. Put a table in front of the first row to be used as an auction desk. Participants take their seats, and the facilitator, playing the role of the auctioneer, announces the auction and briefly explains the rules. The values are called out one by one, and participants bid on them. The winning bid goes to the highest bidder, which is announced by the auctioneer's banging a gavel, like in a real auction. The auction ends when all values have been sold.

Debriefing the Activity

At the beginning of the debriefing, the emotional level of the auction should be explored first, so that the participants can then move on to discuss the process on a more objective level. This is important for the participants to achieve the purpose of the exercise: to recognize values as being important in different ways to other people and to recognize and accept the close link between values and behavior. This is the basis for the development of respect for other people's values. The following are debriefing questions for steps 1 through 3 of the exercise:

- How easy or how difficult was it to choose two proverbs from your culture?
- Are proverbs used often or not often in your home culture and language?
- Were you conscious of the values contained in the proverbs?
- How easy or how difficult was it to explain content and meaning of the proverbs in a foreign language?

The following are debriefing questions for steps 3 and 4:

- Was it easy or difficult to rank your values?
- How easy or how difficult was it to choose the values you felt were worth buying?
- How did you feel when you didn't have enough money to bid for a value that is important for you?
- What did you think when values that mean nothing to you sold at a high price?
- Are you satisfied with what you got and how the auction process went?
- Do the values you bought correspond with those in your proverbs?
- What does your bidding tell you about yourself? Did you learn something new about yourself?

The following are general debriefing questions:

- How do you see the link between values and behavior?
- Why is it important to understand the deeper underlying cultural values in other cultures?

- What insights did you gain from this activity and discussion that can be applied in other cross-cultural situations?

Key Insights and Learnings

- It is quite difficult to rank values.
- It is difficult to choose the values that are worth buying.
- Participants feed badly when they cannot afford to buy values that are important to them.
- Values vary from culture to culture.
- Values are passed on through language.

Variations

Variation 1. Group work. Depending on the participants' willingness to play, the auction of values could be replaced with group work. After every participant has ranked his or her values, small groups of 3 to 4 people discuss the individual rankings. After some time the group makes one final ranking together. This means the debriefing questions will have to be adapted, focusing on how content the single participants are with the group's ranking.

Variation 2. Whole group discussion. If time is brief, this activity could focus primarily on the proverbs each participant contributes and the underlying cultural values represented by those proverbs. A discussion could ensue on the impact of those underlying cultural values on behavior and how those values/behaviors may vary by culture. In this case, values would not be ranked in this activity.

Variation 3. If time is brief, the facilitator can also present some proverbs to the group and let them analyze the values in them. Then the auction can proceed as described. The learnings and key insights are quite similar to those of the original version of the exercise, but they are a little less emotionally based. This variation might be suitable for conflicting groups, as it shortens discussion and leaves out the personal and intimate components of proverbs that were passed on and practiced in group members' families.

Facilitation Tips and Suggestions

- Embed the exercise in a broader context and use it as an introduction to a more theoretical discussion about values.
- During the auction of values, motivate the participants by making use of your acting talent: The more you create an authentic

auction atmosphere the better. You can also make this activity feel more real by using the handout and distributing the valutas currency to participants.

A good summary for ending this exercise might be to give the participants some more context information about proverbs such as the following:

Every culture has features characteristic only for them. The perception and evaluation of the surrounding world belong to these features. These collective evaluations are expressed by language and hence they are expressed in proverbs and sayings, too. With their help, they can easily be incorporated into the cultural memory and saved there. The truth of proverbs' contents is rarely questioned (if consciously thought about at all) and so they are transferred to everyday life. Due to their brevity and memorability, proverbs are very suitable to illustrate the seemingly universally valid values of a culture, its knowledge and wisdom from generation to generation over centuries. (Draheim, 2007)

About This Exercise

The idea for this exercise can be traced to the main features of the exercise "Auction" in Brenner & Brenner (2005). Its current form was created in 2007 and used with various groups of students, monocultural and multicultural. Since then it has been used in different kinds of training programs and workshops (e.g., diversity management, team building in intercultural contexts, or dealing with conflicts in intercultural teams) with very positive results. A similar version of the exercise has been published in Hiller and Vogler-Lipp (2010). Doing the exercise is fun and educational at the same time.

REFERENCES

Brenner, G., & Brenner K. (2005). *Fundgrube Methoden I—für alle Fächer in der Sekundarstufe I und II.* Berlin, Germany: Cornelsen Verlag.

Draheim, K. (2007). *Russische Sprichwörter als Schnittstelle zwischen Sprachen und Kultur—Zum Frauenbild in russischen Sprichwörtern.* Halle/Saale, Germany: Martin-Luther-Universität.

Hiller, G-G., & Vogler-Lipp, S. (2010). *Schlüsselqualifikation Interkulturelle Kompetenz an Hochschulen-Grundlagen, Konzepte, Methoden.* Wiesbaden, Germany: VS Verlag.

HANDOUT S3.4

VALUTA CURRENCY SHEET

19. BUILDING UTOPIASTAN

Lisa Nevalainen and Maureen White

This group role-playing challenges participants to prioritize underlying cultural values and recognize culturally conditioned behaviors connected to cultural values.

Key Focus

Explore cultural values

Type of Activity

Simulation

Objectives

As a result of this activity, participants will

- recognize priorities placed on underlying cultural values and
- identify behavioral characteristics stemming from underlying cultural values and priorities.

Appropriate Audience

Adults

Level of Challenge

Medium

Group Size

5 to 50 people

Time

90 minutes

Materials

- Flip chart paper
- Whiteboards and markers or projector
- Handouts

Preparation

- Print and distribute to each group of participants a copy of the description and guidelines (see Handout S3.5)
- Print the list of assigned roles (see Handout S3.6), and make enough copies to give each participant one of the roles. Cut the roles apart into strips to hand out. (Optional: Place each role in an envelope and distribute them.)

Activity Setup

1. Divide the participants into small groups of 5 or 6. Each group should have flip chart paper or another way to show their final lists to the larger group.
2. Distribute the description and guidelines handout. Read the text from the handout and ask them to prioritize the 10 cultural values for inclusion in a new society. Emphasize that the groups must come to a consensus in prioritizing the values they think are most important from 1 to 10 and list them on the flip chart paper.
3. Ask someone in each group to take on the role of leader, and hand the volunteer that role description.
4. Announce that in addition to prioritizing values, which they must do as a group, several of the members will also be assigned a specific role they must play during the discussion, and this role has to be kept secret. Other members of the group may not be told what each role will do. Randomly pass out the slips of paper with the roles so that each group has one person who is assigned one of the roles. Remind participants they cannot reveal their roles with others, and ask them to do the best they can to play the role well so

their group members will be able to guess their role at the end of the activity.

Managing the Activity

With a time limit of 15 minutes for discussion, the group begins the task of prioritizing a list of cultural values.

1. Move through the groups to observe how the participants are adhering to their roles and in what ways they are portraying their roles by their behavior and ways of communication.
2. Remind participants they will be sharing their choices and their group rationale with the larger group.

Debriefing the Activity

Ask the groups to post their lists for the larger group to see. When presenting their rankings, each group can briefly discuss the top and bottom two or three and make any comments they want on the process involved or the group's discussion. A larger group discussion on the similarities or differences between groups on the top or bottom priorities can also take place.

Following this general group discussion, which is meant to make the groups comfortable talking about their experience, begin to ask more focused questions about the group decision-making process, which may include some of the following:

1. Was it easier to decide which values were most important or least important? Why?
2. Did you find there were certain values everyone agreed on?
3. Were you surprised by any of the differences in opinions? What are some examples of those differences?
4. Were there any definitions of values your group could not agree on? How did you discuss or elaborate on those values so that everyone came to an agreement?
5. What is the impact of particular values on behavior? What are some real-life examples you discussed of how each value might translate into behavior? What are some real-life examples you have where underlying cultural values might have affected individuals' behavior?

6. What was the decision-making process like as diverse participants came together? How did the process evolve? What worked well, and what would you improve about the process?
7. What lessons can be learned in regard to the impact of underlying cultural values on behavior? On group decision-making processes?

Then ask questions to elicit information on communication between members of the groups, potentially including some of the following:

1. How did the group leader attempt to keep everyone involved? Leader, was this easy or difficult? Were there any particular members who displayed behavior that made it difficult to involve them? Examples?
2. Ask the groups: What communication styles did you see at play between members of the group? Individual reactions to the leader? To each other? Which communication styles did you find helpful? Frustrating? Confusing?
3. What strategies, if any, did the group or leader employ to overcome different communication styles?
4. Can you identify the roles that were being played?

Ask the participants to try to guess the roles of the other group members before they reveal their roles by reading the role title and description to the larger group. The facilitator can elicit group comments or a discussion on each role's behavioral characteristics and the impact on group communication.

1. Group: Does learning each person's role shed some light on that group member's involvement?
2. Would that information have been helpful to you before the discussion? How? How would that knowledge have changed the group's interaction?
3. Have you ever encountered someone with those communication characteristics? Reactions/difficulties? Do you see any of those characteristics in your own communication style?

Discuss the approaches or restrictions each of the roles may have brought to the discussion, and guide the group to discuss how those restrictions may play out in future interactions. Include any insights or lessons learned during this activity they can apply in future interactions.

If appropriate, discuss the predominant attitude in the United States in regard to some of the values listed on the handout and the possible behavioral implications of those values. For example, discuss where the predominant U.S. attitude toward the value of independence would fall on a continuum. Do Americans find independence very important or not important at all? And how might that attitude toward independence influence behavior, especially communication and group decision-making processes?

Discuss some culturally conditioned U.S. American attitudes and values that might fall on the opposite end of the continuum. For example, if the group thinks that U.S. culture finds independence very important, discuss an example in which independence is not very important. And how might that attitude toward independence influence behavior, especially communication and group decision-making processes?

Remind participants that these values represent larger patterns found in various cultures; for example, just as each American does not necessarily subscribe to the same values or exhibit behavior based on shared values, individuals from other cultures vary in their own cultural values and behaviors. Be careful to prevent the discussion from stereotyping specific cultural groups. Keep the conversation focused on patterns and the differences in behavior and communication styles, reminding the group that these behaviors and communication styles may arise from cultural values.

Discuss and elicit comments regarding the importance of being aware of the various communication styles that may be at play in a multinational group setting, not necessarily asking about or completely understanding each person's communication style and the relation to culture, but being aware of the differences in interactions.

Key Insights and Learnings

Through this process and debriefing, participants often take away some the following key insights regarding the group decision-making process and communication between members:

- The assumption that universal values can be challenged.
- Not everyone shares your own values or considers them as important as you do.

- Values have different meanings and significant effects on how we live.
- Underlying values have a significant influence on our decision-making process and our ultimate decisions.
- Behavior and values are connected, and it is helpful to understand and respect the connection.
- Navigating differences of opinions and behaviors arising from one's values is challenging, and practice in working in a diverse environment is helpful in developing skills and strategies for being aware, inclusive, sensitive, and ultimately successful in your task.
- Leading groups from backgrounds with various underlying values and communication styles is challenging.
- Heightened sensitivity to working with individuals with various communication strategies is beneficial.

Variation

Divide the participants into groups of 6 or 7 and then hand out the assigned roles, along with a set of two or three discussion questions pertinent to the topic you wish to discuss (i.e., if the topic is cultural values, questions could include: "Discuss two or three cultural values that are very important to you and how those may vary in other cultures.") Allow 10 to 15 minutes for small-group discussion (with each person playing his or her secret role during the discussion). At the end of the discussion, see if group members can guess each other's secret role. Then, debrief the whole group on how the discussion went given the added complexity of the secret roles, pointing out the impact of cultural conditioning on one's behavior and performance.

Facilitation Tips and Suggestions

This exercise can be used with different types of audiences and has proven highly effective with

- U.S. students (graduate or undergraduate) as cross-cultural/multinational communication training program
- incoming international students (graduate or undergraduate) as preparation for communication with U.S. audiences

- faculty, staff, or professionals to highlight cross-cultural/multinational workplace dynamics

Facilitators may want to develop an additional handout that provides more detail on each value (see Hofstede, 2001). It is best for trainers to be fairly familiar with cultural values in different cultures (see Bender, 1989; Hofstede, 1984).

About This Exercise

This activity was adapted from the facilitators' interaction with a variety of cross-cultural training exercises, most specifically, group role playing in which a leader encourages group decision making and prioritizing. It was originally created to bring an international component to a multicultural leadership conference where the majority of participants were U.S. undergraduate students. We think this exercise has the potential to develop participants' awareness of underlying cultural values and priorities through thoughtful discussion of the behaviors that stem from these values, especially in group settings.

REFERENCES

Bender, D. (1989). *American values, opposing viewpoints.* San Diego, CA: Greenhaven Press.

Hess, D. (1994). *The whole world guide to culture learning.* Yarmouth, ME: Intercultural Press.

Hofstede, G. (2001). *Culture's consequences: Comparing values, behaviors, institutions, and organizations across nations* (2nd ed.). Thousand Oaks, CA: Sage.

Hofstede, G. H. (1984). *Culture's consequences: International differences in work-related values.* Beverly Hills, CA: Sage.

Kohls, R. L. (1996). *Survival kit for overseas living: For Americans planning to live and work abroad.* Yarmouth, ME: Intercultural Press.

 HANDOUT S3.5

DESCRIPTION AND GUIDELINES OF ACTIVITY: BUILDING UTOPIASTAN

A brand new nation called Utopiastan is being created. It is your job to determine which values and priorities Utopiastan will focus on fostering among its people.

These values will affect Utopiastan's laws, economy, education system, and culture, which you are just starting to develop. Be sure to discuss the long-term impact of the values below on these national characteristics.

Your task at this meeting is to place the following 10 values in order of priority to Utopiastan. The first value on your list is the value your group has identified as the most important for your new nation, and the last value on your list is the least important.

- Equality/fairness
- Individualism/independence
- Efficiency/practicality
- Competition to bring out the best
- Clearly defined status/hierarchy
- Cooperation/interdependence
- Value in knowledge for the sake of knowing
- Sense of continuity with the past/tradition
- Ability to achieve and excel
- Sense of destiny/fate

 HANDOUT S3.6

LIST OF ASSIGNED ROLES

During the conversation/discussion on prioritizing, the group leader and other members must contend with members acting out the behavioral characteristics of their role. Those roles are listed below. Please make as many copies of these as needed for your group and then separate these roles to hand out to individuals. Optional: Put each role in an envelope before distributing.

Leader: Your role is to keep the group focused on the task at hand and facilitate discussion. You are also the record keeper and are responsible for reporting the final list to the larger group.

Time Keeper: You are concerned with staying on schedule. It is your job to make sure you proceed in a timely manner—keep looking at your watch or a clock. Keep the group aware of how much time they have left at periodic intervals. Be sure to remind the group when you have 10 minutes remaining, 5 minutes remaining, and then 2 minutes remaining.

Non-offender: You are concerned with maintaining good relationships and don't want to upset the balance of the group by arguing. You have strong opinions, but do not feel comfortable strongly stating them. You will start all your sentences gently with, "Well, I don't mean to disagree, but perhaps . . ."

Direct communicator: You are confident in your opinions and believe in being honest and direct. You are a team player and value others' opinions, yet you are assertive (not argumentative) about voicing your opinion. You will start all your sentences with "There is no question that . . ."

Listener: You feel that it is important to hear all opinions before sharing yours. You also may be uncomfortable challenging your team members who have much more experience than you. You can only share your opinion if you are directly asked for it, and then generally you would agree with the leader's opinion.

Fatalist: You feel that much of life is out of anyone's control. You start each sentence with, "Well, there's not really much we can do about that, so . . ."

Individualist: You believe strongly in the power of the individual to make a difference. You try to always be the first one to respond and you start every sentence with, "I think we should . . ." or "I feel that . . ."

SECTION 4

Navigate Identity

20. VOICES FROM THE PAST

Kate Berardo

Voices From the Past provides a creative alternative to standard introductions by having participants share key messages that influenced them, setting the tone for openness, depth, and exploration of values from the start of a program.

Key Focus

Navigate identity

Type of Activity

Introduction

Objectives

As a result of this activity, participants will

- gain insights into what drives fellow team members,
- interact at a personal and powerful level from the start of a program, and
- set the tone for deep discussions on identity and cultural values.

Appropriate Audience

Adults

Level of Challenge

Medium

Group Size

6 to 20 people

Time

20 to 45 minutes

Materials

- Sheets of colored paper
- Pens
- Tape or Sticky Tack
- Handout

Preparation

Pass out pieces of colored paper and pens to participants

Activity Setup

1. Tell participants to introduce themselves in a different fashion than they normally would

(see Handout S4.1). Have them write down on a colored piece of paper

- their name in the top left-hand corner of the paper,
- a culture they identify with (geographical or not) in the top right-hand corner of the paper, and
- their role or profession (however they choose to define this) at the bottom center of the paper.

2. Ask them to write in the center of the paper a comment that contains a key message they heard from someone influential in their lives. Encourage people to think about their past and to listen to the voices that stand out. Perhaps it is a family member, a teacher, a religious figure, or someone else. What message was repeated often or stood out? Ask people to write down this message in quotation marks and indicate who said it, for example: "Rise and shine, seize the day" (My Mother).

3. Do the same thing in advance on a colored piece of paper, or create your responses at the same time as the rest of the group.

Managing the Activity

1. Introduce yourself first to set the tone and the appropriate length of the introduction, which should be short, especially with larger groups. Ask participants to introduce themselves by reading to the group the information they wrote down.

2. When time allows, you can also model good listening and curiosity by asking questions (and encouraging others to do so) that show the type of openness you want to foster in the session and among participants. Most questions will pertain to the messages themselves, but can include

- When did you first hear that message?
- Why is that an influential message for you?
- What value(s) are suggested by the quote?
- How has it influenced you in your life?
- When might we see you being influenced by this quote in our work together?

3. After the participants introduce themselves, take their colored sheet of paper and post it on the wall to create an collage of messages.

Debriefing the Activity

This exercise doesn't require heavy debriefing, as its purpose is simply to enable people to introduce themselves in a different way and model openness and curiosity about the experiences of others. Still, you can effectively close this activity by thanking people for their participation and by reflecting on themes that may have emerged from the messages by asking questions such as

- What do you notice about the messages individuals shared?
- Were there any surprises in what your colleagues chose to share?
- How is this way of introducing ourselves different from how you typically introduce yourself in a training session? What is the impact of this?

Key Insights and Learnings

- Every exercise offers an opportunity to interact with others on a personal level, and in doing so, explore our identities.
- We are flooded with all kinds of messages throughout our lives, but it is the messages that we remember that guide and shape us.
- We have been carrying around many of these messages with us for a long time; we learn many of our values from a young age.
- We often choose what we tell others about ourselves based on trust and how safe we feel it is to share this information.
- We can learn interesting things about each other by interacting in less traditional formats.
- Being curious about yourself and others, and the messages that have helped shape us, is a critical component of intercultural competence development.

Variations

Variation 1. Experiment with and customize the information you ask people to write down. What you ask people to write down is limitless and can include anything from a hope or expectation for the day to a hobby. However, the more the biographical detail is linked to the session itself, the more it will set the tone for the session.

Variation 2. Give the key messages a focus by linking them to topics that will be addressed in a session. For example, when used as a structured introduction for a session on global leadership, ask participants to reflect on a message they received about what it takes to be a good leader; for a session on team building, ask people to reflect on a message about working effectively with others. This more targeted type of message can create good content and a context for further fruitful discussions in the group. It also often demonstrates that not everyone has the same notion about what it means to be on a successful team or to be a good leader.

Facilitation Tips and Suggestions

- This is a particularly effective way to set the tone for deep work on issues of identity and cultural values. It promotes a climate of openness and disclosure among participants. It proves highly effective for team building purposes as well (whether the team has just formed or its members have been working together for some time), when a group would benefit from learning about each other in a nontraditional format.
- While the activity is low challenge, asking participants to disclose personal information from the beginning makes it a medium level of challenge, which should be taken into consideration by the facilitator. In sessions where participants know they will be focusing on issues of cultural identity, they are often primed and ready to start at this level. For others, it may be important to set ground rules before this activity to set the appropriate tone from the beginning (e.g., listening respectfully to each other, taking risks, being open, etc.).
- How you model this will also influence the perceived level of trust as well as the appropriate level of disclosure. When asking people to think about a message that influenced them, consider your audience and set a tone that matches their energy and needs, your goals for the session, and your own style:
  - To keep the energy lighter, simply ask people to think of a message they received over and over in their early years that influenced them, and share your own example in a lighthearted fashion.
  - For more serious and reflective energy, facilitate a guided reflection: Ask people to close their eyes, to think back to their formative years, and to listen to the voices that guided them.
- Show appreciation for all types and levels of disclosure. Some people may reveal messages that reflect deep and formative experiences in their lives, and others may share something lighter. It is important to create an environment that welcomes openness.
- This activity may occasionally bring up a strong emotional reaction for some people (for example, a key message from a participant's father who recently passed away), so it is important to read the energy of the room and the needs of individual participants. Creating safety for an individual who taps into such emotions will be critical, as will balancing the needs of that individual with those of the group.
- Voices From the Past is best for smaller groups (less than 20 people). When the group size is larger, it is best to have everyone post their messages on a wall, then throughout the day after breaks or at key points in the session, have a few individuals read their messages until all messages are shared.
- Use the activity as a frame to talk about how the group is interacting with one another. If the group has been open and constructive in their interaction, ask what enabled that and what do they want to continue doing for the rest of the day. Share other observations you have on how the group has been interacting, and ask whether they want to continue in the same way, or do they want to modify it. Use this to create (or update) a set of norms or ground rules and post these in the room.
- The messages people tend to share often are highly insightful quotes and can create a wall of wisdom when posted together. It can also become something great to take away from the session. You can either
  - compile all the quotes and details from the introductions in a document and send it to participants or
  - take people's photos holding their introductions and create a slideshow to send to the participants.

About This Exercise

The process of identifying key messages from the past that influence us was adapted from the Cultural Detective: Self-Discovery series I wrote with Dianne Hofner Sapphiere, and George Simons (www.cultural detective.com), where it is used as one of several steps in a process to help people identify the core values that influence them. I first thought of using key messages as an alternative and deeper form of introduction while designing a session called Training Methods for Exploring Identity, which I conducted with Tatyana Fertelmeyster for the Summer Institute on Intercultural Communication in 2010, sponsored by the Institute for Intercultural Communication in Portland, Oregon.

 HANDOUT S4.1

SAMPLE INTRODUCTION SHEET

Kate Berardo   **British/Italian**

"To be interesting, be interested."
–My grandmother

Global Leadership Consultant +
Trainer

21. VOICES OF DIVERSITY

Tatyana Fertelmeyster

Through structured introductions, participants move to a deeper level of personal connection with each other, and a constructive climate for addressing cultural diversity is created.

Key Focus

Navigate identity

Type of Activity

Introduction

Objectives

As a result of this activity, participants will

- increase awareness of differences,
- discuss various experiences of diversity, and
- engage in a conversation about diversity on a personal level.

Appropriate Audience

Adults, teenagers

Level of Challenge

Medium

Group Size

5 to 15 people

Time

15 to 45 minutes (3 to 5 minutes per participant)

Materials

None

Preparation

Write questions on a flip chart or a whiteboard.

Activity Setup

1. This exercise is a structured introduction. Ask participants to take turns introducing themselves, providing the following information on a flip chart:

   - name
   - places of birth/growing up/significant travels/current residence
   - place of work/job title
   - if you were to participate in a radio program called *Voices of Diversity*, which voice would you be and why?

2. Read each request for information out loud. Be creative about introducing the last one. You might want to say something like this: "Imagine that your favorite radio station created a show called *Voices of Diversity*. This whole group was invited to participate, and every one of us needs to choose what aspect of diversity he or she wants to represent and be the voice of." The goal of this show is to help listeners understand various experiences of diversity, meaning the stories of those from different backgrounds.

3. It is useful to offer a group a couple of minutes to reflect on the last question. Participants will listen to each other with more attention if they are not busy thinking about their own answers.

Managing the Activity

1. Introduce yourself first as a way to model for the group. The more details you give in your introduction, the more details participants

are likely to provide. The size of the group and an overall time of the program should be taken into consideration.

2. Ask participants to volunteer to introduce themselves following the format you showed them.

Debriefing the Activity

As participants introduce themselves, ask additional questions if necessary making sure that people address their reasons for choosing to be a specific voice of diversity. It is very likely that informal debriefing will start spontaneously as people share their choices. Participants might start asking each other questions and relating to each other's stories. It's important not to make any one participant the center of attention—everybody has a voice and every voice is important.

Ask the following questions for discussion:

- What does it mean to be a voice? To have a voice? To give a voice?
- What does it mean to represent a group or an issue?
- Do you feel you could choose the voice to represent, or that you felt you had to represent a certain voice? What is the impact of this choice (or lack thereof)?
- Did anyone choose to represent a voice he or she does not represent? Why or why not? Can we give voice to a group that we ourselves don't represent?
- Did anybody choose to speak on behalf of somebody else and give a voice to a diversity characteristic as an ally rather than a direct representative? If so, how does it feel to be an ally and to have allies?
- How does it feel to hear others share what voices of diversity they represent?
- Why is it important to understand these diverse voices?
- What are some lessons you learned from this activity?

Key Insights and Learnings

- Participants become more mindful of why certain aspects of diversity might be more important to them and what it means to publicly acknowledge themselves as representative of a certain group or an issue.

- Participants gain insight into their sense of responsibility toward their groups and the level of flexibility in their choices (e.g., if somebody chooses to be a voice of a Black woman does it come from the feeling that she always has to represent her group and she would not feel justified to choose teacher or a young person or a Catholic?)
- Some participants might become aware of the fact that while they have the privilege of speaking freely on their own behalf, other voices are hardly heard.
- Participants experience a sense of empathy as they learn meaning others make out of their experiences of diversity.

Variation

This activity can be used for a quick introduction, which allows acknowledging diversity in the room. However, if it is used with a more in-depth debriefing, it leads to meaningful personal exploration and facilitates team building.

Facilitation Tips and Suggestions

- Even though it is an introduction activity, it is best not to use it in the very beginning of the program. Many people may consider it a high risk because it requires disclosing personal information. It is best used in the afternoon of whole-day training or in the morning of a second day in a two-day program. It is also a good activity to use with groups that meet regularly (like diversity councils, committees, boards, etc.) since it allows people to move to a deeper level of interpersonal understanding and connection.
- Most Americans are used to the metaphor of the voice. However, people from other cultures may not understand it. It is important to clarify what it means during the setup of the activity or to address it as a part of the debriefing if there are people from different cultures in the group. With non-U.S. audiences, using words like voices of differences instead of voices of diversity should be considered.
- This exercise allows participants to get to know each other on a deeper level and create a certain level of openness and vulnerability that are essential for team building, exploring

identity issues, leadership development, and many other group learning processes.

- This activity also provides an opportunity for powerful and at times surprising insights for individual participants. When the group space feels safe, it can lead to a public declaration of a hidden identity or to openly confronting stereotypical perceptions.

- It is best not to use this exercise as a quick introduction activity, as trying to run through it too fast might compromise the debriefing. In training programs that are two days long or more, it might be useful to start the second day with this activity as an opportunity for participants to reintroduce themselves.

About This Exercise

This activity first came out of an improvisation while I was doing a two-day training with a diversity committee of a multiprogram nonprofit agency. A couple of people could not attend the first day. I generally like structured introductions and decided to have the last question be as closely connected to the essence of this group (a diversity committee) as possible. I was blown away by the power of the group's experience. Participants later commented that it allowed them to go a few steps further in a short amount of time. Since then, I have used this exercise many times and always with the debriefing, which is not usually a part of introduction activities.

22. IDENTITY TAG GAME

Darla K. Deardorff

This activity helps participants explore their own cultural self-awareness while getting to know each other better.

Key Focus

Navigate identity

Type of Activity

Introduction

Objectives

As a result of this activity, participants will

- increase their cultural self-awareness,
- reflect on their own culturally conditioned identities, and
- get to know each other better.

Appropriate Audience

Adults, teenagers

Level of Challenge

Low

Group Size

2 to 300 plus people

Time

20 to 30 minutes

Materials

- Blank paper (one sheet per person)
- Markers (one per person)

Preparation

Hand out blank paper and markers, ensuring that each person has one blank piece of paper (white copy paper works well) and a marker. If you don't have markers, you can use crayons.

Activity Setup

1. Ask participants to write their name (what they prefer to be called) in large letters in the middle of the paper using landscape orientation.
2. Then tell participants you have one simple question you want them to write the answer to on the paper: Who are you? Ask them to write their identities in small letters around their name. Be sure to tell them that these should be identities they feel comfortable sharing with others.

Managing the Activity

1. Once they have written their name and identities, ask them to stand up, and holding their paper in front of them so others can read it, walk around the room and read the papers of the others. They should feel free to discuss with each other what they see on others' identity papers. For example, if someone wrote "athlete," then the other person could ask, "What sport do you play?" Encourage participants to try to see as many other participants' papers as possible, so caution them about spending too long talking with any one person.
2. After about 15 minutes (depending on group size), begin to bring the group back together for the debriefing.

Debriefing the Activity

This activity helps people explore their cultural self-awareness. As you debrief the group, ask the following:

1. How did it feel to define yourself in this way?
2. How many of you wrote down family roles? Hobbies? Job titles?
3. What other patterns did you notice? Any surprises?
4. How many identities are readily visible without the identity paper?
5. How well do these identities say who you are? What is it like to try to capture your identities in words and phrases?
6. Which parts of the activity were more challenging and why?
7. What identities did you take for granted and didn't write down (answers are usually "race," "class," or "gender")? This can lead to a discussion on privilege.
8. Ask participants to simply reflect on the following questions and not answer out loud: How many of these identities are culturally conditioned? In other words, how has your culture affected your identity, even that of son or daughter? What does your culture say about being a good son or daughter? How would your responses change if you were at a work event? At a family reunion? How would your responses be different 10 years ago? Ten years from now? What were the first identities you wrote down? Which identities are strongest for you? Why? (You could ask participants to circle one or two identities that are strongest for them.) Which identities are most comfortable? Least comfortable? How do others see you? How would you like others to see you?
9. As you reflect on your culturally conditioned identity, what are some things you can take away from this activity?

End the activity by discussing how important it is to be aware of one's own cultural identity before beginning to explore other cultures. Craig Storti (1998) noted that the essence of cross-cultural knowledge is to begin with understanding oneself.

Key Insights and Learnings

- Culture has great influence on our own identities.
- Each of us belongs to multiple groups, often each with their own culture and identity. We are more than just one identity, which means it is important to look beyond one label when we interact with others, that is, beyond more than just U.S. citizen or female.
- Our identities change over time.
- It is important to get to know others more deeply, beyond initial impressions.
- Understanding ourselves and the lens we use to see the world is essential before we can attempt to understand others.

Variations

Variation 1. If the group is too large, or the room doesn't allow people to physically move around and look at each other's identity papers, then simply invite participants to turn to a neighbor or to those around them and share their papers in pairs or small groups.

Variation 2. To extend this activity further, and before debriefing, invite participants to form groups, but don't say anything about how to form a group. If asked, say, "You decide." Give them 5 or 10 minutes to get into groups. This forces the group into issues of exclusion/inclusion and the concept of in/out group, which can then be included in the debriefing. As part of the debriefing, ask the group members how they decided on how to form a group. In general, they will group based on similarities. Point out that you didn't tell them how to form groups, and they could have grouped themselves based on their differences. You can then discuss what it means to be inclusive and exclusive (for example, a daughters group automatically excludes males in the room, so how does it feel to be excluded?) If U.S. citizens or people from more individualistic cultures are among the participants, don't be surprised to see a group of people who don't want to be in a group. Or if a group's members already know each other well, they may decide to form one big group. During the debriefing, note how cultural identities are about in groups and out groups, and explore what it means to belong to a group or not.

Variation 3. Post the identity papers on a wall and invite participants to walk around and read them as if they were in an art gallery. Depending on the group size, these could even be posted with participants' photos (if time and circumstances permit). Encourage participants to seek out each other and discuss identities further. It is still important to engage in a debriefing using the questions in the debriefing section.

Variation 4. This activity could be used to explore identities and stereotypes further. Based on the Circles of My Multicultural Self activity (Gorski, 2004), encourage participants to think about the judgments and stereotypes they apply to people, and invite them to make a conscious effort to think more deeply about others' identities. This can be done by pairing up participants and having them share stories about one or two of the identities they have listed on their paper. These personal stories can expand on an identity that is especially important to them or that has been painful for them. They can use the statement, "I am a _____ , but that doesn't mean _____." For example, "I am a Christian, but that doesn't mean I try to convert every person I meet" or "I am a teacher, but I do have a social life." Invite the group to share these statements, but be sure to allow for silence during the sharing, and be prepared to debrief them on stereotypes with such questions as: How do the dimensions of your identity that you choose as important differ from the dimensions other people use to make judgments about you? Where do stereotypes come from? Why is it important to see beyond labels and stereotypes? How can we eliminate stereotypes? How can we move beyond assumptions we make about others?

Facilitation Tips and Suggestions

- This activity works well to introduce participants to each other and also helps them begin thinking about identity and culture. It works best with people who do not know each other, so if the participants know each other fairly well, this may not be the best activity to use.
- It's best to develop a sample based on your own identities so you can model what you want the participants to do. While this may create bias in how they answer, it helps make clearer what you want them to do.
- Markers or dark-colored crayons work best so the responses are visible. Pens or pencils do not work, except with Variation 1.
- While many participants write nouns (brother, parent, teacher, etc.), some will write adjectives (friendly, quiet, etc.), and it's interesting to point that out and how some cultures are more focused on what a person does than how someone is as a person.
- Be sure to encourage participants to try to see as many participants' identity papers as possible so they get to talk with as many people as possible (if only briefly).

- Remind participants to only write down identities they feel comfortable sharing.
- Be sure to circulate while the group is interacting so you can make observations about what they have written. Also be sure to listen for comments you can include in the debriefing.
- If your group meets over a period of day or more, it's often helpful to post the identity papers on a wall, so other participants can read them and continue to learn more about each other.
- I usually end with the following sunglasses story:

Imagine, if you will, two groups of people who are born with sunglasses. These two groups of people live on either side of a river (indicate where the river is; ideally it's a center aisle between rows of chairs), and on this side of the river (point to the group on your left) are the yellow sunglass people. You all were born with yellow sunglasses. And you know there is another group of people living on the other side of the river, but you've never met them and you really don't know anything about them. So one day, you decide to send a delegation across the river to meet these other folks. So, you go across the river and you're pleasantly surprised to find that these folks on the other side of the river seem a lot like you. Why? They're even born with sunglasses like you. As you talk longer with them, though, you realize that something is a little different about these folks. And then you take a closer look at their sunglasses and you ask them if you can put on a pair of their sunglasses. Now those are the blue sunglasses people, so what color do the yellow sunglasses people see? (pause a moment). They see . . . *green!*

I adapted this from the sunglass story I saw in an American Field Service (AFS) manual many years ago and have since used this with participants in many different countries and cultures. This story seems to make an impression on many participants and quickly illustrates the notion of different cultural perspectives and how we each see the world through our culturally conditioned lens. (Hence, when trying to understand others, it's like wearing two pairs of sunglasses. It's a real challenge to truly to see the world from others' perspectives. The first challenge is understanding the lens through which we see the world, and thus cultural self-awareness becomes critical.)

About This Exercise

This activity was initially adapted from several different icebreakers, and I have used it for many years now in helping participants begin to think about their own identities in an attempt to help build their own cultural self-awareness. I have used this in training workshops in numerous countries and with participants from many different cultural backgrounds. I have found the activity not only gets the group to be-gin thinking about cultural themes but to also get to know each other a bit better.

REFERENCES

Gorski, P. (2004). *Multicultural education and the Internet: Intersections and integrations* (2nd ed.). Boston, MA: McGraw-Hill.

Storti, C. (1998). *Figuring foreigners out: A practical guide.* Yarmouth, ME: Intercultural Press.

23. CULTURAL ARTIFACT

Darla K. Deardorff

This activity helps participants explore their own cultural self-awareness while getting to know each other better.

Key Focus

Navigate identity

Type of Activity

Icebreaker

Objectives

As a result of this activity, participants will

- increase their cultural self-awareness,
- broaden their perspectives on other cultures (especially if participants are from a variety of cultural backgrounds), and
- get to know each other better.

Appropriate Audience

Adults, teenagers

Level of Challenge

Low

Group Size

2 to 300 plus people

Time

15 minutes

Materials

None

Managing the Activity

1. Group participants in pairs or larger groups of up to 7 or 8 people.
2. Ask them to choose one item or object they have with them (or are wearing) that tells something about their cultural background (not necessarily about them personally). This can be an item in a pocket, purse, backpack, whatever they have with them or may be wearing. Example: A person may say, "My watch, because my life is governed by schedules and because in my culture, schedules are very important." Encourage people to take only about 15 seconds for this (unless you want to use this as an introduction activity in which they can also give their name, organization, and so on, or unless you want to invite participants to tell a story about that particular object that would help provide the cultural context in importance in representing their culture).

Debriefing the Activity

This activity helps people explore their cultural self-awareness. As you debrief, discuss the following:

1. How and why did you choose the object you did?
2. What did you observe as you were listening to others' cultural artifacts? Any surprises?
3. Can you think of other cultural objects or artifacts that could represent your cultural background (even if you don't have it here with you now)?
4. What are the purposes of this activity?
5. What can we learn about others' cultures based on objects or artifacts from those cultures? What did you learn about each other?
6. How important is cultural self-awareness as we interact with others?

7. As you reflect on this activity, what are some things you can take away with you?

End the activity by discussing how important it is to be aware of one's own cultural identity before beginning to explore other cultures, and close with the following observation: According to Craig Storti (1998), the essence of cross-cultural knowledge is to begin with understanding oneself.

Key Insights and Learnings

- It is important to be culturally self-aware, even to the extent of knowing what we wear and carry with us (and what this means), which we often may not think about.
- Cultural objects and artifacts are only a small piece of the larger picture of one's background and identity. It's important to seek more information and understand the context of an individual's cultural background and identity.
- Diversity is in any group, even in groups that look initially the same.
- Understanding ourselves and the lens we use to see the world is essential before we can attempt to understand others.

Variations

Variation 1. If you will see this group again (such as a class that meets regularly), tell participants to bring a cultural artifact to the next meeting that tells a story about their cultural background. Have them give an informal presentation to the group about the artifact (three to five minutes) or have them tell their stories in smaller groups about what they brought and why.

Variation 2. If you will see this group again, have participants write a reflection about the artifact and how it relates to their own cultural background and identity. Encourage them to discuss this assignment with family members, if possible, to learn more about their family's cultural background.

Variation 3. Have participants print photos from the Internet or cut out pictures from magazines and make a collage of photos that represent their cultural background. Then have them share these collages with each other.

Variation 4. Collect an odd assortment of objects (at least one per participant) tailored to the group (these could be objects from their cultural back-

grounds), and put them in a basket. Then ask participants to select an object that represents some part of their cultural background and take turns telling the rest of the group why they chose the object they did. Objects could include a watch, coins, key, pen, timer, photo of a family, membership card, water bottle, business card, calculator, cell phone, a cross, a rosary, an evil eye, and so on. You could also assemble a set of pictures (from magazines) and have them select an image that represents their cultural background. It would be best to laminate those images first so that they are more durable or use a set of photos from VisualsSpeak (www.visualsspeak.com).

Facilitation Tips and Suggestions

- This activity works well as an initial way to introduce participants to each other and also as a way to help participants begin thinking about culture.
- Be prepared to show your own example first, and then give everyone a few minutes to find an object. Then ask for a volunteer to talk about his or her choice of object.
- If the group is 20 people or less, they can talk about their objects with the whole group and then write about the objects, which can be part of the debriefing. For example, if you see several objects representing a particular cultural value, ask participants about that. "I see we have three people who picked watches. What can this say about an underlying cultural value" (i.e., concept of time such as monochronic versus polychronic)?
- Remind participants to discuss their cultural reasons for selecting an object, what it means to them, and how it represents their culture.
- Sometimes participants will want to select objects that represent their personalities, so it may be helpful in the beginning to tell the group about the three levels of human behavior—universal, cultural, individual—and emphasize that in this activity you're looking for artifacts that represent their cultural background, not them individually.
- It's okay if the same cultural object is chosen by another participant, but you may also want to encourage them to pick different objects if possible.
- You may find you are getting groups with individuals from a more multicultural back-

ground (as in global nomads). Encourage them to select an object that represents one of their cultures.

- Other examples of cultural artifacts are credit cards, representing materialism; car keys or drivers' licenses, representing mobility or independence; jeans and sneakers, representing informality; and so on.

About This Exercise

This activity was initially adapted from numerous artifact activities including those found in Kohl L. Robert and John M. Knight's (1994) *Developing Intercultural Awareness: A Cross-Cultural Training Handbook*, and I have used it for many years now. Having used this in training workshops in numerous countries and with participants from many different cultural backgrounds, I have found that this activity is good way to begin group introductions while at the same time having participants begin to think about their own cultures.

REFERENCE

Storti, C. (1998). *Figuring foreigners out: A practical guide.* Yarmouth, ME: Intercultural Press.

24. CRAFTING A VISION STATEMENT

Barbara F. Schaetti, Sheila Ramsey, and Gordon Watanabe

This activity uses the writing of a vision statement as a powerful tool for helping participants set their commitments and align their identities in the context of a training program's larger learning goal.

Key Focus

Navigate identity

Type of Activity

Exercise

Objectives

As a result of this activity, participants will

- make a personal connection to the material through the broader program whatever it may be,
- examine and strengthen their commitment to build their knowledge and skills in the program material, and
- sustain and encourage themselves to apply the knowledge and skills gained through the program in their real world.

Appropriate Audience

Adults, teenagers

Level of Challenge

Medium

Group Size

6 to 60 people

Time

1 to 2 hours

Materials

- A surface (chalkboard, white board, etc.) visible to all participants for writing keywords, with enough space for two to five words per participant); flip chart paper; and appropriate writing implements
- 10 three-by-five-inch index cards per participant (Post-it notes also work well)
- Writing paper, one to two sheets per participant
- A pen or pencil per participant
- Handouts

Preparation

1. Determine how best to introduce the activity. What needs to be said to this particular group of participants, and how it should be said, so they understand the reason, the power, and the potential of crafting a personal or professional vision statement.
2. Decide the type of vision statement you want your group to create and how this links to the session. For example, if the goal is intercultural competence, the visions participants write can focus on what intercultural competence means to them and the qualities they choose to embody. Similarly, if the goal is global leadership or effective teamwork, participant visions can articulate and ultimately sustain their commitments toward those outcomes.
3. Prepare flip charts or other visual aid materials:

   - Crafting a Vision in Context (see Handout S4.2)
   - Four Ps of a Powerful Vision (see Handout S4.3)
   - Template for a Vision Statement (see Handout S4.4)

- Example of a Vision Statement (see Handout S4.5)

Activity Setup

Introduce the activity.

1. Explain that the purpose of the activity is to create a vision statement. Define a vision statement as a one or two paragraph statement of personal or professional aspiration. Note that *vision* in this activity is synonymous with *commitment*.

2. Emphasize the power and potential in crafting a personal or professional vision statement:

   - Writing a vision statement is a powerful tool for helping you define your commitments and how to live them.
   - Something enormously powerful is activated when you craft a vision driven by what you care most about, has clear detail and is focused on success, and that specifies your internal ways of being rather than your external acts of doing.
   - A vision statement serves as a beacon, inspiring you toward your highest and best; it offers relief, comforting and sustaining you in times of difficulty or stress; and it acts as a compass, giving you practical direction for decisions you need to make and strategic guidance for responding effectively to a particular person or situation.

3. Discuss the difference between a *being* vision (focused on internal qualities) and a *doing* vision (focused on external circumstances); emphasize that the attention here is on the former.

4. Give participants the focus of their vision: intercultural competence or global leadership or a good experience doing such and such, or whatever else it might be. If the focus is intercultural competence, you could say: "Intercultural competence requires a translation of knowledge into action. It is not enough to have awareness about a topic area or to have an intellectual understanding of a necessary skill set. Intercultural competence requires practice: doing something with the deliberate aim of learning to do it well. Practice implies the possibility of failure as much as success,

and thus of taking risks outside our normal comfort zones. When we are confronted by that sense of risk, it helps to remember why we care, why it is worth taking the risk to act in a new way, what outcome is possible for ourselves, our teams, our communities and organizations, and even for the world as we develop our competence. Crafting a personally meaningful vision statement provides us with that reminder, and thus serves powerfully to support us in our practice."

5. Reassure participants that they are actually writing a draft of a vision statement.

   - By the end of this activity participants will have made at least a start in writing their vision statements.
   - Although some participants may move to a greater degree of a finished product than others, they should take time over the next few days to refine their statement.
   - It's also important to remember that a vision statement is only temporary. At some point, as participants deepen their understanding and competencies, their vision statements also need to deepen; only in this way will their visions stay alive and offer participants real value.

6. Ask participants to keep two key ideas in mind as they engage in this process:

   - the context for their vision (in the handout and written on the flipchart). They are writing a professional vision, but to be authentic their professional vision must be aligned with their personal commitments, their spiritual or higher-order values, and in effect with everything they do.
   - The vision must be of themselves specifically at their highest and best. Their vision should stretch them to a compelling future; highest and best is much more compelling than lowest and worst and certainly more compelling than mediocre.

7. Tell participants that while there will be an opportunity for those who so choose to read their vision statements aloud, there is no requirement to self-disclose; they are fundamentally writing for themselves. Distribute materials.

- Give each participant 10 three-by-five-inch index cards.
- Ensure that everyone has a writing implement.

Managing the Activity

1. Ask participants to consider the character traits, qualities, and ways of being of someone who is demonstrating what it means to him or her to be interculturally competent (we are using intercultural competence as the example).

   - Give participants two or three examples of qualities or ways of being, for example, authenticity, curiosity, joy.
   - Invite participants to think of times when they have demonstrated a high degree of intercultural competence: What qualities and ways of being were supporting and sustaining them?
   - Invite participants to think of role models, famous or otherwise, who have demonstrated what they would consider a high degree of intercultural competence. Again, what qualities and ways of being might have been supporting and sustaining them?

2. Direct participants to make a list of as many qualities, character traits, ways of being as they can come up with, that people might demonstrate at their most interculturally competent.

   - Have them generate their own list (three minutes).
   - Ask them to turn to a coparticipant, share their lists, and then generate more qualities, character traits, and so on (five minutes).

3. Build a master list, having participants call out the qualities and character traits until as many as possible are recorded on a flip chart, whiteboard, or chalkboard.

4. Direct participants to specifically consider themselves, and their vision of themselves as being interculturally competent at their highest and best.

   - Ask them to choose the 10 qualities or character traits that seem most important

to them, that they most aspire to, commit most to embodying.

   - Tell them they may choose from the master list or use the master list only as a prompt to invoke other qualities. The question is what are the qualities and character traits they each believe they would embody at their highest and best of intercultural competence?
   - Tell participants to write one quality or character trait on each index card. Give them five minutes for this. Tell them that first thoughts are the best thoughts; this is more an intuitive selection than an intellectual one.

5. Direct participants to spread out their 10 cards in front of them so they can see their chosen qualities. Ask them to be sure these are the right 10 for them: Were they able to embody them, would this ensure they are operating at the highest and best of their intercultural competence? (two minutes, again, going with their innermost feeling)

6. When participants are sure they have the right 10 qualities, tell them to choose the five that are really for them the most important. Ask them to set the other cards aside. The five qualities in front of them will form the core of their vision statement.

7. Give participants the instructions for transforming their five qualities into a vision statement.

   - Review the Four Ps of a Powerful Vision Statement (Handout S4.3), duplicated on the flip chart), and encourage participants to carefully ensure their statements account for each P.
   - Show them the template (Handout S4.4, duplicated on the flip chart).
   - Ask participants to consider their own learning style: If seeing an example of a vision statement (Handout S4.5, duplicated on a flip chart) will support their writing rather than curtail it, invite them to step aside to view the statement; otherwise, encourage participants to write first and view the example later if they so choose.

8. Distribute writing paper to participants as needed.

9. Direct participants to write their vision statements (15 to 30 minutes).

10. Invite participants to read their vision statements out loud.

- Assure participants that reading their visions out loud is voluntary.
- Tell them that reading out loud (as with poetry) deepens the understanding; reading out loud is more for the participant who is reading than it is for those listening.
- Those listening are to listen quietly and with open hearts, with no comments or applause.

Debriefing the Activity

1. Ask the following questions and lead a short discussion of each as appropriate:

- What was it like to read the vision out loud?
- What was it like to listen to other people's visions?
- What was it like to write the vision?
- How does it feel to have the vision?

2. Close the activity with an acknowledgement of the power of hearing visions read out loud, if anyone accepted the invitation to read his or her vision. Thank participants for exploring and articulating their deep commitment to being interculturally competent at their highest and best.

- Remind participants that regardless of the condition of their vision statement right now (complete versus a draft), it will be useful for them to revisit and refine their statement that evening and over the next few days.
- Remind participants that their vision will serve them only if they keep it alive: Use it as a guide and compass when they have decisions to make or challenging people or situations to work with; revise and update it as needed to keep it fresh.
- Give participants the handouts along with the bibliography.

Key Insights and Learnings

Reading the vision out loud

- brings up feelings of exhilaration and vulnerability,

- feels like making a powerful declaration,
- provides a different experience from reading the vision internally to oneself—one hears nuance and discovers places for revision and unexpected strengths, and
- is an especially powerful experience when it meets the Four Ps of a Powerful Vision Statement.

Listening to other people's visions

- is wonderful. It's very inspiring and humbling to hear commitments and aspirations about a way of being in the world (interculturally competent) that matters so much, and
- is helpful. It helps to hear that visions can show up in so many different ways with different content, different styles.

Writing a vision

- although not easy, is easier than anticipated. This process actually works well.
- is intriguing. It's stimulating to think about what intercultural competence means, what it feels like and looks like, and to consider honestly one's aspirations and commitments.

Having the vision

- feels good, almost like having a partner on the journey, and
- is very energizing and motivating. This whole process of contemplation and writing and reading and listening is energizing and motivating.

Variations

Variation 1. If time is a constraint, skip the step of writing the qualities into a statement. Instead, direct participants to insert their qualities into the template as a list, and then complete the final "so that" statement of the template.

Variation 2. When working with a multilingual group, invite participants to write in their mother tongue or in another language in which they are fluent. Encourage people who work in multilingual contexts to follow this process for each of their languages and to note which different aspects of themselves come forth. Participants who wrote in a language different from the language of the training program can still read their visions out loud; the rest of the group will receive the energy of what is read even without understanding the specifics.

Variation 3. After each participant reads his or her vision statement, encourage participants to rewrite their statements if they do not conform to the four Ps: personal, present, positive, and passionate. Ask them to note how it feels to them as then they reread it. In particular, be watchful for a statement that might describe what the participant wants to do for others, such as, "I inspire others." Written in this way a vision is not personal, it is rather about the effect one wishes to have on another person. To be personal, such a statement needs to be rewritten; for example, "I am inspired." Similarly, watch for conditional language such as "I will" or "I want" and encourage them to use the present tense. Note: pointing out to the reader that his or her vision is missing one or more of the 4 Ps can dilute the honor and power generated by listening in silence. It may be more appropriate if time allows to offer feedback on a one-to-one basis; participants can support each other in this by reviewing their visions with one another in pairs or triads before you invite them to read their visions to the group.

Variation 4. Invite participants to write a second copy of their vision statement and seal it in a self-addressed envelope. Mail the envelopes to participants (perhaps three months) after the program.

Variation 5. Rather than using this activity as a framing piece for a larger training session, as it is indeed often used, make it an integration piece toward the end of the session as a means for participants to reflect on and articulate how they will be moving forward, incorporating some of the learnings from the training.

Facilitation Tips and Suggestions

- In some contexts, participants may interpret writing a vision statement in the present tense (one of the four Ps) as self-aggrandizing. Be prepared to suggest that the vision statement is actually about holding themselves accountable to their commitments.
- Be careful to link the objectives of this activity to participants' interests and the training program goals. When participants are less

used to being self-reflective, it may be useful to present some of the research on visioning from the leadership or psychological literature (see Handout S4.6).

- Be sure to state at the beginning that participant self-disclosure is not a requirement. At the same time, be willing to model appropriate self-disclosure; consider telling a personal story of how writing a vision statement can support professional effectiveness.
- The activity needs to be appropriately introduced for the specific group, with vocabulary adjusted for the specific situation and the objectives carefully framed to link to participants' interests. With these caveats, this activity is as appropriate for a group of seventh grade American students as for a group of multinational engineers working for a global corporation.

About This Exercise

This activity is one of the core elements in all Personal Leadership: Making a World of Difference training and coaching programs (www.plseminars.com). It motivates participants as they use the Critical Moment Dialogue, the program's core process technology, to access their full intelligence and become more skillful in their lives. It also prepares participants for supplemental activities such as vision mapping, which gives participants direct feedback on whether their relationships, roles, and commitments are aligned with their vision. When they discover areas that are misaligned, participants have the opportunity to consider making changes to what they are doing, the way they are doing it, or to their vision.

We first began asking people in our seminars to create vision statements in 1995 as part of our team building work with the Intern Program at the Summer Institute for Intercultural Communication sponsored by the Intercultural Communication Institute in Portland, Oregon. In the early years, we used many different and often very complex and time-consuming approaches to generate the qualities for participants to use in their visions. In 2004 Personal Leadership Seminars facilitator Jin Abe, now associate professor in the Center for Global Education at Hitotsubashi University in Tokyo, Japan, developed a Q-Sort method of moving participants quickly and elegantly from literally limitless numbers of qualities to 10 and then 5. This is the process now used consistently by all Personal Leadership facilitators. It is the process presented here.

We have used this activity in just about every corner of the world (certainly on every continent), with participants of nationalities and ethnicities too numerous to count, and in relatively monocultural and extremely multicultural settings. It has been well received by corporate engineers, banking leaders, international and study abroad students, K–12 teachers, leaders of nongovernmental organizations, independent consultants seeking professional development, parents of newborns and unruly adolescents, United Nations peacekeepers and community mediators, diversity professionals, university faculty, and with intact and newly established work teams.

The original sources of inspiration for this activity include the work of Kenneth Blanchard and Jesse Stoner (2004), Doc Childre and Bruce Cryer (1999), David Cooperrider (2000), Stephen Covey (1989), Gerald Duffy (2002), and Parker Palmer (1998). Most inspiring, however, has been seeing the impact on participants: they leave focused and with a personal commitment to professional intercultural competence that really makes a difference in how they live and work in the world. Indeed, without exception in our experience, participants find this activity enormously valuable. It's not always easy and is certainly often unfamiliar, but when properly introduced and contextualized they find the process of contemplation, writing, reading, and listening extremely motivating and energizing.

HANDOUT S4.2

CRAFTING A VISION IN CONTEXT

Spirituality or Higher-Order Values

Personal Vision

Professional Vision

Everything You Do

Reproduced from: Barbara F. Schaetti, Sheila Ramsey, and Gordon Watanabe, "Crafting a Vision Statement," in *Building Cultural Competence: Innovative Activities and Models,* eds. K. Berardo and D. K. Deardorff (Sterling, VA: Stylus, 2012), 158–168.

 HANDOUT S4.3

THE FOUR Ps OF A POWERFUL VISION

Personal—it's about you, not about anyone else

Present—it's in the present tense, not a conditional future (even if you don't model it all the time)

Positive—it's what you are committed to rather than what you're not

Passionate—it's alive to you; it makes your spine tingle and gives you goose bumps

Reproduced from: Barbara F. Schaetti, Sheila Ramsey, and Gordon Watanabe, "Crafting a Vision Statement," in *Building Cultural Competence: Innovative Activities and Models*, eds. K. Berardo and D. K. Deardorff (Sterling, VA: Stylus, 2012), 158–168.

 HANDOUT S4.4

TEMPLATE FOR WRITING THE VISION STATEMENT

When I am (insert the program goal, for example: interculturally competent) and operating at my highest and best, I . . .

I do this so that . . .

Reproduced from: Barbara F. Schaetti, Sheila Ramsey, and Gordon Watanabe, "Crafting a Vision Statement," in *Building Cultural Competence: Innovative Activities and Models*, eds. K. Berardo and D. K. Deardorff (Sterling, VA: Stylus, 2012), 158–168.

 HANDOUT S4.5

EXAMPLE OF A VISION STATEMENT

(Note: The words in italics in the following statement represent the words that the author of the statement would have written on the index cards.)

When I am interculturally competent and operating at my highest and best, I am *curious* about the positive intent motivating my own and others' words and actions. I search for points of *authentic connection* even with people who seem the most different from me, and listen deeply with an open heart. I use my *breath* to create space between my experiences and my automatic reactions, remembering to *pause* before interpreting and evaluating. I commit to *joy* and well-being.

I do this so that my thoughts and actions help bring forth a world of peace and justice for all.

Reproduced from: Barbara F. Schaetti, Sheila Ramsey, and Gordon Watanabe, "Crafting a Vision Statement," in *Building Cultural Competence: Innovative Activities and Models*, eds. K. Berardo and D. K. Deardorff (Sterling, VA: Stylus, 2012), 158–168.

 HANDOUT S4.6

A SHORT SELECTED BIBLIOGRAPHY

Why Craft a Vision Statement

Blanchard, K. & Stoner, J. L. (2004). *Full steam ahead: Unleash the power of vision in your company and your life.* San Fransisco, CA: Berrett-Koehler.

Childre, D., & Cryer, B. (1999). *From chaos to coherence: Advancing emotional and organizational intelligence through inner quality management.* Oxford, UK: Butterworth/Heineman.

Cooperrider, D. L. (2000). Positive image, positive action: The affirmative basis of organizing. In D. L. Cooperrider, P. F. Sorensen, Jr., D. Whitney, & T. F. Yaeger (Eds.), *Appreciative Inquiry: Rethinking human organization toward a positive theory of change* (pp. 29–53). Champaign, IL: Stipes.

Covey, S. R. (1989). *The 7 habits of highly effective people.* New York, NY: Fireside.

Duffy, G. (2002). Visioning and the development of outstanding teachers. *Reading Research and Instruction, 41*(4), 331–344.

Palmer, P. J. (1998). *The courage to teach: Exploring the inner landscape of a teacher's life.* San Francisco, CA: Jossey-Bass.

Schaetti, B. F., Ramsey, S., & Watanabe, G. (2008). *Making a world of difference. In Personal Leadership: A methodology of two principles and six practices.* Seattle, WA: FlyingKite Publications.

25. BEFORE AND AFTER: THE DILEMMA

Laura Di Tullio

In this activity, participants use textual and visual hints to explore the concept of identity over time and across space. In philosophy, identity is a dilemma. If something really changes, it cannot be the same thing before and after the change; if it is not one and the same thing before and after the change, nothing has really changed (Gallois, 2011). This activity invites participants to explore the notions of identity and change in time and in space and to discuss whether and how change affects their own values and belief frame of reference as they move across cultures.

Key Focus

Navigate identity

Type of Activity

Exercise

Objectives

As a result of this activity, participants will

- recognize priorities placed on values in their own culture in relation to other cultures,
- explore the concept of identity and relate the concepts of identity and change to identity, and
- develop awareness about the possible responses to change, for example: Change across cultures leads to culture shock; change in oneself leads to self-shock. (For the purposes of this activity, *self-shock* is defined as follows: "an extended reaction to the differences with and within the Self. Self-shock is the intrusion of new and, sometimes, conflicting self-identities that the individual encounters when he or she encounters a culturally different Other" [Zaharna, 1989].)

Appropriate Audience

Adults

Level of Challenge

High

Group Size

2 to 20 people

Time

50 minutes

Materials

Handouts

Preparation

Choose images, short legends, or other written material that effectively highlight the complexity and paradox of identity. These may include

- "The Ship of Theseus" (see Handout S4.7) and
- before and after photographs; for example, the restoration of the Sistine Chapel, images of buildings before and after an earthquake, the new and the old Fiat 500 (see Figures S4.1 and S4.2), or the Volkswagen Beetle.

The goal is to choose examples that allow you to ask, "Is it still the same?" and elicit a good discussion. Use these images or examples on PowerPoint slides or as handouts.

Activity Setup

Ask the participants if they know the legend of the ship of Theseus. You can read it, or ask one of the participants to tell or read the legend to the group.

FIGURE S4.1   Old Fiat

FIGURE S4.2   New Fiat

Managing the Activity

Ask some of the participants to answer the question: Is it still the same ship? Have participants explain their answers. As they answer, write their responses in two columns on a flip chart or on a board at the front of the room. If their answers reflect a synchronic change/identity (given point in time), write them in the first column; if the answers reflect a diachronic change/identity (across time), write the statement in the second column. In the third column, write statements that are factors of change: natural events, technological evolution, human intervention, and so on. Do not put titles on the columns at this point.

- If all the participants give the same answer, provide arguments in favor of another view.
- If there is indecision, point out to the participants that this is a philosophical paradox.

- Have participants reflect on time and space by asking, "Are you familiar with the terms *synchronic* and *diachronic*? Could you explain their meanings?"

If not, tell them that

- synchronic comes from the Greek words σύν (sýn) meaning "with" and χρόνος (chrónos) meaning "time." This refers to the idea of having identity at a given point in time.
- diachronic comes from the Greek words δια (dia) meaning "across" and χρόνος (chrónos) meaning "time." This refers to the idea of having identity across time.

The notion of identity in time has been explored frequently in the history of philosophy. However, when we come across a different culture as expatriates for any amount of time, the punctual (spatial) aspect becomes as relevant as the timepiece such as a wristwatch or clock. The more we are aware of these aspects, the more effective will we be in tackling the identity paradox.

Go back to the activity and write synchronic at the top of the column with the synchronic answers, and diachronic at the top of the column with the diachronic answers. This illustrates how the groups' answers fall into the two categories. Analyze the possible factors of change, and group the answers in a third column (see Handout S4.7). Spend about 15 to 20 minutes on this.

Divide the participants in groups of two to five depending on the size of the class following no particular criteria.

Ask the groups to look at the images of the Fiat and share their reflections on what they see.

The following is an example of a possible interpretation comparing the photo of the old Fiat 500 (Figure S4.1) with the new Fiat 500 (Figure S4.2).

Is it still the same?

Yes. Despite the renovations, the Fiat 500 remains a myth and symbolizes reliable economy cars.

The following is an example of an alternative answer:

Is it still the same?

Don't know. Because of the renovations over time and the changes made at all the levels (from the body to the engine), the Fiat 500 does not look like the same vehicle; however, it still performs the same function and still symbolizes a reliable economy car.

Is it still the same? No. The restyling interventions completely distorted the Fiat 500's essence and changed it.

As we are dealing with a dilemma, there is no right or wrong answer, but further analysis and discussion can generate different perspectives on identity.

Ask the participants to apply the notion of identity and change to a trip abroad. Ask them what they can expect in their experience in the host culture. Similarly, ask them to apply the notion of identity and change to a move or a trip to another state, town, country they had in the past. Relate participants' response to the concepts of culture shock and self-shock, as well as to talk about values and beliefs, and introduce the definition of culture. Go through three or four responses or more if the participants wish to discuss the topic in more detail.

Debriefing the Activity

Briefly summarize the purpose of the activity, which is to develop awareness about identity and change. Ask the following:

- What part of the activity was difficult?
- Did you feel uncomfortable at any point during the activity?
- What did you discover?
- How do you interpret it?
- What happens when people move into different cultural settings?
- What impact does that have on one's identity?
- What is a natural response to change?
- What are some lessons learned in this activity that you can apply in situations of change or in encounters with those who are culturally different?

Key Insights and Learnings

1. Moving across cultures brings about change.

   - Some changes happen on the surface, but other changes are deeper and may influence an individual's perception of his or her values and beliefs.
   - In some cases, the concern for what is right or wrong and good or bad in a foreign country as opposed to one's country of origin may affect individuals to the point that they question their choices and even their own identity.
   - In the world of expatriates, some people cannot find a balance between their identity in their own culture and in the host culture, and in some cases, they absorb so much of the host culture they lose sight of their identity.
   - In both cases, "Who am I?" is the question they are trying to answer.

2. Our response to change is, more often than not, confusion or stress.

   - Change occurs in time (synchronic) and across space (diachronic). Often during a visit abroad these aspects of change come together, causing frustration.
   - Researching the factors of one's uneasiness may help in understanding not only the situation but its underlying factors.

- This reflection is particularly helpful to those individuals who are interested in intercultural studies but have never lived outside their own country.
- "How do you deal with stress?" is the question these individuals try to answer.

3. Change can result in culture shock when "the individual encounters a culturally different Other" (Zaharna, 1989).
4. Change can result in self-shock when the individual faces "differences with and within the Self" (Zaharna, 1989).

Variations

Variation 1. Follow the same procedure with two participants. Give each participant a different set of before/after images and either have them discuss the two images together, or have them describe the images to each other before showing them to each other.

Variation 2. Follow the same procedure with one participant. Give the participant the before and after images one for diachronic identity/change and one for synchronic identity/change. Have the participant write a reflection on the two images.

Variation 3. With two participants, ask them to stand back to back and change something about themselves (e.g., remove their glasses). Ask them to turn around and try to determine what the other person has changed. Discuss how this physical change may or may not have affected one's impression but not the person's identity.

Variation 4. The facilitator can demonstrate change by wearing a hoodie, scarf, or some other type of headgear and then remove it and put on something completely different (like sunglasses). Discuss the participants' impressions of each accessory and how the facilitator's identity remained unchanged.

Facilitation Tips and Suggestions

- The question of identity and change dates from Greek times in Western cultures. It was first reported by Plutarch in the form of the Ship of Theseus paradox. Other Greek philosophers such as Socrates and Heraclitus tackled the issue from different standpoints, but until today the question has no answer.
- The question of identity and change is not perceived as a paradox in every culture. The

Asian cultures, in particular, look at the question from the point of view of "maintaining the essence." The idea of the ship, its intention, and its lines are the essence, and as such they are immutable (Adams & Carwardine, 1992).

- The insight section of this activity may be used to ask participants of different backgrounds to express their views on the paradox. The trainer, keeping the audience's diverse composition in mind, may assist the participants in filtering the different ideas through the lens of culture.

About This Exercise

As a daughter, sister, and wife of expatriates as well as being an expatriate myself, I developed the ability to adapt to diverse situations almost naturally at a very young age. The paradox of identity and change did not grab my attention in its entirety and complexity until fairly recently, when during an intercultural training session, a participant was so scared of change she thought she "would lose touch with herself." Not long after that episode, a cross-cultural facilitator in a meeting said that "everybody chooses how much they change." Finally, an article on identity caught my attention. The juxtaposition of these three occurrences allowed me to look at the philosophical paradox of identity from an intercultural standpoint to develop awareness on the impact the dilemma may have and how deeply it may affect a long-term assignee or an expatriate. This is the activity that ensued.

REFERENCES

Adams, D., & Carwardine M. (1992). *Last chance to see*. New York: Ballantine Books.

Collins English Dictionary: Complete and Unabridged (6th ed.). (2003). New York: HarperCollins Publishers.

Gallois, A. (2011, Spring). Identity over time. *Stanford encyclopedia of philosophy*. Retrieved from http://plato.stanford.edu/archives/spr2011/entries/identity-time/

Theseus. (n.d.). *Internet classics archive*. Retrieved from http://classics.mit.edu/Plutarch/theseus.html

Zaharna, R. S. (1989). *Self-shock: The double-binding challenge of identity*. Retrieved from http://academic2.american.edu/~zaharna/selfshock.htm

 HANDOUT S4.7

THE SHIP OF THESEUS

According to Greek legend, Theseus, the mythical founder king of the Greek capital, Athens, returned to his town by sea in a vintage wooden ship with thirty oars. The ship had undergone several maintenance interventions during which the Athenians took away the old planks and other parts as they wore down and replaced them with newer and stronger timber.

They replaced so many parts the ship became an example among Greek philosophers of the paradox of identity. The logical question they asked was: After all the changes, is this still the same ship? Some philosophers held that the ship remained the same; other philosophers contended it was not the same ship.

(Adapted by L. Di Tullio from Theseus [n.d.])

Reflection:

- suggest a synchronic/diachronic hypothesis
- provide examples of change

Image title:

_____

Is it still the same? _____

Explain: _____

Synchronic aspects, if any	Diachronic aspects, if any	Factors of change

Glossary

Diachronic: used of the study of a phenomenon . . . as it changes through time (http://wordnetweb.princeton .edu/perl/webwn?s=diachronic)

Synchronic: 1. occurring or existing at the same time or having the same period or phase. 2. Concerned with phenomena . . . at a particular period without considering historical antecedents (_Collins English Dictionary_, 2003)

---

26. ME YOU IDENTITY POEMS

Fanny Matheusen

In this activity, individuals create biograms (identity poems) for each other as a tool to explore how we see ourselves, how others see us, and how this affects our interactions across cultures. The poems reflect what people know of each other after working together in a group, which often is surprisingly little. We use poems because they appeal to our imagination, which helps in intercultural communication. The symbolic language we use in the poems is multilayered in significance.

Key Focus

Navigate identity

Type of Activity

Exercise

Objectives

As a result of this activity, participants will

- understand how others may see them,
- expand their perspective on their own identity,
- reflect on how identity and identity perception affects intercultural interactions, and
- reflect on personal interaction in task-oriented groups.

Appropriate Audience

Adults, teenagers

Level of Challenge

Medium

Group Size

6 to 12 is ideal, 16 maximum

Time

45 minutes

Materials

- Paper and pencils
- Handout

Preparation

Make photocopies of the handout.

Activity Setup

- Ask the group if anyone knows what a biogram is. Ask him or her to explain what a biogram is and supplement the description with the following: A biogram is a type of written expression in which the writer expresses the most important aspects of his or her identity and life.
- Explain that the group is going to use the biogram as an exercise to explore concepts of identity and the connection between identity and how we adjust to other cultures.
- Tell the participants that while a biogram is often written about oneself, someone else is going to write a biogram about them.

Managing the Activity

1. Have participants pair off and make sure everyone has paper and a pen to write with.
2. Provide the instructions on writing the biograms. (Distribute Handout S4.8, or display instructions on a PowerPoint slide; it may be helpful to give an example for each instruction.) Inform participants that if they don't know what to write on a line, they should just leave it blank or make an educated

guess. Read the instructions out loud one at a time:

Line 1: Write the person's name.
Line 2: Write four characteristics that describe this person.
Line 3: The person comes from . . .
Line 4: What the person finds important in life is . . .
Line 5: The person gets his or her inspiration from . . .
Line 6: The person feels (name three things) . . .
Line 7: The person needs . . . (name three things) in life.
Line 8: The person gives . . . (name three things) to the world, to this group.
Line 9: The person would like to . . . (name three things) now or in the future.
Line 10: The person's surname is . . .

3. After writing, give the pairs a few minutes to read their biograms to each other. Allow them to react to the biogram that was written about them.

4. Ask for one or two volunteers who are comfortable with their biograms to read them to the group. Ask participants who read their biograms out loud to tell the group what their reactions to the poems are.

Debriefing the Activity

Ask the group the following:

1. What was it like writing a biogram about this other person?
2. What did you assume about the other person before engaging in this activity? How accurate were those assumptions? (If appropriate, discuss the impact of stereotypes on our perceptions of other people.)
3. What do you consider the most important piece of information in this poem? (Highlight how people from different cultures might emphasize different aspects of this poem, and how each of us in different settings may emphasize different aspects of our identity and who we are.)
4. Were you able to see yourself in the biogram? How accurately did this biogram describe you? (Ask those individuals who volunteered

to have their biograms read to the group to talk about this.)

5. How surprising were the observations of your colleague? (It may be useful to highlight how culture also shapes and colors our perceptions of others and ask how the culture of the writer of the biogram may have influenced the writing.)
6. How do you think someone from another culture (name a culture if relevant) might rewrite this poem to describe you?
7. How would *you* want to adapt or change this biogram to make it reflect more how you see yourself?
8. How did the writer's cultural conditioning influence the way in which the biogram was written? What was the cultural conditioning or influence on what was written in the biogram? In other words, what role has your culture and cultural upbringing played in who you are?
9. What would have been the outcome if we did this exercise in your workplace, at your school, with your family? (Explore how important it is to individuals that there is congruency between their identities in these different environments.)

From this discussion go into themes on identity (how we see ourselves, how others see us) and then discuss the implications in terms of identity of how we interact with people from other cultures and how we adjust to living in other cultural environments. Close the activity by highlighting the main themes that emerge from the discussion.

Key Insights and Learnings

- There's a difference between identity (the way we define ourselves) and image (the way others see us).
- A person belongs to different social groups that define a part of one's identity. In different contexts different aspects of identity surface. We call this the concept of multiple identity.
- People are not split; they are not African or Belgian, they are Afrobelgian, and they want to express that multiplicity.
- Within groups, the process of acculturation takes place: People adjust to the values and

norms of a group. Because of this, certain aspects of our identity stay hidden. If the social control in a group is very strong, certain subjects can be taboo.

- Religion is becoming an important theme to discuss in intercultural communication. In some cultures religion is more of a part of daily life than in others, which can be expressed in the biograms (see Variation 2 in the next section).
- Other differences that are probably culturally influenced are

  ○ direct or indirect speech, the way you directly or indirectly address a person in the biogram;
  ○ the use of symbolic language, that is, the use of proverbs; and
  ○ references to places, heroes, and some rituals may differ.

- There's a difference between a stereotype and a prejudice. Stereotypes are often the result of not knowing a person very well. You tend to generalize. Prejudices are maintained fixed ideas (negative or positive) about people that you don't contradict.
- In task-oriented groups, sometimes personal interaction is somewhat superficial, and people do not easily share personal thoughts and feelings.

Variations

Variation 1. If time is short or a self-reflection exercise is desired, have participants create biograms of themselves and then debrief them based on what participants have written about themselves, focusing more on identity and their perceptions of themselves versus how others may perceive them.

Variation 2. If time allows, have participants write biograms about themselves. Then have them write one for another person. Allow people to compare and contrast how they describe themselves with how others describe them. This enables a deeper discussion on the differences between how we see ourselves and how others see us.

Variation 3. If groups are newly formed, you can also use this process as a means for individuals to interact and get to know each other. If used this way, individuals interview one another to gather content for the biograms. They write the biogram for the other

person, using content from what the other person told them. This encourages sharing personal information and can help new groups form more quickly.

Variation 4. If exploring and emphasizing the role of stereotypes using biograms, consider playing a clip from the movie *Crash*. It highlights examples of identity and the inherent biases we all have that result in miscommunication and misunderstanding. This emphasis around stereotypes and biases is important and can result in strong emotions. Strong facilitation skills are required here.

Variation 5. If relevant, connect this identity work to strategies for acculturation. Explore the connection between how we see ourselves and how others see us and how this affects the strategies we choose in how we adjust to living in different cultural environments.

Facilitation Tips and Suggestions

- This exercise works best for small groups, for example, 16 people.
- It is best used with groups whose members have some knowledge of one another but do not know each other well. It works well, though, with newly formed groups and groups whose members know each other well or think they do.
- If people are reluctant to participate in this exercise or keep hesitating because they do not know answers to all the questions, put them at ease by saying the following:

  ○ The purpose of the exercise is not to have a biogram that fully describes the person but is to be used as a mirror.
  ○ If you don't know a line, just leave it open or make your best guess. It shows that you don't know the person as well as you thought, or the person did not allow others to know the answer.

- Do not let people who are already very close work in pairs. Also, avoid pairing individuals who have had difficulties interacting with each other.
- Be aware that people can be offended by what is written about them. Stress the differences between a stereotype and a prejudice, and take into account the purpose of the exercise, namely, knowing the difference between how we see ourselves and how others see us. Give any offended participant the

time and means to correct the image presented to the group. But allow ample time for the debriefing.

About This Exercise

One day I had a training group at the end of a series of theoretical sessions about multiple identity, acculturation and integration processes, values and norms, stereotypes and prejudices, and how they play a role in diversity in the workplace. We planned a session for summarizing and to work through the content in a more personal manner. To find some inspiration I consulted a manual that had just arrived. My eyes fell on the exercise "Biogram" (Bijkerke & Van der Heide, 2006). I felt the variant of this exercise was a good start for the day. This group was ready to go deeper into getting to know each other and I could use the group as a mirror for what's happening in society everyday in dealing with differences among people. I learn the experiential way, so I took a risk, adapted the exercise, and conducted it the next day. It was a great session. Since then I used the exercise in several settings, mostly when there is sufficient time in the training session to conduct this activity. I also had some positive experiences using it as a way to get participants to learn to know each other beyond stereotypes. I often use it when coaching collegial consulting sessions. I thank the authors for their inspiration.

REFERENCE

Bijkerke, L., & Van der Heide, W. (2006). *Activerende werkvormen voor de opleidingspraktijk*. Houten, Netherlands: Bohn Stafleu Van Loghum.

 HANDOUT S4.8

BIOGRAM (IDENTITY POEM)

Instructions: Create a poem about your partner by responding to each of the following lines:

Line 1: Write the person's name.

Line 2: Write four characteristics that describe this person.

Line 3: The person comes from . . .

Line 4: What the person finds important in life is . . .

Line 5: The person gets his or her inspiration from . . .

Line 6: The person feels (name three things) . . .

Line 7: The person needs . . . (name three things) in life.

Line 8: The person gives . . . (name three things) to the world, to this group.

Line 9: The person would like to . . . (name three things) now or in the future.

Line 10: The person's surname is . . .

Reproduced from: Fanny Matheusen, "Me You Identity Poems," in *Building Cultural Competence: Innovative Activities and Models,* eds. K. Berardo and D. K. Deardorff (Sterling, VA: Stylus, 2012), 143–147.

27. SHERLOCK HOLMES

Nagesh Rao

Playing Sherlock Holmes is a cultural self-awareness exercise in which participants learn how they make sense of the world around them, how judgments are made based on the meanings created, and how communication and dialogue can play a role in cocreated meanings.

Key Focus

Navigate identity

Type of Activity

Exercise

Objectives

As a result of this activity, participants will

- understand the importance of the constant self-reflection needed to be interculturally competent,
- explore how each of us sees the world around us and how we make meanings, and
- appreciate that we have multiple cultural identities and that combinations of identities work together in different contexts.

Appropriate Audience

Adults

Level of Challenge

High

Group Size

15 to 30 people

Time

60 to 90 minutes

Materials

- A bell to call time
- Blackboard or whiteboard to write down answers (difficult to do this activity with flip charts)
- Four to six packets of three to four small objects

Preparation

Compile four to six packets (use large envelope or a bag that can hold objects) with each packet containing three or four small objects that belong to you (but don't tell the participants that yet). Ideally, the room should have four to six round tables with three to five participants at each table.

Activity Setup

1. Distribute Handout S4.9. Let the participants know that they will be detectives for the next hour (or 90 minutes). Tell them you asked people you know to give you three or four small objects that represent them. Each group will get one packet, and each participant in the group gets a copy of the instructions to play the game.
2. Inform the participants that they have about 10 minutes to answer all the questions. The participants should not overanalyze the objects and should do their best to reach a consensus if group members differ.

Managing the Activity

1. Walk around the room, observing how each group is answering the questions.
2. After about 10 minutes, and all the groups are ready, draw four to six columns on the board depending on the number of groups.

Invite each group to share its answers for each question and write the answers on the board.

3. After all the responses have been written on the board, admire the range of responses, and tell them that all the objects belong to you.

Debriefing the Activity

First, apologize to the participants for deceiving them and thank them for participating so well. They are generally eager to know why certain objects were included. Take time to answer these questions; it builds trust with the group.

Phase 1: What happened?

1. What were your initial impressions after seeing the objects?
2. In each group, how did the group members decide the answers?
3. How were disagreements handled?
4. What was it like developing the answers?

Phase 2: Key questions for learning

1. How are meanings made? Why did I consciously ask you first to answer the question, "Do these objects belong to a female or a male?"
2. How does one's cultural identity/range of experiences shape our meaning-making process?
3. How are judgments made if a female has the qualities/characteristics of a male (within and across cultures)?
4. If each packet represents one part of my personality, what do the four (or five or six) packets represent?

Phase 3: Relationship to the real world

1. How does this activity reflect what happens in the real world?
2. What does this activity say about assumptions we make about others?
3. What impact does our meaning-making process have on intercultural interactions?
4. How can we begin to use frames other than our own frames to make sense of the world?

Key Insights and Learnings

- Participants understand how we process information.
- They learn how to use communication and dialogue to get multiple perspectives on an issue.
- They learn how to use the describe-analyze-evaluate model (see see Section 1, pp. 53–57) to assess people
- They understand the role of initial impressions, framing, meaning-making processes, ethnocentrism, and multiple sides of self.

Variations

Variation 1. What if we had used photographs instead of objects?

Variation 2. What if we had told the participants that each packet has objects belonging to different patients in a hospital?

Variation 3. What if we informed the participants that the packets belong to different teachers in a middle school (or elementary school, or high school, or college) and that the participants need to evaluate the teacher professionally and personally?

Variation 4: What if we tell the participants that the packets belong to members of a management team from Germany who are coming to visit the United States (these countries can be changed depending on the group).

Facilitation Tips and Suggestions

- When putting the objects together for each packet, you can select objects that are chronological (objects from your childhood, your youth, and the present), based on your interests and hobbies, professional versus personal, based on the group (put medicine in each packet if you are working with health care providers), given to you or bought by you; or picked at random. For example, you can include music CDs, books, photographs, jewelry, toiletries, travel accessories, postcards, travel souvenirs, and so on.
- Be prepared to have participants describe you in multiple ways (anywhere from being generous to anal-retentive, intelligent to sexually oppressed, or gentle to sadistic). This exercise

gives you a glimpse of how others see you, but may not tell you what they are thinking or feeling. The facilitator should be self-assured and have a sense of humor.

- This game does not work well with teenagers. They may become so unhappy in being deceived that they shut down.
- In some training situations, it may not be appropriate for the trainer to reveal this level of detail about himself or herself. In this and the preceding case, use another person's objects for the exercise.
- Plan 5 minutes for setup, 15 minutes for playing, 10 minutes for transcribing, and 30 to 60 minutes for debriefing.

About This Exercise

I created this exercise in 1995 when I was teaching a large undergraduate persuasion class and we were talking about source-credibility. I asked the students to each name one personal characteristic they thought made them credible. After the 150 students did this, a student asked me, "What about you, Nagesh?" I said, "I am sensitive and that is what makes me credible." There was a stunned silence for a few seconds, and then the women in the class said things like, "Aaah, so cute, he said he is sensitive." The men in the class snickered and said nothing. At the end of the class, a student came up to me and asked, "Are you gay?" When I asked her why she thought this, she declared, "You are neatly dressed, you have not mentioned a girlfriend, and now that you say you are sensitive, I wondered if you were gay."

This incident taught me several things: (a) I had clearly transgressed gender lines, as being sensitive is highly valued at home in India; (b) the way we make meaning across cultures varies immensely, based on key observable characteristics; and (c) we each have multiple sides (multiple cultural identities), and depending on where I interacted with someone (home, office, party, etc.), a person could see a different side of me. To explore all these ideas, I created Playing Sherlock Holmes.

I have been using this exercise with audiences all over the world, young and old, and in different contexts (corporate, education, health, etc.) with good results.

 HANDOUT S4.9

PLAYING SHERLOCK HOLMES

Here are three or four things belonging to a real person. You are a group of highly trained and highly skilled detectives. From these objects, what can you tell me about the owner of these objects? Some possible areas to explore:

1. Do these items belong to a male or a female?
2. How old is she or he?
3. Educational level?
4. Relational status (single, married, etc.)?
5. Socioeconomic status?
6. Describe three personality traits (positive and/or negative) of this person (for example, she or he is funny, outgoing, and loves to play with children).
7. What kind of a car does she or he drive?
8. Pet(s)?

Let your imagination flow.

As a professional group, first designate someone to take notes. Take about 10 minutes to answer the questions. Then each group will make a presentation with the objects and the group's mystery person.

Reproduced from: Nagesh Rao, "Sherlock Holmes," in *Building Cultural Competence: Innovative Activities and Models,* eds. K. Berardo and D. K. Deardorff (Sterling, VA: Stylus, 2012), 179–182.

SECTION 5

Manage Cultural Transitions

28. FRAMEWORK: FOUR KEY COMPONENTS OF TRANSITION PLANNING

Kate Berardo

The four key components of transition planning helps individuals understand and prepare for cultural transitions. By exploring what transition stress is, why it happens, how it may manifest itself, and what individuals can do about it, the process offers a thorough and personalized approach to helping participants manage cultural transitions (see Figure S5.1).

Key Focus

Manage cultural transitions

Objectives

As a result of working with this model, participants will

- experience a clear process to help them prepare for and manage a successful cultural transition,
- understand the drivers behind transition stress and how they may affect them, and
- develop personalized, specific strategies for managing the natural ups and downs of cultural adjustment.

Appropriate Audience

Adults

Level of Challenge

Medium

Summary Description

The four key components of transition planning framework outlines a process designed to help individuals

FIGURE S5.1 The Four Key Components of Transition Planning

prepare for cultural transitions by planning to manage associated stresses. Its four main components are

- recognize the What: what transition stress is
- understand the Why: why it is likely to occur for each individual; what specific types of changes an individual is facing with the transition that are likely to cause stress
- personalize the How: how transition stress is likely to manifest itself for the individual, given such factors as their personality, prior experience, and the culture the individual is moving into
- apply the What Now: what detailed, specific, and actionable steps an individual can take to best manage a cultural transition and the accompanying stress of a move

In its simplest form, it is a mental framework coaches and trainers can use to ensure they are comprehensive in covering key components when working with people on transition planning. In its most robust form, the model offers an umbrella process that frames and guides a series of in-depth exercises and discussions on cultural transitions.

The four components model was specifically developed as an alternative to the popular U-curve or W-curve model. The U-curve model is often used for transition planning purposes to demonstrate the emotional dips people often experience and is accompanied by a list of symptoms and strategies to manage culture shock. See Handout S5.1 on the dangers of using the U-curve model.

Key Talking Points

The four components model is a framework to facilitate a guided discussion on cultural transitions. The goal of each component, some general questions each component is designed to answer, and an overview of the types of activities for each component are contained in the following section. (See Suggested Uses section on p. 187 for more examples of exercises.)

Recognize the What. The goal of this component is to help learners develop a deeper understanding of the stress people often face when moving abroad, essentially, what is transition stress? Questions to explore with participants include

- What is transition stress?
- What changes am I likely to face?
- What is the impact of these changes?

Culture shock has become a buzz word, and people may have an inaccurate or incomplete understanding of what transition stress actually is and the variety of ways adjustment challenges may manifest themselves—which is part of the reason this component is important—and also why the term *transition stress* (Bennett, 1998) is preferred and used here.

This component is also designed to help people experience firsthand what it may be like moving across cultures. Within the course of a day, an individual may experience excitement about a new position and the adventure, concern, or worry about how his or her family will make the transition, confusion (that borders on frustration) about how to navigate the new environment, and pangs of longing for the familiarity of certain foods or comforts. Helping participants feel the emotions they may experience helps to establish the need to focus on transition stress and enables individuals to start to get in touch with their own personal reactions to stress. Several processes can help bring this component to life, including

- change exercises—where individuals experience their own reactions to change,
- visual models and analogies that effectively illustrate transition stress, and
- stories, vignettes, and other types of examples that bring transition stress to life.

Generally speaking, the more specific the exercises are to the transition an individual is facing and the more relevant to the culture in question, the easier it will be for people to recognize the complex emotions they may experience in an upcoming transition.

Understand the Why. Next, it is important when discussing transitions to explore the multitude of variables regarding why transition stress occurs so you can more effectively identify the best coping strategies. Essentially, you are exploring the following questions:

- Why does transition stress occur?
- Why am I likely to face this stress when moving across cultures, specifically?

Simply put, to say that culture shock or transition stress occurs because individuals are in a new culture or going through extensive change is inadequate. People need to understand more deeply what's behind the emotions they may experience, or why they may experience stress during transitions—essentially what the changes are that will challenge them most and why? When a facilitator or coach is able to help people effectively identify why they face transition stress, very naturally participants are able to see how they may react and what they can do to mitigate this stress.

A nonexhaustive list of why individuals may experience transition stress includes

- identity shifts,
- daily dilemmas,
- confusing interactions,
- role changes,
- letting go of old ways of doing things,
- the energy required to learn new ways of doing things,
- stress of the unfamiliar and the unknown,
- the drain of constant self-monitoring,
- coping with the fact that your normal behavior does not produce normal predictable reactions,
- the inability to understand others' behaviors,
- calling into question of values and worldviews,
- leaving behind family and friends,
- reevaluation of some of the pillars old relationships were based on,
- the dual excitement and anxiety of a new environment,
- the overwhelming logistical process of moving,
- the responsibility for the satisfaction or well-being of others,
- the perception of being judged or stereotyped,
- exploration of new interests,
- building new relationships, and
- managing the sheer emotional complexity of going through many of these simultaneously.

The list goes on and will vary depending on the type of sojourner (business executive, student, accompanying spouse, refugee, etc.) and individual situation. A business executive may also face the stress of acclimating to a new work environment and managing a dual allegiance to his or her home office and the new office, whereas a student may be emotionally vested in managing relationships back home with concerned parents and friends. Another layer to consider are the elements of the specific culture that may contribute to emotional adjustment challenges. For example, in India, the disparity between wealth and poverty may be troubling for some, while in Japan managing the expectations and perceptions of being viewed as a foreigner in a more homogenous society can be a problem.

It's important not to overwhelm learners with all the possible contributors to transition stress or culture shock but instead to focus on the changes that are most relevant to the individuals in the program. This usually means focusing on changes that may be most relevant to the learner, which you can (a) anticipate prior to the session based on what you know and understand about each person, his or her background, and the targeted culture, and (b) can adjust based on what you hear from participants in order to help them prioritize which changes may have the most impact on them and why. This can be accomplished through

- building on the exercises in the understanding the Why component—hold a second round of processing of each activity to explore why the changes experienced were challenging and how they correlate to likely changes a learner will experience when moving abroad, and
- introducing specific exercises that explore the changes faced when moving abroad, from role changes to changes in routine.

Personalize the How. The goal of this component is to help individuals understand how they may respond to changes and challenges in their move abroad, recognizing that how each of us reacts to changes may be very different. The focus should become highly personalized at this juncture with questions such as

- Which of these are most likely to affect me personally and why?
- How do I react generally in stressful situations?
- How might I react during the upcoming transition?

One person may withdraw and isolate himself or herself; another may try to stay busy to avoid focusing on some of the internal and external changes that are taking place. Some gain weight, some lose it, some see no physical change whatsoever. Rather than providing a laundry list of possible reactions to culture change and transition, this component suggests focusing on the individuals and helping them identify how this stress may manifest itself for them.

Helping people to really understand how these types of changes will affect them can be done in a number of ways:

- Explore through a coaching conversation how individuals react to stress generally.
- Use their past experiences with life changes, big transitions, or particularly stressful times

(getting married, moving home, other cultural transitions) to help them identify how challenges in being abroad might manifest themselves in this new culture. Having them reflect on what was most challenging for them and what they experienced can help prime people to think about how they may react to this new transition.

- Explore the nuanced differences between the upcoming transition and ones in the past. This can also be a good place to integrate other culture-specific information about the culture (e.g., via vignettes, critical incidents, etc.) to examine which specific elements of this particular culture an individual may react to.
- If the upcoming experience abroad is being driven by factors other than the person's interest in going (e.g., the executive thinks it will help his or her career, not because he or she wants to be abroad, or the person is moving for a working spouse), you may also need to spend more time focusing on the individual's motivation and attitude to the move and how change by circumstance rather than choice may affect someone's emotional adjustment.
- Supplement, as appropriate, a person's own known reactions with other typical transition stress reactions (e.g., becoming critical of the host country, withdrawing and isolating oneself, becoming more easily irritated, etc.) so individuals can determine if they might have the same type of reaction.

Apply the What Now. Finally, once you've determined which elements of the transition to a new culture an individual may react to, and how this reaction may manifest itself, the task then becomes to identify effective coping strategies. These coping strategies should be detailed, personalized, specific, and applied and essentially enable a person to answer the following: What are the main steps I can and will commit to take to help me set up my life abroad for success and mitigate and manage transition stress?

For example, assume you are working with an individual, "Rehka," who has recognized through this process that she is a highly social person who has grown accustomed to a strong support network, and one of her greatest fears is losing this support as she moves to a new country where she knows no one. Instead of simply acknowledging that Rekha should focus on building a support network, you would

- have her map out who might be in her future social network, including people from home and her local culture and foreigners and individuals from the host country;
- discuss with her how and when she can stay in touch with people back home so she feels supported;
- share examples of how moving abroad can strengthen some relationships to help alleviate some of her fears of losing contact with people;
- explore with her the advantages and challenges of seeking advice from specific individuals back home who may or may not understand the context or have had a similar experience abroad to relate to, to help her know when to turn to different people; and
- discuss with Rehka where she might be able to meet new people in her new environment to help her start deciding who could be in her new support network.

From this process, several action steps Rehka can take might emerge, for example, she could buy her friend Carol a webcam to use with Skype, invite someone from her language class out for coffee, or join a golf club. As a final step, you would want Rehka to prioritize and sequence these actions. You would also be listening carefully to the expectations and assumptions Rehka might be making to help her ensure that her commitments are realistic. For example, if she says she will complete all her action items within the first two weeks, it is important to review how realistic that is, given the fact that she will be trying to get her house set up and begin her new role. Alternatively, if she suggests she will get settled first, it may be important to tell her that these action steps might be what ultimately helps her settle in, and she should explore how she can effectively integrate them into the settling-in process. As an outcome, Rehka gains a clear set of next steps to help her rebuild her network—and more confidence as well.

The goal here is strengthen any coping strategies you help people develop so they can identify which ones will be most useful for them and determine how they can apply them to their own situation. Taking a question-based coaching approach tends to be one of the most effective ways to apply the What Now. Note too that often as you are moving through the prior components of the transition planning process, strategies to manage stress may emerge. It can be helpful to have the individual record these and synthesize them at this juncture. It is also usually most effective to incorporate planning tools like an action plan at the end of the process to bring together and prioritize the learnings.

Key Insights and Learnings

The main points you want learners to discover during each component are the following:

Recognize the What
- The process of making the transition to a new culture is highly complex and variable.
- The types of and amounts of stress one may experience will depend on the individuals and cultures involved: No two transitions will be the same.
- When going through these transitions it is common to experience various emotions—and often simultaneously.
- Some emotions may dominate at different junctures (more excitement than concern, or more longing than excitement), so it is normal to experience ups and downs as we move through this type of transition.
- While we may not be able to prevent transition stress completely, we can take steps to minimize and manage it for a more successful experience abroad.

Understand the Why
- When making the transition to a new culture, much of our focus is often outside of us—setting up bank accounts, learning how to get around, and such. This can make it hard to be in touch with all the emotions we may be experiencing and even harder to recognize what's behind them—or why exactly we feel the way we do.
- The reasons why we experience transition stress vary, from basic changes in routine to potentially profound changes in how we see ourselves.
- At different junctures in our transition, different types of changes may affect us. At the beginning, we may be more affected by changes in roles and responsibilities, whereas changes

in who we are may surface farther along in our adjustment journeys.

Personalize the How
- How each of us reacts to processes and changes may be very different.
- It is therefore important for each of us to know what types of situations, people, and experiences cause us stress and be aware of how this stress may appear in terms of what we think, say, and do.
- Looking at past transitions we have faced can be helpful in helping us to understand how we may react to upcoming changes.

Apply the What Now
- Knowing (and doing) what helps us manage stress is important.
- Creating realistic and clearly actionable steps to manage the transition is essential.
- Managing transition stress is not about doing everything we could do to manage stress; it's about identifying and committing to the small actions that will most help us to have a successful experience abroad.
- We should continually review, update, and recommit to the action plans we develop as we move into the transition.

Suggested Uses

The main use of the four components of transition planning is to design an effective process for engaging learners in cultural transition planning. When used this way, it provides a framework that coaches and facilitators can use to make sure they are comprehensively and completely covering all key components. The model itself can also be presented to learners directly so they understand more about the process they will go through during transition planning.

It is important when designing a transition planning session to recognize that

- the four components in this model do not need to be addressed linearly or independently of one another. For example, one activity may cover the What and the Why of emotional challenges of adjustment effectively. You may also decide to start with the How component by having people reflect on how they have personally managed past transitions and changes and how stress typically manifests itself for them before looking at the What or Why of culture shock and transitions involving culture change. The point is to ensure that all have been covered completely and creatively during the course of a program or coaching conversation.

- as with all facilitation design decisions, where you start and how you choose to address each of these components should be dictated by your learners, their needs, and preferred learning styles.

A variety of activities can help in achieving the four components effectively during a transition planning session. The following are a few examples, many of which correspond with other activities presented in this book:

Ways to Recognize the What

- William Bridges's (2001) transition model is good for theoretical and conceptual learners and visual thinkers. It shows that during transitions we experience stages of loss, letting go and endings, a neutral zone, and a new beginning. One of its strengths is recognizing that we can experience multiple emotions and stages of a transition simultaneously, and it highlights that this process is normal.
- Duct Tape Hands is a great experiential activity that helps people identify the emotions that can come with change and transitions. It is great for experiential, active learners (see pp. 208–210).
- "Working in Unfamiliar Surroundings" (Brandt, 2000) is another experiential type of activity in which individuals are asked to complete a task where the rules have changed. As a less physical type of experiential exercise, it works well with slightly more reserved groups, for example, engineering and mathematically oriented people.

Ways to Understand the Why

- The 5Rs of culture change (see pp. 193–199) frames five key types of changes we face when we move into another culture: changes in routines, reactions, roles, relationships, and reflections about oneself. It looks at common reactions to each of these changes

and offers strategies that are specific to each change.

- Different Days, Different Ways (see pp. 200–207) is especially effective at looking at the impact of changes in routine and how this affects our stress levels.
- Making a Home (see pp. 211–214) explores in depth the impact of changes on our home life and environment.
- Hats Worn, Torn, and Reborn (see pp. 220–224) explores how the roles we play (or the hats we wear) may change in form and fit when we move to a new culture.

Ways to Personalize the How

- You, Me, and, Stress Makes Three (see pp. 215–219) enables couples to have discussions around how they react to stress, use each other as mirrors to better understand themselves when in stress, and plan together how to manage their individual and collective stress in a healthy fashion.

Ways to Apply the What Now

- Action plans that define next steps at a granular level ask questions such as, What is your goal? What are the key actions you will need to take to reach this goal? What does success look like if you achieve your goal? What is your first step in reaching this goal? When will you take this first step?
- SMART is a well-known acronym that stands for setting goals that are specific, measurable, attainable, realistic, and time bound (see pp. 30–31). It can be used effectively to help ensure that the prioritized goals individuals set are clear, concrete, and actionable.

Facilitation Tips and Suggestions

- Use the preceding activities as a list of potential tools to use once you understand more about the learners' needs. Flexibility is important as this process is emergent and driven by the participant. It can be helpful to bring more activities to a session than you will actually employ; you can decide what will be most useful.
- This model works equally well when working with individuals who are not planning for a

transition but are in the middle of one. When used this way, there is often less need to focus on recognizing the What, as individuals will be sometimes acutely aware of what transition stress is, and more time should be spent on the other three components.

- Remember that the four components can be used as a simple guide for effective transition planning conversations as well. Throughout the formal process, you can continually hold conversations with learners who move through these four components in a cyclical fashion to constantly deepen the focus and impact of transition planning. The following is an example of a conversation using the four components (note that a real conversation would evolve more slowly through these four components):

What concerns do you have about the upcoming move?

Giving up my career is definitely the most stressful component.

Why is that?

I've been working for 20 years and it is how I define myself—I feel competent and productive.

Well, that seems understandable. How do you think this move might affect you?

I probably won't notice the void for the first month or so while we are getting settled in, as there will be so much to do. It will likely be a month or two later. I could imagine I might lose a bit of my sense of confidence and start to isolate myself—I tend to be the type of person who likes to do things really well or not do them at all.

Okay, so knowing all that about yourself, what will help you with this element of the transition (What Now)?

I'm not sure if keeping in touch with old colleagues actively will actually help. I think it could keep me too focused on what I have to give up.

About This Framework

This framework emerged from my master's thesis (Berardo, 2006), which made it clear that the popular U-curve model of cultural adjustment was outdated and ineffective. I was inspired to develop an alternative model and approach from this research and have been using, refining, and expanding this process since 2006.

REFERENCES

Bennett, J. M. 1998. Transition shock: Putting culture shock in perspective. In M. J. Bennett (Ed.), *Basic concepts of intercultural communication: Selected readings* (pp. 215–223). Yarmouth, ME: Intercultural Press.

Berardo, K. (2006). *The U-curve of adjustment: A study in the evolution and evaluation of a 50-year old model* (Unpublished master's thesis). University of Bedfordshire, Luton, UK.

Brandt, M. (2000). Working in unfamiliar surroundings. In G. Simons et al. (Ed.), *Global competence: 50 training activities for succeeding in international business*. Amherst, MA: HRD Press.

Bridges, W. (2001). *The way of transition*. Cambridge, MA: Perseus Books.

Ward, C., Okura, Y., Kennedy, A., & Kojima, T. (1998). The U-curve on trial: A longitudinal study of psychological and sociocultural adjustment during cross-cultural transition. *International Journal of Intercultural Relations*, 22(3), 277–291.

 HANDOUT S5.1

UNDERSTANDING THE DANGERS OF THE U-CURVE MODEL OF CULTURAL ADJUSTMENT

The Four Key Components of Transition Planning has been designed as an alternative process to address adjustment challenges more effectively than the U-Curve model of cultural adjustment.

The U-curve model was first put forth over 50 years ago and was designed to describe the emotional adjustment process of cross-cultural sojourns over time. The U shape suggests the sojourner's emotional well-being begins positively, dips to a negative state, and eventually returns to positive levels of satisfaction. The model is often extended to a W curve (two Us) to depict a second U that individuals presumably go through and is often used as a visual illustration of culture shock. The U-curve is illustrated in various forms, resembling the following:

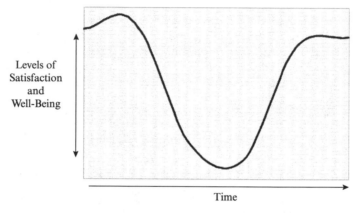

Levels of
Satisfaction
and
Well-Being

Time

THE U CURVE OF ADJUSTMENT

Dangers With the U-Curve Model

There are significant practical and ethical concerns with the U-curve model, which can be summarized as follows:

1. Qualification needed. To use the U-curve model in an ethical fashion, it must be heavily qualified with a number of caveats. These include:

   ○ Adjustment is actually much more complex than this model shows. This is in fact only one of many patterns of adjustment that can be experienced.
   ○ The model does not apply to everyone and may not apply to you.
   ○ It only describes emotional satisfaction levels over time. It does not indicate the degree to which individuals have learned to adapt (skills gained) to the culture or highlight any identity shifts that may be occurring at the same time. While there is a connection for many (e.g., learning how to be effective in the culture helps people to feel more satisfied and improves their mood), this is not always the case.
   ○ Many academics disagree with this model and have a number of criticisms of it. One of the most prominent researchers on the topic has completely dismissed it.

   This takes time and rarely reflects well on the model or the trainer who is presenting it.

Reproduced from: Kate Berardo, "Framework: Four Key Components of Transition Planning," in *Building Cultural Competence: Innovative Activities and Models*, eds. K. Berardo and D. K. Deardorff (Sterling, VA: Stylus, 2012), 183–192.

2. Dismissal by academics. Researchers like Colleen Ward (Ward, Okura, Kennedy, & Kojima, 1998), who has specialized in adjustment theory for decades and written with colleagues perhaps the most influential book on the topic, dismissed the U-curve model in the 1990s because of its lack of empirical support and conceptual issues.

3. Too simplistic. The simplicity that makes the model easy to remember also limits its usefulness. The U-curve does not allow for multiple dips or down periods. It only gives the most zoomed out view of the process of adjustment, where a zoomed in view would be highly irregular, unsmooth, unpredictable—and not necessarily linear. While all models simplify the detail and complexity of the experiences they represent to some degree, the U-curve does so to an extreme degree.

4. No how/why. The U-curve model does not explain how or why adjustment challenges happen; it only describes what happens at a macro level (basically, that you may experience a dip in your level of satisfaction). Its depth and usefulness is therefore limited and its use runs the risk of learners walking away with too basic and superficial of an understanding of adjustment challenges.

5. False One Pattern Assumption. More fundamentally, the U-curve suggests there is only one main pattern of adjustment. However, studies have documented various possible patterns of emotional adjustment over time. With research developments in the last 50 years, we also now know there are a large number of personal and situational variables that affect individuals' adjustment, from personal characteristics like gender and age, to situational dynamics like cultural similarity with the host culture and personal qualities like flexibility and locus of control. To still expect everyone to fall into one same pattern does not recognize research to the contrary or the complexity of variables involved.

6. Inexplicable Elasticity. How the model manages to be so elastic to stretch and apparently fit equally well to a sojourn of 3 months as to a sojourn of 3 years has never been explained. Though adjustment challenges may be experienced by the majority, it cannot be said that these challenges will fall for all different kinds of individuals into the same kind of predictable pattern no matter how long people spend abroad.

7. Poor Quality Photocopies. Descriptions and depictions of the model are often fraught with inaccuracy or are missing detail. Many explanations of the U-curve suggest the model is backed by clear empirical support (which it is not) and some illustrations confuse emotional adjustment, meaning levels of satisfaction and well-being, with other aspects of adjustment such as degree of adoption of host culture values, levels of productivity, or ability to interact effectively in the new culture (which the U-curve *does not* depict).

8. Danger to Participants: Unsubstantiated Predictability. Though trainers report using the model to help people recognize the normalcy of adjustment challenges, the use of the U-curve can have the exact opposite effect. When individual's experiences do not fit into the clean, U-curve shape, they can feel *abnormal*. For example, some may start off their experience with high levels of emotional strain instead of the initial euphoria suggested in the model—which ultimately add to their stress if individuals feel they are not normal in experiencing anxiety from the outset of the experience.

9. Danger to Facilitators. If trainees' experiences do not fit with the U-curve, they may negatively reflect on the rest of the training, wonder what other content was inaccurate, and have a diminished overall opinion of the value of the training.

10. Poor Reflection on the Intercultural Field. Unlike other models that grow stronger with time, the U-curve has only become more porous and problematic. It came out of the infancy of adjustment theory—when data and theories were considered to be disjointed and lacking intricacy and depth. Moreover, its track record of fifty plus years of unclear empirical testing reveals many of the methodological challenges faced by intercultural researchers over the years.

Simply put, the U-curve reflects poorly on the field. It ignores the advancements and sophistication that has been achieved in adjustment theory since the model was developed. Continuing to use the model does a disservice to the depth and complexity of the work that we do and makes our collective approach behind the times, not cutting-edge.

Process Challenges With the U-Curve Model

Beyond the problems with the often used U-curve model, there are also significant limitations to the process typically used with the U-curve model. The U-curve model has often been used to introduce the stress and coping process. After presenting the U-curve model, trainers may give detailed information of the symptoms of culture shock and manifestations of stress in work and relationships. Then, the discussion often moves to providing coping strategies to help trainees prepare for their time abroad. The process in essence often resembles the following figure.

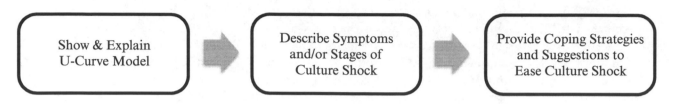

PROCESS CHALLENGES WITH THE U-CURVE MODEL

The two main problems with this process are that 1) it does not go into the why of culture shock beyond the implicit assumption that the amount of change or new culture generally are causing the challenges; and 2) it does not *personalize* the process of culture shock and only provides generalized coping strategies that may or may not be effective, depending on the individual, what lies at the heart of the emotional adjustment challenges they face, and the cultures involved.

In contrast, the Four Key Components of Transition Planning stresses the need to pause both to reflect on the multitude of complex and individual variables that contribute to the why of transition stress and to *personalize* the discussion in order to develop truly effective coping strategies. The Four Components of Transition Planning:

- Encourages and enables conversations. It promotes process over content, and incorporates a coaching approach over traditional training or presenting of information.
- Provides a frame and container to explore dynamics at a personal level and promotes specificity. It does not assume the same challenges, reactions to challenges, or the same coping strategies will be effective for everyone.
- Supports action. The process encourages a continual drive toward the so what? and what now? It ensures not just awareness, but actions—and actions that should have more of a lasting impact because of the preceding focus on the *what, why,* and *how* of the transition process at a personal level.

29. FRAMEWORK: THE 5RS OF CULTURE CHANGE

Kate Berardo

The 5Rs of Culture Change (see Figure S5.2) looks at five key changes we face when we move across cultures. It helps people understand why it is normal to experience ups and downs when moving across cultures and why stress is a part of the transition process.

Key Focus

Manage cultural transitions

Objectives

As a result of working with this model, participants will

- learn a framework to understand five key changes faced when moving abroad,

- understand the impact these changes may have on stress and satisfaction, and
- develop strategies to manage changes and move through transitions more smoothly.

Appropriate Audience

Adults, teenagers

Level of Challenge

Medium

Summary Description

Many descriptions of culture shock (or transition stress) emphasize the symptoms of transition stress

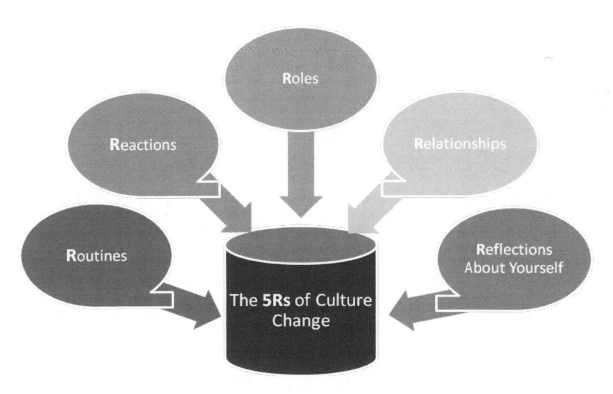

FIGURE S5.2   The 5Rs of Culture Change

(the What) without focusing on the causes of this stress (the Why) beyond noting that it is a result of moving across cultures. This simple model highlights five changes that can cause transition stress when moving across cultures: changes in routines, reactions, roles, relationships, and reflections about oneself. The model enables individuals to explore more deeply why we face transition stress, and as a result, develop effective, personalized strategies for managing it.

This model can be used in coaching and training sessions that focus on transitions—whether before or during a sojourn or as a means to prepare for reentry into one's own country. The model emphasizes understanding the why of the four key components of transition planning (see p. 183). Two handouts are provided for use of this model in facilitation and coaching situations (see Handout S5.2 and Handout S5.3).

Key Talking Points

Step one. Introduce the 5Rs model, explain the purpose and goal of working with this model. Note that experiencing ups and downs as we move to new cultural environments is normal. Show the 5Rs model and give a one-sentence summary of each *R*. Then explain that the goal of this model is to understand

- why we experience these ups and downs and what are the key changes we face when we move abroad,
- the impact these changes can have on us and which changes may influence us the most, and
- how each individual can best handle these changes to manage the transition process most effectively.

Provide additional background on the model if necessary, and explain the process you will take people through as part of this exploration.

Step two. Explore each of the 5Rs by focusing on What the change is, Why this is significant, How it may surface, What Now, and the strategies people can adopt to effectively manage this change.

Two handouts can be used to support this step:

1. The 5Rs of Culture Change (see Handout S5.2): This handout provides the key talking points for each *R*, summarizes common reactions people have to each change, and provides general strategies for how to manage this change effectively.

2. Effectively Managing the 5Rs of Culture Change (see Handout S5.3) is a worksheet that can be used with the model to capture participants' insights, learnings, and plan of action for managing these elements of change.

Suggested Uses

The approach here is to become partners with the people you are working with to explore together likely changes they will face and their potential implications. Rather than simply present this information, it is best to do one or more of the following:

- Provide examples for each *R* that are specific to the cultures participants will be moving to.
- Provide a scenario, example, or story that brings to life each of the 5Rs, and then introduce the model and its main components. You can then hold a conversation with questions such as,

  ○ What if this same thing happened to you?
  ○ What would be your reaction?
  ○ Of the five scenarios, which would bother you the most?
  ○ What would help you to manage stress in each of these situations?

- Continually ask questions about each *R* to help individuals understand them and apply the questions to themselves. This may be anything from, "What types of activities do you do to relax?" to "How much role clarity do you have in your new position?" Generally questions will flow out of your curiosity and attention to helping them make sense of the possible changes they will face and what they can do about them.
- Have individuals rank which type of change they are most concerned with or they feel will likely affect them the most. Use this as a means to build prioritized lists of actions that each individual can take to manage transition stress.
- Link any strategies you discuss to how they address one of the 5Rs. For example, note how unpacking quickly when you arrive or getting out to explore your neighborhood contributes to creating a sense of being anchored and can therefore be a good way to combat the uncertainty that results from changes in routine. The best strategies are

usually developed by individuals themselves, once they have clearly identified the changes that will affect them most.

The preceding suggestions outline a basic process that can be used to introduce the 5Rs model when working with individuals, couples, and even families. The model and process can easily be adapted for groups. For example, rather than present each of the 5Rs of Culture Change, have groups work to identify the What, Why and How, and What Now themselves. For each R, ask participants to answer the following:

- What changes do you think you might experience in each area when moving to another culture?
- Why might this be important?
- How would dealing with these changes likely affect individuals generally speaking? How will dealing with such changes affect you?
- Given this, what now? What strategies do you think can help people to best manage these changes? What will work best for you?

You can either have the entire group discuss all 5Rs or have small groups focus on different Rs and share their findings. Present the What, Why, and How of each of the 5Rs, and then:

- Have individuals or small groups brainstorm the What Now (strategies for managing the transition).
- Divide the main group into five smaller groups, send them to different stations or areas of the room, and assign each group one of the Rs. Tell them they are now investigative reporters who will need to interview other people in the room for suggestions and strategies on what helps to manage the R they represent. For example, someone in the routine group would interview everyone they speak to for strategies for managing the change of routines, asking questions such as, What is the most important routine to establish first? What helps to manage stress when you don't have a routine? Make sure everyone has a pen and something to write on (sticky notes are ideal, with one strategy per sticky note). Ask the five groups to come together in the middle of the room, and tell each member of a group to find someone

who represents another R, pair up, and each interview the other for strategies. Encourage people to provide a new strategy each time they are interviewed rather than repeating the same strategy as a response. Give the group 5 to 10 minutes for these interviews. Then have the groups go back to their stations to share their findings with the other members of their group and create a list of these strategies on a flip chart. If the groups have used sticky notes, they can stick all the strategies they received from their interviews on the wall and group them. Have each group report these strategies to the entire group. Then ask each individual to find one to three strategies that would help him or her the most and commit to applying them.

Facilitation Tips and Suggestions

- As you introduce and discuss each of the 5Rs, the focus should continually return to individuals, their specific situations, how each of the 5Rs may affect them, and what they can do about it. Even in group sessions where you cannot give personalized attention to each person, it is important to create the space and context for people to reflect on how these 5Rs may apply in their own situations.
- There is no one-size-fits-all reaction to these changes. The amount of stress one feels, what triggers stress, how that stress manifests itself, and what helps to mitigate stress will vary by individual. A number of other factors play a role in transition stress, including but not limited to prior intercultural experience, expectations, language, quality of life, degree of difference with home culture, acculturation strategy, living situation, personal dynamics (gender, age, education, characteristics like flexibility and patience), and length of stay.
- Keep a balanced perspective on these changes: Remind people that not everyone faces all these changes nor reacts negatively to them. The goal is not to overwhelm individuals but to help prepare them to address the changes they may face when entering a new culture. Stress the benefits of going through these changes for those who seem to lose sight of this, and help people identify the qualities, resources, and experiences they

already have that will help them manage the adjustment process. Make sure individuals gain confidence through this process by identifying personalized actions they can take to prepare for the transition.

- When safety and trust has been established with participants, you may find people share substantially and personally. Respect cultural norms about how much disclosing is normal and comfortable—it may be more appropriate to keep the conversation at a more general level and important not to push people to disclose more than they are comfortable with. Also, know your own limits. Occasionally, people may share personal challenges that are beyond the scope of focus and beyond your scope of expertise. In these cases, acknowledge their feelings, but also acknowledge your professional limits.

- This model can be effectively used with teenagers and adolescents as long as you appropriately adjust how you describe each R. For example, with teenagers, you can explain the potential changes on what it means to be a teenager in their host country (their roles), and help address concerns they may have about changes in relationships. With adolescents, you can help them identify routines that are important to them and objects that bring them comfort and familiarity, and you can help parents incorporate these into their move.

- Consider employing other transitions-based exercises to go deeper into one or more of these five areas. Encourage learners to keep returning to the 5Rs to see how they are advancing on developing strategies for each of these areas. For example, if it becomes clear that role changes are likely to be one of the biggest concerns for an individual, consider following this discussion with the Hats Worn, Torn, Reborn (see pp. 220–224) activity. Or, to explore routine changes in more depth, try the next exercise in this section: Bruce La Brack's Different Days, Different Ways.

About This Framework

I created the 5Rs of Culture Change after my 2005–2006 master's work in intercultural communication. It became clear through my thesis that there is an ongoing need for easy-to-understand and remember frameworks on cultural adjustment and perhaps, more importantly, great room for improvement on models that not only describe the what of culture shock or transition stress but also the why. The 5Rs of Culture Change was born as a conceptual model to fill this gap. I was influenced by research on cultural adjustment, my own experience making the transition in six different countries, and the stories and challenges I have heard from clients around the globe on what challenges them most about moving to another culture. I have used this model with individuals from various cultural and industrial backgrounds and find it helps to simplify a complex process and still allow for elements of complexity and individuality, which I see as critically important in transition work.

 HANDOUT S5.2

THE 5Rs OF CULTURE CHANGE

	What This Change Is and Why It Is Significant	Examples of How People May Respond	Examples of the What Now
Routines	When we first move across cultures many of our routines are disrupted: we eat different foods at different times of the day, we have to navigate a new environment, and we may be without a regular schedule for some time as we get settled. At the same time, even the most basic of routines, from turning on lights, to getting on a bus, to shopping at the grocery store—which we normally do on auto-pilot without much thinking, may suddenly require more (and in some cases our full) focus and energy.	• Not feeling as "anchored" or "grounded" as normal • Feelings of low-grade, but constant stress • Generally being more tired or stressed, without an easily identifiable cause	• Create new routines as quickly as possible • Realize and plan for things to take more time as you spend more energy on these routine-establishing activities • Build in from the beginning mini-routines, habits, and hobbies that help you to relax
Reactions	We do things we are accustomed to doing in our own culture—but we get a very different reaction than we expect in our new culture. We tip 10%, and to our surprise, the waiter demands to know what was wrong with the service. We shake hands with all colleagues in our office area when we arrive in the morning, and we are met with a strange look. We present a gift to a customer, who seems offended rather than pleased. We request that a team member completes a task by a certain deadline, but our team member doesn't deliver. While we recognize we have probably acted out of the norm for the culture we are in, we don't have the "key" to unlock this situation and understand exactly why people have reacted in the way they did. At the same time, we experience a different way of working, interacting or engaging. We ourselves try to react appropriately but find ourselves lacking the appropriate skills to do so effectively, be it a command of the language or the ability to shift styles.	• Higher levels of confusion and uncertainty • Our sense of competence and confidence decreases, especially if these reactions continue over time • Withdrawal or isolating ourselves to minimize the frequency of these reactions • Become critical of other ways of doing things, preferring our ways of acting because we know them better	• Learn as much about the culture as possible before you go—learn as many "keys" to unlocking reactions as possible • Start to build needed skills to interact effectively in that culture • Identify people who can help you make sense of others' reactions and help you determine your best reaction to different situations • Set realistic expectations for the time and energy it will take to learn these skills • Remind yourself of what you are good at
Roles	We often experience changes in our roles and responsibilities when we move across cultures. We may carry out the same role professionally but in another culture. We take on a new or expanded role. We lose roles that are important to us if we, for example, have to give up our job in support of a spouse and their move. We find some roles do not change, but our ability to fulfil these roles does: for example, being a caretaker for parents who remain in the home country or being the person close friends call without a moment's notice for help and advice. Or, others see us as playing a particular role, whether or not we define ourselves in this way ("the foreigner," "a stay-at-home parent," a representative of your home culture). We are likely to experience many forms of role changes—and simultaneously—creating mixed emotions.	• With new roles: excitement, anticipation, and enthusiasm mixed with anxiety, apprehension, sense of responsibility • With unwanted roles: pressure, defensiveness, and rejection of being defined in a certain way • With lost roles: sadness, mourning, and loss of identity	• Hold discussions to gain clarity (as much as possible) on your new role and its responsibilities • Set and manage expectations about how you will perform in different roles • Strategize how to live out the same roles in a different location (e.g., taking care of parents who remain in your home country) • For roles that you no longer are living out, reflect on what you gain from that role, and where and how else you might experience that type of feeling

Reproduced from: Kate Berardo, "Framework: The 5Rs of Culture Change," in *Building Cultural Competence: Innovative Activities and Models,* eds. K. Berardo and D. K. Deardorff (Sterling, VA: Stylus, 2012), 193–199.

Relationships	Relationships are arguably always in motion and evolving, but moving to a new culture often accelerates this process. When we move to another culture with a spouse or with families, we discover how to live out our relationships in a new environment and are often challenged not to let the stresses around us enter into these relationships. Our relationships with those we transition with may get stronger, deeper, and more profound as a result of going through this change, but they also take work. At the same, we find other relationships around us changing—we may drift apart from certain friendships back home, be surprised at the newfound sense of closeness and kinship we experience with others despite the distance, and be challenged to recreate relationships in our new environment so we have a sense of community and support.	• Excitement, enrichment, satisfaction as new relationships built—though energy intensive • Worry, guilt, pangs of loss, frustration or tension as relationships change • Loss of support system, especially initially as we seek to recreate our support network • A sense of satisfaction, ultimately, as we realign relationships and deepen the connections	• Determine the relationships that are most important for you to maintain back home and devise a plan (e.g., Sunday Skype calls) to stay in touch • Keep dialogues open about hopes, needs, concerns in existing relationships • Be proactive in building new relationships, seeking connections via new networks, events, and support systems • Leverage technology tools (online photo albums, blogs, social media, Skype) to stay connected
Reflections About Yourself	As we experience culture change, we may start to notice that we ourselves change in some subtle and not so subtle ways: we may realize we actually really enjoy a certain aspect of the lifestyle here that we didn't know we would; or, we realize just how important certain values are to us that we might not have articulated before. We may pick-up certain habits, gestures, ways of being that are now natural to us, but also may surprise and disarm family and friends back home who start to wonder what else has changed about us. We are growing, evolving, and developing—trying to become more aware of who we are culturally and individually speaking—which brings many benefits, but often also some confusion and uncertainty.	• Find ourselves oscillating between being critical and accepting of the new culture • Surprise ourselves as we learn things about ourselves that we did not know—some of which we may not be able to make total sense of • Explore and grapple with deep, identity-based questions: Who am I? What's most important to me? Where do I feel at home?	• Acknowledge that these changes are a natural part of the transition process for many • Stay in touch with what is going on inside you by reflecting, writing in a journal and noting what you are learning about yourself • Share and seek support from other expatriates who may have faced similar situations in the culture you are heading to

 HANDOUT S5.3

EFFECTIVELY MANAGING THE 5Rs OF CULTURE CHANGE

Instructions: Reflect on each of the 5Rs of Culture Change for your situation specifically. What are the changes you will likely face in each of these areas? Be as specific here as possible. List the routines you will not be able to continue, the relationships that will change the most, etc. Then note why this is significant for you. If you find this change stressful, how might this stress manifest itself in you? Rank the impact of these changes on you, from 1 being most significant, to 5 being least significant. What now: What are the 1–2 things you can commit to doing that will best help you manage this element of culture change?

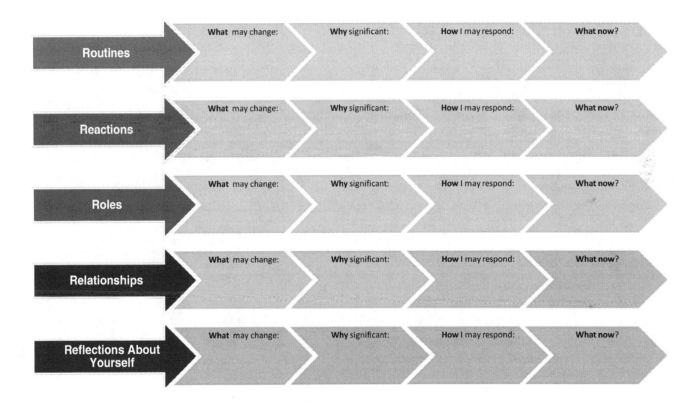

Reproduced from: Kate Berardo, "Framework: The 5Rs of Culture Change," in *Building Cultural Competence: Innovative Activities and Models,* eds. K. Berardo and D. K. Deardorff (Sterling, VA: Stylus, 2012), 193–199.

30. DIFFERENT DAYS, DIFFERENT WAYS

Bruce La Brack

This exercise allows individuals to anticipate and reflect upon the impact of making the transition to another culture and explore the differences between their typical home schedule and a typical day abroad by comparing their schedule of daily activities with a 24-hour grid.

Key Focus

Manage cultural transitions

Type of Activity

Exercise

Objectives

As a result of this activity, participants will

- gain a more accurate assessment of the similarities and differences they will face in their daily lives after entering a new cultural context,
- consider the psychological and behavioral alterations it might be necessary for them to make as they seek to adjust to the new realities, and
- think about how cultural and social values of the host society and home society are reflected in these historical patterns and preferences.

Appropriate Audience

Adults, teenagers

Level of Challenge

Low

Group Size

1 to 60 plus people

Time

30 to 60 minutes

Materials

Handouts

Preparation

1. Decide which will likely be more insightful in highlighting the changes participants will face: a daily or weekly schedule comparison. For a daily schedule, see Handout S5.4, for a weekly schedule, see Handout S5.5.
2. Print out copies of the schedule grid you will use for the exercise.
3. Customize grid titles depending on the specific focus. For example, for a corporate executive the title could be Typical Office Workday; for a nongovernmental organization worker, A Typical Project Workday; or for medical personnel, Typical Clinical Day.

Activity Setup

This activity involves having individuals complete a schedule for their current culture and the culture they are moving to, and using these two contrast sets to explore the impact of changes they will face. The exercise can be conducted at any or all four of the following stages in an international move or sojourn:

1. Predeparture, to anticipate the impending change of place and pace
2. In country, to reflect on the initial experience of a change of place and pace
3. Prereentry, to reflect on an international experience and anticipate the return home
4. Reentry, to bring closure to an international experience and plan for a new life back home

Set up the exercise as follows:

- Distribute two schedule grids per participant (one for the home culture, one for the host culture). Allow sufficient time for participants to think about and record their schedules. This can be done either as part of the session or in advance with participants completing the schedules on their own and bringing them back for debriefing.
- Ask participants to complete the schedules in whatever level of detail you want (e.g., for only one day making notations only every hour, or for an entire typical week). Generally, the greater the detail the better the exercise may work, but even general comparisons can yield interesting and useful insights and points of comparison between two different lifestyles.
- For predeparture, participants are likely to have only a vague idea of what the specifics of their new schedule abroad might be. In such a situation they can be helped by prompting with questions such as, "Given what you know about the country you are going to, what are some ways your schedule might be different from your current patterns?"
- For in country, participants will need to complete a grid from memory for their comparable schedule at home.
- For prereentry, have participants complete their current schedule and anticipate their future schedule once they return home.
- For reentry, participants complete their current schedule and contrast this with their past schedule in their sojourn culture, which they complete from memory.

Managing the Activity

Have a few participants discuss their current schedules and what features are likely to be very different in the other culture. Then choose a couple of schedules that will provide maximum contrast for a more in-depth discussion. See Table S5.1 for a brief example from Japan.

The following is a basic set of questions (adjusted accordingly to reflect the appropriate phase of the stay abroad) to start the debriefing:

1. What differences can you anticipate while abroad in terms of time (i.e., meal times, shopping hours, etc.)?
2. What do you think some of the reasons are for these differences?
3. Have you ever been in other situations where there were such differences?
4. If so, how did you feel and what did you do?
5. How do you feel about these differences that you'll encounter abroad?
6. What will be difficult for you and what will be more easy for you to adapt to?
7. How can you develop realistic expectations of times and schedules and other routine items?
8. What are some specific adaptation strategies you can use as you adjust to these different expectations and realities?

Predeparture—anticipating the impending change of place and pace. Raise the awareness of how entry into another culture will affect participants' personal daily routines. These fundamental changes may initially feel uncomfortable, restrictive, and incomprehensible—often all three—depending on the degree of difference between their current patterns at home and the expectations of themselves and those around them.

Explain how even the most routine things one does at home may either not be possible or may be seen as inappropriate elsewhere. Discuss the myriad of details that will likely be different while abroad: differences in meal times and staple foods, local transportation systems, bathing times and etiquette, cost of utilities (phone, electricity, gas), recreational opportunities, amount of free time or time alone, and host family expectations. This gives the participants something to think about, an impetus for further research on what the actual conditions are likely to be while abroad, and a reason to consider in advance what they might have to adjust to after their arrival. If possible, you may even want to bring in someone from that country (as a country/culture expert) to respond to questions about schedules.

Additionally, to the extent of your knowledge, explore why, for example, these Spanish, Kenyan, Russian, or Japanese daily or weekly patterns exist. Demonstrate how politics, history, economics, demographics, aesthetics, geography, belief systems, and so on have all contributed to shape the present patterns and give the culture its particular unique form. It is often a bonus that once participants begin considering why another culture has different approaches

Table S5.1   Comparison of a U.S. and Japanese School Day

Typical U.S. School Day	Typical Japanese School Day
9 a.m. Participant rises	6:30 a.m. Participant rises with family
Long, hot shower (15 minutes)	No shower (*ofuro* the night before)
Eats minimal breakfast alone	Eats Japanese breakfast with family at 7 a.m.
Drives to school (15 minutes)	Walks to train station; takes commuter train to university (1 hour plus)
In class for five hours	At school for four hours
Recreation 1 hour (soccer)	Recreation facilities unavailable or sparse (club-oriented)
Drives home or to meet friends	Commuter train home (1 hour plus); if late, must notify family
Dinner (often alone/often fast food/often away from home)	Eats with family if possible
Studies for a couple of hours	Studies for a few hours
Watches television, DVDs, plays video games, listens to music, cruises Internet, hangs with friends	May spend time with family watching TV; not much time alone
Go to sleep between midnight and 1 a.m.	Go to sleep around 11 p.m.

to behavior or communication from one's home culture, they will frequently begin to consider (perhaps for the first time) what historical and social circumstances led to patterns in their own culture.

In country—Initial experience of a change of place and pace. At this point the impact is likely to be more visceral, and differences may loom larger than similarities. The exercise is a good starting point to discuss cultural reactions (culture fatigue, culture shock), the cultural reasoning behind the new patterns, ways to enhance culture learning through observation and inquiry, and how to find adjustment strategies that will work for the individual participants in their immediate circumstances. It also helps to sort out what cannot be changed and how to deal with difficult issues.

Pre-reentry—Reflecting on the international experience and anticipating the return home. Direct the focus during the debriefing more toward thinking about leaving

the host culture and whatever routines one has adjusted to during the visit and beginning to evaluate the time retrospectively. This works particularly well for international students who are completing academic programs of several years' duration, international aid workers in the last stage of project completion, and business executives (and their spouses and families) returning from a successful corporate assignment abroad.

In these situations, the exercise can be adapted to help participants contemplate closure in their host culture (and the sudden loss of their current daily life patterns) and to anticipate what resumption of routines at home will mean. The difference at this stage is that participants often resist the notion that there will be any problems once back home. This is particularly true of international students who may already have some concerns and anxiety about what the return home will bring and may seek to avoid any discussion or consideration of potential negative issues. The use of this exercise is a relatively low-risk way to help such participants at a minimum to recognize to some extent the magnitude of alterations in their daily lives that returning home will entail to and consider some of the specifics involved.

In prereentry, this exercise can be used to raise awareness of how living in another culture has affected participants' personal daily routines and in what ways the return will be different from their current practices. At this stage, the in-country experience has taken on some semblance of reality and may even become to some extent a kind of home. Participating in this exercise tends to help participants who are soon to return home to think about the changes they have undergone in the process of adapting overseas and to anticipate what going home will mean in terms of their daily life once back. Additional questions to explore include:

- What will they be happy to leave behind?
- What will they particularly miss about life abroad?

Discuss cultural reactions (reverse culture shock), the major cultural values the two schedules reflect, the necessity of bringing culturally appropriate closure with friends and community members, and how they feel about the changes. Discussions can be initiated about what kinds of behaviors they have adopted abroad that can be successfully brought back home (e.g., taking off shoes in the house, practicing a language, attending the opera) and what items, good or bad, must be left behind. What knowledge gained will be less useful or irrelevant (e.g., knowledge of the Tokyo subway system, negotiating in a market)? How will they feel about that? A wide range of issues including personal safety, public transportation systems, and urban versus rural communities can be spun from a consideration of the daily schedule and extrapolating to larger adjustment issues and challenges.

Reentry—Bringing closure to an international experience and planning for a new life back home. Debriefing in the reentry stage is more complex than in any of the previous three stages because it is based on extensive experiential knowledge as well as the attendant feelings associated with all prior stages of the transition.

In reentry, the debriefing can take place on several levels and be used to explore different aspects of the overseas experience at different times. It can be used to contrast what participants thought the experience

was going to be like on a daily basis with what it actually turned out to be. Or it could be used to compare daily life overseas with what they are currently experiencing during reentry.

In addition, at this stage of the experience, the exercise can be used to focus on everything from earlier phases by asking questions such as:

- What strategies were developed to cope with everyday activities?
- How realistic were expectations about initial entry into the culture?
- How realistic were expectations about the return home?
- What has been most surprising or disconcerting about daily life since you returned?

Variations

With appropriate alterations, this process can be a valuable exercise for people who are not going abroad but are facing a significant transition in a wholly domestic context, such as a change of job or company or moving to a new area or state in their home country.

A variation of the exercise could also be used to sensitize individuals and offices responsible for adjusting international participants or scholars to their campuses to the types and degrees of adjustments such populations face on a daily basis. Similarly, the exercise could be used by agencies assisting refugee and immigrant populations to begin conversations about the salient differences between their clients' former daily life and their new circumstances.

Adjust the grid to suit the purpose of the exercise, providing the necessary detail to conduct a practical and specific debriefing. This could be as simple as a 24-hour grid for a single day or for up to a week, depending on which stage the participants are about to face or are in (e.g., predeparture, in country, predeparture, or reentry) and the degree of detail desired. The type of grid can vary somewhat so long as the result is a daily or weekly schedule (or a contrast set listing home and abroad time allocations) and is sufficiently detailed to be able to make comments on the most important and potentially salient differences between the two daily patterns.

Facilitation Tips and Suggestions

- In orientation and in-country phases the exercise works best when the trainer has detailed knowledge of the target overseas cultures as well as participants' home culture.

- In prereentry with corporate participants, they are frequently unable to visualize what their new work context will look like, as they may not have a specific new assignment, or it may be so different the specifics may be unknown. In such cases they should use the previous patterns as a rough guide to discussing potential reentry conflicts.

- This exercise may be introduced at just about any time in a program with predictably interesting and engaging results. All that is required is to distribute the blank schedules and have participants fill them out and discuss them.

- Debriefing can take place in one session, allowing perhaps an hour or so depending on the size of the group, or aspects may be stretched out over several weeks or even months. One can return to the exercise again and again as a reference point indicating cul-

tural change, skills involved in cultural adaptation, the role of expectations in successful and satisfying transitions, and any other subjects the instructor or participants raise.

- It is simple to administer and is relatively quickly completed, is low risk, costs nothing but class or training time, and requires only thoughtful participant involvement.

About This Exercise

The use of a 24-hour grid to compare and contrast typical home and international patterns was first employed in the University of the Pacific's cross-cultural orientation class (Cross Cultural Training I) in the mid-1990s as an extension of discussions about how the participants' new routines would significantly differ from their current lives. It was expanded in 2001 for use in the Training for Transitions class at the Summer Institute and adapted for in-country, prereentry, and reentry situations.

📄 HANDOUT S5.4

TYPICAL DAILY SCHEDULE

	AM		PM
12:00		12:00	
12:30		12:30	
1:00		1:00	
1:30		1:30	
2:00		2:00	
2:30		2:30	
3:00		3:00	
3:30		3:30	
4:00		4:00	
4:30		4:30	
5:00		5:00	
5:30		5:30	
6:00		6:00	
6:30		6:30	
7:00		7:00	
7:30		7:30	
8:00		8:00	
8:30		8:30	
9:00		9:00	
9:30		9:30	
10:00		10:00	
10:30		10:30	
11:00		11:00	
11:30		11:30	

Reproduced from: Bruce La Brack, "Different Days, Different Ways," in *Building Cultural Competence: Innovative Activities and Models,* eds. K. Berardo and D. K. Deardorff (Sterling, VA: Stylus, 2012), 200–207.

 HANDOUT S5.5

TYPICAL WEEK

	Monday	Tuesday	Wednesday	Thursday	Friday	Saturday	Sunday
5:00am							
6:00am							
7:00am							
8:00am							
9:00am							
10:00am							
11:00am							
12:00pm							
1:00pm							
2:00pm							
3:00pm							
4:00pm							

Reproduced from: Bruce La Brack, "Different Days, Different Ways," in *Building Cultural Competence: Innovative Activities and Models,* eds. K. Berardo and D. K. Deardorff (Sterling, VA: Stylus, 2012), 200–207.

	Monday	Tuesday	Wednesday	Thursday	Friday	Saturday	Sunday
5:00pm							
6:00pm							
7:00pm							
8:00pm							
9:00pm							
10:00pm							
11:00pm							
12:00am							
1:00am							
2:00am							
3:00am							
4:00am							

31. DUCT TAPE HANDS

Stephanie Pollack

In this exercise, participants experience firsthand some of the challenges of cultural transitions as a means to open a discussion on effective cultural adjustment.

Key Focus

Manage cultural transitions

Type of Activity

Exercise

Objectives

As a result of this activity, participants will

- increase their awareness of feelings that may accompany their transitions and adjustment to different cultural environments,
- gain insight into their personal level of adaptability to change, and
- learn strategies for effectively managing cultural transitions.

Appropriate Audience

Adults, teenagers

Level of Challenge

Medium

Group Size

8 to 40 people

Time

25 to 40 minutes

Materials

- Cut pieces of duct tape about four to six inches long, totaling four pieces per participant
- Whiteboard or flip chart
- Markers

Preparation

- Place precut duct tape pieces throughout the room close to where the participants will be sitting—on the back of their chairs or on nearby windows. Four pieces of tape are needed per person, all between four to six inches long.
- Setting up chairs in a U shape or a circle without large tables or desks works well.

Activity Setup

Do not do any framing; just jump into the exercise. The key to facilitating this experience successfully is providing an opportunity for participants to experience all their natural feelings, thoughts, and behaviors that accompany not knowing what is happening.

Managing the Activity

Round one:

1. Ask participants to untie and tie their shoes, or unbutton and button their jacket, or unbuckle and buckle their computer bag—anything they can do with their fingers that they do all the time.
2. Ask participants what it felt like to do it, and write the responses on the board. Sample responses are "normal," "usual," "Why did you have us do this?" "rote," and so on.

Round two:

1. Instruct participants to take a piece of duct tape and bind their fingers on both hands so they cannot use their fingers separately.
2. Once complete, ask participants to repeat the action in round one—untie and tie their shoes or unbutton and button their jacket or unbuckle and buckle their computer bag.
3. While they do this the second time, write any of their relevant verbal comments on the board.
4. Once complete, ask participants what it felt like, and write the responses on the board. Sample responses are "harder," "weird," "it took longer," "a bit awkward," "still easy," "I felt clumsy," and so on.

Round three:

1. Instruct participants to bind their thumb to their palm on each hand with another piece of duct tape.
2. Once complete, again ask participants to repeat the action in round one.
3. Write down any of their relevant verbal comments or nonverbal communication on the board; there will probably be more comments during this third round, for example, "I can't do this," "I give up," laughter, grunts, people using mouths and knees, people helping each other, and so on.
4. Again ask participants what it felt like, and write the responses on the board. Sample responses are, "frustrating," "annoying," "I had to be creative," "That was hard," and so on.

Debriefing the Activity

1. Ask participants why they think you asked them to go through the process and discuss it.
2. Take participants through the steps of the activity, and ask some version of the following:

   • What did you think about the first stage, the first time you did your manual activity?
   • How did you handle the second stage when your fingers were taped together? What do you think about how you handled it? What surprised you? What did you see others doing that was helpful?

• How did you handle the third stage when your thumbs were taped down? What do you think about how you handled it? What surprised you? What did you see others doing that was helpful?

3. After reviewing the activity itself, move the conversation to a "so what" discussion on how to effectively manage cultural transitions. Questions you can ask during this portion include

   • What are some similarities between this exercise and making the transition into a new culture?
   • What past experiences have you had that are the equivalent of needing to button, tie, and buckle things in a new cultural environment? How did you handle them? What did you do well? What do you wish you had done differently? What coping mechanisms did you use?
   • Through this exercise, what did you learn about your natural feelings, attitudes, thoughts, and behaviors that could help you when moving into a new culture? What did you learn about your natural feelings, attitudes, thoughts, and behaviors that could be challenges for you when moving into a new culture?
   • Based on this exercise, what thoughts, tips, tricks, ideas, and coping mechanisms could increase your cultural adjustment proficiency in managing future cultural transitions? What can you do to ensure you have this knowledge at your fingertips to use when you are most in need?

Key Insights and Learnings

• Making a transition into different cultures can be filled with strong emotions that can alter the performance of simple tasks.
• It is normal for feelings to change throughout the different stages of cultural transition.
• Knowing personal natural reactions in advance of a cultural transition can shed light on the feelings, attitudes, thoughts, and behaviors people might have during the transition.
• Determining various possible coping mechanisms in advance of a cultural transition can support people during the transition.

Facilitation Tips and Suggestions

- Duct tape works the best, as it does not stick to the skin or hair as much as other types of tape.
- Keep visible the written responses and notes from all three rounds so participants can see the progression of feelings or actions throughout the activity.
- The tape can either remain on or be taken off during debriefing. If nothing is said about it, inevitably a participant will ask if he or she can take it off. Treat this as a learning moment and bring it into the debriefing. It's interesting to point out to the participants that some people don't mind the tape, while others want to take it off with urgency. Note that we all have different types of triggers that take us out of our comfort zone. For some, keeping the tape on may not be an issue but having to stand on a crowded train will. Ask people to reflect on what types of tasks might be the hardest for them as they enter a different cultural environment.

About This Exercise

I first experienced Duct Tape Hands as a participant in 1998 as a part of my master's degree program in a course on creative teaching methods at the C. W. Post campus of Long Island University. Over the years, I have adapted it for intercultural learning purposes. I have used it with various populations including study-abroad students preparing for their trip, volunteers at the beginning of a cross-cultural service program, business people in the midst of organizational change, and fellow interculturalists during training of trainers sessions.

32. MAKING A HOUSE A HOME

Nancy Longatan

Through a series of questions, individuals reflect on what it means to set up a new home abroad, discussing practical considerations and the deeper meaning of home. Questions facilitate a discussion on how individuals can set up their new home in a way that supports their transition.

Key Focus

Manage cultural transitions

Type of Activity

Exercise

Objectives

As a result of this activity, participants will learn to

- reflect more deeply on their personal needs while living in another culture, and
- become aware of issues and areas in which further planning may be needed.

Appropriate Audience

Adults

Level of Challenge

Low

Group Size

1 to 8 people

Time

30 to 60 minutes

Materials

Handout

Preparation

Make one copy of the two-page questionnaire (see Handout S5.6) for each participant. The room may need to be arranged for privacy, depending on group characteristics (see Variations on p. 212).

Managing the Activity

1. Distribute the questionnaire to each participant and allow 15 to 30 minutes to complete it.
2. Invite participants to form dyads or small groups to share their responses to the questions.
3. Debrief the the group as a whole (if appropriate).

Debriefing the Activity

General debriefing questions include the following:

1. Were there questions here that surprised you? Issues you hadn't thought of before that may be important?
2. Were there questions you couldn't answer because of lack of information about your destination? If so, how can you get them answered?
3. Were there questions you couldn't answer because you haven't considered them before, or that you will have to wait to see before answering them? If so, how will you prepare to deal with them?
4. Did you find specific items or areas that make you believe that life overseas will be

uncomfortable for you? If so, what coping strategies do you think you will need?

5. Supposing that you have a community or support group whose members give very different responses to these questions, how will you get and give support? (For example, in an expatriate community some members are comfortable with the living conditions of the host country, while others strive to replicate their home conditions.)

6. Considering what home means to you, what is important for you to re-create in your new space? What are the first steps you need to take to make this happen?

Key Insights and Learnings

• Living arrangements may turn out to be more complex and critical than expected.

• Responsibility for living arrangements and homemaking may need to be shared among family members after consultation.

Variations

The debriefing discussion should depend on the participants.

Variation 1. If participants are similar in origin and destination cultures, set up the debriefing so it takes the form of nurturing from a support community. Encourage participants to support one another after the program as well and discuss mechanisms for them to do so.

Variation 2. If participants are similar in culture but diverse in life stage (single, married, etc.) or destination, build connections in the discussion on what is similar and what is different in everyone's expectations. Discuss the role life stages or the destination plays.

Variation 3. If participants are diverse in origin but similar in destination (e.g., international students entering a new program), supplement the discussion with information about the destination environment, conditions, and cultural notions of home.

Variation 4. When participants are diverse in origin and destination, consider having people reflect on the debriefing questions and write down their answers rather than discuss them out loud. Then hold a general and shorter debriefing.

Variation 5. If spouses or partners are participating together in the debriefing, discuss these issues with both. Be prepared to have a discussion with couples on roles and responsibilities in making a home together.

Variation 6. If you are coaching an individual, use this questionnaire to hold a deeper coaching conversation, and establish clear actions the individual can take to support a successful transition.

Facilitation Tips and Suggestions

• Full-group discussion of the issues raised may or may not be appropriate. It is important for the facilitator to assess the energy of the room to decide the best way to debrief the group.

• Responses are very personal. It is unlikely a group of participants will arrive at any kind of consensus, nor need they be encouraged to.

• Facilitators may choose to modify the questionnaire itself to make it more relevant to particular groups.

• The main desired outcome is that each person will reflect on these questions for his or her own unique situation.

About This Exercise

I developed this reflective exercise as a result of my own experience as a teenager moving with my family to Guyana from Northern California. My family's experience convinced me that the details of daily life always need careful attention in new cultures. Since then I have been listening to the stories of numerous sojourners—singles and families, moving with the family, leaving the family behind, coping with living standards up, down, or sideways—and have come to believe that the experience of homemaking holds important lessons for reflection and learning about oneself and about life in general.

 HANDOUT S5.6

MAKING A HOME

INTERNATIONAL SOJOURNER VERSION

Both for families and for those living alone, making a home for oneself and others is an important task. Many people, such as students or singles living alone may not have given much attention to homemaking in the past, and others have lived with family members who handled daily living tasks without much discussion.

However, moving to a new environment and culture can make simple chores such as washing clothes or cooking food into complex challenges that may have to be negotiated in new ways within the family, and sojourners may find themselves handling personally tasks such as water treatment that may not have been necessary, or personal care tasks that were handled by domestic employees or relatives before. For everyone, making a home in a foreign culture involves intense challenges, and especially those for whom the move means a change of role from full-time homemaker or student to employed outside the home, or vice versa, some personal reflection and preparation will be meaningful.

These questions are designed to get you thinking about some basic issues related to homemaking both at home and overseas. You may need to do some more research to answer some of these questions, and the exact living situation you are going to may or may not be clearly defined yet, but the questions should alert you to issues that you may need to make decisions about or adjust to. It is recommended that you fill out this sheet now, and keep it to read again as you get settled in, and even later, when you are preparing to leave. The intent is to stimulate deeper reflections at any stage of the adjustment process.

1. (a) What is the primary meaning of "home" for you? Choose one or your top three or rank them all.
   - A serene retreat from the chaos of the outside world
   - A place to nurture children and visitors
   - A hub of many activities for many people
   - A congenial meeting place for friends and guests
   - A display or showcase of my design skill and artistic style
   - A plain backdrop for my life requiring little attention
   - A place where my roots and traditions are preserved
   - A safe space where I can drop the mask and be myself
   - Other_____

   (b) Do you expect the place you are going to to have these characteristics or meanings, or will it be more of a temporary dwelling? What aspects of home may be difficult to build or make in your new environment?

2. What is necessary for a comfortable residence?
   ___ Electricity
   ___ Water supply
   ___ Hot running water
   ___ Refrigerator
   ___ Stove (with/without oven)
   ___ Toilet separate from bathroom
   ___ Shower/bathtub
   ___ Separate bedrooms for each family member
   ___ Rooms with/without interior doors that lock
   ___ Play/study space for children
   ___ Washing machine for clothes
   ___ Dryer for clothes

Reproduced from: Nancy Longatan, "Making a House a Home," in *Building Cultural Competence: Innovative Activities and Models,* eds. K. Berardo and D. K. Deardorff (Sterling, VA: Stylus, 2012), 211–214.

___ Household help/servants (live in/live out)
___ Substantial natural lighting
___ Windows that open/don't open/are barred/screened
___ Yard or garden
___ Porch or balcony
___ Entry area (for shoes) separate from front room
___ Fence/wall/gate around property
___ Heating/air-conditioning
___ Other:_____

3. Employees at home. If you
   a) Have never had domestic help and don't expect to have it in the new place, you can skip this section.
   b) Have had domestic help before but don't expect to have it in the new place:
      What tasks do you need to learn? (e.g., use of washing machine, or washing clothes by hand)
   c) Have never had domestic help before and expect to have it in the new place:
      How many domestic helpers will you employ?
      How will you find them?
      What will they do?
      How will you train them?
      What language will you speak with them?
      How much power distance[1] do you expect? Do they expect?
   d) Have had domestic help before and expect to have it in the new place:
      What cultural similarities and differences do you expect to have with your new employees?
      Will there be differences in power distance in the new culture compared with the culture(s) in which you have had domestic help before?
4. What kind of water supply will you have? Will the water be treated adequately or will that be your task? If necessary, how will you treat water for home consumption?
5. What proportion of your income do you now spend on daily living necessities? What proportion will you be spending in the new place? What proportion of income do you personally see as ideal to be used for daily living (food, water, energy, home entertainment, etc.)?
6. Who will do the daily or weekly food shopping in the new place? How will they learn where to go and what to buy?
7. Do you know how to drive a car? Do you need to learn in the new place? How do you feel about driving? If you already drive how much difference will there be in the system there? If you are not planning to drive yourself in the new place will you feel a sense of lost independence?
8. To what extent will you be dependent on members of the host culture for household and daily living requirements that you have been able to handle independently before? International sojourners often find that they simply cannot provide independently for needs that they covered by themselves at home. Could there be any value in this dependency (loss of independence?)?
9. What expectations do you have for yourself and others about the speed and extent of your learning to be independent in the new culture, and how do you define independence?

1. Power distance: "The extent to which the less powerful members of [society] expect and accept that power is distributed unequally" Hofstede (2001, p. 98). In low power distance cultures, employers and employees see authority as a pragmatic arrangement to get work done for remuneration, whereas in high power distance cultures, employees see their employers as on some higher plane, with the God-given right to exercise authority over them. Obviously, a very different quality of relationship and a potential source of conflict will result if the employer and employee have differing cultural values on the subject. For more information, see Hofstede, G. (2001). *Culture's consequences: Comparing values, behaviors, institutions, and organizations across nations* (2nd ed.). Thousand Oaks, CA: Sage.

33. YOU, ME, AND TRANSITION MAKES THREE

Kate Berardo

This exercise, specifically designed for couples moving abroad, helps each person in the relationship identify and express what causes his or her stress, how this stress manifests itself, and what the person and those around that person can do to help manage stress. It promotes necessary conversations between couples on how they can support one another during stressful times.

Key Focus

Manage cultural transitions

Type of Activity

Guided discussion

Objectives

As a result of this activity, a couple moving abroad will learn to

- recognize stress triggers for each person in a relationship,
- hold an open dialogue on how stress manifests itself in their relationship, and
- build strategies as a couple on how to support each other through a cultural transition.

Appropriate Audience

Adults

Level of Challenge

High

Group Size

2 people

Time

60 to 90 minutes

Materials

Handout

Activity Setup

1. Emphasize the need and importance of having open dialogues with our spouses and partners on transition stress. The following are some key points:

   - Couples are like buoys tethered together in the ocean. In a calm sea, they may happily bob around together. Yet when the water gets rough, and when one person gets down or stressed, one of two things can happen: One pulls the other down, or the other lifts the other up.
   - To ensure that people in a couple can effectively lift and support one another, it's important to have healthy conversations about what stresses each is susceptible to, what helps, and how each can support the other through the transition.
   - These discussions are important because we all have different stressors, react differently to stress, and may need different things from our spouse or partner to most effectively move through transitions.
   - These conversations as a couple are a key step in the transitioning planning process and is the focus of the next part of the session.

2. Provide the couple with copies of the worksheet (see Handout S5.7). Explain that the goal will be to give them some time to reflect

on how they see stress surfacing for themselves, their partner, and as a couple—and then to compare their reflections and discuss what each one of them can agree on to ensure they are managing the transition effectively as a couple.

Managing the Activity

Ask both of them to think about the following questions and record their responses in the corresponding box in the handout:

1. Stress triggers

   - What situations, types of people, responsibilities, or domains (finances, work, and personal life) typically cause you stress? Be as specific as possible.
   - If people get stuck here, ask them to reflect on the last few times they were stressed and what caused the stress.

2. How stress surfaces

   - How does stress affect you? What do you think, feel, and do as a result of this stress?
   - What happens to you physically when this stress surfaces?
   - What happens to you emotionally and mentally when this stress surfaces?
   - How would someone else see that you were stressed?

3. Likely stressors

   - Think about the stress triggers you wrote down. Which of these are likely to be present during your upcoming transition and cause you stress? How and when do you see them surfacing?
   - What other elements of the upcoming transition are most likely to cause stress?

4. What I/we can do

   - What helps you feel balanced and manage stress?
   - What kinds of activities most help you relax?
   - What is it important for you to say or think to yourself to help manage these stressors?

- What steps and strategies can you commit to now to help manage and minimize transition stress?

Repeat the process and guided questions two more times, one for how each sees his or her partner (e.g., What triggers stress in your partner, How does he or she react while stressed?) and another for how both people see themselves as a couple (e.g., What causes stress for you as a couple, How does stress surface in your relationship?). The preceding questions can be used with slight modifications for each of these subsequent rounds. Usually, by the second and third round, fewer prompting questions are needed, and the individuals may pick up speed in completing each section.

Debriefing the Activity

Initiate a discussion with the couple, moving sequentially but fluidly through each of the components of the handout.

- Start with one of the two individuals, and ask what he or she identified as stress triggers. Make this a dialogue rather than reading a list by asking questions and asking for examples. Ask the other person if he or she identified the same stressors for as the spouse or partner.
- Continue in this format until you have addressed stress triggers, reactions, likely stressors, and what I/we can do for each person and for them as a couple. Keep the focus in the conversation on the stress management commitments they can make to themselves and each other.
- Ensure participants leave with key actions they can take to support one another. Other questions you can ask to help drive these conversations are

   ○ What does your spouse do that helps you in times of stress?
   ○ What does your spouse do that does not help you in times of stress?

Key Insights and Learnings

- Stressors are different, and so are our responses.

- Our life partners may observe how stress manifests itself for us in ways we are not aware of. They therefore serve as good mirrors to help us identify our stress triggers and reactions.
- When our partners are stressed, how we react and respond can either help reduce their stress or add to it.
- We need to be aware of what helps and what we may do that may only add to our life partner's stress.
- It's important to have conversations about what we can do for each other that is truly helpful in times of stress.
- Holding open dialogues of this nature can help us keep external stress from entering too much into our relationship. We should keep having these dialogues.
- Both have a better sense of their stressors, those of their partners, and how they can support one another to manage stress during their transition.

Variations

Variation 1. Rather than go through the worksheet person by person and then as a couple, you can also go through by level. Explore stress triggers for each person and then the couple, and then do the same for stress reactions and stress management strategies.

Variation 2. After participants complete the worksheet as a couple, have the couple fill out the boxes for any children they have, keeping in mind how stress manifests itself for their kids and what each one of them does that helps the children and what each may do that may add to the children's stress.

Variation 3. This process can be highly effective when a couple is in the midst of a transition (this will require an even higher level of facilitation given the stress that may surface). The same overall process can be followed, omitting the likely stressors in the new environment sections (since the stressors in the new environment will be covered in the stress triggers section).

Variation 4. This process can be used in group trainings when the partner is not present by doing the following:

- Provide participants with two copies of the worksheet. Have individuals in the session complete one of the worksheets themselves.

- Once completed, facilitate a group discussion.

  ○ First, have them pair up or form trios to discuss what stresses them out, how stress manifests itself, and what helps. Encourage people to serve as coaches for each other to develop effective strategies to manage stress.

  ○ Then as a group, ask individuals to share a few examples of what tends to stress their partners and how they react. See if anyone else in the group has the same experience with his or her partner and can say what seems to help, or if anyone has the same stressor as the partner and can say what helps the most.

  ○ Finally, encourage individuals to go home and have these conversations with their partners as one of their next steps in preparing for the move abroad.

Facilitation Tips and Suggestions

- This process is usually best introduced toward the end of a coaching session when trust and disclosure levels are high and after other elements of the transition (e.g., culture-specific information, critical incidents, etc.) have been discussed that can help individuals contextualize their potential stress.
- As a facilitator of this conversation, your role is to listen deeply and help the couple listen carefully to each other. You want to guide this process almost invisibly and allow the focus to remain with the couple as much as possible.
- However, as you are explaining and setting up each box you want the couple to complete in the worksheet, it can be helpful to provide examples. At these times, sharing examples of other transitioning couples and personal examples (e.g., what stresses you and how it manifests itself) can help create a spirit of disclosure, model self-awareness, and normalize the notion of being stressed by transition dynamics. It is important as you give these examples to be short, specific, and swift in moving the focus back to the couple.
- This exercise is often a highlight for couples in a session on transition because they are given tools and a process to hold healthy, meaningful

conversations that are constructive and action focused. At the same time, it is a higher-order form of facilitation and should be carried out by well-practiced facilitators who need to be prepared and able to facilitate deep, moving conversations in the face of strong emotions and laughter, moments of potential disconnect, and opportunities for growth, which can all occur in a short period of time.

- When safety and trust have been established, you may occasionally find that couples share deeper challenges that are beyond the focus of the session and beyond your scope of expertise. In these cases, it is important to acknowledge their challenge but also acknowledge your professional limits (unless you are a trained couples counselor or a psychologist) and make recommendations for further professional support as needed and appropriate.

This exercise addresses in depth the Personalize the How and Apply the What Now elements of the Four Key Components of Transition Planning (see pp. 183–192). It also follows the What, Why, How, What Now process to ensure effective transition planning.

About This Exercise

I have been building, developing, and conducting this exercise for the last five years. It first came out of my master's research that was focused on the outdated and ineffective use of the U-curve model of cultural adjustment. At the time it was clear we needed more effective ways to help people plan for transitions abroad. This exercise is one such tool and is specifically focused on helping couples manage transitions effectively. I have used it with my husband in our moves to five countries and with countless couples moving across the globe with good results.

HANDOUT S5.7

YOU, ME, & TRANSITION STRESS MAKES THREE

	Stress Triggers What situations, types of people, responsibilities, or domains (finances, work, and personal life) typically cause you stress?	**How Stress Surfaces** What happens physically, emotionally, mentally when this stress surfaces? What do you think, feel, and do as a result of this stress?	**Likely Stressors** What elements of the upcoming transition are most likely to cause you stress?	**What I/We Can Do** What helps? What steps and strategies can you commit to now to help manage and minimize transition stress?
Me				
You				
Us				

Reproduced from: Kate Berardo, "You, Me, and Transition Makes Three," in *Building Cultural Competence: Innovative Activities and Models,* eds. K. Berardo and D. K. Deardorff (Sterling, VA: Stylus, 2012), 215–219.

34. HATS WORN, TORN, REBORN

Kate Berardo

Role changes are an often overlooked cause of transition stress. This exercise helps people explore how various roles they play—friend, colleague, parent, or child—may change as they move across cultures and how to proactively plan for these changes.

Key Focus

Manage cultural transitions

Type of Activity

Exercise

Objectives

As a result of this activity, participants will

- understand how work and life roles may change when making the transition to another culture,
- gain clarity on the impact these role changes may have, and
- visualize and plan to manage the impact of role-based changes.

Appropriate Audience

Adults

Level of Challenge

Medium

Group Size

1 to 10 people

Time

45 to 90 minutes

Materials

Index cards (7 per person will be ample)

Preparation

Distribute stacks of index cards to all participants.

Activity Setup

1. Provide a few examples of how we often experience changes in our roles and responsibilities when we move across cultures:

   - We may take on a new or expanded role professionally or may carry out the same role but in another culture.
   - We may lose important roles if, for example, we have to give up our job to move with a spouse.
   - We may find some roles do not change, but our ability to fulfill them does (e.g., being a caretaker for parents who remain in the home country or the person close friends call without a moment's notice for help and advice).
   - Others may see us playing a particular role, whether or not we define ourselves in this way (the foreigner, stay-at-home parent, a representative of one's culture). (Adjust these examples so they are real and relevant to the group you are working with).

2. Tell the group how we are likely to experience many forms of role changes simultaneously, which can create everything from excitement, anticipation, and enthusiasm to anxiety, apprehension, pressure, loss, and a sense of responsibility.

3. Stress the need to anticipate and plan for the role changes we face when we move abroad, and introduce Hats Worn, Torn, Reborn as a means to do this.

Managing the Activity

Identify the Hats You Wear
Have individuals:

1. Take a small stack of index cards from the pile.
2. List their current roles (call this "the hats they wear"), for example, wife, daughter, project manager, sister, friend, board member. Have them write down one role per index card, with the role title at the top. Create or show them an example so these instructions are clear.
3. Once they have completed the cards, ask participants to identify what they gain from wearing each hat (each role). Alternatively, you can ask people what would be missing in their life if they didn't wear this hat. Have them write down whatever words or phrases that come to mind on the index card. See figure S5.3 (front side) for an example.
4. Finally, conduct a mini debriefing of this step. Ask the participants to share an example of one of the roles they play. Try to find out what they gain from the role. If working with a group, ask the rest who can relate to the meaning associated with the role. Discuss what is similar and different about the roles and the meaning of these roles to the group.

Carry the Hats Into a New Culture
1. Have individuals visualize their life in the culture they are moving to in as much detail as possible. Encourage them to think about their day-to-day activities, how they may spend their time, what the average week will be like, and who they will be connecting with.
2. Then return their focus to the roles on their index cards. Ask the participants to remove any index cards that represent hats and roles they will no longer wear when they move abroad and set these aside (hats torn). These could be, for example, a specific role the individual will no longer perform because he or she has accepted a promotion in the new country, or an accompanying partner has given up a career for the transition. Acknowledge that many of these hats may be cherished roles, and you will come back later to explore what to do with them.

3. Review the remaining roles one by one, asking people to share how they see the role in the new country. Supplement their descriptions with relevant culture-specific information. For example, discuss how a good mom is viewed in the destination country, what expectations are of students, or what it means to be an effective manager in the host culture.

Hats Worn: Resizing to Fit
1. Note how these examples show that when we move to a new culture, even when our roles don't change, how we live them out and the expectations others have of this role may also change.
2. Ask people to focus on their top three roles, one by one, and answer the following:

   - What will stay the same? What will change?
   - What is the impact of these changes? What are the implications of these changes for your upcoming move?
   - What steps and action do you need to take now and when you arrive to ensure you are best prepared to wear this hat in the new culture?

Encourage them to record their reflections on the back of the index card. For group programs, you can also pair up and give them 15 minutes to discuss these questions with their partner. If time allows, you can have people complete this step for all their hats rather than their top three.

Hats Born
1. Ask individuals to reflect on whether they will start wearing any new hats when they enter the new culture. These may be new job roles or hats others may see you wearing (the foreigner, Canadian, or Spaniard).
2. Have individuals create a new index card for any new hats they will likely start wearing and also record words or phrases to describe how they feel about wearing this new hat. Discuss again the implications of their new role, and help participants identify any next steps or action they should take to be best prepared to wear this hat in the new culture.

Hats Torn: Looking for a Chance to Be Reborn

1. Have participants look at all the roles they will play when they are in their new culture. Ask them to think about (and express if desired) what they think and feel as they look at these different hats. Reflect with participants on how meaningful an experience they will have in their new culture, including what's complete and what's missing in the picture of their new life abroad.

2. Have people return to the hats they set aside as being torn. Tell them to set aside any index cards that represent torn hats they are comfortable with. Ask them to focus on any torn hat that gives them a sense of loss. Acknowledge the loss individuals feel and that it is natural to have such feelings.

3. Encourage them to look back at the specific words they associated with the torn hat. Ask them to compare these words to the words they wrote for other roles. Have them note any overlap in words, which can help people see they will likely experience the same emotions or meaning when playing another role, which can be reassuring.

4. Then have them note what words remain. Ask them to think of other activities or roles that might give them the same sense of meaning they identified with a particular role. For example, if you are working with a spouse who was giving up a career to follow his or her spouse and feels competent and organized when wearing his or her professional hat, start to explore other types of activities (e.g., taking classes, volunteering to organize school events, etc.) that can lead to similar feelings of competence through another activity.

5. Have the individuals write answers to the following questions on the back of the torn role index card:

   - What are the implications of your not wearing this hat in your upcoming move?
   - What steps or action do you need to take now and when you arrive to ensure you are best prepared to substitute this hat with other roles or activities in the new culture?

See Figure S5.3 (back side) for an example.

Packing Up the Hats for the Move

Finally, ask people to turn over all their index cards to reveal their notes and the action they are going to take. Ask them to highlight or circle their top three actions that have emerged from this reflection. Then, encourage them to put a timeline on these actions to help turn them into realistic action plans.

Debriefing the Activity

Debriefing generally occurs throughout this discussion as you look at each role type. To close the activity, ask participants:

1. What they are taking away from the activity in terms of insights and realizations
2. What they are taking away in terms of next steps or action?

Key Insights and Learnings

- Even roles that stay the same change in a transition. How we live every role can shift.
- How others see the same role can also shift as one moves into a new culture. What makes a manager good in one culture may be the exact opposite in another culture. Or, how one supports a partner may be viewed differently by that partner in another culture.
- When we move to other cultures, new roles are also often born. We may be happy to take on some of these roles, but we may also have less choice about others. It is therefore important to be in touch with our emotional response to wearing new hats when we enter another culture.
- Even if you can't live certain roles in a new culture, there are other ways to minimize loss and ensure you are able to gain a similar sense of meaning in life.
- With all role changes, visualizing what these roles will look like in another culture is a key step in setting realistic expectations for a transition.
- Establishing the implications of role changes can help us identify needed steps we can and should take to help manage the impact of role-based changes during transitions.

Project Manager

A sense of competence

Connection to professionals

Chance to be detail-oriented

Results! A sense of accomplishment

Knowledge of different parts of the business

✓ REWORN   ○ BORN   ○ TORN

[Front]

Impact + Implications of Move on This Role

Different scope of responsibilities, somewhat unclear right now

Don't have established network in parts of the business: will have to rebuild, may face some red tape

Need to balance desire to show results with really understanding new environment

My Next Steps:

1. Set up meeting with Jerry – see who he can introduce me to before he transitions back.
2. Have an expectation setting meeting with my boss on scope of responsibilities and realistic timelines!

[Back]

Friend

Gain and give support

Advice and venting of frustrations!

Someone to explore with: a sense of fun

People who love me and get me

✓ REWORN   ✓ BORN   ✓ TORN

[Front]

Impact + Implications of Move on This Role

Have to rebuild friendships. Feels like it will be energy intensive.

Like that I am moving to a relationship-oriented culture!

Grieving losing chance to speak regularly to friends back home.

My Next Steps:

1. Test Skype video with Maria before we leave.
2. Invite a mother from the school to coffee within the first two weeks.
3. Reach out to neighbors within the first week.

[Back]

FIGURE S5.3   Sample Index Cards

Variations

Variation 1. Have individuals order their roles, for example, put the number 1 next to the role they see as the most defining, 2 next to the second most defining role, and so on until all roles have been numbered. Have them do this for their current roles, and then again after they have reviewed and born, torn, or reworn their roles. Seeing that not only do the roles change but the order of the roles may also change can often provide interesting additional insights.

Variation 2. Be creative in bringing to life the metaphor of the roles we play as the hats we wear:

- Bring to the session real hats of different types (e.g. beret, bowler, cowboy hat, chef's hat, bolero, straw hat, fedora, etc.). Have participants assign a role to each hat and then have them try on the hat in another culture or try on a new hat. The physical act of putting on a hat can help people get in touch with the meaning of the role for them and to visualize living this hat (role) in another culture.
- Alternatively, provide index cards with pictures of hats attached or printed on them. Then people can choose the hat they feel represents the type of role they are playing.

Facilitation Tips and Suggestions

- This exercise works best with individuals and couples. It requires more of a coaching approach and to go toward the individual's or couple's interest and energy. When used in this way, it can be an extremely insightful and powerful session for individuals.
- Allow people to have roles that fall into multiple categories. For example, with the role of a friend, it can be torn (some friendships lost), reworn (friendships continued virtu-

ally), and born (new friendships made) simultaneously. The richness of this exercise will become apparent in the discussion about these differences.

- For groups it is important to keep the group size to less than 10 people so you can give individuals personalized attention and make sure you continually bring everyone's voice and experience into the room. Take advantage of the power of the group: Have individuals coach each other and discuss different aspects with each other as often as possible.
- Note that this process follows the Four Key Components of Transition Planning (see pp. 183–192). It can be used in a larger transition process framework to cover the Why component in more detail.

About This Exercise

In my own experience making transitions between six countries and my work with transitioning individuals and couples, I have found it important to identify role changes that occur with a transition, reflect on the impact of these changes, and plan accordingly to help manage transition stress. This exercise was developed with this need in mind.

REFERENCES

Hofstede, G. (2001). *Culture's consequences: Comparing values, behaviors, institutions and organizations across nations.* Thousand Oaks, CA: Sage.

Ward, C., Okura, Y., Kennedy, A., & Kojima, T. (1998). The U-curve on trial: A longitudinal study of psychological and sociocultural adjustment during cross-cultural transition. *International Journal of Intercultural Relations, 22*(3), 277–291.

SECTION 6

Communicate Successfully

35. FRAMEWORK: THE SCORE COMMUNICATION PRINCIPLES

Kate Berardo

The SCORE Communication Principles are a set of guidelines for communicating effectively and appropriately across cultures (see Figure S6.1). It is designed to be an easy to remember checklist for communicating in global settings and can be used by speakers and listeners to minimize miscommunications.

Key Focus

Communicate successfully

Objectives

As a result of working with this model, participants will

- understand how to improve two-way understanding when communicating across cultures,
- learn five ways to improve the quality of communication as a speaker and a listener, and
- have a clear model to guide their communication forward

Appropriate Audience

Adults, teenagers

Level of Challenge

Low

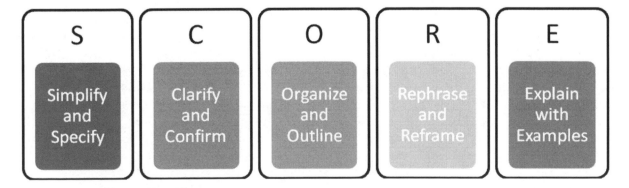

FIGURE S6.1   SCORE Communication Principles

Summary Description

The acronym SCORE stands for

S—Simply and specify
C—Clarify and confirm
O—Organize and outline
R—Rephrase and reframe
E—Explain with examples

This acronym can help individuals remember some of the key principles of communicating effectively across cultures, can be used by a speaker and listener in a conversation, and ideally should be employed by both. The model is explained further in Handout S6.1.

Key Talking Points

Each SCORE principle can be introduced by telling participants

- what the concept is,
- why it is important in global communication settings, and
- tips and strategies to employ the principle.

In addition to describing each of the SCORE principles, tell participants the following:

- The point is not necessarily to employ all these principles at all times but to think about which have the highest likelihood of increasing the chances of clear communication at a given moment. For example, imagine you are trying to explain a complex process to a colleague located across the globe, and you realize that he or she is struggling to understand all the components of the process. At this juncture, rather than give examples and further explain the process, your best strategy is likely to organize and outline it by numbering the main steps: "Essentially, there are four steps in this quality control process." Once the overall structure has been clarified, it may then be helpful to bring in examples and explain each step in the process. These principles can be used by speakers and listeners alike, with slight modifications. For example, a speaker can clarify by saying, "What I am trying to say is . . ." A listener can achieve the

same thing by asking, "I think I understand. Are you saying that . . .?" A speaker can organize his or her thoughts by saying, "There are two main challenges here." If the speaker doesn't do this, the listener can also organize and outline what is being heard with a similar statement, "So it sounds like there are two main challenges here." When both communicators apply these principles and work to develop a common understanding, the chances for miscommunication are reduced.

- What each principle looks like in different cultures and contexts will vary. Rephrasing in a low-context culture, for example, will often simply involve stating the same message again with slightly different wording. In a higher context culture, the use of analogies and even nonverbal body language may be most effective and appropriate to rephrase the communication so it is understood.

- Moreover, we need to adapt how we achieve these principles to the situations, contexts, and cultures we are in. For example, if an indirect speaker is subtly giving feedback about the quality of a meeting, it could cause loss of face to clarify and confirm what the person is saying by asking, "Are you saying you don't think this was a good meeting?" To be more effective, the best approach may be to approach the person after the meeting to try to gently confirm the feedback. In this way, you are still clarifying understanding, but in a culturally appropriate way.

Facilitation Tips and Suggestions

- It is best to introduce the model in an interactive format, for example, presenting the concept, asking the group why it is important in global communication, and asking participants how they could demonstrate this principle in their own communication.

- It can be highly effective to bring these principles to life with stories and examples. Usually the most poignant and humorous examples are those in which this principle has not been employed. For example, an e-mail with a lot of jargon, idioms, and acronyms can quickly establish the importance of being simple and specific when communicating.

- As an alternative way to introduce the model, consider demonstrating two short versions of a conversation. In the first, have the speaker and the listener model ineffective communication (e.g., complex language, little organization, no confirming). Discuss with the participants why this is not effective. In the second demonstration have the speaker and listener model the principles of SCORE effectively. Have the group discuss what both the speaker and the listener did that enabled more effective communication. Then introduce the model and point out moments in the conversation where one or both of the communicators employed this as a strategy.

- Start with exploring what the SCORE principles are, focusing on how a speaker or writer would use them. Ask how you could apply these principles whether you are the speaker or the listener. Have the group come up with types of questions the speaker or the listener can ask or statements that can be made by the speaker or the listener to ensure that each of the SCORE principles are met.

- Move quickly to apply this model—participants usually grasp what is meant by each principle quite quickly. The value comes in understanding how to apply these principles and actually doing so. After briefly introducing each principle, divide participants into small groups, assign them one of the SCORE principles, and have them generate a list of best practices, statements, or questions that can be used to help apply each strategy. Then give them a chance in the training session to practice applying the things on their list.

Suggested Uses

- Let them keep the handout as a reminder on how to communicate effectively and appropriately across cultures.
- Apply the model as a framework to identify communication skills to practice in role playing. After introducing the model, have individuals role-play phone calls or meetings with counterparts in different locations. Have observers "SCORE" their colleagues and give feedback on how they were able to practice these communication skills (see Handout S6.2).
- Use the SCORE principles as an assessment or checklist to evaluate e-mails. Provide an example of a poorly written e-mail. Have individuals rewrite the e-mail using these principles as a guideline.
- Employ the principles as a set of ground rules a team can decide to adopt to improve its communication. It can be helpful to post the SCORE principles so team members can see them to facilitate a discussion about what this means for the group (e.g., specifying in e-mails all the time zones for meetings), and to encourage team members to coach each other to increase the frequency of these principles in their communication.

About This framework

I developed this framework while exploring and working with clients on communication issues. I was seeking an easy to remember, handy set of communication principles that could be equally applied to speakers and listeners. I started playing with different mnemonics until I decided on SCORE. I have found program participants appreciate the ease of use and clear application of this model.

 HANDOUT S6.1

THE SCORE COMMUNICATION PRINCIPLES

The SCORE Principle	The Rationale	Suggestions
S — Simplify and Specify	Much miscommunication happens across cultures because the language is hard to understand or details are not specific.	Make your communication as easy to understand as possible: • Aim for short sentences that are 12 words or less. • Simplify complicated language. "If it wouldn't be too much trouble, would you mind?" becomes "Could you please . . . ?" • Make time zones, locations, and deadlines clear in e-mails. • Limit use of acronyms and idioms, and when used, specify what they mean. "By 'ballpark figures,' I mean a general estimate of pricing."
C — Clarify and Confirm	It is not uncommon for two people to think they understand each other when each has a different understanding of the situation. It is therefore important to continually clarify what you are intending to communicate and confirm that this is in fact what the other person understands.	Ensure the message you are delivering is clear and understood: • Clarify often what you are trying to say: "What I mean is . . ." / "To clarify . . ." • Check regularly that you understand the other person: "So what you are saying is . . ."/ "Could you clarify that last point?" • Check to ensure the other person has understood you: "What is your understanding so far?"
O — Organize and Outline	When our communication is structured and organized into different sections and key points, it becomes easier for others to understand the main points we are making and to follow our communication.	Structure your communication: • Number or letter key ideas to divide them into the main points. • When face to face, use your hands and gestures to help structure key points you are making. • State the purpose of your e-mail in the subject line. • Use headings to organize different topics within an e-mail.
R — Rephrase and Reframe	Providing multiple ways of saying the same thing increases the chances of our being understood.	Provide alternative ways of saying the same thing: • If saying something one way doesn't work, try a different way. • Use analogies, metaphors, and stories when helpful in making a point: "It's a lot like a software update . . ."
E — Explain with Examples	Providing the rationale behind our thinking can make our intentions clearer to others. By using examples to illustrate our points (and sometimes literally illustrating our point through drawings and visuals), our message becomes clearer.	Reinforce key concepts with explanations and examples: • When you present an idea or make a request, provide the why behind it: "Here's why getting this step right in the process is critical . . ." • As much as possible, provide examples that bring these to life. • Provide visual examples by drawing ideas on paper or showing images.

Reproduced from: Kate Berardo, "Framework: The SCORE Communication Principles," in *Building Cultural Competence: Innovative Activities and Models,* eds. K. Berardo and D. K. Deardorff (Sterling, VA: Stylus, 2012), 225–230.

 HANDOUT S6.2

SCORE COMMUNICATION

Use the items listed below to review your own or others' communication. First, note whether the following strategies have been employed by marking Yes, Somewhat, No, or Not Applicable (not all may apply, depending on the nature of the communication). Give an overall rating to the use of this principle on a scale of 1–5 (1 = *principle not employed*, 5 = *principle very effectively employed*), and record observations and suggestions in the box provided.

Simplify and Specify

Uses short sentences that are 12 words or less.	❏ Yes	❏ Somewhat	❏ No	❏ Not Applicable
Uses simple language. For example, "If it wouldn't be too much trouble, would you mind?" becomes "Could you please . . .?"	❏ Yes	❏ Somewhat	❏ No	❏ Not Applicable
Time zones, locations, and deadlines are clear.	❏ Yes	❏ Somewhat	❏ No	❏ Not Applicable
Use of acronyms and idioms are limited, and when used are explained.	❏ Yes	❏ Somewhat	❏ No	❏ Not Applicable

Overall rating: 1   2   3   4   5

Additional notes and observations on what was done well and/or suggestions for improvement:

```




```

Clarify and Confirm

Clarifies often what is being said: "What I mean is . . ."/"To clarify, . . ."	❏ Yes	❏ Somewhat	❏ No	❏ Not Applicable
Regularly checks understanding of the other person: "So what you are saying is . . ."/"Could you clarify that last point?"	❏ Yes	❏ Somewhat	❏ No	❏ Not Applicable
Checks to ensure the other person has understood: "What is your understanding so far?"	❏ Yes	❏ Somewhat	❏ No	❏ Not Applicable

Overall rating: 1   2   3   4   5

Additional notes and observations on what was done well and/or suggestions for improvement:

```




```

Reproduced from: Kate Berardo, "Framework: The SCORE Communication Principles," in *Building Cultural Competence: Innovative Activities and Models,* eds. K. Berardo and D. K. Deardorff (Sterling, VA: Stylus, 2012), 225–230.

Organize and Outline

Numbers or letters key ideas to divide them into the main points	❏ Yes	❏ Somewhat	❏ No	❏ Not Applicable
Has a clear beginning, middle, and end	❏ Yes	❏ Somewhat	❏ No	❏ Not Applicable
E-mail: States the purpose in the Subject line	❏ Yes	❏ Somewhat	❏ No	❏ Not Applicable
E-mail: Uses headings to organize different topics	❏ Yes	❏ Somewhat	❏ No	❏ Not Applicable

Overall rating: 1   2   3   4   5

Additional notes and observations on what was done well and/or suggestions for improvement:

Rephrase and Reframe

If saying something one way doesn't work, tries another way to make sure he or she is understood	❏ Yes	❏ Somewhat	❏ No	❏ Not Applicable
Uses analogies, metaphors, and stories when helpful in making a point	❏ Yes	❏ Somewhat	❏ No	❏ Not Applicable

Overall rating: 1   2   3   4   5

Additional notes and observations on what was done well and/or suggestions for improvement:

Explain with Examples

When presenting an idea or making a request, explains why it is important	❏ Yes	❏ Somewhat	❏ No	❏ Not Applicable
Provides examples of ideas and concepts	❏ Yes	❏ Somewhat	❏ No	❏ Not Applicable
Uses visuals such as drawing ideas on paper or showing images	❏ Yes	❏ Somewhat	❏ No	❏ Not Applicable

Overall rating: 1   2   3   4   5

Additional notes and observations on what was done well and/or suggestions for improvement:

36. MODEL: THE MÖBIUS MODEL

Emma Bourassa

This model demonstrates the evolution of understanding of cross-cultural communication. It uses a progression of images to relate to various experiences of intercultural communication and Bennett's (1993) developmental model of intercultural sensitivity to explore the complexity of intercultural communication as an ongoing process of learning and experimentation (see Figure S6.2, Figure S6.3, and Figure S6.4).

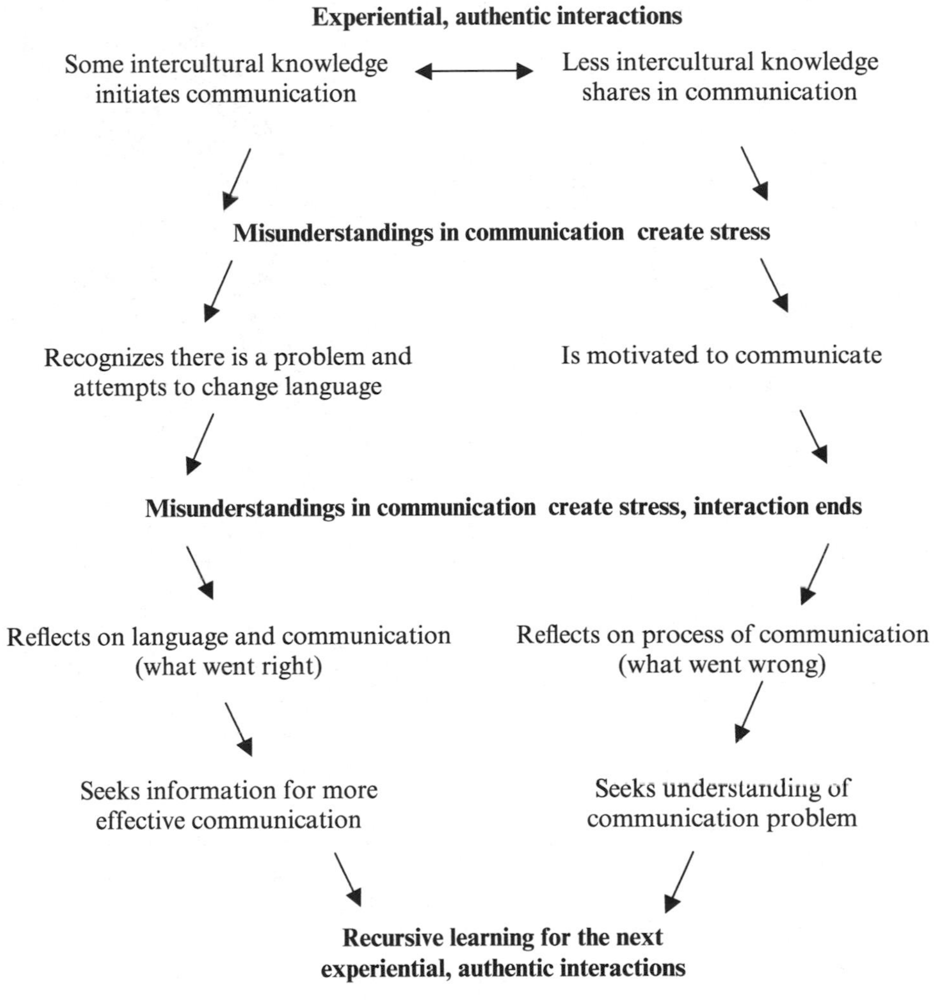

Experiential, authentic interactions

Some intercultural knowledge ⟷ Less intercultural knowledge
initiates communication shares in communication

Misunderstandings in communication create stress

Recognizes there is a problem and   Is motivated to communicate
attempts to change language

Misunderstandings in communication create stress, interaction ends

Reflects on language and communication   Reflects on process of communication
(what went right)   (what went wrong)

Seeks information for more   Seeks understanding of
effective communication   communication problem

**Recursive learning for the next
experiential, authentic interactions**

This would be reiterated as a pattern of out and in and out and in as the interlocutors go away from the communication and begin the next interaction somewhat like an hourglass.

FIGURE S6.2 Hourglass Interactions

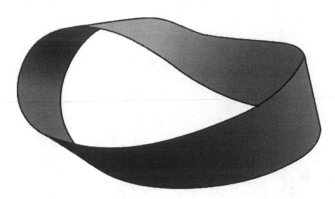

FIGURE S6.3   Möbius 1

Key Focus

Communicate successfully

Objectives

As a result of working with this model, participants will be able to

- identify the constraints of using limited knowledge of a culture in communication,
- explore how culture is dynamic, and
- explore how Bennett's (1993) model can be one way of relating to this model.

Appropriate Audience

Adults

Level of Challenge

Medium

Suggested Uses

This model can be used to

- explore the complexity of intercultural communication and interaction;
- explore one's responsibility to engage in intercultural communication in an open way; and
- acknowledge that models are a starting point of discussion, but more exploration is welcome.
- Provide participants with Handout S6.3. Show participants the hourglass model (see Figure S6.2). Explain that cultural encounters at their simplest could been seen as two people coming together for the first time, going

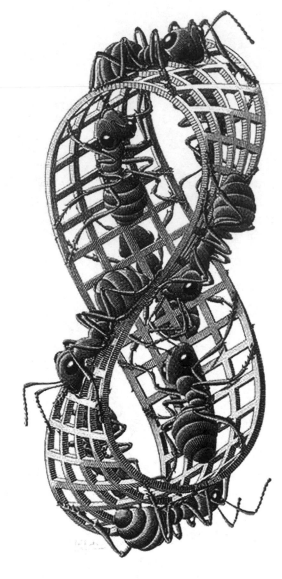

FIGURE S6.4   Möbius 2

Note: M. C. Escher's "Moebius Strip II" © 2011 The M. C. Escher Company-Holland. All rights reserved. www.mcescher.com.

away, and then meeting under new circumstances. This could be, for example, during a job interview and later in a job-related exchange such as an employee seeking clarification about a deadline. Ask what challenges a job interview might involve: language, power distance, high/low context, and so on. Tell participants to assume the first meeting in the job interview went well. In the next exchange, the employer and employee meet to talk about a timeline for a job. Again, language is not a problem, but both leave wondering if they've understood what specific date the job needs to be completed on. Although the language may be understood, underlying cultural differences may not be recognized. Use a Craig Storti (1994) dialogue such as "Dr. Spetsos" or a personal example to bring this concept to life.

- Show the first Möbius Strip (Figure S6.3), and ask how it differs from the hourglass model (e.g., the Möbius is a continuous connection between the two communicators and not as two-dimensional and separate as the hourglass). Tell participants that with this added connection between the communicators, it could be assumed that at times they would spend more time trying to figure out what is happening. This may occur from self-reflection, research, or opening a dialogue with another. As the intercultural challenges are resolved, each may build a category or stereotype of how to work with people from that culture. By practicing under the same circumstances, the communicators may have some success, but it may be limited, leaving them to wonder why. Tell participants to recognize that assumptions of what the other is doing or thinking based on norms is part of the communication challenge because it does not address other important aspects, such as being in the Minimization phase of Bennett's (1993) model. While there may be some successes, it is likely the communicators are behaving from a limited cultural lens. Have participants look at the model and raise questions about its applicability as a model for intercultural communication.

- Introduce the second Möbius model (Figure S6.4) as being fleshed out from the first two models. Ask what participants can interpret from this three-dimensional flexible model. Tell participants this model represents a different, richer experience of intercultural interactions. Draw attention to the ants and their representation of movement. Link this to the dynamism of culture, which also affects intercultural communication. There are points of contact but also spaces, somewhat like a web, which could be interpreted as increasingly making connections between oneself and the other. The spaces could be seen as openness and more likely curiosity and interest to make connections. The model illustrates the experience of learning how to

cognitively and behaviorally shift (e.g., acceptance and adaptation in Bennett's developmental model of intercultural sensitivity, 1993).

- After viewing the three models, ask participants to summarize the challenges in creating a model for intercultural communication or interactions. For example,

  - a phenomenon such as communication patterns is not easily dissected;
  - culture is in flux, and therefore what is known today might best be used as a base but not as the truth; and
  - we are simultaneously in a role (spouse, teacher, employee, etc.) or represent something (power, mistrust, etc.) to the other that may shift depending on the context (job interview, hospital, bus stop, etc.). (Proulx, 2006)

Facilitation Tips and Suggestions

1. Participants may see the models as very linear and restricted to cultural norms. This is true, as my own style of organizing ideas is based on cultural models. Explore and acknowledge what other possibilities exist and acknowledge them.

2. Participants may not agree with the notion that one interlocutor, especially one with more cultural learning, would react as demonstrated in the hourglass model. Note that this is just one possibility, and other elements may be present for either or both of the interlocutors. Both might go away to read or to talk to people about the situation, or one might be direct enough to identify a problem and attempt to work it out immediately.

3. The model does not focus on a particular theory such as high context, power distance, and such. It is a tool to explore the process of becoming more interculturally aware.

4. This model works well with those who can use and relate well to the use of metaphors and abstract ideas.

5. It may be useful to have participants find their own metaphors or models to explore the nature of intercultural communication.

About This Model

This model or metaphor for culture has come through a number of iterations because I agree with Dahl (2000), who states that

> basically static models of culture, as largely favored in intercultural research, are inadequate to explain and predict current culture situations. There is hence a need to develop a more interactive model of cultural transformation that is capable to explain the shifts in the cultures that we are experiencing in the world today. (p. 47)

The model I present here has evolved from my master's in education work that articulates my understanding of curriculum from a phenomenological perspective of learning. It begins with an examination of interactions and builds on the complexities of those interactions. There is an assumption that at least one of the communicators in the models accepts that cultural difference exists and is curious.

NOTE

Proulx's communication idea was first presented to me in an intercultural communication workshop at the University of British Columbia. Jacques Proulx is in the Department of Psychology at Sherbooke University, Quebec. For more on Proulx, see www.usherbrooke.ca/psychologie/nous-joindre/personnel-enseignant/proulx-jacques/

REFERENCES

Bennett, M. J. (1993). Towards a developmental model of intercultural sensitivity. In R. Michael Paige (Ed.), *Education for the Intercultural Experience* (pp. 21–72). Yarmouth ME: Intercultural Press.

Bourassa, E. (2006). *A curriculum for intercultural travellers* (Unpublished masters thesis). University of Victoria, Canada.

Dahl, S. (2000). *Communications and culture transformation: Cultural diversity, globalization and cultural convergence.* London, UK: ECE Publishing.

Molinsky, A. (2007). Cross-cultural code-switching: The psychological challenges of adapting behavior in foreign cultural interactions. *Academy of Management Review, 32*(2), 622–640.

Storti, C. (1994). *Cross-cultural dialogues: 74 brief encounters with cultural difference.* Boston, MA: Intercultural Press.

HANDOUT S6.3

MODELS FOR INTERCULTURAL COMMUNICATION

One common model of culture is an iceberg, which draws attention to the visible aspects of surface culture such as food, clothing, and language as well as the unseen, deeper cultural aspects such as values. Another model uses the metaphor of the onion—that core values are the foundation of the other layers of life experience such as ritual, relationships, and so on. These two models have been used to provide a visual representation of the challenging questions about what is culture and to segue into the challenges of intercultural communication/interactions. They provide a foundation to understand that assumptions of cultural interactions must include what is seen and not, and that the unseen aspects can be challenges when people of different backgrounds interact. The following exploration of a new model focuses on the evolution of the intercultural learner's knowledge and skills during an intercultural communication interaction (Bourassa, 2006). The hourglass model attempts to illustrate a simplistic representation of intercultural interaction. The first Möbius model builds on the hourglass model but still lacks important dimensions of the intercultural interaction. The final Möbius model provides a more robust explanation of the dynamism of culture and intercultural communication.

Consider the model in Figure S6.2. Assume there are two communicators. They begin with a purpose to communicate. In this representation we can assume that one speaker has more intercultural knowledge than the other:

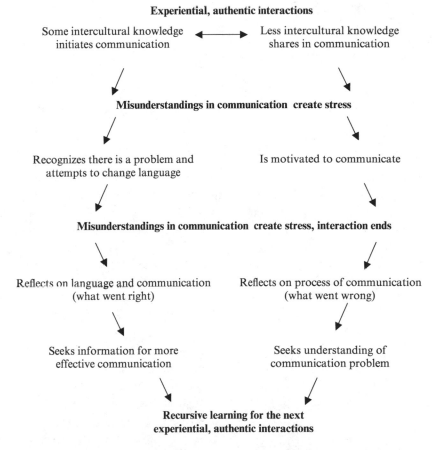

FIGURE S6.2   Hourglass Interactions

The diagram in Figure S6.2 may be viewed as a repetitive circle, or spiral, where the interaction pattern repeats. Note that the areas of convergence are minimal and limited. The communicator is in contact, makes attempts to communicate clearly, but within the communication itself, may not be able to manage and must go away to prepare for the next encounter. The model is a coming together and going apart, which is two dimensional. This is likely how many interactions proceed: an exchange of words but perhaps not an adequate understanding. In intercultural understanding, there are more dimensions that encompass more fullness than this model allows.

Rather than a two-dimensional model, the interactions can be better captured in a Möbius strip model (see Figure S6.3). Each side of the strip represents the communicators' experience of intercultural communication. On the edge of the strip is the outside border, which can represent cultural interactions, while on either side of the strip, the communicators' experiences are occurring. If you follow one side of the strip you will always wind up on the other and come back to the side where you started. In other words, the communicators are interconnected, and there is a fuller sense of the possibility for understanding compared to the first model because there are more contact points and iterations that allow for different experiences. The reality is that the path is unpredictable, and will likely never be the same, much like authentic communication between varying cultures. Although there is more chance for the communicators to build communication competency, the possibility that the change in cultural understanding won't change much remains because the model is still constrained. This calls for a more dynamic model.

To build on the Möbius model, we could consider the following:

Side A of the Möbius strip represents the concepts in intercultural learning that one could experiment with:

Etic, emic, space, silence, direct, indirect, negotiate meaning, high/low context, cultural understanding, risk, motivation, authenticity, confidence, respect, participation, lived experience, reflect, expand, roles.

Side B represents the story of how the concepts evolve through the interactions that shape the intercultural communicators' lived experience:

Before I began to learn about cultural difference, I didn't give much thought to the power of its existence in interactions. After gaining cognitive knowledge, I expanded my learning to include the authentic voices of those I was trying to interact effectively with and to shift cognitively and behaviorally. It was important to not assume I knew that the words were the complete communication. Now I know every interaction is a knowledge opportunity and holds some mystery.

In the following Möbius strip (Figure S6.3) the outside becomes the inside and the inside becomes the outside in endless connection. This illustrates the flow of the communication between the concepts and the story or lived experience of the participants. Each person could also represent one side of the Möbius strip. This is a more accurate representation because in culture, there is constant connection and interaction. However, it is not as flexible as it should be. Additional details, which are better shown in M. C. Escher's Möbius Strip II (1963; see Figure S6.4) where the communication (strip) is woven, producing solid and open areas, indicates potential for flexibility (or movement) of the solid area. The solid area would represent that knowledge and ability gained from recognizing difference and being curious about the other's communication needs. While an individual is solidifying the intercultural knowledge and skill set,

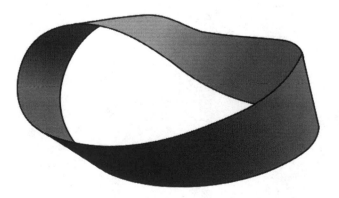

FIGURE S6.3   Möbius 1

building a foundation that is represented by the solid parts, there is recognition that the space holds a place that remains open to the idea that there is not one definitive answer. To relate this to Bennett's (1993) developmental model of intercultural sensitivity, this model could represent intercultural communicators who are building the cognitive and behavioral aspects of intercultural understanding. Whereas a person in the Ethnocentric stage of Denial in Bennett's model may not notice or be interested in difference, and one in Minimization might notice a difference but rely on the assumption that we are all the same in the end and let things go (as with the second Möbius model), this model demonstrates a more ethnorelative response to intercultural communication. A person who is in Acceptance and Adaptation would communicate, using the skills previously learned (the solid parts); the individual also works with the unknown (space) engaging in intercultural communication and attempting to adjust behavior (Bennett). This model better represents how the ongoing work to understanding cultural communication can be a challenge and the importance of experimenting with new knowledge for language and code shifting (Molinsky, 2007).

This is different from the solid Möbius and is still limiting as a model for intercultural communication. What is missing from the first Möbius strip is the energy of culture. A crude attempt is to say that any model must include some kind of reference to movement or energy that could be realized by including symbolism such as an ant. Because the energy is unpredictable (individuals are in charge of their experience), the concept of culture and cultural learning is not stagnant. The ants/energy/learner can move in and out of the porous areas (unknown), weaving between concepts and the stories of cultural understanding, or they can

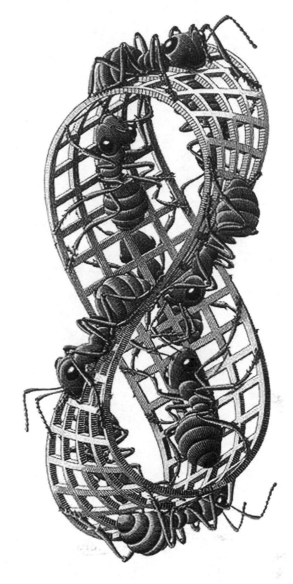

FIGURE S6.4 Möbius 2

Note: M. C. Escher's "Moebius Strip II" © 2011 The M. C. Escher Company-Holland. All rights reserved. www .mcescher.com.

remain where they are (stuck in the solid, known) or indeed jump off (with each new cultural communication context, there is an opportunity to build another Möbius, extending the cultural understanding). Perhaps the jumping off could be seen as engaging in communication at the Adaptation level of Bennett's model where one knows there is a miscommunication and uses cultural clues to shift behavior to meet the need of the other communicator. Perhaps jumping into the larger space leads to creation of new solid learning—a reiteration that then becomes an attempt to grow cognitively, emotionally, and socially. In other words, stretching and growing the Möbius of richer experiences with the other.

In short, the model represents those things we know about and are comfortable with (solid), the openness to exploring other perspectives (the spaces), and the realization that culture is not static (there is much more space outside of the Möbius). While one might investigate what we currently understand about culture and cultural interactions, what the future of both is, is not necessarily within reach at this time. A recognition that we are not done and that any model is useful in a limited way is critical.

37. THREE CHAIRS

Darla K. Deardorff

This activity, done in triads, illustrates how communication styles affect our communication with others, especially those from different cultural backgrounds.

Key Focus

Communicate successfully

Type of Activity

Exercise

Objectives

As a result of this activity, participants will

- practice different communication styles and
- experience different communication styles.

Appropriate Audience

Adults, teenagers

Level of Challenge

Medium

Group Size

3 to 99 people

Time

20 to 25 minutes

Materials

None

Activity Setup

1. Have participants form groups of three and set up three chairs, with one chair facing the front of the room and the two other chairs on each side, facing the middle chair.
2. Tell the group the chair on the left is the position of the expert, the middle chair is the listener's place, and the right chair is the real story.
3. Assign a relevant topic, such as "Life in the United States" (or another country relevant to the makeup of the group).
4. Tell the group that the expert and the real story person will talk to the listener simultaneously, while the listener tries to listen and respond to both as best as possible. The two talkers are intentionally competing (realistically) for the listener's attention, and the goal is to see which talker holds the listener's attention more. The expert talks as if he or she were a specialist and may cite statistics and give factual information. The real story person talks like someone you would meet on the street. This participant can tell a true story from his or her life or even make up a story related to the topic, but the story should be personal.
5. Make sure the instructions are clear, and start the activity.

Managing the Activity

1. After two minutes, call time and then have the participants change chairs and repeat the procedure with each person in a different role.
2. After two more minutes, have the participants change chairs one more time and repeat the activity.

Debriefing the Activity

This activity helps people understand the importance of resolving cultural differences together. As you debrief the group, discuss the following:

1. How did you feel in this activity? Which role did you find most comfortable? Most uncomfortable?
2. Which roles did you find yourself listening and responding to more attentively—the person in the real story chair or the expert chair? Why?
3. How can different styles be used to increase effectiveness with people from different cultural backgrounds?
4. How does one's own communication style affect the way one receives information? Gives information?
5. What are some lessons learned, or what can you take away with you from this activity?

Key Insights and Learnings

- This activity illustrates different communication styles. For example, two people talking at once could be an example from a polychronic culture. Factual versus personal information is indicative of another style of communicating in different cultures.
- The styles of communication can affect us as much or more than the words.
- Communication styles are not right or wrong, just different, and it's very important to be aware of those different styles and how those styles ultimately have an impact on the content being conveyed.
- Communication styles are culturally conditioned, and we often tend to resonate more with styles that are similar to the ways we have been culturally conditioned.

Variations

Variation 1. After the people in the two chairs talk simultaneously, you could then have a second round where the two people in the expert and real story roles take turns speaking. This encourages focusing more on the actual style and deeper listening instead of on competing styles. Be aware that since the people in both roles are not talking at once but rather taking turns, this variation will take more time.

Variation 2. Assign nonverbal styles to the different roles. For example, the real story person could talk excitedly and loudly using hand gestures. The expert could talk more quietly with minimal gestures, with or without eye contact. Discuss the impact these different styles also have on commanding attention based on one's cultural conditioning.

Variation 3. With groups over 75 or 100, you may want to demonstrate this activity by asking six to nine volunteers to do the activity in the front of the room with the rest observing as in a fishbowl activity. Be aware that some volunteers may find this to be a little uncomfortable with so many observers.

Facilitation Tips and Suggestions

- It's important to have a spacious room with movable chairs so that the chairs can be moved into groups of three and ideally with space between the groups so they're not immediately next to each other.
- If chairs are not available, participants can do this activity standing up, but the chairs help to keep the roles clearly distinguished. Participants should move among the chairs and not physically move the chairs themselves.
- If there are one or two people left after triads are formed, they can be observers.
- Be sensitive to those who are not using their first language in this activity. It may be more challenging for them because they must focus not only on which style to use but also on the language being used, whereas first language speakers would focus more on the style. In this case, consider using Variation 1, as it allows for more time to think and be heard. If language seems to be a definite barrier, you could also have participants write out what they'll say first before they do the activity.
- It's important for the assigned topic to be relevant and one that all participants know about and can relate to. Some examples are how to make your favorite dish, directions to your home, your position on global warming, and so on.
- This can get a bit noisy, so be aware of others who may be affected by the noise.
- Be sure to tell participants not to exaggerate the roles, even if they are competing for the listener's attention.

- This activity works well after a discussion on different communication styles, as it provides a concrete way for participants to experience those styles.
- This activity really works better in groups under 50, although it has been used quite successfully with larger groups using Variation 3.

About This Exercise

I developed this activity by combining a number of different ones. I was seeking a way for participants to be able to experience some of the communication styles so we could move from simply knowing about them to actually experiencing different styles of communication, especially for those who learn best by doing.

38. VISUAL COMMUNICATION PATTERNS

Emma Bourassa

In this activity participants investigate different communication styles by analyzing and trying on a communication pattern, which may challenge assumptions that speaking the same language is the most important aspect of intercultural communication. This game leads to negotiating meaning in communication styles and can lead to a deeper conversation on the values that determine specific cultural patterns of communication.

Key Focus

Communicate successfully

Type of Activity

Exercise

Objectives

As a result of this activity, participants will

- recognize there are differences in cultural communication styles (e.g., direct and indirect),
- understand that by examining communication styles of themselves and others they may be able to recognize communication barriers,
- realize that shifting communication styles is a challenge, and
- understand that intercultural communication involves more than speaking the same language.

Appropriate Audience

Adults, teenagers

Level of Challenge

Low

Group Size

10 to 40

Time

15 to 30 minutes

Materials

- Handout
- Blackboard, whiteboard, or flip chart that is large enough for everyone to see

Preparation

Handout S6.4 has five communication patterns on it. Each group will receive one of these five communication patterns. Make one copy of the handout if you have five groups and two copies if you have between 5 and 10 groups. More than one group can have the same communication pattern. Cut out each of the five communication patterns.

Activity Setup

1. Have participants form groups of two to four.
2. Ideally, have these groups sitting at separate tables. They do not need any writing materials.
3. Write on your whiteboard or other surface: Visual Communication Pattern. Tell participants that each group will receive an image that represents a communication style. Instruct participants to look at the image with their group and describe what the communication pattern or style is. At this point, you can either tell the group that they will eventually be asked to communicate effectively using this communication style, or you can let the groups discover this themselves in a few minutes.

4. Distribute one communication pattern image per group. Draw attention to the black dot in each image: This represents the topic or main point of what is being communicated. Make sure they understand that they are trying to identify the style of communication that revolves around the main point. Allow 5 to 10 minutes for groups to analyze and describe the pattern of communication. For example, the circle with a dot in the center may be described as when the speaker never identifies the point explicitly, and it looks like talking in a circle or around the point (depending on the intercultural knowledge of the group, they may identify this as an indirect or high-context communication style, but they can use any manner to explain how the speaker is dealing with the point, e.g., talking around it, etc.).

5. Circulate and ask questions to help prompt each group's thinking, as needed. For example, if the group is looking at the spiral the facilitator might ask, "If the point is at the bottom, what kind of information might the speaker begin with and continue with until reaching the end point of this communication style?"

6. Stop the groups and give them a topic to apply the image's pattern to. The topic should be relevant (e.g., marketing for a business group), not necessarily have a definitive answer (e.g., how to launch a new product), and one they are sufficiently knowledgeable about to start the analysis. Tell the groups they will need to use the communication style represented by their image to tell the rest of the group about the topic—and emphasize that their goal is to use this style effectively.

7. While groups are working, circulate and offer guidance. Participants may benefit from questions such as: "Given your image, how might you start the discussion and how might you get to the point about pollution?"

Managing the Activity

After 5 to 10 minutes of planning their communication, stop the participants. Ask one group to show their communication pattern image to the rest of the participants. Draw a larger version on the board and ask the group to talk about the point or topic using the visual to guide their communication style, while others listen and watch. Ask the group to explain what its visual communication style required (e.g., start on the topic, then go off on a tangent, then come back to the topic, etc.).

Continue this process until all groups have shown their images and talked about the selected topic using their assigned communication pattern. Note that when two groups have the same communication pattern, they may have different interpretations of the pattern and use it differently. This is okay and will create a good discussion in the debrief.

Debriefing the Activity

After all groups have spoken, ask the following debriefing questions:

- What was it like participating in this activity?
- What was easy or difficult? Why?
- How difficult was it to figure out the communication pattern? (Allow for examples.)
- How difficult was it to figure out how to apply the pattern to the topic? (Allow for discussion.)
- What does this mean for communicating with people whose communication style may not be the same as our own?
- What does this tell us about the assumption that having the same language does or doesn't mean effective communication is a given?
- Do any of these ways of communication say something about how we (Canadians, Americans, etc.) perceive time (or another cultural value)?
- Ask for experiences from participants who speak more than one language: Do they notice a shift in the pattern of communicating when speaking a different language? This may also include more body language, silence, and so forth. How did they learn to shift their communication for the new language group? And, what questions remain about another group's communication style?
- Which style do you relate to or would best describe your communication style? How can you adapt your style specifically to others' styles? Give a concrete example of adaptation. (This adaptation question is a very important one, so be sure to spend adequate time exploring responses.)

- Have participants draw a picture that represents how they think their cultural group tends to communicate. (You may need to give a specific context, such as making a presentation.)
- What cross-cultural lessons can you take and apply from this activity?

Depending on the group, there may be an opportunity to ask participants to apply intercultural theory to the visuals, for example, high/low context, direct/indirect, building a relationship before getting down to business.

Key Insights and Learnings

- Words alone may not be enough to overcome an intercultural communication challenge.
- Understanding that various patterns of communication exist may help one to stop and consider that this is the reason for a miscommunication.
- Shifting communication styles is not a simple task. This could build empathy for those working with different cultures and when the language in use is not the speaker's first language.
- Depending on the participants' background, a deeper look at the underlying values for communication styles could emerge: Cultural values can be reflected in communication styles (e.g., North Americans tend to be linear and direct, which could be linked to individualism and values of time, while collectivists tend to be more high context and indirect, take time to build relationships, don't need specific words because of shared knowledge or history, etc.).

Variations

Variation 1. Reveal the visual communication pattern of each group only after group members have spoken using their style. See if the rest of the group can guess what style they were demonstrating. Then have the group reveal its visual and explain how group members tried to use it.

Variation 2. One person from each style group could form a new group and have the conversation in his or her prescribed communication style. The listeners guess what the communication pattern might

be and respond to the ease or challenge of being in such an interaction as a speaker and as a listener.

Variation 3. At the end of the activity, have participants draw a visual on their name tags (if used) that represents their own style.

Facilitation Tips and Suggestions

- Keep the activity moving.
- Be prepared to acknowledge a communication style is from your perspective. Invite people from different language groups to draw an image representing their interpretation of what communicating in English is like.
- The ambiguity may frustrate some. Remind participants these communication patterns are subject to interpretation, and this is an exercise in trying on another communication style to understand where communication challenges may originate.
- It is likely that participants will rightly identify that communication preferences or patterns are not only cultural but also personality driven.
- Wherever possible, use the participants' comments to recognize the challenges in trying to understand the complexity of intercultural communication. Point out that although we are all speaking the same language, there are other aspects to communication that affect understanding the message.
- As this is an experiential activity, more time may be necessary to allow for empathy building. Experience has shown that the best conversations around communication differences have happened when there has been some challenge in negotiating how to do something. Check participants for too much stress or frustration.
- Note that the use of the phrase *What's the point?* is linguistically and culturally loaded. Participants from other language or cultural groups may need to use a different term.
- Have a visual that represents your perception of your culture's communication style (see Figure S6.5). For example: "This horizontal line illustrates that I start with my point or focus. Attached to the top line is a vertical line that represents all the things I may say connected to this first point (e.g., I may give examples, provide the rationale for my first

point, etc.). The second horizontal line illustrates that I am finished talking about this point and often represents the conclusion I may end with." Note that this visual is based on giving a presentation in English in a Canadian academic context.

Notes regarding the visual representations of communication shown in Handout S6.4a:

1. The first visual is a spiral that starts very broadly and eventually gets to the point. This could represent taking time to get to know someone instead of getting down to business. This model could represent an Asian or aboriginal value of setting the context or building a relationship before discussing the topic of the conversation. It may also indicate a need to establish one's credibility on the topic prior to getting to the point, as with some European groups and Russians. (Note: This visual came from a Russian student of mine, and an Italian student identified with it as well).

2. The second visual is the circle with the dot in the center. This indicates a high context communication style where the point doesn't have to be identified because the information around the point is enough, and the participants share that unspoken information. It could also be viewed as indirect communication. In both cases, the listener has to work to figure out the point as opposed to being given all the words and details. This can be seen with Japanese and some other Asian communication styles.

3. The third visual begins with a focused message, then presents the same information four different ways prior to getting back to the point. This can be perceived as repetition without apparent reason. The final completion does not have to be a summary or even relate to the previous details. This has been self-selected by some of my Chinese students to represent their common style of communication.

4. The fourth visual is a switchback, a curved or flowing line punctuated with different points (A, B, C, etc.) indicating that the message is not linear and can be interrupted. The curvy line that appears to go off topic has been

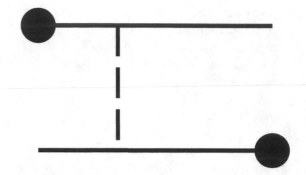

FIGURE S6.5   Example of Communication Style

identified by some Hispanic students who state they spend more time telling the story, which can allow for spontaneously adding other information. This may connect to a polychronic sense of time and message, as opposed to a direct, one idea at a time style.

5. The fifth visual illustrates three separate but related threads of the communication that come together at the end of the message. In this instance, the receiver has to do some work to understand the communication. While not necessarily high context, it is not as direct as a typical linear style of communication (e.g., as is common in Canada and the United States, among other places). One may consider it being similar to poetry, fables, or parables. This communication pattern was one that a Japanese student of mine identified as being most like their communication style.

About This Exercise

This exercise has evolved from my classroom struggles to find a way to help students understand the required style of writing in an academic class. It comes from my research using visuals to analyze English and other languages' communication styles, which was inspired by a student in *Writing Across Borders* (2005), a film by Wayne Robertson at Oregon State University. It also builds on Robert Kaplan's (2001) visuals, although it does not match any visual with any particular culture. The exercise was first used in 2008. Three of the visual representations in this task were produced by my students, and the interpretations are based on their conversations as well as faculty development sessions cofacilitated with Kyra Garson of Thompson Rivers University (TRU). The exercise has been used with intercultural groups of students, faculty, and staff at TRU and other faculty development sessions in other Canadian universities. The aim for students is to help them understand a communication pattern to emulate, which has been met with much success as it does not diminish the students' primary communication pattern; rather it enhances their understanding of behavioral shift for intercultural communication. In terms of faculty development, it has been used as a tool to build empathy. When experientially challenged with shifting our own preferred learned style of communication, faculty have a stronger understanding of what they are expecting other cultural groups to be able to do. The task itself can be frustrating for one who does not shift easily.

REFERENCES

Kaplan, R. B. (2001). Cultural thought patterns in inter-cultural education. In T. J. Silva, P. K. Matsuda (Eds.), *Landmark essays on ESL writing* (pp. 11–25). Mahwah, NJ: Erlbaum.

Oregon State University (Producer), & Robertson, W. (Director). (2005). *Writing across borders.* [Video/DVD]. Corvallis: University of Oregon.

HANDOUT S6.4

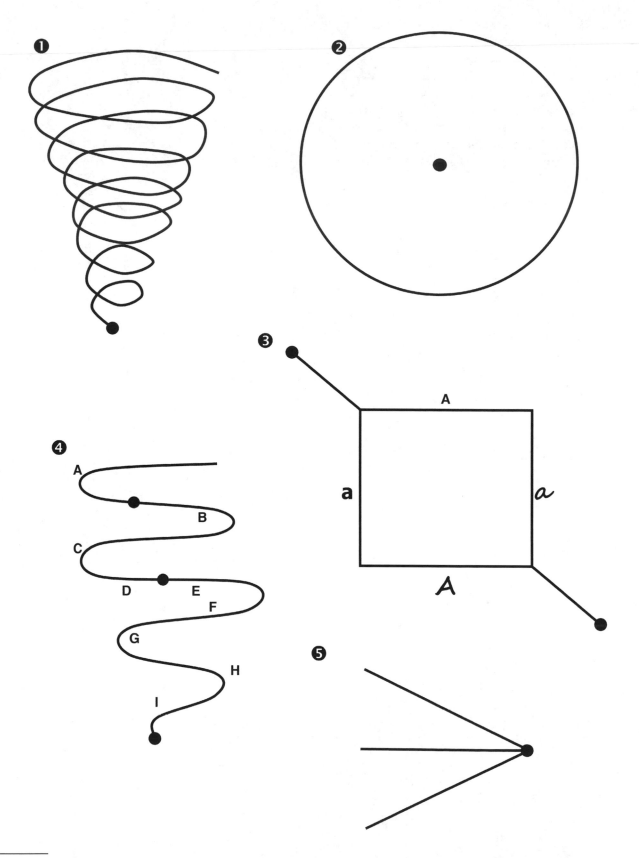

 HANDOUT S6.4a

NOTES REGARDING THE VISUAL REPRESENTATIONS OF COMMUNICATION

1. The first visual is a spiral that starts very broadly and eventually gets to the point. This could represent taking time to get to know someone instead of getting down to business. This model could represent an Asian or Aboriginal value of setting the context or building a relationship before discussing the topic of the conversation. It may also indicate a need to establish one's credibility on the topic prior to getting to the point, as with some European groups and Russians. (Note: This visual came from a Russian student of mine, and a fellow Italian student identified with it as well).

2. The second visual is the circle with the dot in the center. This indicates a high context communication style where the point doesn't have to be identified because the information around the point is enough, and the participants share that unspoken information. It could also be viewed as indirect communication. In both cases, the listener has to work to figure out the point as opposed to being given all the words and details. This can be seen with Japanese and some other Asian communication styles.

3. The third visual begins with a focused message, then presents the same information four different ways prior to getting back to the point. This can be perceived as repetition without apparent reason. The final completion does not have to be a summary or even relate to the previous details. This has been self-selected by some of my Chinese students to represent their common style of communication.

4. The fourth visual is a switchback, a curved or flowing line punctuated with different points (A, B, C, etc.) indicating that the message is not linear and can be interrupted. The curvy line that appears to go off topic has been identified by some Hispanic students who state they spend more time telling the story, which can allow for spontaneously adding other information. This may connect to a polychronic sense of time and message, as opposed to a direct, one idea at a time style.

5. The fifth visual illustrates three separate but related threads of the communication that come together at the end of the message. In this instance, the receiver has to do some work to understand the communication. While not necessarily high context, it is not as direct as a typical linear style of communication (e.g., as is common in Canada and the United States, among other places). One may consider it being similar to poetry, fables, or parables. This communication pattern was one that a Japanese student of mine identified as being most like their communication style.

39. SPEED DATING ACROSS CULTURES

Maria Jicheva

Speed Dating Across Cultures is a communication and influencing exercise in which individuals pair up and practice short role playings and try out different styles to do this effectively. This is a highly energizing and fun exercise that avoids afternoon slow training moments. It helps translate cultural dimensions into easily understandable terms for practical everyday scenarios, thus bringing them to life.

Key Focus

Communicate successfully

Type of Activity

Role playing

Objectives

As a result of this activity participants will

- understand clearly the meaning of the two poles of a cultural dimension (e.g., direct and indirect communication),
- practice communicating using both sides of each dimension,
- develop a good understanding of how to influence others using different cultural styles, and
- build confidence to flex or adapt their style to be successful across cultures.

Appropriate Audience

Adults

Level of Challenge

High

Group Size

8 to 50 people

Time

60 to 90 minutes

Materials

- Handouts
- Noisemaker

Preparation

- Print out the Tent Cards (see Handout S6.5), so you have one set of tent cards for every two people. Take each set, fold the tent cards, and stack one on top of the other to create a tent card stack for each pair. Every stack should be identical, so ensure you stack each set in the same way.
- Print one copy of Influencing Strategies (see Handout S6.6) per participant.
- Create a long line of tables.
- Line up chairs on both sides of the table to form two long rows of chairs.
- Place tent card stacks on the tables, with all the Influencing Strategies cards facing one row of chairs, and the Being Influenced cards (see Handout S6.5) facing the other row of chairs.
- Set up a separate timekeeper table with noisemaker.

Activity Setup

1. After introducing clearly the cultural dimensions, introduce the activity:

   - You are about to embark on an activity called Speed Dating Across Cultures.
   - The goal of this exercise is to practice a variety of ways to influence others.
   - You will have a chance to practice influencing others using cultural styles.

2. Invite participants to take a seat in one of the chairs. Participants should be seated across from someone else, with a set of tent cards between them.

3. Tell them that one side of the tent card describes the task of the person who will try to influence the other person (the influencer). The other side gives clues to the person who is being influenced (the influencee) on how to respond. Designate one row as the influencers, the other as the influencees.

4. Explain the activity as follows: You are on the same team with the person sitting opposite you. You need that person to write a report on X, Y, Z (participate in a green initiative, provide you with a day of their time as an expert on a project you are working on, run a marathon for charity, convince another student to help you on a student project, etc). Provide an influencing situation according to the type of participants (business, academic, etc.) and a realistic situation in which they might need to influence someone.

Managing the Activity

1. Give each participant a copy of the Influencing Strategies (Handout S6.6) and introduce the first dimension, for example, direct communication style.

2. Instruct the participants to read the description of the strategies for influencing someone in this cultural dimension (allow two minutes). Influencers should be thinking about which strategies they might employ, and influencees should be reading the instructions on their tent card and can also look through the influencing strategies to anticipate what their counterpart may try.

3. Signal to the influencers to start influencing the person sitting opposite using the strategies in their handout for the designated dimension (allow two minutes).

4. After two minutes, stop the participants using the noisemaker.

5. Ask participants the following:

   - How many of the influencees agreed to take on the task?
   - Why? What worked?

6. Briefly summarize key insights and then move to the next round.

7. Instruct influencers to stand up and move a chair to the left. The last person in this row will need to walk to the beginning of the row and take the first chair.

8. Instruct participants to place the top tent card at the bottom of the stack, revealing the next focus, which will be the opposite style of the same cultural dimension (e.g., indirect style after practicing a direct style).

9. Repeat this process (practice one style, shift one seat to the left, flip a new card, practice new style) with the next dimension.

10. Halfway through the dimensions, ask the influencers to switch with the influencees. The easiest way to do this is to simply turn around the tent cards, so those who previously had the being influenced instructions are now look at the influencing instructions.

Debriefing the Activity

The group is debriefed on each dimension during the activity. After participants have gone through all the dimensions, ask the following questions:

1. What worked for you when you were in the role of the influencee?
2. What worked for you when you were in the role of the influencer?
3. How did you feel during the activity?
4. What helped (skills, resources, past experience)?
5. How was this exercise helpful? What are you taking away from this activity?

Key Insights and Learnings

- We can all expand our influencing repertoire.
- Switching styles to adjust to the other is not as challenging as one might think: Once someone's preference is understood, a few adjustments in how one communicates and frames things can help connect to the other person and his or her needs.
- Our cultural values affect the way we influence others or are being influenced by others.

Variation

This exercise was created to work with four of the dimensions in the tool ArgonautOnline (www.argonautonline.com), which provides self-awareness and information on 12 cultural dimensions. It provides descriptions of each dimension and tips for adapting one's personal style in each dimension. You can create your dimensions and your own tips that focus on influencing others in other dimensions of cultural difference. Make sure the tips are written in simple and clear language. Also, choose dimensions that easily translate into skills practice: For example, communication style differences are likely easier to practice in influencing situations than attitudes toward conflict.

Facilitation Tips and Suggestions

- This activity is a logical step in the learning progression to ensure learners move from awareness to action. Awareness and knowledge of cultural differences should be covered in detail before engaging in this skill-practice type of exercise.
- It is important to keep the exercise moving and energetic. Hold short influencing rounds followed by quick and to-the-point debriefings.
- While you can use negative questions in the debriefing (What didn't work? What makes it difficult to be indirect?), this focuses the attention of the participants on deficiencies rather than the resources they have, which can erode their confidence. Since one of the objectives is to build confidence, it is usually best to keep the focus on what works.

- The amount of time you will need on this exercise depends on the number of cultural dimensions practiced. Allow seven minutes for each influencing style on the tent card, that is, two minutes to read, two minutes to practice, and three minutes for debriefing.

About This Exercise

The activity was inspired by an influential Myers-Briggs Type Indicator exercise developed by the LORE group (now part of the Korn Ferry group, www.kornferry.com) about adapting to different personal styles (rather than cultural patterns). I adapted the exercise to reflect the dimensions of ArgonautOnline and used it for the first time in 2004, adjusting and fine-tuning it over the years. At Coghill and Beery International, we have used the exercise with numerous groups of participants and teams. The feedback from participants has been invariably positive. They report being relieved to see they can adapt their style easily and be more effective in their influencing.

REFERENCES

Bourassa, E. (2006). *A curriculum for intercultural travellers* (Unpublished masters thesis). University of Victoria, Canada.

Molinsky, A. (2007). Cross-cultural code-switching: The psychological challenges of adapting behavior in foreign cultural interactions. *Academy of Management Review, 32*(2), 622–640.

 HANDOUT S6.5

DIRECT COMMUNICATION

Influencing

Key Variables: Hard information, Clear Statements

DIRECT COMMUNICATION

Being Influenced

You respond well to clear precise statements. You mistrust "fluffy" language.

Use Expressions like: What exactly is your point? Let's not beat about the bush. To be perfectly honest...

Reproduced from: Maria Jicheva "Speed Dating Across Cultures," in *Building Cultural Competence: Innovative Activities and Models,* eds. K. Berardo and D. K. Deardorff (Sterling, VA: Stylus, 2012), 248–260.

Influencing

INDIRECT COMMUNICATION

Key Variables: Body Language, Statement Phrasing and Choice of Words, Hints and Suggestions

---

Being Influenced

INDIRECT COMMUNICATION

You respond well to diplomatic language. Direct statements seem offensive.

Examples: I wouldn't necessarily see the immediate need to go in that direction. I will look into this further.

Your input is appreciated, but perhaps we should discuss it later.

TIME SPAN—PAST ORIENTATION

Influencing

Key Variables: Appreciation for Tradition, Past Results, Past Achievements

---

TIME SPAN—PAST ORIENTATION

Being Influenced

You value tradition. Changing things for the sake of changing things seems unnecessary.

Examples: How is it relevant to my experience? How is it connected to what we already do? Will this make use of my existing skills?

Influencing

TIME SPAN—FUTURE ORIENTATION

Key Variables: Company Vision, Change = improvement

Being Influenced

TIME SPAN—FUTURE ORIENTATION

You are motivated by new solutions, progress and change.

Examples: Does this change fit with our corporate vision? What is the impact of the change? What will be the impact for our work in the future? This is an opportunity to do things differently.

Influencing

HIGH POWER DISTANCE

Key Variables: Respect for Status, Consult Superiors, Direct Orders

Being Influenced

HIGH POWER DISTANCE

You respond to authority and are more willing to listen to someone with power.

Examples: Who said this is the plan? Have you checked with the department head? Maybe I need to check with my boss? Isn't this the responsibility of the Managing Director?

Influencing

LOW POWER DISTANCE

Key Variables: Empowerment, Encourage and Inspire, Taking Initiative

Being Influenced

LOW POWER DISTANCE

You are put off by hierarchy. You feel people contribute their best when they are treated equally.

Examples: What would I be responsible for? What can I contribute to the project?

<u>Influencing</u>

RELATIONSHIP FOCUSED

Key Variables: Familiarity, Relationship-Building, Your Colleague's Identity

---

<u>Being Influenced</u>

RELATIONSHIP FOCUSED

You prefer to get to know people before you get down to business.

Examples: How are you? How is the family? Let's have some coffee and talk about this more.

Influencing

TASK-FOCUSED

Key Variables: Practicality, Goals and Objectives

TASK-FOCUSED

You work best if you focus on the project at hand without distractions.

Being Influenced

Examples: What is the deadline? How will this affect our work? What outcomes do you expect?

 HANDOUT S6.6

INFLUENCING STRATEGIES

Below are strategies for adjusting how you act in the workplace to work more effectively with people from other backgrounds. Use these strategies along with your knowledge of these cultural dimensions to help you understand how you can work more effectively with others.

Communication	
If you deal with people who are **more indirect** in their communication than you	If you are dealing with people who are **more direct** in their communication than you
• pay extra attention to the way you phrase your requests or statements—directness may be interpreted as being abrupt or even rude • try to watch and decipher the meaning of the nonverbal communication (body language, pauses, intonation); the speaker's message is partly sent in this way • choose a private not a public moment when you need to disagree or crit icize • deliver your message partly by hints and suggestions, not by final-sounding statements • find an indirect way to communicate disagreement ("Shall we look at this later?" instead of "We could never agree to this") but check for reactions in body languag e and tone • leave room for interpretation in what you are saying, and expect to interpret what is said to you • use private meetings to get extra information • do not deliver uncomfortable facts openly	• pay extra attention to hard information you are delivering and less to phrasing and style—hard information is what your audience is listening for • do not always wait for a private moment when you need to disagree or criticize • make very clear proposals—hints and suggestions may be missed • find a direct way to communicate disagreement ("I'm sorry but we don't agree" will be more effective than "Shall we look at this later?" unless you really plan to resolve it later) • do not leave much r oom for interpretation in what you are saying —vague, open statements may be considered confusing and unhelpful • rely more on public meetings to get key information • do not bury uncomfortable facts—honesty will be appreciated more than diplomacy
Time Spans	
If you deal with people who are **more past oriented** than you are	If you are dealing with people who are **more future-oriented** than you
• show your appreciation for tradition • use arguments and examples based on past results and achievements • use established (not new) concepts and terminology where possible • make sure you show appreciation for their experience • look into their history—it will help you understand them and they will welcome your historical knowledge	• try to demonstrate how your activities fit into the overall vision for the future • consider the positive aspects of change • look for opportunities to make improvements through change • use more references to the future (aims, vision, direction) when trying to persuade people • give them your personal view of the future • use new concepts and terminology—not established ones—where possible • pay at least as much attention to positive future scenarios as negative ones

Reproduced from: Maria Jicheva "Speed Dating Across Cultures," in *Building Cultural Competence: Innovative Activities and Models*, eds. K. Berardo and D. K. Deardorff (Sterling, VA: Stylus, 2012), 248–260.

Power	
If you are dealing with people who **tolerate greater power distance** than you	If you are dealing with people who **tolerate less power distance** than you
• show respect for people with higher status • make sure that you understand the chain of authority and its implications • accept that employees may like strong supervision and feel com fortable with a directive, persuasive supervisor • do not put employees in a position where they have to disagree with their managers • do not expect your being available to build your authority—your staff will respect you even if you are distant • do not try to mix informally with your superiors unless the idea comes from them • actively encourage your staff to take the initiative, if you do not want to them to follow your lead closely • consult your superiors before taking the initiative yourself • be ready to give direct orders to get things done	• make sure your staff feel empowered, if you want to get the best performance out of them • avoid close supervision—it is likely to be counterproductive and seen as offensive • focus on encouraging or inspiring your staff, not controlling or instructing them • make yourself available to your staff more often and share some informal occasions with them • do not always wait for orders or authority to act—others may be waiting for you to take the initiative • do not expect automatic respect and obedience • find out how much authority you have—and exercise it fully

Tasks	
If you deal with people who are **more relationship-oriented** than you are	If you deal with people who are **more task-oriented** than you
• make relationship building one of your key tasks • give time getting to know your partners • do not wait to get to know your partners through your cooperation, get to know them beforehand • don't let deadlines and other pressures endanger the relationship • remember that your partners may judge a project to be a success if your relationship is strengthened at the end, even if some deadlines and milestones were missed • allow time for small talk • give away some personal information—even if it does not seem relevant to your work • when discussing business, remember that your partner is paying attention to the kind of person you seem to be —not just to the subject you are discussing	• try to use the practical work as a way of getting to know your partners • be ready to make agreements before you are fully familiar with the partners • remember that achievement of your joint objectives may be the best way to build relationships • your partners may not calculate time for socializing into the plans • remember that your partner may believe that not discussing personal matters shows greatest respect • to find out more about your partner, you will have to sensitively and actively ask questions • offer objective views as well as personal opinions • be clear about the mutual advantage in the partnership—it will be the whole basis of the relationship in the mind of your partner

SECTION 7

Build Global Teams

40. SNOWBALL

Stephanie Pollack

This creative alternative to traditional introductions helps participants get to know one another and deeply dive into important topics quickly.

Key Focus

Build global teams

Type of Activity

Introduction

Objectives

As a result of this activity, participants will

- create a positive group memory with a non-traditional form of introductions;
- increase their awareness of and camaraderie with fellow participants; and
- be able to explore any topic while simultaneously being in an inclusive, fun, interactive, and safe environment.

Appropriate Audience

Adults, teenagers

Level of Challenge

Low

Group Size

8 to 35 people

Time

25 to 50 minutes

Materials

One sheet piece of paper and a pen for each participant

Preparation

Identify five general questions on any topic to ask participants. The first question should be the lowest risk and the fifth question the highest risk.

Although described here as more of an introduction, Snowball can be played at any stage of a group's formation and existence by varying the questions. If the facilitator wants the group to focus on a specific topic or wants to find out certain information about the participants, the questions can be varied accordingly. Questions can be tailored so the answers provide value for the group, the facilitator, or even the client (e.g., surveying the participants to provide information for the client). The facilitator can also ask participants for a list of questions they want to ask each other. In this case, pick five and use those.

The following are sample questions for cultural team building:

1. What is your favorite afternoon snack?
2. When was the last time you laughed incredibly hard, and briefly, what were the circumstances?
3. Who has been a big role model in your life?
4. What is the worst time of day for you to have a meeting?
5. If you could have a super power, what super power would you want and why?

The following are sample questions for cultural transitions (job relocation, study abroad):

1. What are you most excited about in this transition?
2. What do you think will be your biggest challenge in this transition?
3. What do you do to reduce stress?
4. What was a big transition for you in your life, and what did you do to cope?
5. What do you most want to learn in this new phase of your life?

The following are sample questions for intercultural leadership:

1. Who was a great role model for intercultural leadership for you, and what did that person do?
2. What quality do you feel is most important in being a successful intercultural leader?
3. What environment do you need around you to do your best work while bringing your full cultural self to work?
4. What did a former supervisor do to make you feel comfortable (or what do you wish he or she had done) in an intercultural atmosphere?
5. What do you wish could happen in your current situation to display the most appropriate style of intercultural leadership?

Answers to all questions are placed in various locations on the sheet of paper (1 = upper left, 2 = upper right, 3 = lower left, 4 = lower right, 5 = center).

Activity Setup

1. Give each participant a sheet of paper and a pen.
2. Ask participants to use their papers in landscape mode.
3. Tell participants they will be asked to write answers to five different questions in different areas on the paper. Ask them to not put their name on the paper, and to please write legibly because someone else will be reading the answers.
4. Ask the five questions, pausing between each one so participants can write their answers. Give them the following instructions: "In the upper left corner, write the answer to . . ., In the upper right corner . . ., In the lower left corner . . ., In the lower right corner . . ., and In the center of the paper, write the answer to . . ."
5. Once all the questions have been asked and answered, ask participants to put their pens down, take their papers, and move to an open area of the room. Tell them no other materials are needed other than their papers.

Managing the Activity

1. For the next step, the facilitator says, for example, "I'm now going to ask you to do something you are normally not asked to do once you've put your hard work onto paper: Crumple up your papers." The facilitator quickly and playfully crumples a sheet of paper into a small ball, and the participants will do the same. Continue, speaking more loudly over the sound of crumpling paper. "The name of this activity is Snowball. We're about to have a snowball fight! You can chuck these things at each other as hard as you want to because, hey, it's paper and it's not going to hurt. We're going to keep throwing these at each other, picking them up and throwing them until I tell you to stop, and then I'll tell you the next step. Ready?" The facilitator then gets into a hard throwing stance, and says, "Go!" The facilitator throws the ball or fakes it (see Facilitation Tips and Suggestions on p. 264).

2. The snowball fight can last as long as the facilitator wants and ends when he or she calls out, "Stop!"

3. Instruct everyone to pick up a snowball and begin reading the answers. Tell them that if someone happens to pick up his or her own paper, let the group know, and if this happens, begin the fight again to shuffle the snowballs.

4. Tell participants they are to figure out whose paper they have based on the answers. Ask them to walk around reading the answers out loud without directly asking other participants if the answers belong to them. Tell them that once they find their author, they are to keep that person on their left.

5. Watch as participants try to find each other, and offer help as necessary.

6. Eventually participants will find each other and will be in a circle (or a few circles). Once this happens, tell them they are going to introduce the person whose paper they have to the group. The person introducing should say the author's name and then read the list of answers to each question. The introduction circle continues until all participants have been introduced.

7. Thank everyone for their participation. If desired, collect the papers (if you want to know who wrote the answers, ask participants to write their name on the back of their paper).

Debriefing the Activity

The debriefing for this activity can be used as a beginning for larger discussions based on answers to the questions. General debriefing questions might include:

1. What do you think of this exercise?
2. What did you learn about your fellow participants in this exercise? Is there anything you'd like to try based on answers you heard?
3. What did you learn from your fellow participants in this exercise? How might this influence the way you communicate with them?

Topic-specific questions might include:

1. Cultural team building: What did you learn you have in common with your fellow partici-

pants? How might this influence the way you communicate with them?

2. Cultural transitions: How do your feelings about the upcoming cultural transition compare with those of your fellow participants? What did you learn from your fellow participants' answers that could be useful to you during the upcoming cultural transition?

3. Intercultural leadership: What did you learn about intercultural leadership after hearing your fellow participants' answers? What new intercultural leadership ideas might you want to try?

Key Insights and Learnings

- Introductions can be fun rather than the usual boring "My name is . . ."
- It is possible to learn a lot about fellow participants in a short period of time.
- Unexpected similarities exist between people.
- People are full of surprises.
- Certain people may seem interesting, and others may desire to get to know them better.

Topic-specific learnings include:

- Cultural team building: Participants realize they have things in common with people they didn't expect or previously realize, and will follow up with those people. They understand new ways to best communicate with specific people (time of day for meetings, what makes them laugh, what foods we can share, etc.).
- Cultural transitions: Through other participants' answers, they learn new things to be excited about while going through a transition. They also learn new ways (coping mechanisms) to reduce cultural transition stress, and may follow up with the people who suggested them so they know exactly what to try.
- Intercultural leadership: Participants learn about some people's role models and want to know more about them. People value different qualities when it comes to being an intercultural leader. Work environments need to be inclusive to work for people with diverse backgrounds. They learn a few specific ideas

to try out to be an interculturally proficient leader.

Facilitation Tips and Suggestions

- If doing this activity with a new group, do it first, do not do any prior introductions or sharing of names. The facilitator should introduce himself or herself and let the group know that official introductions will occur as part of the activity.
- If the facilitator wants to be introduced, and it makes sense to play with the group, play along. If it doesn't make sense for the facilitator to answer the same questions or play with the group, the facilitator should pantomime throwing the snowball; participants will be so into throwing their own snowballs they'll never notice.
- Do not introduce the activity by name until partipants are holding their crumpled pieces of paper. If the name is given away earlier, the surprise will be spoiled. The big revelation should occur only once the participants are ready to throw their snowballs.

    If the activity is in a location without snow, or the participants are not familiar with snow, rename the activity (e.g., Falafel Ball in the Middle East, Paper Ball in Southeast Asia, etc.).
- Don't worry about everyone not wanting to throw paper balls at other people. While it is possible someone might start slowly, once he or she sees how much fun everyone else is having, the person will inevitably break into a smile and participate.
- Give participants the choice to either link arms or keep the person whose paper they have on their left; when given the choice, participants almost always link. It's effective to underplay the instructions: "You can link arms if you're comfortable, or just keep the person to your left, whatever you want." This delivery works the best; if it is only suggested that participants link arms, they will feel uncomfortable.
- This activity hits multiple learning styles: visual—the placement of the answers on the page, auditory—hearing instructions and in-

troductions, and kinesthetic—throwing the snowballs and physically linking up with others.
- This activity gradually increases risk: Sitting and writing is low risk; disclosing information about oneself can be low or moderate or high; throwing snowballs can be low, moderate, or high depending on the participant, but it's usually low because everyone is doing it at the same time; finding each other by asking questions—moderate; and introducing each other—low moderate or high depending on the participant (but it would be high if participants were speaking for themselves about themselves).
- When participants are introducing each other, the facilitator supports them by reminding them what the questions are (they may only have one word written on the paper).
- This activity can be easily altered for whatever time is available by changing the number of items participants share at the end. Not much time? Ask participants to share one specific item (based on program goals). Lots of time? Share them all.

About This Exercise

I first played Snowball as a participant in 1998 as a part of my master's degree in a course on creative teaching methods at the C. W. Post campus of Long Island University. Over the years I have adapted it for numerous intercultural learning purposes. It can be used as an icebreaker, a debriefing tool, or to delve deeply into any one particular subject or issue. I have played it with various populations including corporate marketing departments, environmental and social change organizations, deans of global universities, professors and teachers, museum interns, summer camp staff, high schoolers and college students, recent refugees, and fellow interculturalists during training of trainers sessions. One specifically memorable Snowball experience involved playing it first thing in the morning with representatives from the University of California, Berkeley, when I was working for The Scholar Ship and we were seeking a U.S. academic partner. Berkeley's administrators agreed to become our partner and cited the creativity of Snowball as one reason why.

41. INSIDE CIRCLE, OUTSIDE CIRCLE

Basma Ibrahim DeVries and Barbara Kappler Mikk

In this activity participants form one large circle and are then invited to step forward to make a general statement about themselves (e.g., "I speak two languages."). All others who who can say the same thing about themselves then step into the middle, and participants see who has stepped to the inside circle and who has remained in the outside circle. Once everyone has had a chance to observe who has stepped into the circle, inside circle members can step back and rejoin the outside circle until the next person makes a statement. The movement in this activity helps create a visual picture of the interplay of different ideas, interests, experiences, and challenges that participants have encountered. This activity can be used in multiple ways and for multiple purposes: introductions of participants and their interests, generating cohesiveness in groups, and showing similarities and differences on a variety of levels.

Key Focus

Build global teams

Type of Activity

Introduction

Objectives

As a result of this activity, participants will

- learn the similarities and differences in their group,
- reflect upon emotional reactions to better understand responses to in-group and out-of-group experiences, and
- be challenged to confront biases, stereotypes, and assumptions about other group members.

Appropriate Audience

Adults, teenagers

Level of Challenge

Medium

Group Size

10 to 20 plus people

Time

15 to 60 minutes

Materials

None

Activity Setup

1. Have all group members stand in a circle. Introduce the main reason for this exercise, either

   - to introduce group members' interests (or work experience, travel experience, etc.) to one another or
   - to understand in-group and out-of-group dynamics and to confront biases we might have about one another.

2. Indicate that when they have something to share, they should step to the middle of the circle, turn around slowly so they can connect with the whole circle, and make their statement (for example, "I have traveled to the Middle East" or "I am the youngest child in my family.").

Managing the Activity

1. Demonstrate the activity by stating something about yourself.
2. Anyone else who has had the same experience steps into the middle, and everyone can

---

265

observe who has stepped to the inside circle and who has remained in the outside circle.

3. Once everyone has seen who stepped into the circle, inside circle members can rejoin the outside circle until the next person steps into the middle to make a statement. The activity concludes either when each participant has made a statement or when the activity seems to have reached a stopping point.

Debriefing the Activity

Ask the following debriefing questions:

1. What was it like for you to participate in this activity?
2. How was it to step forward and make a statement about yourself? To step forward when someone else made a statement? To remain in the outer circle?
3. What did you learn about your fellow group members?
4. What assumptions did you have about your group members that have changed as a result of this activity?
5. How might what has been learned today help our group work together? What might you need to do next to learn more about someone in this group? What can we do as a group to learn more about each other?

If you are using this exercise to talk about stereotypes,

1. Tell participants that talking about stereotypes will be a challenging conversation for the group and one that the group is hopefully ready to have.
2. Ask participants:

   - What stereotypes do they believe others had of them that were challenged?
   - What stereotypes did you have of others that were challenged?

Key Insights and Learnings

- Participants learn they are not accurate in their assumptions of their similarities and differences.
- It's a big risk to focus on oneself in examining culture; it's easier to stay distant and pre-

tend that intercultural communication is about someone else.

- Participants learn they do have much in common with others in unexpected ways.
- They need to reach out to several members to understand them better and to help the team work together better.
- They have stereotypes of others in the room.
- Others have stereotypes of them.
- It's uncomfortable to talk about stereotypes, and it takes courage to admit to others that one harbors stereotypes.
- It's exhausting to realize that even today others carry stereotypes that should have disappeared already.

Variations

Variation 1. Facilitators could add another dimension to this activity by asking participants to step back when the statement does not apply to them OR when they grew up with an opposite message (e.g., "I was told that looking someone directly in the eyes was a sign of respect"). By allowing participants to step back when statements are counter to what they experienced, more visual—and potentially powerful—information is added.

Variation 2. Facilitators can preselect the topics for the activity instead of relying on the participants to supply the topics, which might work especially well for a group that might not be familiar with this type of open-ended and personal activity.

Variation 3. Facilitators can use this activity to move from introductions of group member experiences to a specific topic. For example, the activity can be started by instructing participants to share something about themselves in the circle format as a means of introduction, and then the facilitator may instruct the group to shift their statements to apply to the specific topic of the training, for example, offering ideas about culturally appropriate behaviors based on their experiences. This could work very well to quickly move a new group from introductions to the topic of the training session.

Facilitation Tips and Suggestions

- This activity should not be rushed, because participants need time to decide if the statement applies to them and if they wish to step forward. Set a calm tone as you introduce the exercise, and when others are making statements, model taking time to think about the statement before moving.

- Hold the debriefing until the end to ensure that the participants have ample time to make statements and step forward. Also, debriefing too early not only makes the activity feel disjointed, it might end up favoring a particular topic (language or gender, etc.) and unintentionally allocating a significant amount of time to one or two participants. This may be what the group needs, but you want to be sure you have completed the activity first so all participants take part in the activity and the debriefing.

- It may come up in the debriefing that some statements by participants "pushed" others to disclose information they might not have chosen to share on their own. For example, if a participant says he or she was adopted, and another participant was also adopted but was not planning to tell that to the group, that participant may feel conflicted when deciding whether to step into the circle. This can lead to some great discussions in terms of self-disclosure, choices, visible and invisible aspects of identity, and so on. Facilitators should be prepared to respond if this comes up and may even add debriefing questions that target this type of situation.

- This exercise works well for group members who are getting to know one another or who know each other well. With intact groups who work together, encourage them to offer information beyond what others may already know about them.

- Sometimes stepping into the center (or not stepping into the center) can be quite insightful about a particular group and the individuals in the group. As a facilitator, you can choose to allow these types of observations to be made during the circle time or during the debriefing at the end. We have found it often moves the group to deeper thinking if observations are allowed during the process. At times it seems useful for the facilitator to make such observations. For example, in one session participants were asked to share messages they received while growing up about

appropriate communication behaviors. One participant stepped into the middle of the circle and said, "If you do not have anything nice to say, don't say anything at all." Sixteen of the 18 participants stepped inside the circle, except the only Korean woman and the only East Indian woman in the group. These two women looked at each other from their outside circle positions and giggled knowingly. Another participant asked them why they were giggling, which led to a very insightful discussion about some important communication style tendencies within specific cultural groups. Facilitators must be prepared to appropriately manage discussions based on simple observations that could potentially become volatile or alienate some participants.

- If the facilitator chooses the topics (e.g., "Please step forward if you speak more than one language."), he or she should be sure to carefully choose the kinds of topics used and their training purposes when deciding how to implement the activity. Some topics can be quite sensitive, and some may elicit stronger than expected emotional reactions from participants. Potentially controversial topics should be avoided when the activity takes place at the beginning of a training session.

- Larger groups work well.

About This Exercise

Our training focuses on hearing in the participants' own words how they are responding to the challenges and opportunities of intercultural interactions. This activity was inspired by working with a group that had several silent members who seemed to be left out of the organization and yet had so much to contribute. The activity allowed all participants in the group to choose their level of participation and provided a space for greater group cohesion to develop. Because the activity was successful in that setting, we used it many times since over the past several years. Over time, we have discovered the levels of depth that can be achieved by this simple activity and the many ways it can serve as a bridge to other aspects of a training session.

42. CULTURAL COMPETENCE diversophy®

George Simons

Through an interactive and enjoyable game of cards, participants explore the awareness and practices needed to develop cultural competence and discover how to build them.

Key Focus

Build global teams

Type of Activity

Game

Objectives

As a result of this activity, participants will

- become aware of several dimensions of cultural competence, and
- realize that cultural competence is a matter of heart, head, hands, and community engagement, that is, managing feelings, gaining knowledge, and choosing appropriate behavior to cohabit and collaborate effectively with others.

Appropriate Audience

Adults

Level of Challenge

Medium

Group Size

The game is played in groups or teams of four to seven, with six being ideal. The total number is unlimited, but a set of materials is necessary for each small group that will be playing together as a team.

Time

60 minutes

Materials

- Handouts
- Post-it notes
- Pencils

Preparation

Print and cut the cards (see Handout S7.1a–e) and provide one set for each group along with a block of Post-it notes and a pencil. Allow 20 minutes for first-time creation of materials, which can be reused. Read the game rules (see Handout S7.2). For ease in printing, full color PDF sets of cards are available at www.diversophy.com/buildingculturalcompetence.htm. A single printing creates two sets of cards, enough for up to two groups of six players. Here you will also find printable copies of the game rules and the Facilitator's Guide.

Activity Setup

1. Form groups of four to seven people.
2. Explain the purpose of the exercise and ask a member of each group to read the rules of the game out loud. Ask if there are any procedural questions. Distribute cards, Post-it notes, and pencils.
3. Ask participants to attach a Post-it note to any card they want to discuss further during the debriefing. Tell them to start playing.

Managing the Activity

1. Observe the group, or circulate among the groups if there is more than one.

2. Be available to answer questions about how to play the various card types, but do not respond to game content questions. The downloadable facilitator guide will help you do this.

Debriefing the Activity

The following are some useful questions for the debriefing session following the game:

1. What did you learn? From the game cards? From each other?
2. What struck you as particularly interesting, questionable, or otherwise noteworthy while playing the game?
3. How did the way your team played the game reflect diverse orientations to learning through playing, competition versus collaboration, and other dynamics of discussion and exchange?
4. Given this experience, what do you feel you would need or like to learn next about becoming more culturally competent?
5. What specific issue or questions did you write on the Post-it notes that you would like to discuss further now?
6. How can you apply what you learned from playing and discussing the game to your work or life?

Key Insights and Learnings

Participants usually learn from the game materials and from discussions with each other

- the relevance and importance of developing cultural competence and important clues and processes for doing it,
- interesting and memorable facts and attitudes and skills required for living and working with people of other cultures, and
- even a small team quickly develops a culture of how it plays, how competition or collaboration

develops in the team's style of play. It is useful to reflect on how the team itself and its diverse members understood and played the game.

Variation

A full game consisting of 250 cards, which may be played with just the cards or with the cards and dice, is available from www.diversophy.com. This website also contains links for playing customized games, online versions, and android phone games if the facilitator wants to coach or tutor individuals or groups. Customized versions are available for classroom use or training sessions.

Facilitation Tips and Suggestions

The purpose of this game is to provide insight not just from the cards themselves but from the exchanges of the participants with each other. Therefore,

- try to make your groups as diverse as possible,
- your role is not to play the expert but to stimulate exchange and facilitate sharing even where there is disagreement with the card content or when participants disagree with each other,
- discourage lengthy exchanges during the game (if a discussion seems lengthy or unproductive, tell the participants to mark the card for discussion during the debriefing session), and
- allow 5 minutes for setup, 35 minutes for playing time, and 20 minutes for the debriefing.

About This Exercise

Cultural Competence is one of the newest in the award-winning series of over 60 diversophy® games that began to appear in 1993. Games address specific cultures as well as critical intercultural themes, such as Negotiating Globally and Global Teamwork.

HANDOUT S7.1a

A   diversiCHOICE

B. Finding people from the new culture to accept you, interact with you and bring you into their social circles should be your primary concern. A. and sometimes C. can help, but they will not automatically integrate you. Lack of B. may actually keep you from feeling like you belong to your new surroundings. Common interests have short term value, but will not by themselves integrate you in the long term.

If you chose the the best answer, keep this card. If not, discard it.

3 Points

CC-EN-0015

A   diversiCHOICE

False. While we might say that respect is a universal value, how people expect to be respected may differ substantially from one culture to another. Words and gestures of respect may differ according to the age and status of the persons involved. What might be respect in one culture might be an insult in another.

If you chose the better answer, keep this card. If not, discard it.

3 Points

CC-EN-0020

Q   diversiCHOICE

In order to become integrated into the society or worklife of another country, the most critical factor is:

A. Learning the language and cultural differences.

B. Finding people from the new culture to accept you, interact with you and bring you into their social circles.

C. Having clearly something new and different to offer to the new culture.

D. Having common interests.

3 Points

CC-EN-0015

Q   diversiCHOICE

You can be sure that if you respect people and demand respect of others as you do in your own culture, you will be accepted wherever you are in the world.

True or False?

3 Points

CC-EN-0020

Reproduced from: George Simons, "Cultural Competence diversophy®," in *Building Cultural Competence: Innovative Activities and Models,* eds. K. Berardo and D. K. Deardorff (Sterling, VA: Stylus, 2012), 268–295.

diversiCHOICE   A

A. is the least useful, as "putting up" or "suffering through" with the words or actions of others is usually accompanied by negative judgments and feelings. Not giving offense to others is important, but refusing to take offense is even more critical for resolving culturally conflicted situations. Choose to be curious rather than resentful!

If you chose the better answer, keep this card. If not, discard it.

CC-EN-0022

3 Points

diversiCHOICE   A

C. provides the best starting point of the options given. Both A and B might hinder more than improve individual and team performance. Starting with A might give the impression that you don't know your job and B might send the message that you don't care about them.

If you chose the best answer, keep this card. If not, discard it.

CC-EN-0027

3 Points

Q   diversiCHOICE

We are often told to *be tolerant.* Which of these behaviors is the *least useful* when exercising or learning tolerance?

A. "Putting up" with things that annoy you.

B. Avoiding words and behaviors that give offense to others.

C. Refusing to take offense when the words or behaviors of others are difficult to accept or understand.

CC-EN-0022

3 Points

Q   diversiCHOICE

You are working in an organization where people are used to hierarchical leadership. You want to empower the people who work for and with you. You should:

A. Give them vague assignments so that they have to think and exercise creativity.

B. Make yourself unavailable, so they have to make decisions on their own.

C. Praise their willingness to follow direction and engage them in more conversations about their work and its objectives.

CC-EN-0027

3 Points

HANDOUT S7.1a *(continued)*

Q   diversiCHOICE

When a cultural conflict occurs, the best way to resolve it is to insist on maintaining one's own values and arguing for their logical validity, while letting the other party do the same. Rational persuasion is the best way to resolve the conflict.

True or False?

CC-EN-0034

3 Points

A   diversiCHOICE

False. While a clear statement of values may be a starting point for a discussion, it is often necessary to understand the history, geography and economics that lie behind them. Each culture has a story that can remain hidden if the only dialog is rational persuasion.

If you chose the better answer, keep this card. If not, discard it.

CC-EN-0034

3 Points

Q   diversiCHOICE

To build a smoothly functioning multicultural organization, you should:

A. Establish clear quotas to assure the diversity of those employed in the organization.

B. Test candidates and employees for cultural sensitivity.

C. Benchmark best practices for cultural competence.

CC-EN-0041

3 Points

A   diversiCHOICE

C. Benchmarking best practices is the most comprehensive and continuing way of evaluating your progress and setting standards and directions for a multicultural and inclusive organization. Both A and B are likely to cause personnel problems and may be illegal as well.

If you chose the best answer, keep this card. If not, discard it.

CC-EN-0041

3 Points

A diversiCHOICE

A. is the best definition. Knowing and respecting people's differences and similarities will tell you when and where B. and C. are appropriate and helpful.

If you chose the best answer, keep this card. If not, discard it.

3 Points

CC-EN-0042

A diversiCHOICE

C. You may move or seek legal support, but the most practical thing to do might be to take the opportunity to learn their language. Everyday fluency will make you more comfortable, create good will and help you seek positive solutions, along with your new neighbors, to the challenges they face.

If you chose the best answer, keep this card. If not, discard it.

3 Points

CC-EN-0049

Q diversiCHOICE

Behaving "inclusively" is making sure that you:

A. Know, respect and use the similarities and differences in your group to effectively meet your goals.

B. Invite everyone to meetings and events.

C. Copy everyone on e-mails and correspondence.

3 Points

CC-EN-0042

Q diversiCHOICE

Most people where you live are immigrants and refugees and speak a language different form the national language that you speak. You should:

A. Move house.

B. Insist on laws that require all public and commercial signage to be in the national language.

C. Learn some of their language.

D. Associate only with your own kind.

3 Points

CC-EN-0049

HANDOUT S7.1a *(continued)*

Q diversiCHOICE

Given the effects of globalization and the mobility of people in today's world, you should not expect to find identifiable ethnic or regional cultural characteristics in the people you meet and work with.

True or False?

CC-EN-0054

3 Points

A diversiCHOICE

False. There is a high degree of cultural exchange and fluidity in cultural identity and behavior, but behaviors that we see are often driven by deeper cultural values consistent with the past. Like good detectives, we look for the clues that tell us about these values. This will help us understand, respond and adapt to others appropriately.

If you chose the best answer, keep this card. If not, discard it.

CC-EN-0054

3 Points

Q diversiCHOICE

You can largely resolve problems in recruiting workers from non-dominant groups in the culture by establishing objective job qualifications.

True or False?

CC-EN-0055

3 Points

A diversiCHOICE

False. Objective may not be very objective at all unless based on well-defined competencies. Even so, culturally competent hiring requires understanding of how work is accomplished across cultures and the commitment of those whose responsibility it is to develop workers from nontraditional sources.

If you chose the best answer, keep this card. If not, discard it.

CC-EN-0055

3 Points

HANDOUT S7.1b

diversiGUIDE

"I suppose leadership at one time meant muscles; but today it means getting along with people."

Indira Gandhi (1917 – 1984), thrice Prime Minister of the Republic of India

After you read this card aloud, any team member, including you, may comment on how it can add to our sense of cultural competence. Keep this card.

CC-EN-1018

1 Point

diversiGUIDE

"Ubuntu, ungantu, ngakanye, abantu."
(People are people through other people.)

Xhosa proverb

After you read this card aloud, any team member, including you, may comment on how it can add to our sense of cultural competence. Keep this card.

CC-EN-1019

1 Point

diversiGUIDE

"I suppose leadership at one time meant muscles; but today it means getting along with people."

Indira Gandhi (1917 – 1984), thrice Prime Minister of the Republic of India

After you read this card aloud, any team member, including you, may comment on how it can add to our sense of cultural competence. Keep this card.

CC-EN-1018

1 Point

diversiGUIDE

"Ubuntu, ungantu, ngakanye, abantu."
(People are people through other people.)

Xhosa proverb

After you read this card aloud, any team member, including you, may comment on how it can add to our sense of cultural competence. Keep this card.

CC-EN-1019

1 Point

HANDOUT S7.1b *(continued)*

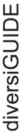

diversiGUIDE

"National culture's influence on organizations is as inevitable as getting wet when swimming."

A business student in Moldova

After you read this card aloud, any team member, including you, may comment on how it can add to our sense of cultural competence. Keep this card.

CC-EN-1026

1 Point

diversiGUIDE

"...beneath the skin, beyond the differing features and into the true heart of being, fundamentally we are more alike, my friend, than we are unalike."

Maya Angelou, African American poet

After you read this card aloud, any team member, including you, may comment on how it can add to our sense of cultural competence. Keep this card.

CC-EN-1036

1 Point

diversiGUIDE

"National culture's influence on organizations is as inevitable as getting wet when swimming."

A business student in Moldova

After you read this card aloud, any team member, including you, may comment on how it can add to our sense of cultural competence. Keep this card.

CC-EN-1026

1 Point

diversiGUIDE

"...beneath the skin, beyond the differing features and into the true heart of being, fundamentally we are more alike, my friend, than we are unalike."

Maya Angelou, African American poet

After you read this card aloud, any team member, including you, may comment on how it can add to our sense of cultural competence. Keep this card.

CC-EN-1036

1 Point

diversiGUIDE

"Three-fourths of the miseries and misunderstandings in the world will disappear if we step into the shoes of our adversaries and understand their standpoint."

Mohandas K. Gandhi, (1869–1948)

Indian political & spiritual leader

After you read this card aloud, any team member, including you, may comment on how it can add to our sense of cultural competence. Keep this card.

CC-EN-1039

1 Point

---

diversiGUIDE

"Three-fourths of the miseries and misunderstandings in the world will disappear if we step into the shoes of our adversaries and understand their standpoint."

Mohandas K. Gandhi, (1869–1948)

Indian political & spiritual leader

After you read this card aloud, any team member, including you, may comment on how it can add to our sense of cultural competence. Keep this card.

CC-EN-1039

1 Point

---

diversiGUIDE

"If you talk to a man in a language he understands, that goes to his head. If you talk to him in his language, that goes to his heart."

Nelson Mandela, former President of South Africa

After you read this card aloud, any team member, including you, may comment on how it can add to our sense of cultural competence. Keep this card.

CC-EN-1041

1 Point

---

diversiGUIDE

"If you talk to a man in a language he understands, that goes to his head. If you talk to him in his language, that goes to his heart."

Nelson Mandela, former President of South Africa

After you read this card aloud, any team member, including you, may comment on how it can add to our sense of cultural competence. Keep this card.

CC-EN-1041

1 Point

HANDOUT S7.1b *(continued)*

diversiGUIDE

"Values are like fingerprints. Nobody's are the same, but you leave 'em all over everything you do."

Elvis Presley (1935-1977), US pop singer

After you read this card aloud, any team member, including you, may comment on how it can add to our sense of cultural competence. Keep this card.

CC-EN-1044

1 Point

diversiGUIDE

"We must love them both, those whose opinions we share and those whose opinions we reject. For both have labored in the search for truth and both have helped us in the finding of it."

Thomas Aquinas (1225-1274),

Regent Master, University of Paris

After you read this card aloud, any team member, including you, may comment on how it can add to our sense of cultural competence. Keep this card.

CC-EN-1045

1 Point

diversiGUIDE

"Values are like fingerprints. Nobody's are the same, but you leave 'em all over everything you do."

Elvis Presley (1935-1977), US pop singer

After you read this card aloud, any team member, including you, may comment on how it can add to our sense of cultural competence. Keep this card.

CC-EN-1044

1 Point

diversiGUIDE

"We must love them both, those whose opinions we share and those whose opinions we reject. For both have labored in the search for truth and both have helped us in the finding of it."

Thomas Aquinas (1225-1274),

Regent Master, University of Paris

After you read this card aloud, any team member, including you, may comment on how it can add to our sense of cultural competence. Keep this card.

CC-EN-1045

1 Point

diversiGUIDE

"Only when I stop judging can I start discovering."

Virginia Satir (1916-1966)

US family therapy psychologist

After you read this card aloud, any team member, including you, may comment on how it can add to our sense of cultural competence. Keep this card.

1 Point

CC-EN-1051

---

diversiGUIDE

"Human beings seem to like to give themselves a sense of security by forming simplistic notions about the culture of other countries."

Masakazu Yamazaki, contemporary Japanese philosopher

After you read this card aloud, any team member, including you, may comment on how it can add to our sense of cultural competence. Keep this card.

1 Point

CC-EN-1052

---

diversiGUIDE

"Only when I stop judging can I start discovering."

Virginia Satir (1916-1966)

US family therapy psychologist

After you read this card aloud, any team member, including you, may comment on how it can add to our sense of cultural competence. Keep this card.

1 Point

CC-EN-1051

---

diversiGUIDE

"Human beings seem to like to give themselves a sense of security by forming simplistic notions about the culture of other countries."

Masakazu Yamazaki, contemporary Japanese philosopher

After you read this card aloud, any team member, including you, may comment on how it can add to our sense of cultural competence. Keep this card.

1 Point

CC-EN-1052

📄 HANDOUT S7.1c

diversiRISK –

You have embarrassed yourself by asking someone whose facial features are quite different from yours, "Where do you come from?" It turns out that this person is a native of your own country with deeper roots than your own.

Think this over and share your thoughts before taking your next turn. Discard this card.

CC-EN-2015

4 Points

diversiRISK –

You are having a hard time figuring out how to combine your organization's official practices with locally important values, resources and behaviors. You feel guilty both when you impose your organization's priorities as well as when you don't insist on them.

Think this over and share your thoughts before taking your next turn. Discard this card.

CC-EN-2021

4 Points

diversiRISK –

You have embarrassed yourself by asking someone whose facial features are quite different from yours, "Where do you come from?" It turns out that this person is a native of your own country with deeper roots than your own.

Think this over and share your thoughts before taking your next turn. Discard this card.

CC-EN-2015

4 Points

diversiRISK –

You are having a hard time figuring out how to combine your organization's official practices with locally important values, resources and behaviors. You feel guilty both when you impose your organization's priorities as well as when you don't insist on them.

Think this over and share your thoughts before taking your next turn. Discard this card.

CC-EN-2021

4 Points

diversiRISK –

You must work in a cultural context in which everyone seems to feel very sure of themselves and has strong, positive and negative opinions on just about everything. You are feeling increasingly less sure about yourself and feel that accepting much of what you hear would be very risky.

How might you think, feel or react in this situation? Tell your team, and then discard this card.

CC-EN-2030

4 Points

diversiRISK –

Your immigrant parents experienced bias in the new country and wanted the best for you. As a consequence, they went to great effort to hide the "old country" identity and language. Only later in life did you realize what you had lost.

How might you think, feel or react in this situation? Tell your team, and then discard this card.

CC-EN-2036

4 Points

diversiRISK –

You must work in a cultural context in which everyone seems to feel very sure of themselves and have strong, positive and negative opinions on just about everything. You are feeling increasingly less sure about yourself and feel that accepting much of what you hear would be very risky.

How might you think, feel or react in this situation? Tell your team, and then discard this card.

CC-EN-2030

4 Points

diversiRISK –

Your immigrant parents experienced bias in the new country and wanted the best for you. As a consequence, they went to great effort to hide the "old country" identity and language. Only later in life did you realize what you had lost.

How might you think, feel or react in this situation? Tell your team, and then discard this card.

CC-EN-2036

4 Points

HANDOUT S7.1c *(continued)*

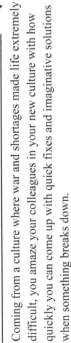

diversiRISK +

Coming from a culture where war and shortages made life extremely difficult, you amaze your colleagues in your new culture with how quickly you can come up with quick fixes and imaginative solutions when something breaks down.

How might you think, feel or react in this situation? Tell your team, and then keep this card.

CC-EN-2044

4 Points

diversiRISK +

Coming from a disadvantaged minority in your country, you resist the temptation to dismiss the cultural pain experienced and expressed by others whom you feel were less disadvantaged than your own group. With your empathy for them, the dialogue continues.

How might you think, feel or react in this situation? Tell your team, and then keep this card.

CC-EN-2048

4 Points

diversiRISK +

Coming from a culture where war and shortages made life extremely difficult, you amaze your colleagues in your new culture with how quickly you can come up with quick fixes and imaginative solutions when something breaks down.

How might you think, feel or react in this situation? Tell your team, and then keep this card.

CC-EN-2044

4 Points

diversiRISK +

Coming from a disadvantaged minority in your country, you resist the temptation to dismiss the cultural pain experienced and expressed by others whom you feel were less disadvantaged than your own group. With your empathy for them, the dialogue continues.

How might you think, feel or react in this situation? Tell your team, and then keep this card.

CC-EN-2048

4 Points

diversiRISK –

You just can't take it any more! Ignorance, negative attitudes, little insults about your cultural identity have built up to the point where you feel rejected, dismissed and so frustrated that you feel like angrily attacking the people around you. Instead, you withdraw and no longer contribute actively to your work team.

Think this over and share your thoughts before taking your next turn. Discard this card.

CC-EN-2051

4 Points

diversiRISK +

You come to realize that both positive and negative stereotypes are inevitable in our own minds as well as in the beliefs of groups we belong to. It is not possible for us to grasp the complexity of the individuals and groups we meet. You refuse to blame yourself and continue to learn.

How might you think, feel or react to this? Tell your team, and then keep this card.

CC-EN-2053

4 Points

diversiRISK –

You just can't take it any more! Ignorance, negative attitudes, little insults about your cultural identity have built up to the point where you feel rejected, dismissed and so frustrated that you feel like angrily attacking the people around you. Instead, you withdraw and no longer contribute actively to your work team.

Think this over and share your thoughts before taking your next turn. Discard this card.

CC-EN-2051

4 Points

diversiRISK +

You come to realize that both positive and negative stereotypes are inevitable in our own minds as well as in the beliefs of groups we belong to. It is not possible for us to grasp the complexity of the individuals and groups we meet. You refuse to blame yourself and continue to learn.

How might you think, feel or react to this? Tell your team, and then keep this card.

CC-EN-2053

4 Points

HANDOUT S7.1c *(continued)*

diversiRISK +

Being abroad and meeting someone from your own country you remember not to automatically assume common values by realizing that there are many subcultures within your own culture.

How might you think, feel or react in this situation? Tell your team, and then keep this card.

CC-EN-2055

4 Points

diversiRISK +

You regularly hold discussions of organizational goals, exploring how these can be effectively translated into action according to the values and language of several national cultures who are represented in your general staff. This pays off in increased motivation and synergy in the organization and better outreach to the people you serve.

How might you think, feel or react in this situation? Tell your team, and then keep this card.

CC-EN-2065

4 Points

diversiRISK +

Being abroad and meeting someone from your own country you remember not to automatically assume common values by realizing that there are many subcultures within your own culture.

How might you think, feel or react in this situation? Tell your team, and then keep this card.

CC-EN-2055

4 Points

diversiRISK +

You regularly hold discussions of organizational goals, exploring how these can be effectively translated into action according to the values and language of several national cultures who are represented in your general staff. This pays off in increased motivation and synergy in the organization and better outreach to the people you serve.

How might you think, feel or react in this situation? Tell your team, and then keep this card.

CC-EN-2065

4 Points

HANDOUT S7.1d

diversiSHARE

Describe briefly one improvement (or new approach) which you have seen resulting from pooling local and foreign talent and experiences, e.g., in communication, negotiation, decision making, community or team building. Each player in the group is invited to add one experience of her or his own.

Give a round of applause to the entire group. Keep this card.

CC-EN-3001

5 Points

diversiSHARE

Tell your team one or two things you would do to try to encourage someone you have begun to work with to trust you.

Any teammate who would find one or the other of these behaviors uncomfortable will tell you. Keep this card.

CC-EN-3023

5 Points

diversiSHARE

Describe briefly one improvement (or new approach) which you have seen resulting from pooling local and foreign talent and experiences, e.g., in communication, negotiation, decision making, community or team building. Each player in the group is invited to add one experience of her or his own.

Give a round of applause to the entire group. Keep this card.

©2009. GSI. All rights reserved.
www.diversophy.com

CC-EN-3001

5 Points

diversiSHARE

Tell your team one or two things you would do to try to encourage someone you have begun to work with to trust you.

Any teammate who would find one or the other of these behaviors uncomfortable will tell you. Keep this card.

©2009. GSI. All rights reserved.
www.diversophy.com

CC-EN-3023

5 Points

HANDOUT S7.1d *(continued)*

diversiSHARE

How would you draw the line between tolerating words or behaviors that you dislike and cowardice in confronting such things?

When you are done, any member who knows a slang word for "coward" in their culture will mention it. Keep this card.

CC-EN-3029

5 Points

diversiSHARE

Share with your team one of the core values that you bring from your cultural background and one example of how it drives your behavior.

Any teammate who feels that she or he shares this value may give an example of one way he or she behaves because of it. Keep this card.

CC-EN-3044

5 Points

diversiSHARE

How would you draw the line between tolerating words or behaviors that you dislike and cowardice in confronting such things?

When you are done, any member who knows a slang word for "coward" in their culture will mention it. Keep this card.

CC-EN-3029

©2009. GSI. All rights reserved.
www.diversophy.com

5 Points

diversiSHARE

Share with your team one of the core values that you bring from your cultural background and one example of how it drives your behavior.

Any teammate who feels that she or he shares this value may give an example of one way he or she behaves because of it. Keep this card.

CC-EN-3044

©2009. GSI. All rights reserved.
www.diversophy.com

5 Points

diversiSHARE

Showing irritation or stress in intercultural situations is more than likely to reduce your ability to react appropriately. Share with your team one thing you do to reduce stress when working with others.

Any teammate who wishes may share how this stress reducing behavior would work for him or her or in his or her culture. Keep this card.

CC-EN-3045

5 Points

diversiSHARE

In some cultures, people make jokes when they are uncomfortable in a group situation; in others they become silent. How do people in your culture tend to show or betray that they are uncomfortable? Share with your team.

As you speak, your teammates will each imagine that what you say makes them uncomfortable and will react by showing discomfort in a way common to their culture. Keep this card.

CC-EN-3046

5 Points

diversiSHARE

Showing irritation or stress in intercultural situations is more than likely to reduce your ability to react appropriately. Share with your team one thing you do to reduce stress when working with others.

Any teammate who wishes may share how this stress reducing behavior would work for him or her or in his or her culture. Keep this card.

CC-EN-3045

5 Points

diversiSHARE

In some cultures, people make jokes when they are uncomfortable in a group situation; in others they become silent. How do people in your culture tend to show or betray that they are uncomfortable? Share with your team.

As you speak, your teammates will each imagine that what you say makes them uncomfortable and will react by showing discomfort in a way common to their culture. Keep this card.

CC-EN-3046

5 Points

HANDOUT S7.1d *(continued)*

diversiSHARE

Tribes, groups, teams, nations, and organizations often try to express who they are by the use of totems, symbols, coats of arms, mascots, logos and other artifacts or images. Tell your team about one image used by a group you belong to and how you feel it expresses the spirit or behavior of the group's culture.

After you share, each teammate will mention, in a single word and without commenting on it, the name of a symbol or image that describes a group she or he belongs or identifies with. Keep this card.

CC-EN-3047

5 Points

diversiSHARE

How are channels of communication in your organizational or social culture structured? What are the official channels, what are the unofficial ones, and how are they used? Give at least one difference and an example.

After you share, the other players thank you by telling you how informal communication is called or described in their culture or organization. For example in English people often speak of "the grapevine." Keep this card.

CC-EN-3052

5 Points

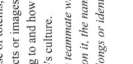

diversiSHARE

Tribes, groups, teams, nations, and organizations often try to express who they are by the use of totems, symbols, coats of arms, mascots, logos and other artifacts or images. Tell your team about one image used by a group you belong to and how you feel it expresses the spirit or behavior of the group's culture.

After you share, each teammate will mention, in a single word and without commenting on it, the name of a symbol or image that describes a group she or he belongs or identifies with. Keep this card.

CC-EN-3047

5 Points

diversiSHARE

How are channels of communication in your organizational or social culture structured? What are the official channels, what are the unofficial ones, and how are they used? Give at least one difference and an example.

After you share, the other players thank you by telling you how informal communication is called or described in their culture or organization. For example in English people often speak of "the grapevine." Keep this card.

CC-EN-3052

5 Points

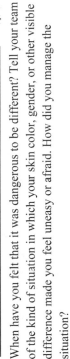

diversiSHARE

Share with your team a perspective or life, a skill or strength that you feel you have developed as a result of a culture you belong to that you feel helps you to work with people who are different from you or when in unfamiliar environments.

After you share, any teammate who wishes may tell you about a situation in which he or she thinks this cultural perspective or skill would be valuable. Keep this card.

CC-EN-3058

 5 Points

diversiSHARE

When have you felt that it was dangerous to be different? Tell your team of the kind of situation in which your skin color, gender, or other visible difference made you feel uneasy or afraid. How did you manage the situation?

After you share, any teammate who wishes may tell you something he or she tells him or herself internally to cope with such a discomfort. Keep this card.

CC-EN-3060

 5 Points

diversiSHARE

Share with your team a perspective on life, a skill or strength that you feel you have developed as a result of a culture you belong to that you feel helps you to work with people who are different from you or when in unfamiliar environments.

After you share, any teammate who wishes may tell you about a situation in which he or she thinks this cultural perspective or skill would be valuable. Keep this card.

©2009. GSI. All rights reserved.
www.diversophy.com

CC-EN-3058

5 Points

diversiSHARE

When have you felt that it was dangerous to be different? Tell your team of the kind of situation in which your skin color, gender, or other visible difference made you feel uneasy or afraid. How did you manage the situation?

After you share, any teammate who wishes may tell you something he or she tells him or herself internally to cope with such a discomfort. Keep this card.

©2009. GSI. All rights reserved.
www.diversophy.com

CC-EN-3060

 5 Points

HANDOUT S7.1e

Q   diversiSMARTS

When interacting with people from cultures different from our own, the Golden Rule, "Do unto others as you would have them do unto you," is still the best advice.

True or False?

CC-EN-4007

2 Points

Q   diversiSMARTS

People who speak English as a second language tend to find it easiest to converse with:

A. Other speakers of English as a second language

B. Speakers of Oxford English.

C. Other native born English speakers, such as US Americans, and Australians.

CC-EN-4011

2 Points

A   diversiSMARTS

False. The traditional Golden Rule works to the degree that others are like you. E.g., most people want to be respected by others, but how one culture shows respect can be just the opposite of how another shows it. A cross-cultural "Golden Rule," some call it the "Platinum Rule," might be, "Do unto others as they would have you do unto them."

If you chose the correct answer, keep this card. If not, discard it.

CC-EN-4007

2 Points

A   diversiSMARTS

A. Generally speaking, other speakers of English as a second language, even though they are from different backgrounds. Often native English speakers talk too quickly, use too large a vocabulary and too many slang expressions, and assume the content of their speech is familiar to everyone else.

If you chose the correct answer, keep this card. If not, discard it.

CC-EN-4011

2 Points

A diversiSMARTS

False. This often used strategy usually backfires. Guilt can make people respond in the short term, but in time they are likely to turn against the victim or those who point the finger of guilt against them. Help everyone understand the key issues and their impact on the group, their role in the dynamic, and how they can collaborate.

If you chose the correct answer, keep this card. If not, discard it.

CC-EN-4013

2 Points

A diversiSMARTS

C. People in power oppose them and support a positive climate. Many harassers see the silence of leadership as permission to harass.

If you chose the correct answer, keep this card. If not, discard it.

CC-EN-4034

2 Points

Q diversiSMARTS

One of the most effective ways to benefit groups that are being treated unfairly is to make those you feel are speaking or behaving unfairly feel guilty about what is happening.

True or False?

CC-EN-4013

2 Points

Q diversiSMARTS

Prejudice and harassment in organizations are significantly reduced when:

A. Perpetrators are publicly made to apologize.

B. Particular words are banned in the workplace.

C. People in power oppose them and support a positive climate.

CC-EN-4034

2 Points

HANDOUT S7.1e *(continued)*

A   diversiSMARTS

True. Such a thing is called a "social construct." An example might be "social class," which results in people being seen and treated differently because of the category they are placed in. Another example is "money" whose worth is created by common consent. Much of culture is "socially constructed."

If you chose the correct answer, keep this card. If not, discard it.

2 Points

A   diversiSMARTS

False. While knowledge is needed, the culturally competent person is the one who has developed both the skills and attitudes needed to interact successfully with people of different cultures and even more today with people who have mixed cultural backgrounds.

If you chose the correct answer, keep this card. If not, discard it.

2 Points

Q   diversiSMARTS

Some things can actually become "real" just because people agree to believe in them.

True or False?

2 Points

Q   diversiSMARTS

The shortest road to cultural competence is knowledge of other cultures.

True or False?

2 Points

A diversiSMARTS

B. 20% seems to be the tipping point when the group begins to realize that it is multicultural. Until this point the "different" people are seen as token and rarely affect the culture, its development pattern or its behavior.

If you chose the correct answer, keep this card. If not, discard it.

CC-EN-4041

2 Points

A diversiSMARTS

True. In taking care of themselves in the new environment, the group is likely to recreate and preserve familiar cultural elements in their lives in order to care for themselves. Further, they are likely to be lumped together in the perception of their hosts and seen as a threat, hence slowing their acceptance into the new society.

If you chose the correct answer, keep this card. If not, discard it.

CC-EN-4047

2 Points

Q diversiSMARTS

A group starts to feel and behave in a multicultural way:

A. When 10% of its members are of a different ethnicity or gender.

B. When 20% of its members are of a different ethnicity or gender.

C. Only when 50% of its members are of a different ethnicity or gender.

CC-EN-4041

2 Points

Q diversiSMARTS

When a large number of immigrants from one country or region of the world settle together in a new place, their assimilation is likely to be slower than if they come in small numbers.

True or False?

CC-EN-4047

2 Points

HANDOUT S7.1e *(continued)*

A   **diversiSMARTS**

B. Choosing how to present yourself while simultaneously reading the self presentations of others, a challenging process when working across cultures. C. might be one action in the process and A. might also involve presenting ourselves in the most fitting way, both being examples of the practice of "negotiating identity." Usually unconscious, it is much more conscious in cross cultural interactions and in the virtual world.

If you chose the correct answer, keep this card. If not, discard it.

2 Points

CC-EN-4052

A   **diversiSMARTS**

True. Stress causes us to revert to self and group protective survival thinking strategies. One example of this is how anti-immigrant attitudes are likely to emerge in times of economic crises.

If you chose the correct answer, keep this card. If not, discard it.

2 Points

CC-EN-4066

Q   **diversiSMARTS**

Negotiating identity means:

A. Approaching a foreign government to receive a long-stay visa or a passport.

B. Adjusting one's self presentation in reaction to the self presentations of others one is engaged with.

C. Changing one's name to better fit in a new cultural environment.

2 Points

CC-EN-4052

Q   **diversiSMARTS**

Under stress, people are likely to revert to the values and behaviors of their earliest upbringing as well as engage in stereotyping, prejudice and bias towards outsiders.

True or False?

2 Points

CC-EN-4066

 HANDOUT S7.2

QuickStart
How to play Cultural Competence diversophy®

Read these instructions aloud to your team.

1.   The object is to win as many points as you can for yourself and your team before the game ends. You win points by responding to the cards. Each card's point value is at the bottom left. Keep cards you win. Discard the rest in a pile in the center of the group.

2.   The person to my left starts. Play goes clockwise. When it is your turn take the top card from the pile. Read the card aloud to the group.

   - If you draw a CHOICE or SMARTS card, respond to the question, then turn the card over and read the correct or best answer aloud. Keep or discard the card as instructed.

   - For GUIDE, SHARE and RISK cards, follow the instruction below the question on how to respond. Keep or discard the card as instructed.

3.   If you choose not to respond to a card, another player may volunteer to do so. If no one volunteers, discard the card and lose that turn. If a volunteer responds and carries out the instruction, the next turn still belongs to the person on your left.

4.   When the facilitator ends the game, add up your points. The person with the most points is team champion. The team with the most points wins the game.

Reproduced from: George Simons, "Cultural Competence diversophy®," in *Building Cultural Competence: Innovative Activities and Models,* eds. K. Berardo and D. K. Deardorff (Sterling, VA: Stylus, 2012), 268–295.

43. VIRTUAL CONSTRUCTION SITE: A VIRTUAL TEAM PROBLEM-SOLVING SIMULATION

Rita Wuebbeler

Teams build structures blindly, based on instructions given to them by team members who are sitting back-to-back with them, which simulates the challenges of virtual communication in a multicultural team environment

Key Focus

Build global teams

Type of Activity

Simulation

Objectives

As a result of this activity, participants will

- understand the challenges and opportunities of virtual team communication,
- analyze and appreciate the influence of cultural differences on virtual team communication, and
- create strategies for effective virtual team communication.

Appropriate Audience

Adults

Level of Challenge

Medium

Group Size

8 to 24 people

Time

50 to 60 minutes

Materials

- Sets of Tinkertoys or building blocks (number of sets depends on number of groups) in clear, resealable plastic bags
- Smartphone with a camera

Activity Setup

1. Form teams of four to six players, then divide each of these teams in half. For example, if you have 16 participants, divide them into four teams of four and then divide each team into pairs (e.g., Group A and Group B) so that two pairs play against each other. If you have 20 participants or more than 20, you can make slightly larger teams. It is not important for all teams to be exactly the same size. However, the two groups within each team should be roughly the same size. For example, with 22 participants, have three teams of six and one team of four. The six-person teams will split into trios playing against each other, whereas the team of four will split into pairs.
2. Ask the people in Groups A and B to sit with their backs to each other so no one can see what the other is doing, or, if possible, send one group from each team to another room.
3. Hand each group an identical number of Tinkertoys or building blocks (about 15 to 20).
4. Tell them their task is to design and build a prototype of a new product for their company using the Tinkertoys or building blocks; they must use all the pieces they were given. They are to keep their end product hidden from the other group (if they are in the same room). They have about 15 minutes to think of a design and build their product.

Managing the Activity

1. If they are in the same room, the groups will stay back-to-back for the length of the activity. Make sure one group does not see what the other one is building. You might also ask the groups to keep their conversation low so they don't give away their design.

2. When time is up and both groups have completed their product, tell them to take a photo (or several) of it (or draw it), disassemble it, and put the pieces back in the plastic bag. If the groups worked in separate rooms, call everyone back into one room and have them sit back-to-back.

3. Tell them they have just joined a new design team and half of their colleagues are in a remote location. They are charged with building the prototype for a new product for their company (if you don't want to use a corporate context, think of another story), and they will get the building instructions verbally.

4. Tell Group A to give Group B exact instructions on how to assemble the product they have designed and constructed (participants are still sitting with their backs to their colleagues). They cannot tell the other group what the design is (e.g., a lamp, a table, a car), but they can refer to the photo or their drawing. Group B has 10 minutes to complete the task. Have group members put the finished product to the side.

5. Tell Group B to do the same with Group A.

6. When both groups are finished building, invite them to the big unveiling in which both groups show their designs and compare them to the photos or the drawings of the originals.

Debriefing the Activity

After participants have had a chance to reveal and discuss their completed products, facilitate a discussion with questions such as the following:

1. What happened?
2. How did you accomplish your task? What steps did you follow?
3. How did sitting back-to-back with your counterparts and not being able to see what they were doing affect your performance?
4. How did you change or adjust your communication style while sitting back-to-back?
5. What does this activity teach you about virtual communication?
6. What role did cultural differences play in this activity? If so, what were the differences?
7. What was helpful in accomplishing your goal? What was a challenge?
8. What did this activity remind you of?
9. What did you learn from this activity?
10. How might your learning influence or change your behavior with your remote colleagues in the future?

Key Insights and Learnings

The groups discover what has meaning for them, but typical insights and themes that emerge include the following:

- Virtual team communication is challenging.
- Culture and personal styles affect how we approach virtual communication.
- Creativity and flexibility help.
- The lack of visual clues can significantly affect the efficacy of the communication process; people should use video conferencing more.
- Having clear roles and a clear process enables better communication.
- Trust is foundational; without it on either side, things break down.
- Participants from culturally diverse backgrounds can bring a broader range of perspectives to the table, or they can slow down the communication process. Usually, having strategies like using similar terminology are helpful to ensure that the diversity of the group is a strength rather than a limitation.
- Language differences can play a role in the communication process and need to be considered if team members' first languages are different.

Variations

Variation 1. Increase the complexity of the activity by providing a larger number of pieces for the designs.

Variation 2. Making the groups slightly larger results in a more complex team in which team dynamics of leadership, followership, and so forth come into play.

Variation 3. Ask the teams to think of a creative name for their product and give it to their counterparts before they start building. Later ask them how having a name for their creation affected their strategy and what assumptions the other group made based on the name of the product.

Facilitation Tips and Suggestions

- It is advisable to keep things fairly simple so the participants have a positive virtual communication experience instead of feeling frustrated by a task too hard to accomplish.
- This activity also works with Legos. Whatever type of building toy is used, make sure there are at least 10 to 15 pieces that one can use to build a relatively simple, recognizable object in about 5 to 10 minutes. The advantage of Tinkertoys or something similar is that the

pieces are different in color and shape and can be assembled in a variety of ways. The more versatile the toys and the more versatile they are to assemble the better.

About This Exercise

I use this activity with intact teams that work across cultural and geographic boundaries using predominantly virtual communication tools such as e-mail, phones, or web meetings to accomplish their tasks. I have also used it with participants in open-enrollment classes on managing a virtual workforce or managing global virtual teams. Credit goes to my friend and diversity trainer and consultant Cynthia East, who first introduced me to using Tinkertoys in multicultural team training and to George Simons, who uses a different version of the back-to-back exercise in his global virtual team programs.

44. TEAM SIMULATION

David Goddard

This simulation can be used in various sizes of groups to help participants realize the impact of culture on teamwork and develop strategies to work efficiently in diverse teams.

Key Focus

Build global teams

Type of Activity

Simulation

Objectives

As a result of this activity participants will

- heighten their cross-cultural awareness and sensitivity in the workplace,
- recognize the impact culture has on the way we work, and
- develop strategies for efficient multicultural teamwork.

Appropriate Audience

Adults

Level of Challenge

Medium

Group Size

12 to 60 people

Time

90 minutes

Materials

- Flip charts and markers for each team
- Handout

Preparation

Prepare teamwork instructions for each team, customized to their interests and needs (see Handout S7.3 for examples).

Activity Setup

1. Organize participants into teams of 5 to 10, selected on the basis of their common cultural background such as professional, generational, geographical (e.g., high- or low-context cultures, individualist or collectivist cultures, or high-power distance or low-power distance cultures).
2. Select three to five people who will be observers and provide feedback on the simulation.

Managing the Activity

1. Give teams an identifying name (Number 1, 2, 3, or red, blue, green, etc.) and tell them they have five minutes for team building that they can use in any way they wish prior to being given a task shortly.
2. During these five minutes, tell the observers

   - they are going to watch and give feedback on a teamwork simulation. The teams have been selected on the basis of a common cultural background that should affect how they work together as a team. The observers' task is to observe differences in teamwork styles and provide feedback at the end of the exercise.
   - halfway through the teamwork task the facilitator will move two or three people from each team into another team, thus changing the team composition from monocultural to multicultural. The observers' task is to watch and provide feedback on what

happens after this job rotation. Specifically, ask the observers to make notes on three issues:

- How do participants react to the task, look for differences between the teams?
- How do participants carry out the task, look for differences between the teams?
- What happens after the job rotation? How does it change the dynamics in each team? Does it have a positive or negative impact on the teamwork? Are new members successfully integrated? Do they try to change the working practices of the team they join?

3. Go back to the teams, bringing the observers along, and give each team the task instructions. Each team gets the same task and the same instructions. Instructions can be in writing and the task is to produce a design for an exhibition space representing the team's organization, company, department, or institution at a fair or expo. Teams have 30 minutes for the task.

4. After 15 minutes, when the teams are well into their tasks, invite two or three participants from each team to move to another team. Tell them it is part of a new corporate initiative on job rotation, and they have been selected to work elsewhere in the organization.

5. At the end of the 30 minutes, ask participants to finish up. Allow them a couple of extra minutes to complete what they are doing and to decide how they would like to present their work to the other teams. During the last few minutes of the simulation bring the observers together for a moment so they can swap notes and decide how they will present their feedback.

6. Let teams take turns to present in two or three minutes the output from their work. Ask for a round of applause for each team's presentation, but don't make any comments at this stage.

Debriefing the Activity

Ask participants how it felt to carry out this task. In particular, ask about the job rotation and how it felt

for participants who moved from one team to another. What happened? Ask the teams they left or joined how they felt, and what they felt happened. Sometimes people make very strong statements, such as, "I felt I had gone to another planet," "I didn't feel comfortable leaving my team," "It was chaos in their team when I got there," "I was made very welcome and immediately felt able to contribute," or "They ignored me, I couldn't find a way into the team."

Get feedback from the observers, prompting them as necessary:

- Did you notice any differences in the way each team reacted to the task?
- What differences did you notice in working styles between the teams?
- What happened when people were moved into other teams?
- How did the group dynamic change?

Encourage the observers to keep the feedback constructive. Generally the observers find very strong differences between the teams and do not need much prompting. Peer feedback is very powerful, so don't lead.

If all has gone well, the facilitator shouldn't need to offer too much feedback, although often participants and observers have concentrated on the actual task so much they miss a couple of things, for example, the output from the task and the way it is presented are both often strongly influenced by (the original) cultural composition of the team.

The following are some follow-up questions for the whole group:

- How was the simulation similar to or different from real life?
- What did the simulation teach you about intercultural interaction?
- What actions should participants take at the organizational, team, and individual levels to ensure efficient intercultural collaboration and teamwork?

Key Insights and Learnings

- Culture has a strong impact on the way people work.
- Teams develop a distinctive cultural style very quickly.

- When someone from a different cultural background joins the team it affects the team dynamics.
- The impact of this diversity can be creative or chaotic, producing synergy or disharmony.
- For productive teamwork to take place team members need to make adaptations to different cultural styles.
- Cross-cultural collaboration does not take place automatically; rather it takes active work, mindfully and purposefully.

Variations

Variation 1. Team tasks should be relevant to participants' backgrounds, for example, keeping in mind the employer's image for corporate groups or the university's image for academic groups.

Variation 2. If the focus is on collaboration, a variation would be to merge entire teams in the middle of the task, rather than just swap a couple of participants among the teams.

Facilitation Tips and Suggestions

- Try to make the original teams as culturally similar as possible.
- Don't overbrief the observers, such as telling them too much about what they are likely to see.
- Make sure the observers are not making judgmental criticism of the teams.

- Don't interfere with the team tasks after the teams have been given the instructions, let the simulation unfold on its own but keep a careful eye on the time, ask teams for a time check every now and then to ensure they keep to the 30-minute limit.
- Always begin the debriefing by listening to the participants first and then the observers.
- Ensure you have enough time after the simulation to debrief the group thoroughly and discuss how participants can apply the learning to their own organization, department, or institute.
- This simulation is especially suited for any cultural setting in which people work in teams—corporate, academic, institutional.

About This Exercise

I came up with the idea 10 years ago when working at a company that wanted an activity that would illustrate the different behavioral styles of the three cultural types of the Lewis model (2005). The simulation was refined for use at the World Bank in train the trainer sessions and to over 1,000 participants.

REFERENCE

Lewis, R. (2005). *When cultures collide: Leading across cultures* (3rd ed.). Boston, MA: Nicholas Brealey.

HANDOUT S7.3

EXAMPLE TEMPLATES OF TEAM INSTRUCTIONS

The World Bank has decided to exhibit at a World Expo taking place in Hawaii next year. Your team has been selected as the design committee that must come up with the idea of how to fill the exhibition space. The theme for the exhibit is "The Intercultural Nature of the World Bank." You should produce a mockup of the design (not just a verbal presentation). You have 30 minutes. Use any materials you can find. At the end of 30 minutes be prepared to make a short presentation (2 or 3 minutes) of your ideas.

Your company will be exhibiting at a diversity expo taking place in Hawaii next month. Your team has been selected to design an exhibit booth for the expo. The theme of the expo is "Developing Human Capital in the Workplace." The theme of your exhibit is "Cultural Diversity in Your Company." The objective is to demonstrate the multicultural nature of your company. Delegates at the expo will come from around the world.

    You should produce a mockup of the design. Use any materials you can find. You have 30 minutes. At the end of 30 minutes, please be ready to make a short (maximum 3 minutes) presentation including some kind of a visual.

The Turku Region Development Foundation would like to attract the best talent in the world to join the dynamic workforce of southeast Finland. The foundation will be exhibiting at an employers fair for university graduates taking place in Paris next month. Your team has been selected to design the stand for the fair.

    Your stand should represent Turku as offering interesting and inspiring challenges for an international working environment. How would Turku be attractive to young talent?

    You must produce a visual representation of the stand. Use any materials you can find. You have 30 minutes. At the end of 30 minutes, please be ready to make a short presentation (maximum 3 minutes) on your design.

Reproduced from: David Goddard, "Team Simulation," in *Building Cultural Competence: Innovative Activities and Models,* eds. K. Berardo and D. K. Deardorff (Sterling, VA: Stylus, 2012), 299–302.

45. MARKET EXPANSION

Monika Chutnik and Marta Nowicka

Various leadership styles are differently received depending on the cultural backgrounds of team members and the country where the team is based. This exercise makes it possible to experience reactions to different leadership styles and to understand them depending on one's own and the team's cultural setup.

Key Focus

Build global teams

Type of Activity

Simulation

Objectives

As a result of this activity, participants will

- understand how culture influences the preferred way of leading a team,
- understand and experience different perceptions of leadership styles depending on their own cultural backgrounds,
- experience different leadership styles present across cultures, and
- become more flexible in a multicultural team setting.

Appropriate Audience

Adults

Level of Challenge

Medium

Group Size

10 plus people

Time

60 minutes

Materials

Handout

Preparation

Participants should have an understanding of different leadership styles and culture dimensions for this exercise. Provide participants with this overview if it has not been covered elsewhere in a program.

Activity Setup

1. Divide the group into an even number of smaller teams, ideally five to seven people each.
2. Set the scene by saying: "You are working in a company manufacturing exclusive writing tools. You have recently received an award for the best design of your products. In business for 10 years already, you are now a leading company in the national market. You have been considering going international."
3. Talk about the task (see Handout S7.4): "Your company is about to start expanding to a foreign market. Your task will be to prepare a detailed plan of the activities of your team for the coming three months. You will have 20 to 25 minutes to complete the plan."
4. The facilitator assigns team roles at random (the roles are one leader and one observer per team, the rest are employees) or the team members pick their roles themselves.
5. Give participants a copy of the handout, which describes their roles. Make sure half the teams receive the leader and team instructions from the handouts marked with (A), and the

other teams receive the instructions marked with (B).

Managing the Activity

1. Give participants 10 to 15 minutes to work in their groups.
2. After 10 to 15 minutes, switch the leaders of two teams: The leader from a team with instructions A takes the place of the leader of a team with instructions B. At this point, the facilitator could say: "There has been an organizational change. You are getting a new project leader."
3. Let the groups continue 10 more minutes with their new leaders.
4. At the end of this period, have observers briefly share their observations (allowing two to three minutes each).

Debriefing the Activity

1. The group listens to the observers' report.
2. Ask the following debriefing questions:

   - What happened? How was it for you to work in the team before the change in leaders?
   - To what extent do you personally associate with your role?
   - How did you perceive the change?
   - What happened after the leader exchange?
   - What reactions appeared after the leader exchange?
   - How did you react to the changed leadership style? What did you do? What were you saying? What did you hear others saying?

3. Ask the leaders the following questions:

   - How did the group behave when you started working? What worked well?
   - What did not work? What could have been the reason?
   - How did you react to the leader exchange?
   - What first steps did you take with the new group? How did your actions reflect your assigned leadership style?
   - How did the group react to you as the new leader?

   - What did you do in return? What helped you? What were some obstacles?

4. Finally, focus the debriefing on organizational structure, values, and leadership styles by asking the following:

   - Have you experienced a situation of this kind in your professional life? If so, what lessons did you learn in that particular situation that are transferrable to other similar situations?
   - Where do you think such a situation is most likely to occur?
   - What can be done to adapt one's communication and leadership styles to different situations?
   - What can you personally do if you are in such a situation in real life? What lessons can you apply, especially as you work with those from different backgrounds?
   - What insights can you gain and use from participating in this activity?

Key Insights and Learnings

- Various leadership styles are culturally conditioned.
- No leadership style is better or worse than another.
- Adaptation and communication skills are required if one changes his or her leadership style or starts working with people from a different cultural background.
- Adaptation and communication are necessary elements of intercultural competence.

Variations

Variation 1. In this version, there are no leader exchanges. The groups share their experience from inside their own team with the whole group.

Variation 2. For specific groups, the task description itself can be adjusted, for example, for financial controllers: "Identify key features of a new finance system you are going to purchase for the whole company"; for teachers: "Create a new curriculum for your students."

Variation 3. In a culturally mixed group, divide the participants into teams according to cultural origin and then ideally let someone from a different background be involved in the leader exchange. In the debriefing, try to uncover and highlight any visible cultural patterns. It can be useful to explore perceptions of leadership (i.e., what worked, what didn't) before and after the leader exchange. Be careful not to have the leaders feel exposed or embarrassed during the discussion of leadership styles.

Facilitation Tips and Suggestions

- While debriefing, connect participants' observations and insights to relevant cultural dimensions and leadership styles. For example, the facilitator can explore power distance distribution among countries—people from cultures with higher power distance measures will likely prefer a more autocratic style (instructions A), while those from low distance cultures would likely prefer a more facilitative leadership style (instructions B).
- This exercise can open a good discussion on the culture(s) and structure(s) of the participants' organization, and provide a forum to discuss organizational change and strategic thinking. This can be done following the debriefing with questions such as:

  - How would you describe the preferred leadership style in your organization (can be a mixture or a way between the two styles from the exercise)?
  - How many layers are there between an individual contributor and an executive? What message about the organizational culture do these layers send to a newcomer?
  - What are official organizational messages, and how do those messages reflect various

layers of culture (national culture, organizational culture, departmental culture)?
  - What can we do if we have a multicultural organization whose leaders represent various cultures? What would be the right way to do something? Who is to decide? How can a team influence that decision?

- The role of observer is important; the observer should be able to record specific sentences and behaviors.
- Extend the time for working in groups to reduce the pressure.
- This exercise works well for large groups. The only requirement is an even number of groups since there are two leadership styles in this activity. For example, if a leader with a certain style switches to a group with the same style, no change would be noticed by the group members.
- This exercise can be used in a number of contexts: culture differences and values, differences in organizational culture, differences in leadership styles, and reaction to change.

About This Exercise

While working in teams run by leaders from different cultures, we experienced situations in which we had to adjust to different leadership styles. Frequently, we were finding that some leadership styles were more or less appropriate to the cultural environment of the team. We used our conclusions from these experiences to create the Market Expansion exercise. Outcomes of this exercise prove to be especially valuable for working with teams or leaders in multinational organizations or those preparing to merge with another company, acquire a new big business partner, and so on.

 HANDOUT S7.4

MARKET EXPANSION

Observer sheet

The task of the group is to prepare a detailed plan of the activities of the team for the coming three months.

Please observe the group carefully. Please note any specific behaviors you observe and any specific words or sentences you hear.

The following questions will help you make good observations.

How did the group behave when they started working?

What worked well?

What did not work?

What were the first steps the new leader took in the new group?

What reactions appeared after the leader exchange?

How did the group members react to the leader exchange? What did they do? What were they saying?

(A) Instructions for the leader

You are working in a company manufacturing exclusive writing tools. You have recently been awarded for the best style of your products. In business for 10 years already, you are now a leading company in the national market. You have been considering going international.

Your company is about to start an expansion to a foreign market. Your task will be to prepare a detailed plan of the activities of your team for the coming 3 months.

You are the leader of the team. As a leader, your role is to make sure that tasks are well divided among team members and that the good balance in the group is kept. You expect your decisions to be respected. As you are the most senior person in the team, you are to be addressed with respect. Your decisions will not be questioned as the team members trust your professionalism completely.

You are patient and ready to take sufficient time in order to get the desired results.

(B) Instructions for the leader

You are working in a company manufacturing exclusive writing tools. You have recently been awarded for the best style of your products. In business for 10 years already, you are now a leading company in the national market. You have been considering going international.

Your company is about to start an expansion to a foreign market. Your task will be to prepare a detailed plan of the activities of your team for the coming 3 months.

You are the leader of the team. Your team consists of highly skilled individuals who are highly committed to work on the project. As a leader, you need to make space for their opinions to be expressed and to meet to identify the best solution possible. It is a usual thing that a team member will be questioning your opinion if their expertise would suggest a different course of action. You seek contrasting options in order to understand all the different points of view from within your team.

Not everyone needs to be happy with the final solution selected. Above all, you and your team need to be efficient and ready to face any competition in a timely manner so as not to lose out to the competition. In case something is unclear, you need to be informed directly and you also use direct feedback toward your team members. Clarity and openness are what matter most.

(A) Instructions for a team member

You are working in a company manufacturing exclusive writing tools. You have recently been awarded for the best style of your products. In business for 10 years already, you are now a leading company in the national market. You have been considering going international.

Your company is about to start an expansion to a foreign market. Your task will be to prepare a detailed plan of the activities of your team for the coming 3 months.

As a member of the team, you are observant and open to the situation of the others. The task is as important as the harmony in the group. Your leader is the most senior person in the team and you trust his or her professionalism completely. You accept any decision or suggestion which is made by your leader. You address your leader with appropriate respect.

You are patient and ready to take sufficient time in order to achieve the desired results.

(B) Instructions for a team member

You are working in a company manufacturing exclusive writing tools. You have recently been awarded for the best style of your products. In business for 10 years already, you are now a leading company in the national market. You have been considering going international.

Your company is about to start an expansion to a foreign market. Your task will be to prepare a detailed plan of the activities of your team for the coming 3 months.

As a member of the team, you are aware that your personal contribution matters and will be acknowledged in a performance review later. You will do your best to make sure that you have enough space to share your expertise. It is quite natural that your colleagues have different opinions and together with the leader you will choose the best option. Not everyone needs to be happy with the final solution selected. In case something is unclear, you need to be informed directly and you also use direct feedback toward your team members. Clarity and openness are what matters most.

Your leader is here to support you and to provide enough space for every team member to share his or her perspective and expertise on the team. Above all, you and your team need to be efficient and ready to face any competition in a timely manner so as not to lose out to the competition.

SECTION 8

Resolve Differences

46. TOOL: A 360 DEGREE VIEW ON CULTURAL DILEMMAS

Kate Berardo

This tool helps people solve complex intercultural challenges in a structured, holistic way. It provides a clear process and set of questions to reach more effective and appropriate solutions.

Key Focus

Resolve differences

Type of Activity

Tool

Objectives

As a result of this activity, participants will learn to

- look at challenging intercultural situations holistically,
- identify contextual elements beyond sheer cultural differences that affect dilemmas, and
- develop more effective strategies for resolving challenging intercultural situations.

Appropriate Audience

Adults

Level of Challenge

Medium

Group Size

2 to 50 people

Time

60 to 90 minutes

Materials

Handouts

Activity Setup

1. Set up the activity by telling participants the following:

   - Often when we are facing cultural dilemmas, we lose our perspective of the bigger picture and of potential avenues to aid us in establishing how to move forward in a relationship or situation.
   - Rarely is a dilemma purely a cultural one. Other factors like personalities, histories, and the general environment affect a

situation, so we need to take these into consideration. (These points can also be mentioned to the group by holding a short discussion on what makes solving cultural dilemmas challenging.)

2. Pass out copies of the 360 degree tool (see Handout S8.1) and offer it as a framework to look holistically at cross-cultural situations, and appreciate the inherent complexity of dilemmas to enable us to reach our desired outcomes.

The goal during this session is to show participants how to use the 360 degree view tool and apply it to their own situations.

Managing the Activity

1. After setting up the activity, begin by having people document a current challenging intercultural situation (often some form of conflict) they are facing with another individual. (If they cannot think of a current example, have them choose a past situation.) Ask people to record the situation in the first box of Handout S8.1, Mapping a 360 Degree View of an Intercultural Challenge.
2. Then have them identify and describe what success would look like in the situation, filling out the second box of the same handout.
3. Distribute Handout S8.2, Gaining a 360 Degree View of an Intercultural Challenge, and tell them these questions can serve as a structured means to look more holistically at a situation. Explain the worksheet and then allow people some time (and ideally, a quiet space) to reflect on and analyze their situations.
4. Once individuals have completed their analyses, have people pair up to discuss their findings with each other and share strategies.

Debriefing the Activity

Bring the group back together and conduct a general debriefing on the process:

1. Have one or two people share their scenarios and their next steps. Compare and contrast the different situations and solutions generated by the group.

2. Then facilitate a general discussion using the following questions:

   - What was the impact of taking this holistic focus?
   - What factors were you not originally thinking about that the 360 degree view revealed?
   - What was the impact of discussing the situation with someone else?
   - What else did you learn through the process?

3. Explore the value of the tool itself by asking the following:

   - What does it take to work effectively with this tool?
   - How can it be useful to you moving forward?

4. End the activity by adding your own reflections and insights.

Key Insights and Learnings

1. Taking a structured approach in complex intercultural situations can help prevent us from spinning around a situation or getting stuck in analysis paralysis.
2. By looking at the factors in a situation such as the stakeholders, history, values, climate, and organizational structure, we can generate more effective and expansive solutions that may not otherwise be obvious.
3. Keeping a balanced focus on potential barriers (e.g., different communication styles, history of problem encounters) and potential enablers (e.g., shared values, common acquaintances you both trust) is important to find well-rounded solutions for moving forward.
4. Stopping to reflect on your own motivations and your own role in challenging intercultural situations is important.
5. Sharing our situations with others is often revealing; others see things from a different perspective and can therefore offer good insight on how to move forward in a challenging situation.
6. The 360 degree view tool allows us to take into account the natural complexity of working across cultures by highlighting and orga-

nizing all the various influencing factors rather than ignoring them or oversimplifying them.

7. It gives us clarity on the information we need and questions we need answered to move forward and therefore confidence in what our next steps should be.

8. The more you work with the tool, the more you will naturally start to look between, within, behind, to others, and around when faced with a challenging situation.

Variations

Variation 1. As an alternative introduction, share a personal example of a challenge you faced working across cultures. Use a flip chart or a board to display and fill out the 360 degree mapping tool (replicating what is in the handout). As you describe the various elements in the situation, fill in the various boxes of the mapping tool (a second facilitator can write while you talk if you are working in pairs). Have the group ask you questions from Handout S8.2 and essentially coach you through the situation. Then highlight the different forces that could be enabling and restraining the situation, and ask the participants what they think the best solution would be. This enables everyone to work with the same case from the beginning and familiarize themselves with the tool before they apply it to their own situation.

Variation 2. This exercise can also be conducted in pairs who coach one another. Give each person 15 minutes to describe the situation to his or her partner, and then the other person asks questions to help explore the various forces at play and identify next steps. Once the pair have completed their analysis for one of them, they then switch to the other person's situation. This approach can be powerful, because talking through these types of situations with others is often very revealing and useful.

Facilitation Tips and Suggestions

- This exercise is a high-order, challenging exercise. It should be introduced toward the end of a program when individuals have learned the basics about cultural dynamics (such as key cultural differences) and once they are more comfortable talking about their own situations.

- Especially in group settings, remind participants they are committed to confidentiality to one another, which helps to ensure participants' willingness to talk about their own situations.

- Many individuals recognize the need to have subsequent conversations with the other individual they are in conflict with. When this is the case, consider having individuals use role playing as their next step so people can practice the conversations they will have in real life.

About This Exercise

The inspiration for this tool came from an early experience I had working in Japan that taught me that most intercultural challenges are complex and not solely influenced by culture. I was also influenced by the work of Kurt Lewin and his Force Field Analysis. While our field is rich in content that helps people become aware of cultural differences, there are fewer resources to help people solve intercultural situations, especially in a structured holistic way. This tool was developed to help fill that void.

 HANDOUT S8.1

MAPPING A 360 DEGREE VIEW OF AN INTERCULTURAL CHALLENGE

The Task: Gain clarity on a challenging situation you are facing by taking a structured approach to looking at the situation.

Instructions:

1. Describe a current situation you are facing with another individual that is challenging you. Include who is involved and a few key details about the challenge you are facing.
2. Document what success looks like in the situation.
3. Use Gaining a 360 Degree View of an Intercultural Challenge (see Handout S8.2) to map out various potentially influencing factors in the situation. Record your thoughts, questions, and insights in the space provided here.
4. Identify your next steps to move toward a successful resolution of the situation.

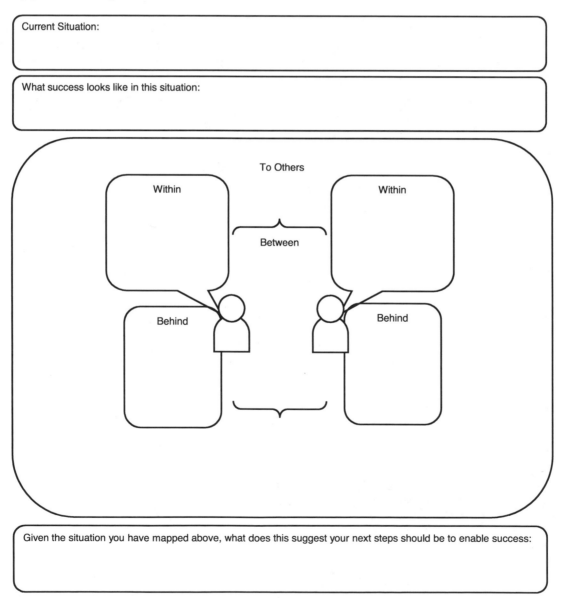

Reproduced from: Kate Berardo, "Tool: A 360 Degree View on Cultural Dilemmas," in *Building Cultural Competence: Innovative Activities and Models,* eds. K. Berardo and D. K. Deardorff (Sterling, VA: Stylus, 2012), 311–315.

📄 HANDOUT S8.2

GAINING A 360 DEGREE VIEW OF AN INTERCULTURAL CHALLENGE

The Task: Use the following questions to help you look at an intercultural challenge with a 360 degree view, in other words between, within, behind, around the situation, and how it looks to others. Keep a balanced focus on potential barriers (e.g., different communication styles, history of problem encounters) and potential enablers (e.g., shared values, common acquaintances you both trust) as you think through your situation.

Note: Knowing the answer to all these questions is not essential; part of the value should be in thinking through what *might be* influencing the situation and also identifying *how* you can find out more about the potential influence of some factors.

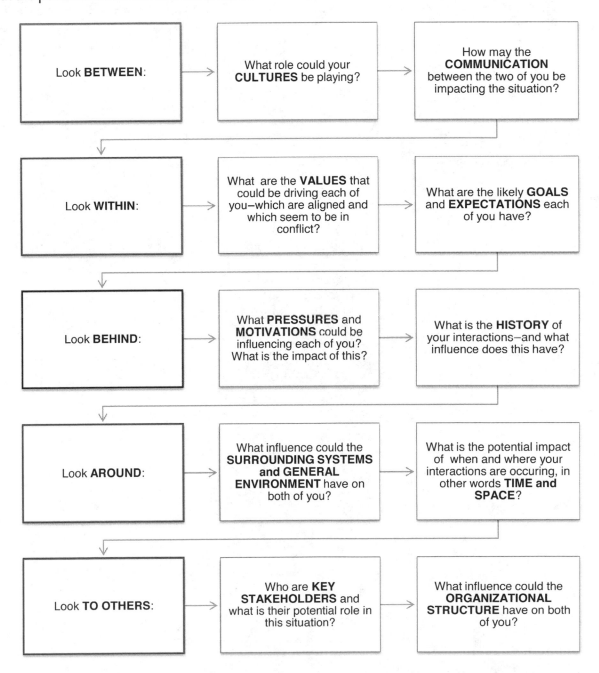

Reproduced from: Kate Berardo, "Tool: A 360 Degree View on Cultural Dilemmas," in *Building Cultural Competence: Innovative Activities and Models,* eds. K. Berardo and D. K. Deardorff (Sterling, VA: Stylus, 2012), 311–315.

47. FRAMEWORK: MULTICULTURAL COMPASS MODEL: A TOOL FOR NAVIGATING MULTICULTURAL SPACE

Jacqueline Wasilewski

The Multicultural Compass (see Figure S8.1) is a conceptual tool to help people decide how to behave when they have to choose between culturally marked behaviors.

Key Focus

Resolve differences

Objectives

As a result of working with this model, participants will

- know the six possible choices available to someone faced with choosing between culturally marked behaviors in a given cultural context, and
- be able to choose the most effective behavior (as in allowing people to continue toward their goals) for a particular context based on four guidelines.

Appropriate Audience

Adults, teenagers, children

Level of Challenge

Medium

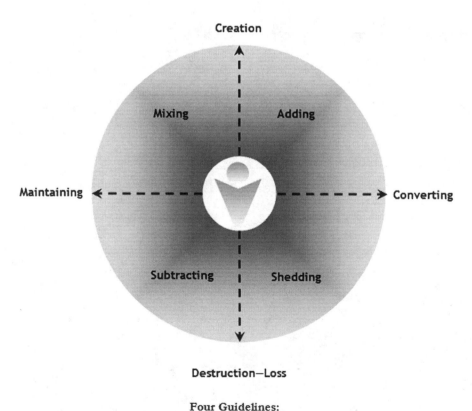

Creation

Mixing   Adding

Maintaining ← → Converting

Subtracting   Shedding

Destruction–Loss

Four Guidelines:
* Goals   * Context   * Choice   * Continuation

FIGURE S8.1   The Multicultural Compass

Summary Description

In the globalized networked world of the 21st century, even if we stay at home, we are faced with cultural choices. Sometimes these new choices come to us via TV, the Internet, or some other medium. Sometimes these new choices come to us via newcomers to our home environments. Sometimes we encounter them because we leave our homes and sojourn elsewhere in the world. And sometimes we are faced with cultural choices because we embody a multicultural heritage and have a diverse set of relatives, directing us to go in different directions simultaneously.

When faced with these options, when do we keep on behaving the way we have always behaved or are presently behaving? When do we adapt to another way and adopt a new behavior? Are there other choices?

A culturally marked behavior makes a cultural difference. Do we eat our meals with our hands, with *ohashi* (chopsticks in Japanese) or a fork? Which set of spiritual practices should we follow? Should we greet each other with a bow, by shaking hands, with a kiss on the cheek? In which language should we say hello? Is it okay for women and girls to go out by themselves? Is public bathing modest?

As we move about the globe, we are constantly faced with these kinds of choices. The Multicultural Compass identifies six kinds of choices, options, or directions we can move in when we are faced with having to choose how to behave; they are maintaining, converting, adding, subtracting, mixing, and creating. These directions are based on an analysis of 192 life histories, autobiographies, and autobiographical novels and the kinds of choices diverse urban and rural dwellers, sojourners, migrants, immigrants, refugees, and their descendants made when faced with having to make these kinds of decisions.

Key Talking Points

- Maintaining/sticking with the familiar means not changing one's behavior or staying with one's first or current behavior. To use a linguistic example, this would mean that if English is one's first language, one just keeps on speaking English and does not learn any other language. If a person speaks a global language like English, this might be a workable choice (although this could blind the person to the privilege it entails), but if one's first language is Lithuanian, such a choice

limits one's interactions to a very small linguistic community. However, sometimes concentrating on maintaining one's first language is really important, especially if one comes from a community, like many Native Americans, whose languages are in danger of disappearing. Some communities have selected some individuals to remain linguistically pure to preserve the language. This may not be the optimal choice for the individual, but it may be the optimal choice for the long-term identity maintenance and welfare of the entire community. Thus, whether a choice is effective depends on one's goals.

- Converting /assimilation means giving up one's first behavior completely and replacing it with another. To continue with the linguistic example, it means stopping to speak English at all and using another language, say, Chinese, all the time. Converting or assimilation is usually the result of power dynamics in the larger world, where converting or assimilating is supposed to give one better access to the dominant culture's goods. In the Western Hemisphere this has been the preferred choice ever since the Europeans arrived and became dominant. They also struggled over which group of Europeans and which languages should be dominant where. These struggles continue in domestic U.S. politics today. In addition, in giving up one's diversity, the dominant cultural world is also impoverished. For instance, by insisting on an English-only education system, we have turned potentially bi- and multilingual children into monolingual adults, when given the immigrant roots of most people in the United States, we could have been a population who could speak to most of the people of the world in their own languages.

- Adding means adding other behaviors to existing ones, that is, expanding one's repertoire of behaviors. Linguistically, one keeps on speaking English where appropriate, but learns Chinese, Spanish, and Hindi to communicate with people outside a person's first linguistic community and uses each language in the appropriate context. This is the most common choice of skilled intermulticulturalists. It also maintains maximum choice in the human community. However, sometimes this choice is complicated to implement. If one is becoming bilingual and biliterate, for instance, in French and Spanish, this is rather easy. Both are alphabetic languages, and they belong to the same linguistic family. However, becoming bilingual and biliterate in English and Japanese is more complicated. One is an alphabetic language, and one is not, and they belong to totally different linguistic families. Even the reasons for opening one's mouth to say something are totally different. So, sometimes we cannot implement our ideal choice, but we can still approximate it. One individual cannot learn all the world's languages, but we can learn to speak, read, and write two or three, maybe speak a couple of others, and in specific contexts understand yet others. For instance, traditional Aborigines in Australia all grew up in bilingual families because husbands and wives came from different groups. People were monolingual for speaking but bi- and multilingual for listening. So we may not be able to implement our ideal choice, but the goal of maximum participation and inclusion can always be approximated.

- Subtracting/destruction, loss/shedding means giving up a behavior and not replacing it with anything. Subtracting is usually not a free choice. It is usually the result of oppression, but making this choice has often been necessary for survival. Subtracting means, for example, ceasing to speak one's first language but not immediately replacing it with any other language. In the United States, Native American children who were kidnapped by government officers and sent to government boarding schools to be detribalized were forced into this option. They were forbidden to speak their tribal languages at school, even with their friends, and were physically punished if they did so. Many were in this languageless state for three or more years while learning English. It left deep psychological scars. Shedding on the other hand, indicates a free choice rather than a forced one. In the life histories this compass is based on, the most common cultural element that was shed in the United States was religion, although sometime later in life a person sometimes acquired another spiritual orientation (conversion) or

returned to his or her original spiritual tradition (maintenance). This subtractive choice is extremely connected to the power dynamics going on at the societal level, and sometimes it involves the almost total destruction and loss of one's original culture, as in the institution of slavery in the United States. This option is always closely connected to societywide power dynamics. However, this forced choice at one point in history is also strangely connected to the creative choice described later.

- Mixing/synthesis means taking one strand of behavior from one cultural context and another strand of behavior from another cultural context and creating a new one. This is often the preferred choice in times of rapid societal change. It is much easier to recombine existing behaviors than to invent totally new ones. Every lingua franca is the result of such mixing or synthesis of diverse linguistic elements to create, relatively rapidly, a widely intelligible means of communication. We also do this very often in the realms of food and music. We combine different gastronomic traditions (Tex-Mex food of the Texas/Mexican borderlands) and different musical traditions (jazz) to create new things that taste good and sound good. Maybe not doing this in the realm of politics is simply a failure of imagination.

- Creating means creating totally new human behavior for new circumstances. It is always difficult to separate innovation from creation. For example, chop suey was invented in the Western United States by Chinese cooks for railroad workers. It consisted of U.S. ingredients cooked in a Chinese way. When does a simple novel combination (as in mixing or synthesis) become creation as in current fusion cuisines worldwide? True creation is a little difficult to do at this point in time with four billion plus of us on this planet, but it is still necessary and possible from time to time. English was once a lingua franca that eventually became a separate language. The Chinese ideograms were created so Chinese administrators could manage a multilingual empire. In the present, how do we create human spaces in which we can all be ourselves together? In Malaysia, for instance, when citizens from different communities, Indian Hindus, Malay Muslims, and Chinese Taoist-Buddhists-Confucians gather to share a meal, a protocol has been created that consists of two simple rules: Everyone should have something to eat, and nothing that would be offensive to anyone present should be served. Currently, the most active area of cultural creation globally is in the realm of all kinds of human behavior associated with the Internet.

Suggested Uses

This model can be used

- with participants of all ages,
- in any educational, training or therapeutic context,
- when participants are struggling with how to choose between culturally marked behaviors,
- when participants are trying to maintain a sense of personal authenticity, and
- when participants may have to explain contested behavioral decisions to important others in their interpersonal networks

This model was derived from and used in Native American, African American, Hispanic American, and Asian American communities in the United States where multiculturalism is not a choice but a matter of survival. It has also been extensively used in Japan with third culture kids and their families, international students, and Japanese students who want to lead international lives, that is, they want to become multicultural by choice as the result of an enrichment process, not in order to survive (Wasilewski, 1982).

This model has most often been used as part of a self-reflective process in which participants examine the directions they and the members of their families and peer groups have chosen across time and space (see Handouts S8.3 and S8.4). Sometimes this has involved participants who are in the midst of some kind of inter- or multicultural experience for the first time, and sometimes this has involved participants who come from a generations-long inter- or multicultural experience. If the participants are young children I often introduce the exercise with my mother's experience of having to switch hands when using her fork depending on whether she was eating at home (left hand, European style) or at school (right hand, American style). Her father and her teachers thought

the other way was eating like a farmer, while their own way was good table manners. With teenagers the introductory example could be about dating. With adults the example could be about gender expectations. But for each age group, the example is simply a warm-up to enable each participant to reflect on his or her own experience. The results of the reflection can be shared with other participants in the group or serve as the basis of a self-reflective essay to be handed in.

Typical Questions and Two Additional Points

- *Isn't this range of options rather obvious?* Not if you are in the middle of choosing across all dimensions of your behavior. For example, I come from a multicultural family that carried seven different lines of history. When I was 10 years old and trying to please all my relatives it would have been very handy to have this conceptual model so I could have been aware of all my options, whether I was dealing with religion, language, or the degree to which I could express my personal opinion. In this latter realm, it would have been very helpful to me to be aware of the adding option. At school I could give my opinion to my teacher (in fact, I was encouraged to do so), but at home giving my opinion was considered to be talking back and impolite and disrespectful. So it would have been helpful to know that switching behaviors between home and school and using the appropriate behavior in the appropriate context was an acceptable choice.

- *I don't understand the subtracting option. Can you give more of an explanation?* Again this option is usually not a free choice. And it is important to remember that it means giving up a behavior and not replacing the given-up behavior with any other behavior. This is why in the three-dimensional model of the compass, the subtracting/shedding option is associated with loss and destruction. It's as if a person has fallen through the floor, is in free fall, and quite literally, is nowhere.

- *However, there is a curious connection between subtracting/destruction, loss/shedding, and creation.* When a person or whole populations have been through harrowing subtracting processes, like slavery among African Americans in the United States, the emptiness generates tremendous creativity. Just look at the contributions of African American culture to global popular culture.

- *The best choice*. Best means the choice that is effective in the context in moving toward one's goals.

About This Model

This model developed from five sets of experiences: my own multicultural upbringing in a family that carried seven lines of history; my 1982 doctoral dissertation that analyzed effective multicultural coping and adaptation by Native American, African American, Hispanic American, and Asian Americans based on life histories, autobiographies, and autobiographical novels; the years of collaborative research with H. Ned Seelye, the first director of bilingual education for the state of Illinois and the founder and head researcher until his death in 1997 of International Resource Development; my own work with the Spanish Education Development Center and with Americans for Indian Opportunity; and finally, my 17 years of teaching intercultural communication and relations and conflict resolution at International Christian University in Tokyo.

REFERENCE

Wasilewski, J. (1982). *Effective coping and adaptation in multiple cultural environments in the United States by Native, Hispanic, Black and Asian Americans* (Unpublished doctoral dissertation). University of Southern California, Los Angeles.

 HANDOUT S8.3

THE PLUSES (+) AND MINUSES (–) OF EACH DIRECTION

+   –

Maintaining (or Sticking With the Familiar)
Is familiar   Can result in rigidity
Enables us to maintain our culture   Can result in isolation

Converting (or Assimilating)
Allows us to blend in   Often is the result of oppression.
Allows us to access dominant society resources   Have nothing different to offer society
                                                     Results in the loss of overall diversity
                                                     Leaves society with fewer sources of innovation

Adding (or Learning Other Cultural Behaviors)
Enables us to be flexible   There are many skills to learn
Enables us to be at home many places   We risk appearing foolish (while we are learning)
                                                     We can be seen as arrogant, slick, untrustworthy
                                                     (because we change behavior depending on the
                                                     context, that is, we are not "stable")

Subtracting (or Shedding)
Aids assimilation in the short run   Can result in self-alienation marginalization
                                                     Can have feelings of shame because we "gave up"
                                                     our culture
                                                     Can result in low self-esteem

Mixing (or Synthesis)
Can access existing behaviors   Can result in weird combinations
Enriches our lives   Can be seen as not "pure"
                                                     Can be associated with low status

Creating (or Inventing a Totally New Human Behavior for New Times)
Enables us to meet new circumstances   Is anxiety producing
                                                     Can be misunderstood
                                                     Is risky

Reproduced from: Jacqueline Wasilewski, "Framework: Multicultural Compass Model: A Tool for Navigating Multicultural Space," in *Building Cultural Competence: Innovative Activities and Models,* eds. K. Berardo and D. K. Deardorff (Sterling, VA: Stylus, 2012), 316–323.

 HANDOUT S8.4

MULTICULTURAL COMPASS WORKSHEET

Situation:
Identify a particular situation in which you had to or are trying to figure out how to behave, that is, a situation where your behavior makes a cultural difference:

Goals:
What are you trying to accomplish in this situation?

Context:
What is the larger social context in which this situation is taking place? Identify the power dynamics inherent in the particular situation and in the larger social context.

Choice:
Examine each direction in terms of

1. The pluses and minuses of each direction (see Handout S8.3)
2. Your personal strengths and weaknesses (Are you good at learning languages? Can you sit on the floor? etc.)
3. The way the larger context supports or obstructs your chosen behavioral direction (Does it only support assimilation? Is it assumed that people can command more than one language? Are your people considered to be "uncivilized"? Is your religion seen as violent? etc.)

Maintaining/sticking with the familiar:

1.

2.

3.

Converting/assimilation:

1.

2.

3.

Adding:

1.

2.

3.

Reproduced from: Jacqueline Wasilewski, "Framework: Multicultural Compass Model: A Tool for Navigating Multicultural Space," in *Building Cultural Competence: Innovative Activities and Models,* eds. K. Berardo and D. K. Deardorff (Sterling, VA: Stylus, 2012), 316–323.

Subtracting/destruction, loss/shedding:

1.

2.

3.

Mixing/synthesis:

1.

2.

3.

Creating:

1.

2.

3.

Continuation:
The final question is:

Will this choice of direction enable you at least to continue toward your goal?

48. PUSH BACK

Darla K. Deardorff

This activity gets participants physically engaged in conflict to introduce ways to resolve cultural difference.

Key Focus

Resolve differences

Type of Activity

Icebreaker

Objectives

As a result of this activity, participants will

- gain awareness of the results of imposing one's cultural views on another (win/lose) and
- experience the value of thinking creatively about resolving cultural differences.

Appropriate Audience

Adults, teenagers

Level of Challenge

Low

Group Size

2 to 200 plus people

Time

5 to 10 minutes

Materials

None

Activity Setup

1. Have participants pair up and face each other. It's helpful to pair those of similar height. Tell them to make sure their feet are planted firmly on the floor.
2. Ask participants to hold their hands up at shoulder height, palms facing their partner, and then place their palms lightly against their partner's palms.
3. Tell them their goal is to get their partner to move their feet first, doing whatever it takes. Remind them to keep their hands palm to palm the whole time, and then say, "Go!"

Managing the Activity

1. Give them a few seconds to try to get their partner to move their feet.
2. Observe what happens around the room.
3. Stop the activity, and then ask those who were successful to raise their hands.

Debriefing the Activity

This activity helps people understand the importance of resolving cultural differences together. Ask the following debriefing questions:

1. What happened?
2. What strategies did you use to get the other person to move his or her feet?
3. How could this be a win-win situation? Response: Note that if both persons moved their feet, then both of them succeeded.
4. What assumptions were made that prevented a win-win solution? What role do assumptions play in our interactions with others, especially when we're in conflict situations?

5. How can we mutually adapt to others when we may come from different backgrounds?
6. What stood out to you from this activity?
7. As you reflect on this activity, what are some things you can take away with you?

Key Insights and Learnings

- Assumptions can prevent us from developing creative solutions.
- When we impose our cultural values and ways on others (adaptation that takes place in one direction only), it may be viewed as a win-lose situation
- When we think creatively of win-win situations, it benefits both of us (mutually adapting to each other).

Variation

Have participants do this activity without talking, which creates an extra challenge and possibly causes the perceived tension to escalate. Include the role of communication in the debriefing.

Facilitation Tips and Suggestions

- It's important to have a room with enough space for participants to move around.
- This serves as a good energizer.
- A creative solution is when both people simply dance, and in that way, it's a win-win solution.
- Be sensitive to participants who may not wish to physically touch others (possibly for religious reasons) or to those who have physical limitations.

About This Exercise

I saw Peggy Pusch lead this activity, originally from Sivasailam "Thiagi" Thiagarajan, at an Intercultural Toolbox session at an international education conference in Europe, and I have since adapted it to addressing intercultural conflicts. It's an excellent activity for getting people up and moving, as well as a good way to introduce conflict resolution topics.

49. ON THE TRAIN

Gundula Gwenn Hiller

Through a nuanced critical incident, participants learn to identify and resolve situational, cultural, and individual factors that influence intercultural interactions. *Critical incidents* are interaction situations an individual finds "conflictual, puzzling, or which he is likely to misinterpret; and . . . which can be interpreted in a fairly unequivocal manner, given sufficient knowledge about the culture" (Fiedler, Mitchell, & Triandis, 1971, p. 97).

Key Focus

Resolve differences

Type of Activity

Case Study

Objectives

As a result of this activity, participants will

- learn to explore situational, cultural, and personal factors that influence intercultural interactions, and
- learn to analyze a critical incident and interpret the situation from various perspectives.

Appropriate Audience

Adults, teenagers

Level of Challenge

Medium

Group Size

Up to 30 people

Time

45 minutes

Materials

Handouts
Paper
Pens
Masking Tape

Activity Setup

1. Introduce the concept of the critical incident and explain that we will now practice analyzing a critical incident with an exercise.
2. Give participants Handout S8.5 and about five minutes to read it.

Managing the Activity

1. Ask the participants to reflect on and respond as spontaneously as possible to the following questions (encourage people to write down their answers on a sheet of paper):

   - Is this an intercultural critical incident?
   - What was the conductor's point of view?
   - What was Angelika's point of view?
   - What were the fellow travelers' points of view?
   - Do you think this critical incident exhibits accurate cultural attitudes? Or do you find something stereotypically Polish or German?
   - What other factors could also have influenced the situation?

2. After this short period of reflection, ask for the group's general opinion: Who believes this critical incident is intercultural in nature? With paper and masking tape label one area of the room "Agree," another area "Undecided," and the third area "Disagree." Ask participants to go to the area in the room that represents their answer to the question. Once individuals have chosen their location, ask a

few of them why they have chosen that particular area as their answer. You do not need to debrief much here. Ask all the participants to return to their seats after a few have provided their reasoning.

3. Introduce the culture-person-situation (CPS) model (see Handout S8.6) so participants can explore the situational, cultural, and personal factors in the situation.

4. In groups of four to five people, have participants identify the situational, cultural, and personal factors that could have influenced the situation, using the key questions provided in Handout S8.6

Debriefing the Activity

After exchanging their results with others in their group, bring the participants back together to discuss their perspectives and interpretations.

For this particular critical incident, the facilitator may ask the following questions:

- Which institutional aspects may have influenced the situation?
- What role could power have played?
- What role could language have played within the situation?
- Would culturally specific knowledge about successful Polish communication strategies have helped Angelika in this situation?
- What was the role of the fellow travelers?

  1. What would Angelika possibly expect from her fellow travelers?
  2. In what way did the presence of the fellow travelers or their action influence the interaction between Angelika and the conductor?

- Is it possible to understand whether the protagonist's and the conductor's behavior are an action or reaction?

Close with a few final reflection/debriefing questions:

- What was surprising in this exercise?
- What, if anything, was difficult?
- What general learnings or applications does this give you about working or interacting across cultures?

Key Insights and Learnings

- Interactions are very complex. They can be influenced by cultural, situational, and personal factors.
- By analyzing a situation in detail, we can reflect on the role of language, verbal misunderstandings, and different communication strategies that might be more successful in a situation.
- Knowing a foreign language does not guarantee that one can communicate appropriately in a given situation. Often, specific cultural knowledge, such as knowing successful communication patterns, is needed to be effective when working in global situations.
- Interaction has its own unpredictable dynamics and can create new cultural spaces.

Variations

Variation 1. Following the CPS analysis, discuss other alternatives: What could Angelika have done differently to avoid buying an extra ticket and convince the conductor to cooperate with her? Can you think of any strategies?

Variation 2. After the analysis, ask participants to act out the situation on the train using the communication strategies that were developed in the analysis. After this reenactment, discuss what worked and if any other strategies could help ensure success.

Variation 3. Ask participants to put themselves in the shoes of one of the people in the scenario. Ask the participants to tell the story from the perspective of that person to help participants develop empathy and understand the situation from different perspectives.

Variation 4. After working with this critical incident, have people apply the CPS model and its analysis process to their own situations.

Facilitation Tips and Suggestions

- The critical incident used in this exercise was purposely chosen because it is not easily explained through the culture criteria but rather consists of a variety of culture-specific behaviors. The learning objective here, however, is that the participants understand the complexity of communicative interaction. This critical incident contrasts a classic critical incident, which may only use culture to make sense of the incident (for more information, see Fischer, Dünstl, & Thomas, 2007).

- Moreover, this critical incident offers the opportunity to explore how cultural norms influence our actions and expectations. In this example, the cultural norm of following all rules (which generally pertains to Germans) and loosely following the rules (which generally pertains to the Polish) is compared. This allows a rich discussion on what happens, for example, if you know the cultural norms in a situation, just like Angelika did, and thus expect certain behaviors from others.
- The activity can last between 45 and 90 minutes, depending on the learning objective and the complexity of the analysis. Time and complexity can be increased using the suggested variations.
- Variations 1 and 2 (discovering alternative actions or communicative strategies), can help teach additional competencies such as flexibility of one's behavior and perspective-switching.

About This Exercise

This activity has been translated, modified, and revised from a German version in a textbook on innovative intercultural activities (Hiller & Vogler-Lipp, 2010). I was inspired to develop this activity after discussions with my colleagues about the limitations of traditional critical incident analyses. Having studied German-Polish interactions in terms of critical incident analysis, I was encouraged to develop an approach that simultaneously entertained cultural and noncultural influencing factors in the interaction. The story presented here (based on a real experience) clearly reveals that a number of different factors influenced the incident, including culture (Polish notions of hospitality, solidarity, and harmony), institutional frameworks, power dynamics, and misunderstandings in verbal communication.

REFERENCES

Bosse, E. (2010). Vielfalt erkunden—ein Konzept für interkulturelles Training an Hochschulen. In G. Hiller & S. Vogler-Lipp (Eds.), *Schlüsselqualifikation Interkulturelle Kompetenz an Hochschulen: Grundlagen, Konzepte, Methoden* (pp. 109–133). Wiesbaden, Germany: VS Research.

Fiedler, F. E., Mitchell, T., & Triandis, H. C. (1971). The culture assimilator. An approach to cross-cultural training. *Journal of Applied Psychology, 55*(2), 95–102.

Fischer, K., Dünstl, S., & Thomas, A. (2007). *Beruflich in Polen. Trainingsprogramm für Manager, Fach- und Führungskräfte. Handlungskompetenz im Ausland.* Göttingen, Germany: Vandenhoeck & Ruprecht.

Hiller, G., & Vogler-Lipp, S. (Eds.). (2010). *Schlüsselqualifikation Interkulturelle Kompetenz an Hochschulen: Grundlagen, Konzepte, Methoden.* Wiesbaden, Germany: VS Research.

 HANDOUT S8.5

CRITICAL INCIDENT: ON THE TRAIN

Tuesday, April 22, approximately 4:30 p.m., Wrocław, central station
Professor Angelika Schiller takes the train from Berlin to Poland in order to conduct a two-day workshop at a university in Wrocław. In Wrocław she is welcomed by her colleague Manuela Pinska. Following Manuela's advice, both decide to buy Angelika's return ticket to make sure she will be able to leave on Thursday afternoon. At the counter was a sign stating *szkolenie* (training), and a young woman is serving the customers, while in the background an older, more experienced colleague is sitting behind the younger woman looking over her shoulder. Angelika, who speaks Polish very well, asks for a return ticket for the date and time she needs it, and in front of Manuela buys the ticket.

Thursday, April 24, approximately 5 p.m. Passenger train (pociąg osobowy)
Wrocław—Poznań
Angelika is sitting in a compartment of eight passengers on the train ready to go home after accomplishing very hard work. The seminar went well, and that makes Angelika very happy. Only the fact that the university will not reimburse her for the train tickets makes her angry, since she only found out after she had arrived in Wrocław. After all, the transportation costs a fifth of her honorarium.

There are other women in the compartment besides Angelika; two might be students, and one lady in her forties who is very communicative might be a businesswoman. In a short conversation it becomes obvious that she has a leading position in an international company.

After a short while the conductor, who is a very serious-looking, 50-year-old man, enters the compartment. When Angelika presents her ticket, he shakes his head and says in a very unfriendly voice that the ticket is not valid. Surprised, Angelika asks why, and he responds that the ticket is issued for April 22. Angelika is outraged and says that they sold her the wrong ticket. She tries to explain to the conductor with her almost perfect Polish, but with a German accent, that she bought the ticket at the counter, and the woman serving her was being trained and this might be the reason for the wrongly issued ticket. She can prove it. She wants to show the conductor her ticket for her journey to Wrocław, which would demonstrate that she arrived in Wrocław on April 22 at 4:30 p.m., and—the conductor interrupts her and says it is the responsibility of the customer and not the clerk to double-check the ticket. This is procedure and thus there is nothing to be discussed. He is not interested in the evidence. She now has to buy a new ticket. Again very outraged, Angelika says she feels unfairly treated and does not agree with her having to buy a new ticket if the clerk made a mistake and did not issue the right ticket. The conductor's facial expression hardens, and he tells her that if she does not buy a ticket, she will have to get off the train at the next station.

At this moment the Polish businesswoman interrupts and offers to pay the ticket. One of the two young women suggests that the three ladies could divide the cost among themselves to buy the ticket for Angelika. Angelika, however, won't allow that. Why should the Polish women have to pay for a mistake made by the railroad? Very absurd. She thankfully declines the offer and pays for another ticket. The conductor leaves without saying anything. Angelika is angered by the fact that the conductor would not listen to her. She speaks Polish so well, and yet the communication failed. And besides, aren't the Polish known for being flexible when it comes to laws and rules? Very frustrated, Angelika begins thinking of strategies she could have used to convince the conductor.

The Polish women sitting in the compartment are very concerned and seem to have been embarrassed by this situation.

Reproduced from: Gundula Gwenn Hiller, "On the Train," in *Building Cultural Competence: Innovative Activities and Models*, eds. K. Berardo and D. K. Deardorff (Sterling, VA: Stylus, 2012), 326–330.

HANDOUT S8.6

REFLECTION AND ANALYSIS OF CRITICAL INCIDENTS: CULTURE-PERSON-SITUATION MODEL

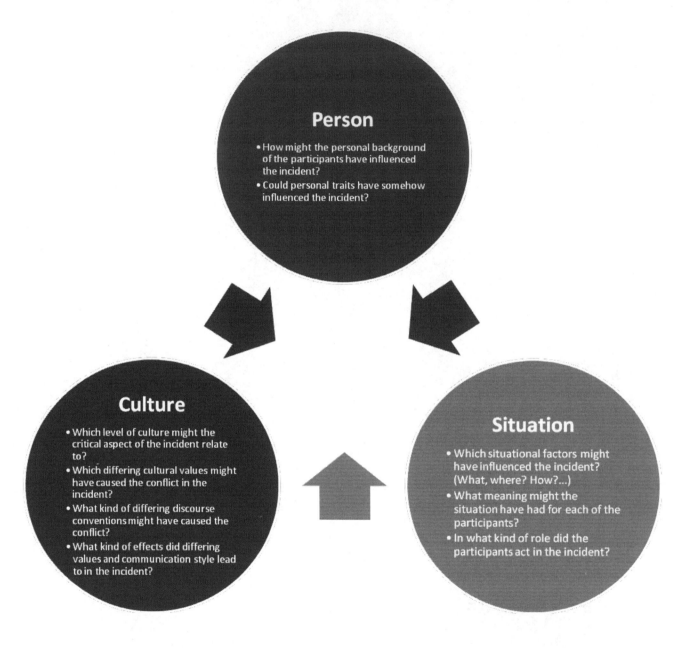

Person
- How might the personal background of the participants have influenced the incident?
- Could personal traits have somehow influenced the incident?

Culture
- Which level of culture might the critical aspect of the incident relate to?
- Which differing cultural values might have caused the conflict in the incident?
- What kind of differing discourse conventions might have caused the conflict?
- What kind of effects did differing values and communication style lead to in the incident?

Situation
- Which situational factors might have influenced the incident? (What, where? How?...)
- What meaning might the situation have had for each of the participants?
- In what kind of role did the participants act in the incident?

Note. Adapted from "Vielfalt erkunden—ein Konzept für interkulturelles Training an Hochschulen," 2010, by E. Bosse, in G. Hiller & S. Vogler-Lipp (Eds.), *Schlüsselqualifikation Interkulturelle Kompetenz an Hochschulen: Grundlagen, Konzepte, Methoden*, pp. 109–133), Wiesbaden, Germany: VS Research.

---

50. METEORITE

AFS Interkulturelle Begegnungen e.V. (AFS)

This simulation involves inhabitants of three cities with three very different perspectives. Through this simulation, participants practice communicating clearly, as well as understanding the value of different perspectives.

Key Focus

Resolve differences

Type of Activity

Simulation

Objectives

As a result of this exercise the participants will

- realize the value of different perspectives,
- learn how to reconcile different perspectives to solve challenging dilemmas, and
- practice clear communication skills.

Appropriate Audience

Adults, teenagers

Level of Challenge

Medium

Group Size

6 to 18 people

Time

30 minutes

Materials

- Handout S8.7 with illustration (drawing/ photo) of the ice meteorite or a 3D model created from Play-Doh or modeling clay

- One blank sheet of paper and a pen per person
- One copy of the handout of the ice meteorite story for the relevant village for each person in that village (e.g., each person in Tricity gets a copy of the Tricity story) (see Handout S8.8)
- One copy of the plan of the site for each small group (see Handout S8.9)

Preparation

1. Set up three groups of chairs in the room, one for each village.
2. Put an empty sheet of paper and a pen on each chair.
3. Keep the illustration of the meteorite (Handout S8.7) or the 3D model hidden.

Activity Setup

1. Separate participants into three groups and have them take their seats.
2. Give each group a town name: Roundville, Tricity, and Squareburgh (see Handout S8.8).
3. Introduce the participants to the story as follows:

   - A gigantic ice meteorite hit the earth near the towns of Squareburgh, Tricity, and Roundville.
   - The inhabitants of Squareburgh discovered that the meteorite had a quadratic shape.
   - The inhabitants of Tricity could see that the meteorite was triangular in shape.
   - The inhabitants of Roundville couldn't see the meteorite. When they got to the impact point, the meteorite had already completely liquefied. They could only see that the meteorite left a round indentation.

4. Distribute the site plan (see Handout S8.9) and the appropriate partial views of the meteorite site (see Handout S8.8) as follows: give the circle for Roundville, the triangle for Tricity, and the square for Squareburgh.

5. The activity continues in the following stages:

- Stage 1: Village Visits. Tell participants they will now have the chance to talk with people from neighboring villages to determine the shape of the meteorite before it melted. They need to choose one or more village representatives to travel to other villages to discuss the shape of the meteorite before it melted. Village representatives are allowed to share and add their own perspectives on the shape of the meteorite and ask at least one inhabitant of

  - Tricity and Squareburgh to discuss the shape of the meteorite before it melted,
  - one inhabitant of Tricity and Roundville to discuss the shape of the meteorite before it melted, and
  - one inhabitant of Squareburgh Roundville to discuss the shape of the meteorite before it melted.

- Point out to the group that neither the specific location of the towns nor the material of the meteorite is important. Each of the three groups received different information about what the meteorite looked like, and you need to talk to other villages to determine the correct shape of the meteorite. Have the groups decide who will be staying in their town and who will be visiting the other towns to find out more about the meteorite.

- Stage 2: Meteorite Re-creations. After a few minutes of discussion, have participants return to their village and explain to the rest of the group what they learned from their visits. The group then should re-create the meteorite either by drawing a picture or by forming a model with Play-Doh.

- Stage 3: Presentations. After about 10 minutes, have one representative of each town present its results to the whole group.

Debriefing the Activity

Show the illustration in Handout S8.7 or the 3D model to the whole group, pass it around, and compare it with what the groups came up with. Tell them the shape of the meteorite appears different to each group, and the exact shape of the meteorite can only be reconstructed by combining what the other groups know about it. Tell the group the essence of the task: The meteorite can be described precisely only with the knowledge of all three parties.

Ask the following debriefing questions:

- What happened in this exercise?
- How did you feel during the exercise?
- Which strategies did you use to solve the problem?
- What was the value of different perspectives in this exercise?
- What did you learn as a result of this exercise, and why does what you learned matter?
- How can this be compared to similar situations that you have experienced before?

Key Insights and Learnings

- The knowledge of the individual sometimes isn't enough to comprehend a complex circumstance. Extensive insight can be gained with the help of other views, even if at first they seem wrong, improbable, or implausible.
- Only a change of perspective enables us to see the whole picture.

Variations

If you work with children you can use a shape that is simpler (e.g., a cone) that has only two different perspectives (the view from the side, which will be a triangle; and the view from the indentation it will leave on the ground, which will be a circle).

Facilitation Tips and Suggestions

- Using a model of the meteorite and a drawing helps participants who have different ways of perceiving or interpreting a two- or three-dimensional object.
- A model can also easily be carved out of a large candle.

About This Exercise

This exercise was developed by a group of German volunteers of the student exchange organization AFS. The aim of the group is to develop training materials for host families who participate in a German-U.S. student exchange program.

 HANDOUT S8.7

THE ICE METEORITE WITH COLOR-CODED SURFACE

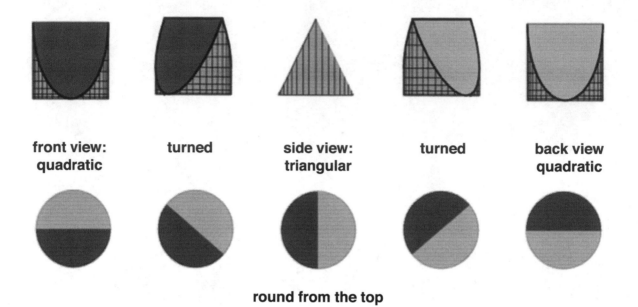

| front view: quadratic | turned | side view: triangular | turned | back view quadratic |

round from the top

 HANDOUT S8.8

STORY

- A gigantic ice meteorite hit the earth between the towns of Squareburgh, Tricity, and Roundville.
- The inhabitants of Squareburgh discovered that the meteorite had a quadratic shape.
- The inhabitants of Tricity could see that the meteorite was triangular in shape.
- The inhabitants of Roundville couldn't see the meteorite. When they got to the impact point, the meteorite had already completely liquefied. They could only see that the meteorite left a round mold.

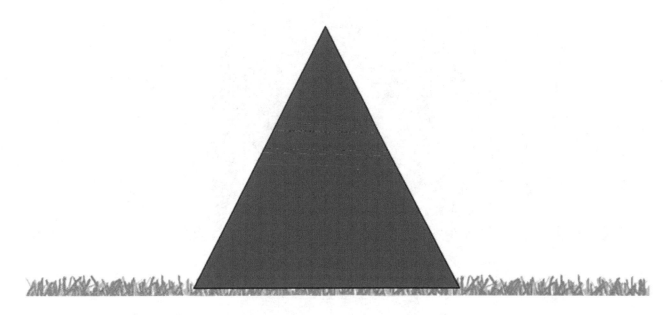

VIEW OF THE ICE METEORITE FROM TRICITY

STORY

- A gigantic ice meteorite hit the earth in-between the towns of Squareburgh, Tricity, and Roundville.
- The inhabitants of Squareburgh could discover that the meteorite had a quadratic shape.
- The inhabitants of Tricity could see that the meteorite was triangular in shape.
- The inhabitants of Roundville couldn't see the meteorite. When they got to the impact point, the meteorite had already liquefied completely. They could only discover that the meteorite left a round mold.

VIEW OF THE ICE METEORITE FROM SQUAREBURGH

STORY

- A gigantic ice meteorite hit the earth in-between the towns of Squareburgh, Tricity, and Roundville.
- The inhabitants of Squareburgh could discover that the meteorite had a quadratic shape.
- The inhabitants of Tricity could see that the meteorite was triangular in shape.
- The inhabitants of Roundville couldn't see the meteorite. When they got to the impact point, the meteorite had already liquefied completely. They could only discover that the meteorite left a round mold.

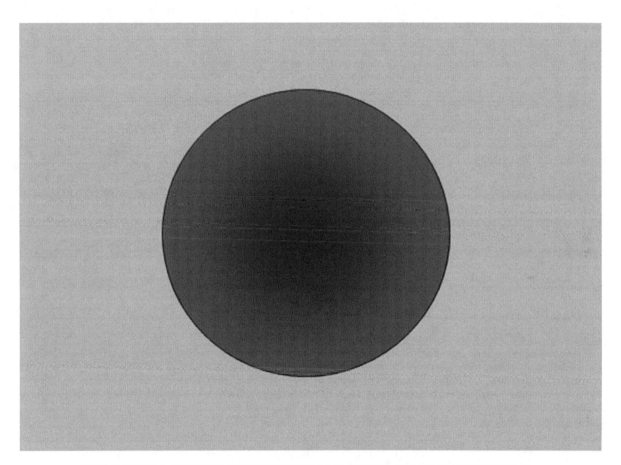

MOLD FROM THE METEORITE IN THE GROUND NEAR ROUNDVILLE

 HANDOUT S8.9

PLAN OF SITE

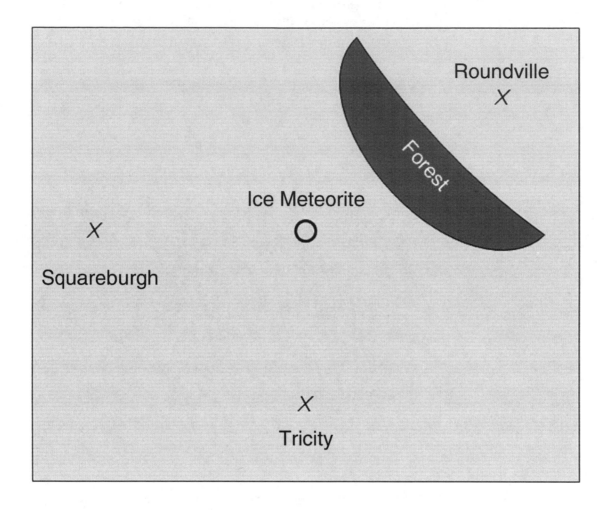

51. ARCHIVUM 2060

Maja Woźniak

In this simulation, two teams from different cultural institutes plan an art exhibit, *archivum 2060*. Without knowing it, these teams have different ideas about how to arrange the artwork in three exhibition rooms. One team believes the pieces of art should be grouped by category and the other believes the artwork should be grouped by color. The two groups meet to decide how to arrange the artwork, and an interesting discussion ensues, allowing a rich reflection on intercultural competence.

Key Focus

Resolve differences

Type of Activity

Simulation

Objectives

As a result of this activity, participants will

- raise their awareness of culture-specific forms of perception,
- practice changing perspectives and dealing with ambiguous situations,
- learn to make culturally appropriate decisions in a situation, and
- receive feedback on their own intercultural competence in terms of tolerance of ambiguity, empathy, and behavioral flexibility.

Appropriate Audience

Adults, teenagers

Level of Challenge

High

Group Size

3 to 15 people

Time

60 to 90 minutes

Materials

- Handouts
- 12 art cards
- A drawing of the rooms to be used for the art exhibit
- Chairs for participants
- At least one table
- Computer and projector for a PowerPoint presentation of the artwork

Preparation

1. Go to http://dl.dropbox.com/u/26016813/archivum%202060.zip to download the PowerPoint presentation and 12 artwork cards. Open the 12 artwork cards file, print this document in color, and cut out each artwork piece so you have 12 artwork cards.
2. Draw a draft of the exhibition rooms (see templates in Handouts S8.10 and S8.11) on a chart or enlarge the template in the handout so that it is large enough for the 12 cards of artwork to be moved around on the drawing.
3. Print the information sheets for all participants as follows:

   - one copy of the Introduction per participant (see Handout S8.11)
   - three to five copies of Team A materials (see Handout S8.12)
   - three to five copies of Team B materials (see Handout S8.13)

- three to five copies of the observer information and evaluation sheets (see Handout S8.14)

4. Organize the room with a table and chairs in the center and chairs on the outside for the observers. Set up the computer on the table and open the PowerPoint presentation file. Do not put out the artwork cards yet—keep these hidden from view initially.

Activity Setup

1. Form a group of three to five participants for Team A, three to five participants for Team B, and three to five participants who will be the observers. Distribute Handout S8.11, Introduction to *archivum 2060* and provide the following background information:

   - Teams A and B, you are the organizers of the renowned international art exhibition *archivum 2060*, which is organized every year by two teams of different cultural institutes. This year you are responsible for the success of the exhibition.
   - Today your teams are meeting to arrange the artwork in the three exhibition rooms (point to large exhibit room poster on table).
   - Team B, these exhibition rooms are located within your institute, so you will host the exhibit and welcome the members of Team A as partners in this exhibit.
   - Team A, you will have the chance to demonstrate and practice intercultural competence as you work with Team B.
   - Your meeting will start in roughly 20 minutes. At that time, Team A, you will arrive to Team B's institute. You all will first review a PowerPoint presentation of each of the artwork pieces briefly. Then both teams will need to come to an agreement about where to place each piece of art in the exhibit rooms.

2. Pass out the instruction sheets for each team and for the observers and tell all participants to read their instruction sheets carefully. Send Team A to a separate room to read its instructions and prepare for the meeting. Tell Team A it has about 20 minutes to prepare

and that you will join the team to answer questions in a few minutes.

3. After Team A has left the room, begin briefing Team B members (the observers can also listen in on this briefing). Explain to Team B that

   - it will create the context for Team A to practice intercultural competence by demonstrating unexpected behaviors (e.g., unexplained emotions) that challenge Team A's degree of empathy, tolerance of ambiguity, and behavioral flexibility.
   - Team A will want to arrange the artwork according to category (e.g., animals), but that Team B strongly believes the artwork should be organized according to the emotions that are triggered by different colors, as follows:

     ○ Blue artwork triggers sadness.
     ○ Red artwork triggers anger.
     ○ Green artwork triggers happiness.

   - In fact, Team B will show the emotions prompted by the colors of the artwork verbally and nonverbally whenever the artwork is shown. For example, when talking about a green piece of artwork (green = happiness), the person should do it in an upbeat, enthusiastic way. When speaking about the blue artwork, the person should act sad. (Model this as you are giving these instructions.)

     Make sure they are clear about their task, the emotional meaning of the colors, and how the meeting with Team A should be conducted. Encourage Team B to continue to practice its show of emotions while you brief the other participants. Have them run the PowerPoint presentation of the artwork and encourage all team members to respond appropriately.

4. Next, brief the observers. Make sure they have read their instructions and the evaluation chart. Each observer should be focused on one individual from Team A as well as observing the interactions of both teams generally. Ask the observers to decide which one of them will observe which team member and advise them to sit where they have a good view of the person they are observing. Review

and check the observers' understanding of the three definitions of intercultural competence. Be sure they understand the scales for the evaluation, and answer any questions they may have about how to observe the meeting.

5. Finally, go to the room where Team A has been preparing. Ensure that Team A has understood its guidelines. Point out to Team A members that the meeting will give them a chance to practice their intercultural competence and help them prepare for this by reviewing their answers to the questions on their instruction sheet. When no further questions arise, invite Team A into the art institute of Team B in the other room.

Managing the Activity

Place the 12 artwork cards on the table before Team A arrives. The simulation starts when Team A enters the room. Take a seat with the observers and watch what happens. The general course of action will likely resemble the following:

1. The teams take their seats around the table.
2. The PowerPoint presentation is shown, and Team A is confronted with Team B's emotional roller coaster for the first time.
3. After the PowerPoint presentation, Team A unveils its concept of the arrangement by placing the 12 cards with the artwork on the drawing of the exhibition rooms. At this point, Team A is confronted with the emotional behavior of Team B for the second time.
4. Team B then presents its idea of the arrangement, and a lively discussion takes place.
5. The outcome depends on the stage of development of Team A's degree of empathy, behavioral flexibility, and tolerance of ambiguity.

Debriefing the Activity

Conduct the debriefing by asking the following questions:

- How did the members of Team A and Team B and the observers feel during the interaction?
- What was it like to be in a particular role?
- Which behaviors of Team A demonstrated greater degrees of intercultural competence?

- Which behaviors could be considered as less interculturally competent?
- Is there any behavior of Team A or Team B that could have made the interaction more efficient and adequate?
- Based on this exercise, what enables individuals with different perspectives to create mutual understanding in intercultural encounters?
- What did you learn from this exercise?

Key Insights and Learnings

- Different cultural groups have unique perceptions and ways of expressing these perceptions.
- Our own views and communication styles, which seem so natural and normal to us, may not be clear or even understood by others.
- Being exposed to an entirely different way of thinking and acting can cause us to react in different and sometimes emotionally charged ways.
- It is important to learn how to work with different behaviors and communication styles and to find common understanding.
- Participants now have a better gauge of their intercultural competence. They know where they are strong and where they can improve in terms of empathy, tolerance for ambiguity, and behavioral flexibility.

Facilitation Tips and Suggestions

- Take your time to familiarize yourself with the activity and the materials because clarity and understanding are important.
- Keep in mind that you will be dealing with three groups, so it might be helpful to have a cofacilitator who can brief one group.
- Be aware that not every participant will be comfortable receiving his or her feedback in front of the entire group. The debriefing questions should be general and focus on certain behavior, not on the person who showed it. Feedback should be addressed to the entire team and not to the individual participants. If a participant wishes to receive individual feedback, provide it to him or her at that moment or after the activity.
- Enjoy the exercise. You will be surprised how creative the participants will be.

About This Exercise

I developed the first version of *archivum 2060* while I was a student at the European University Viadrina in 2008. During my studies, I often participated in intercultural trainings and I found that the role playing was quite similar. Therefore, I wanted to develop something new to contribute to the existing portfolio of activities. The idea was to have a unique scenario applicable to everyday intercultural encounters that would encourage practicing three central skills of intercultural competence: empathy, tolerance of ambiguity, and behavioral flexibility. The activity *archivum 2060* enables the participants to develop and test these skills.

HANDOUT S8.10

DRAFT OF EXHIBITION ROOMS AND ART CARDS

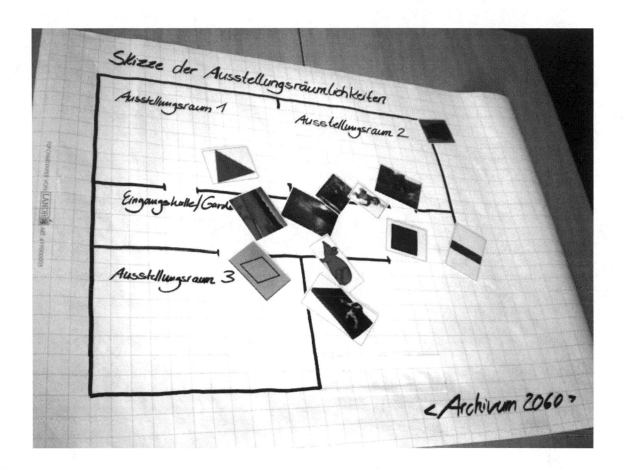

HANDOUT S8.11

INTRODUCTION ARCHIVUM 2060

You are the organizer of the renowned international art exhibition *archivum 2060*, which is put together every year by two teams from different cultural institutes. This year you are responsible for the success of the exhibition.

Today your teams (Team A and Team B) are meeting in order to arrange the pieces of art in the three exhibition rooms.

The exhibition rooms are located in Team B's institute. Therefore Team B is the host, welcoming the members of Team A.

Both of your teams know the art pieces, which have been selected by a jury. You appreciate the fine selection.

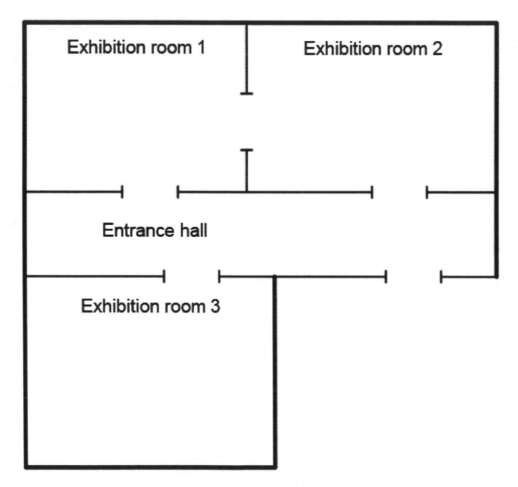

DRAFT OF EXHIBITION ROOMS

Reproduced from: Maja Woźniak, "Archivum 2060," in *Building Cultural Competence: Innovative Activities and Models*, eds. K. Berardo and D. K. Deardorff (Sterling, VA: Stylus, 2012), 339–353.

 HANDOUT S8.12

INFORMATION SHEET FOR TEAM A

Today you are going to meet with your partners, Team B, in order to organize the art exhibition *archivum 2060*.

The purpose of the meeting is to find a way to arrange the pieces of art in the exhibition rooms. You have acknowledged and appreciate the 12 pieces of art (see compositions of the images at the end of this handout), which are categorized as follows:

- animals
- landscapes
- geometrical figures

Being a fan of art you should already be able to determine how you would display and organize these pieces of art in the exhibition rooms. You have decided to arrange them as follows:

- One room will contain all pieces of art relating to animals (Composition 1).
- One room will contain all pieces of art relating to landscapes (Composition 2).
- One room will contain all pieces of art relating to geometrical figures (Composition 3).

The exhibition rooms are located at your partner's cultural institute (see Handout S8.11). Your team is free to decide which room will display which composition provided that the pieces of art are grouped in the three categories of animals, landscapes, and geometrical figures.

The Task
Take another good look at the pieces of art. The meeting will start with a brief review of each piece of artwork, so you will want to be able to discuss what you think are the merits of each piece of art. You should then be prepared to present your proposal for where the art pieces should be placed in the exhibit rooms. You will need to explain and defend your decision regarding the arrangement to Team B.

The Challenge
When two teams from two different cultural institutions meet, you can be pretty sure that the meeting will be exciting. Both teams have their specific opinions, views, and ways of expressing themselves. This applies particularly to the art scene, where unique thinking is the way to be. Therefore, some unexpected situations might arise during the meeting. Keep in mind that Team B is your partner and friend and you have the common goal of creating a great exhibit.

How to Prepare Yourself
In order to prepare yourself adequately for the meeting, try to imagine the entire meeting from the beginning when you enter Team B's institute to the discussion about the arrangement of the art pieces and up to your departure.

The following questions may be helpful:

1. What are your expectations regarding
   - the way Team B will greet and treat you,
   - the negotiation process, and
   - the outcome of the meeting?

Reproduced from: Maja Woźniak, "Archivum 2060," in *Building Cultural Competence: Innovative Activities and Models*, eds. K. Berardo and D. K. Deardorff (Sterling, VA: Stylus, 2012), 339–353.

2. What unexpected things could occur during this meeting? Try to identify and list the things that could be different.
3. How can your team benefit from these differences?
4. What will you do if you encounter these differences?

COMPOSITION 1: ANIMALS

COMPOSITION 2: LANDSCAPES

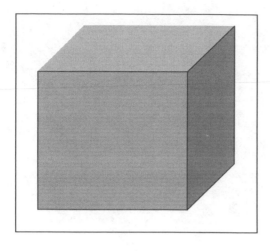

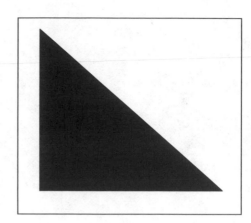

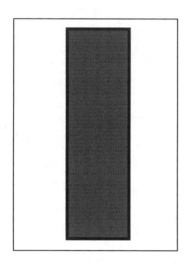

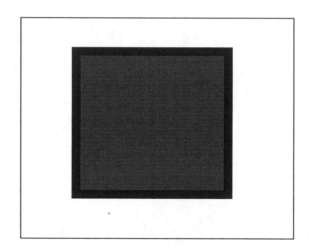

COMPOSITION 3: GEOMETRICAL FIGURES

 HANDOUT S8.13

INFORMATION SHEET FOR TEAM B (HOSTS)

Your Task

Your task is to show surprising behavior to the members of Team A in order to give them a chance to practice and demonstrate intercultural competence.

Being the hosts, you have prepared well for the arrival of your partners. You are looking forward to meeting Team A.

The purpose of the meeting is to arrange the pieces of art in the exhibition rooms.

Team A has decided to display the pieces of art in the three exhibition rooms as follows:

- One room will contain all pieces of art relating to animals (Composition 1).
- One room will contain all pieces of art relating to landscapes (Composition 2).
- One room will contain all pieces of art relating to geometrical figures (Composition 3).

Team A will try to convince your team to arrange the pieces of art in accordance to this classification. Your team has a different idea regarding the arrangement of the art pieces in the exhibition rooms.

You do not want to arrange the pieces of art according to category (animals, landscapes, geometrical figures). Instead, you are going to group the pieces of art according to the emotions these pieces of art trigger in you.

Important: The pieces of art stir up the following emotions because of their eye-catching colors:

1. Sadness (Blue)
2. Anger (Red)
3. Happiness (Green)

Course of Action

The meeting will start with a PowerPoint presentation of all 12 pieces of art, one after the other. The presentation will be followed by the discussion to find a way to arrange the pieces of art in the exhibition rooms.

1. Please welcome Team A, and have them take a seat at the table. Express your appreciation to Team A for its cooperation.
2. Announce the presentation as a means to discuss each piece of art briefly before deciding where it should be placed within the exhibit rooms.
3. When everyone has taken their seats, start the PowerPoint presentation.
4. While the presentation is running, you will express the three kinds of emotions verbally and nonverbally:

Sadness (Blue)	nonverbal: e.g.: You look down, you sigh.
	verbal: e.g.: "This is somehow depressing."
Anger (Red)	nonverbal: e.g.: You become agitated and act slightly irritated.
	verbal: e.g.: "There is something about this piece that bothers me!"
Happiness (Green)	nonverbal: e.g.: You laugh, clap your hands.
	verbal: e.g.: "This is wonderful!", "Great!"

Note: The emotions *do not* correspond to the categories (animals, landscapes, and geometrical figures) but only to the actual color of the pictures.

Reproduced from: Maja Woźniak, "Archivum 2060," in *Building Cultural Competence: Innovative Activities and Models*, eds. K. Berardo and D. K. Deardorff (Sterling, VA: Stylus, 2012), 339–353.

5. After the PowerPoint presentation , ask Team A to present its idea for the arrangement of the pieces of art in the exhibition rooms. Provide them with cutout pieces of the artwork (your facilitator will provide these) so they can show you directly on the exhibit floorplan their suggestion. Their concept will differ from yours. Take this into consideration, but show you are not really satisfied with their suggestion.
6. Present your concept of the arrangement to Team A as follows:
   • Sadness room: 5 images (Blue: cat, cow, sea, rectangle, triangle)
   • Happiness room: 4 images (Green: cube, jungle, mountains, square)
   • Anger room: 3 images (Red: mouse, seal, desert)

Note: Remember to show your emotions during the discussion as well. Emphasize your arguments with emotional expressions. For example:

When talking about the image of the blue cat (blue = sadness) try to be restrained.
When talking about the anger room (red = anger) try to do it in an outrageous way.
When talking about the image of the green jungle (green = happiness) be cheerful.

Team A has to find out that certain emotions are attached to the art pieces. Do not explain anything at the beginning. For example, if they ask you why you have arranged them in this way, say something like, "You know, it feels right to us." Only when Team A poses specific questions about your behavior are you allowed to give away information, bit by bit, saying, for example, that the art pieces are highly charged with emotions.

Insist on your idea about grouping the pieces of art and on your idea about how to arrange them in the exhibition rooms. After a while, for example, when Team A is willing to question its decision and deviate from its approach, you could and should compromise or find other possible solutions.

 HANDOUT S8.14

INFORMATION SHEET FOR OBSERVERS

Your task as the observer is to watch and to evaluate the behavior of the members of Team A, who will have the opportunity to practice their intercultural competence by interacting with Team B.

The intercultural challenge in this situation is that there are different perceptions and different forms of expression between the two teams. This will result in different ways of classifying the artwork and different ideas about the arrangement of the pieces of art.

While Team A is instructed to group the pieces of art according to three categories (animals, landscapes, and geometrical figures), Team B is instructed to arrange the pieces of art according to colors (red, green, blue).

What makes this more complex is that for Team B colors are associated with emotions (red = anger, green = happiness, blue = sadness), which they will also show when they are talking about the different pieces of artwork.

Your goal as an observer is to provide useful feedback for Team A to help the team members understand how well they are able to demonstrate intercultural competence. In particular, you will be looking for how much these individuals are able to demonstrate empathy, behavioral flexibility, and tolerance for ambiguity.

Use the following feedback sheets to record your observations. Note specific behaviors and moments in the conversation where you saw intercultural competence or a lack of it. At the end of the interaction between Team A and Team B, you will be asked to give your feedback. Remember your goal is to help others learn and develop their intercultural competence as you give this feedback.

1. Please decide first who is going to observe which member of Team A.
2. Make sure you have a good view to observe the person you have picked to observe.
3. Read the observations sheets carefully before the role playing starts.

Observation Sheet: Empathy
Definition: Empathy is the willingness and ability to switch one's own perspective and to successfully try to understand the feelings, expectations, and wishes of the other person. It is the ability to interpret the behavior of the other person correctly at that time and place. Empathy is connected to knowing that the behavior of the person one is interacting with often can't be evaluated and interpreted with one's own cultural standards. People with interculturally competent empathy are able to take culture-specific perspectives that have been developed through interaction with people with different cultural backgrounds.

Reproduced from: Maja Woźniak, "Archivum 2060," in *Building Cultural Competence: Innovative Activities and Models*, eds. K. Berardo and D. K. Deardorff (Sterling, VA: Stylus, 2012), 339–353.

Please indicate by marking on the scale provided the extent to which the following statements apply:

The participant

	strongly disagree		strongly agree***	
recognizes quickly the "different" behavior of Team B (+)*	1	2	3	4
remains in his/her own perspective (–)**	1	2	3	4
shows curiosity and interest in understanding the perspective of Team B (e.g., is asking for the reason of the behavior) (+)	1	2	3	4
notices that the members of Team B are angry, sad, or happy (+)	1	2	3	4
shows appreciation for the different perceptions held by Team B (+)	1	2	3	4
discusses and compares the different ways to classify the artwork (+)	1	2	3	4

Note. *The plus (+) refers to the positive occurrence of the interculturally competent empathy.
  **The minus (–) refers to its negative occurrence.
***Scale: 1 = strongly disagree, 2 = disagree, 3 = agree, 4 = strongly agree

Notes:

Observation Sheet: Behavioral Flexibility

Definition: Behavioral flexibility is the ability to adjust fast to changing conditions with appropriate behavior. People with behavioral flexibility are aware of the impact of their own actions and are able to reflect on them. They are able to act appropriately in interactions with people with different cultural backgrounds. They do this by understanding the situation, recognizing expectations, and responding appropriately. At the same time the interculturally competent person only adjusts his or her behavior when sure that adjustment is required.

Please indicate by marking on the scale provided the extent to which the following statements apply:

The participant

	strongly disagree		strongly agree***	
takes on a defensive stance toward the situation (–)**	1	2	3	4
views the different approach of Team B as an enrichment for the exhibition and his/her own team (+)*	1	2	3	4
is willing to adjust (+)	1	2	3	4
imitates the reactions of Team B during the PowerPoint presentation and discussion without making fun of it (+)	1	2	3	4
is open-minded and flexible with regard to diverse suggestions and solutions for the arrangement of the artwork (+)	1	2	3	4

Note: *The plus (+) refers to the positive occurrence of the intercultural competent empathy.
**The minus (–) refers to its negative occurrence.
***Scale: 1 = strongly disagree, 2 = disagree, 3 = agree, 4 = strongly agree

Notes:

```

```

Observation Sheet: Tolerance of Ambiguity

Definition: Tolerance of ambiguity is the ability to embrace ambiguous and unknown situations. People who are tolerant of ambiguity can cope and deal with the emotional stress that arises in such situations. They accept and tolerate the complexity and ambiguity of intercultural interactions and deal properly with them.

Please indicate by marking on the scale provided the extent to which the following statements apply:

The participant

	strongly disagree		strongly agree***	
reacts calmly to the surprising behavior of Team B (+)*	1	2	3	4
is open to the different perception and classification of Team B according to colors/emotions, even if they don't fully understand it yet (+)	1	2	3	4
finds the approach of Team B interesting and accepts it (+)	1	2	3	4
is desperately trying to establish a system within the experienced chaos (–)**	1	2	3	4
is pushing the others to find a fast solution (–)	1	2	3	4

Note: *The plus (+) refers to the positive occurrence of the intercultural competent empathy.

**The minus (–) refers to its negative occurrence.

***Scale: 1 = *strongly disagree*, 2 = *disagree*, 3 = *agree*, 4 = *strongly agree*

Notes:

```

```

SECTION 9

Develop Professionally

52. TOOL: THE WHEEL OF INTERCULTURAL SKILLS

Kate Berardo

The Wheel of Intercultural Skills (see Handout S9.1) is a planning tool that helps individuals understand which skills and experiences are relevant and necessary for building a career in the intercultural field. Individuals can map out their current intercultural skill levels, plan for their future development, and evaluate current and future opportunities in the intercultural field with this tool. The wheel can be used as an aid in writing an effective résumé or curriculum vitae (CV), to track one's development over time, and as a personal assessment tool for workshops on careers in the intercultural field.

Key Focus

Develop professionally

Objectives

As a result of working with this tool, participants will be able to

- articulate their expertise in six key intercultural professional development areas,
- understand what it means to be a well-rounded interculturalist,
- map current strengths and future development needs for furthering an intercultural career, and

- plan for and evaluate different opportunities to develop their intercultural knowledge and skills.

Appropriate Audience

Adults

Level of Challenge

Medium

Suggested Uses

The tool can be used as a

- personal development guide that individuals use to map their own experience levels over time,
- coaching tool to help individuals set goals and plan for a career in the intercultural field, and
- group training tool for workshops on intercultural career building.

Key Talking Points

About the Tool

With no clear standards or processes for becoming an intercultural professional, the question of what it takes to become successful in this field is one that many interculturalists—whether aspiring, new, or highly experienced—have been discussing for decades. And, while we all may have our own opinion on which experiences and training are most important, most agree it requires a balance of different types of expertise to truly be a well-rounded interculturalist. The necessary expertise falls into one of six areas, each of which represents a section on the Wheel of Intercultural Skills:

- Formal education: the formal training and education you bring to your work in the intercultural field, the courses you have taken, the subjects you have studied, the credentials you carry that advance your work
- Life experience: the intercultural experiences that have shaped you and constitute your own experiences working across cultures, including time living abroad, working globally, being in an intercultural relationship, having a diverse cultural background, and daily intercultural interactions
- Work experience: actual experience you have working in different sectors, industries, organizations, and departments; those areas where you have applied your skills
- Personal qualities: your traits and skills that help you demonstrate the skills we help others develop, such as openness, flexibility, good communication skills, style shifting, and intercultural sensitivity to name a few
- Application area: the topics and areas you specialize in and where you apply your intercultural expertise, including team building, relocation, conflict resolution, global virtual teams, study abroad, cultural identity, or global leadership
- Methods skills: the methods and approaches you use in your intercultural work, including, but not limited to, teaching, training, coaching, consulting, mediating, and advising

The Wheel of Intercultural Skills is designed to help you think about, plan for, and articulate the qualifications that matter in an intercultural career.

Using the Wheel of Intercultural Skills

The wheel can be completed in multiple ways and at multiple times by individuals and groups. When you work with the wheel with groups or individuals, begin by passing out the wheel and introducing it by speaking briefly about its background and purpose. Then explain each of the six key skill areas and why they are important for a career in the intercultural field, and provide several examples of relevant experience in each to bring them to life.

Activities Using the Wheel

Once you have introduced the wheel, participants can complete one or more of the following activities.

1. Current skills inventory: Ask individuals to list their relevant experience and expertise in each section of the wheel, using the questions in Handout S9.1 as a guide. Under life experience," write, for example, "Lived in Togo for 3 years" or "am in a cross-cultural relationship." This will help people recognize their current experience, point out obvious gaps, and serve as an effective aid for specific activities such as writing a biography, résumé, or CV. You can also formalize this activity by asking people to bring their résumés or CVs to the session. After they complete the current skills inventory, have them review their résumés and update the language and list of relevant experiences. Have people work in pairs to help one another.

2. Pulse check on your current skill levels: Once participants have listed their skills in each area, ask them to rate the amount of experience they have on a scale from 1 to 6 for each skill or knowledge area, with 6 being *highly developed*. Have people fill out the My Wheel of Intercultural Skills: Current Skills Inventory (see Handout S9.1) and connect the lines and color in the area. This will visually indicate current strength areas as well as help individuals identify the areas needing further development to balance their intercultural skills. Discuss with individuals and groups what their interest is in developing more in these areas and what opportunities are available to do so.

3. Wheel networking event: Have people in the room share their wheel of skills with each other. This may even include, for example, posting their wheels around the room. Give people time to review each other's wheels and ask questions. This can be a structured activity as part of the session or something you encourage people to do over breaks. Point out

how there are a lot of resources in the room, and encourage people to share what experiences have helped them most. For example, for those who have an advanced degree in intercultural studies, what programs did they look at? How did they ultimately decide on the program they went with? Would they recommend it to others? Have people identify others who can complement their skill set by offering new areas of expertise and explore how they might support one another in moving forward.

4. Profession wheels: Have individuals use the tool to focus on a particular profession in the intercultural field and map the needed skills. If doing this in a group training session with multiple professions, first divide the group into professional interest groups (e.g., one group of trainers, one of teachers, etc.). If doing this with one group of professionals (e.g., all intercultural coaches), have people form small groups of three to four. Give each group a piece of flip chart paper to create a wall-size Wheel of Intercultural Skills. Have the small groups

- list the types of experiences, qualifications, and expertise participants can develop under each area;
- discuss or rate (on a scale from 1 to 6, with 6 being *most important*) which areas are most critical for being a trainer, coach, teacher, etc.; and
- identify specific opportunities that exist to further develop in this role.

Bring the groups back together. Have each group report its findings, or allow the group to simply walk around and observe and ask questions about each other's work. Then facilitate a general discussion to debrief the activity by asking the following questions:

- What stands out when you look at or hear these different types of experiences?
- What similarities and differences do you notice on these lists?
- How was it to complete this wheel for a particular profession? What was easy to do? What was more challenging?
- What does this mean for you? (Have individuals compare their individual wheels to others' wheels.)

5. Future development action planning: Use the tool for setting goals and developmental planning. Ask individuals to think about specific steps they can take over the next one to three years to develop in each of the six skill areas. Use the wheel to help people create an action plan, with specific development opportunities either in each category or the two or three categories where they need the most development. Encourage people to identify their first steps to take advantage of these opportunities and set dates to do this.

Facilitation Tips and Suggestions

- Complete the tool yourself first. It will help you give relevant examples in each category, anticipate any concerns that might arise as you apply this with individuals and groups, and determine the activities that will be of highest value to those you are working with.
- The Wheel of Intercultural Skills is designed to be time-flexible. It can be used for as little as a half hour during a session, with participants being able to complete other activities on their own, or it can be used for as many as six hours. To make a full day's session of career planning with this tool, you can conduct all these activities and add a few other supplementary sessions, for example:

  - To frame the session, provide a profile of the intercultural field that includes the field's history, influences, application areas, and overview of the different professions in the field. The following three sources can be helpful:

    - Pusch, Margaret D. (2004). Intercultural training in historical perspective. In D. Landis, J. M. Bennett, & M. J. Bennett (Eds.), *Handbook of intercultural training* (3rd ed., pp. 13–36). Thousand Oaks, CA: Sage.
    - *Professional knowledge center: What are intercultural services?* Retrieved from www.grovewell.com/pub-intercultural .html
    - Berardo, K. *The intercultural profession in 2007: Profile, practices and challenges.* Retrieved from www.culturosity.com/

pdfs/Intercultural%20Profession%20
Report.%20Berardo.%202008.pdf

- Bring in seasoned intercultural experts whom groups can interview for further insight and perspectives on the skills needed for particular professions.
- Hold a wider session on what it takes, beyond expertise, to be successful in the field (e.g., how and where to build networks, the importance in certain professions to be active writers or contributors, pitfalls to avoid, etc.).

- A healthy debate can often emerge on which of these categories is most important and what constitutes valuable experience in each of these areas. It is important for individuals to recognize that no one set of variables qualifies a person for work in the intercultural field, and much will depend on the exact profession one is seeking.
- It is also worth discussing a few ethical questions with a group. Questions you can explore include:

  - When can you call yourself an intercultural professional?
  - What constitutes enough intercultural experience in each of these areas?
  - Do some experiences count for more than others?

  - When does our expertise expire? If we lived in a country 10 years ago, can we or should we still consider ourselves a specialist in that country?
  - What should you do if you are asked to work on a project that is beyond the scope of your expertise?

About This Model

The Wheel of Intercultural Skills is an adaptation of the Wheel of Life developed by the Coaches Training Institute (www.thecoaches.com) and designed to look at an individual's life balance. I developed the first skeleton version of this tool for the Young Society for Intercultural Education, Training, and Research (Young SIETAR) as part of a master workshop training session for the SIETAR USA Annual Conference in November 2006. Much has been added and changed since this first version. The wheel was created as a tool that could simplify the seemingly complex set of expertise needed for a career in the intercultural field. My journey in exploring a career in the intercultural field also served as an inspiration: I was searching for a tool like this one in my own (ongoing) development in this field, and through probably hundreds of casual conversations on what it takes to be successful in this field, along with research into the field itself and intercultural competencies, this six key skill areas pattern emerged.

📄 HANDOUT S9.1

The Wheel of Intercultural Skills

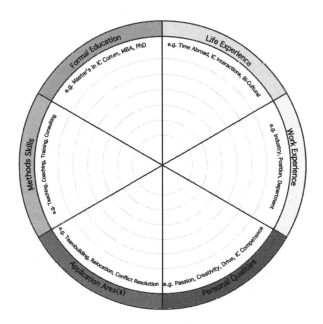

Planning a Career in the Intercultural Field
A tool by Kate Berardo

Reproduced from: Kate Berardo, "Tool: The Wheel of Intercultural Skills," in *Building Cultural Competence: Innovative Activities and Models*, eds. K. Berardo and D. K. Deardorff (Sterling, VA: Stylus, 2012), 355–370.

The Wheel of Intercultural Skills

What does it take to become successful in the intercultural field? This a good question, and one that aspiring and highly experienced professionals have been discussing for decades. Without any standards or defined processes for becoming an intercultural professional, the path to move forward isn't always clear. What is clear, however, is that a successful career in the intercultural field requires a balance of different types of skills so that you can become a truly well-rounded interculturalist.

About this Tool

The Wheel of Intercultural Skills is a tool that will help you identify and build well-rounded expertise in six key areas that are critical to success in the intercultural field:

Formal education	**Personal qualities**
Life experience	**Application areas**
Work experience	**Methods skills**

You can use this tool to map your own skills in each of these areas, plan and evaluate different career opportunities, and match your skill set to different roles and positions within the field. You can also use the wheel as an aid in effective résumé or curriculum vitae (CV) writing or as a tool to track your development over time.

Background of the Tool

The Wheel of Intercultural Skills was created by interculturalist Kate Berardo, who recognized the need for a tool that could simplify the seemingly complex set of expertise needed for a career in the intercultural field. She developed the first skeleton version of this tool in November of 2006 as an adaptation of the eight-sectioned Wheel of Life developed by the Coaches Training Institute to look at an individual's life balance. At that time, she had been asked by the Young Society for Intercultural Training, Research and Education (Young SIETAR) to deliver part of a Master Workshop career training session for the SIETAR USA Annual Conference. She has been adding and adjusting elements of this tool in the five years since.

Kate's own early journey in exploring a career in the intercultural field was also a motivation behind the creation of this tool. In her own development exploration, Kate was looking for a process and instrument like this one that would help her identify the skills she needed for different types of professions in the field, inventory the current skills and experiences she was bringing to the field, and help her identify what steps she could take to further advance her career. It was through what were probably hundreds of casual conversations on what it takes to be successful in this field—along with research into the field itself—that these six key skill areas emerged as being the most important to gaining a fruitful career in the intercultural field.

The Six Key Intercultural Skill Areas

1 Formal education

- The formal training and education that you bring to your work in the intercultural field, the courses you have taken, the subjects you have studied, the credentials you carry that advance your work in the intercultural field.
- *Examples: A Masters Degree in Intercultural Communication or International Relations, a PhD in a related subject matter, global leadership courses taken during an MBA, Intercultural Communication courses taken while pursuing an undergraduate degree, professional development courses.*

2 Life experience

- The intercultural experiences that have shaped you and constitute your own experiences working across cultures, including time living abroad, working globally, being in an intercultural relationship, having a diverse cultural background, and daily intercultural interactions.
- *Examples: living abroad, working globally, having intercultural interactions, having a diverse cultural background.*

3 Work experience

- The "on-the-ground" or "in the field" experience you have working in different sectors, industries, organizations and departments; those areas where you have applied your skills.
- *Examples: Experience in a certain industry (banking, agriculture, high tech, pharmaceutical, study abroad); Organizational experience (having been a line manager, worked internally for a learning and development department); Knowledge of departmental dynamics (the culture of the IT department, marketing individuals, finance).*

4 Personal qualities

- The traits and skills you bring that help you "walk the talk" and demonstrate the skills we help others to develop. Openness, flexibility, good communication skills, style shifting, and intercultural sensitivity are just a few of the types of qualities needed to work in the intercultural field.
- *Examples: style-shifting, flexibility and adaptability, open-mindedness, passion, creativity, and curiosity, drive.*

5 Application areas

- The topics and areas that you specialize in and where you apply your intercultural expertise.
- *Examples: teambuilding, relocation, conflict resolution, global virtual teams, study abroad, cultural identity, global leadership.*

6 Methods skills

- The methods and approaches you use to carry out your intercultural work.
- *Examples: teaching, training, coaching, consulting, facilitating, mediating, and advising.*

Why These Six Areas?

1. **Formal education.** To work in the intercultural field, it is increasingly important to have an in-depth understanding of the theoretical frameworks and research that influences the intercultural field. As formal education opportunities in the intercultural field have grown in the last two decades, so too, has the need to demonstrate that you have this formal education, especially as a newer entrant to the field. Having this background demonstrates the seriousness of your commitment to the field and enables you to stay abreast of pertinent changes in the research driving our field. Continuing to refresh this experience through professional development courses is also of critical importance.

2. **Life experience.** To be credible in the intercultural field, you certainly have to have lived and be constantly living the experience, not just have theoretical knowledge of it. Life experience is one of the best balances to formal education, and a critical first and ongoing step in the intercultural field. What exactly constitutes enough experience and the right experience is often under debate, but what is certain is that it is essential to have lived the types of experiences you are helping others to understand, whether this is moving abroad, working in global teams, or communicating across cultures, so that you can share relevant personal examples of what works, what doesn't, and guide others on a similar journey of discovery. Building a combination of daily life experience (interacting across cultures) and life path experiences (moving abroad) creates the richest of experience in this area.

3. **Work experience.** Working in the field enables you to speak from a place of authority and connect to the reality of those you are working with. Whether this means spending time working for a multinational organization, being an engineer, or working as a line manager, the more relevant work experience you have, the better off you generally are. When you have specialized work experience in a particular area (e.g., IT specialist), it also offers the opportunity to develop a niche expertise to better serve particular audiences.

4. **Personal qualities.** Walking the talk is a critical part of being an intercultural professional. Having and showing high levels of intercultural sensitivity, self-awareness, and intercultural competence (an admittedly highly loaded term that encompasses a number of different skills and qualities) is important in this field. You can build the personal qualities needed in this field through other development areas including life and work experiences. That said, conscious and intentional ongoing development of yourself as an individual and intercultural professional is important in advancing in this field, as there is perhaps nothing that can as quickly eradicate your credibility as not showing the skills and sensitivities that you are helping others to develop.

5. **Application areas.** As the intercultural field is a highly applied one, individuals in this field also need to develop expertise well beyond general cultural awareness and into how culture affects different areas from leadership to identity. Successful interculturalists typically specialize early in a few key application areas and become known as experts in these particular application areas. Keeping abreast of developments within and outside the intercultural world in these application areas is paramount to advancing in this field.

6. **Methods skills**. The final of the six skill areas are method skills, meaning having expertise and demonstrated competence in the methodology you use to impart your intercultural knowledge and help others to build their own, whether in research or keynote speaking. While programs often exist that are specific to the intercultural application of a particular method (e.g., intercultural coaching, teaching intercultural competence), professionals will be well served to continue to develop their method skills at a more general level. This can include getting certified as a facilitator, joining associations like the American Society for Training and Development (ASTD) for training or International Coaching Federation (ICF) for coaching.

Note that:

- Different professions (e.g., transitions coach, trainer for global teams) will require different skill set combinations.

- There are no hard rules on what constitutes enough expertise in each of these areas.

- Similarly, what constitutes the best type of experiences and expertise will also be subject to opinion.

- Generally speaking, the more experience in each of the areas, the better.

My Wheel of Intercultural Skills
Current Skills Inventory

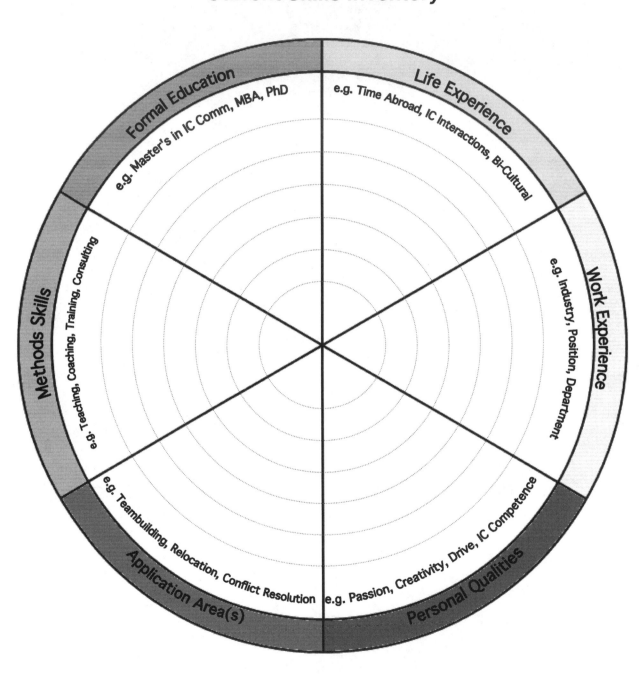

Completing the Wheel of Intercultural Skills

Step 1: Create a Current Skills Inventory

The Wheel of Intercultural Skills can help you identify the specific skills you have to offer. In each of the six areas on the wheel on the previous page, write in the experiences you have that contribute to your expertise in this area on the wheel. Use the following questions to guide you:

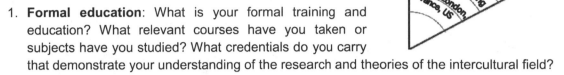

1. **Formal education**: What is your formal training and education? What relevant courses have you taken or subjects have you studied? What credentials do you carry that demonstrate your understanding of the research and theories of the intercultural field?

2. **Life experience**: What intercultural experiences have shaped you and constitute your own experiences working across cultures, such as time living abroad, working globally, being in an intercultural relationship, having a diverse cultural background, or daily intercultural interactions?

3. **Work experience**: What is your relevant experience working in different sectors, industries, organizations and departments?

4. **Personal qualities**: What traits and skills do you bring that help you "walk the talk" and demonstrate the skills we help others to develop?

5. **Application areas**: What are the topics and areas that interest you most and that you have experience with (e.g., teambuilding, relocation, conflict resolution, global virtual teams, study abroad, cultural identity, or global leadership)? Note the experiences that have helped you develop skills in these application areas.

6. **Methods skills**: What methods and approaches do you/will you use to carry out your intercultural work (e.g., teaching, training, coaching, consulting, mediating, and advising)? List any associations you belong to, method-specific certifications you have received, and any other experience that demonstrates your expertise for each of the methods you use in your work.

Tip: If you have experiences that have contributed to your building expertise in multiple areas, you may choose to either put it in a best fit area or list it in all relevant areas. For example, if you worked as a country manager abroad, you could either list this experience solely under work experience or you could list the country manager position under work experience and then record the time you spent abroad under life experience.

Once you have completed a Skills Inventory for the Wheel of Intercultural Skills, share and compare your profile with others. Use the wheel to help when you write or update your CV, résumé, or bio. Compare your skills inventory with the background and expertise listed on your résumé and ensure you include the various experiences and expertise that you have recorded on your skills inventory.

Step 2: Rate Your Current Skills Level

What's your current skill level in each of these areas? To get a big picture view, mark how much experience you have in each of the six intercultural areas currently on a scale of 1 to 6, with 1 being low and 6 being high. For example, if you have little to no relevant experience or expertise in the methods area, you would draw a line next to the 1 for this area. You might at the same time put a line next to the 6 in personal qualities if you feel this is one clear strength you bring to your work as an interculturalist. Then, connect these lines and color in the area. This will visually indicate where your current strength areas are and help you identify the areas you need to develop to balance your intercultural skills.

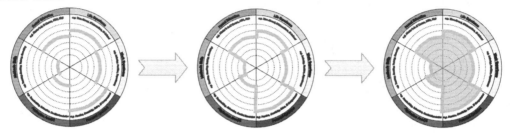

My Current Skills Level: A Quick Glance

***Evaluate future opportunities using the Wheel of Intercultural Skills.** Come back and use this wheel when weighing in job and professional development opportunities to help you determine the value of each role you may be considering. Take another pen color and mark this time on a scale of 1 to 6 how much a specific job or role is likely to help you grow and round out your skills in each area. Aim for "stretch" experiences—opportunities where you bring enough existing qualifications to do the job well but that will simultaneously help you develop new expertise in areas of the wheel where you may be less strong currently.*

Step 3: Map the Skills Needed for a Specific Profession

Choose a specific job, role, or profession in the intercultural field. Then map what types of experiences, qualifications, traits and expertise you believe would best prepare someone for this role. *Tip: As you have conversations with others in the intercultural field, seek to understand what they view would be most important as well.*

Skills Profile: _____

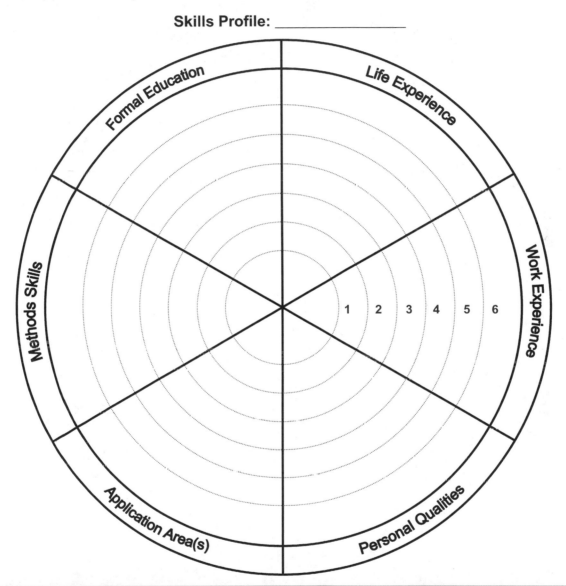

Discussion Questions

As you mapped these skills, were there some that you believe are more important for this role than others?

What would you consider to be the minimum type of experience you need in each of these areas for this role to qualify someone for this position?

How does this list of needed skills compare to your own skills? What similarities and differences do you notice between your current skills inventory profile and this profile?

My Future Wheel of Intercultural Skills
Opportunities to Develop in the Intercultural Field

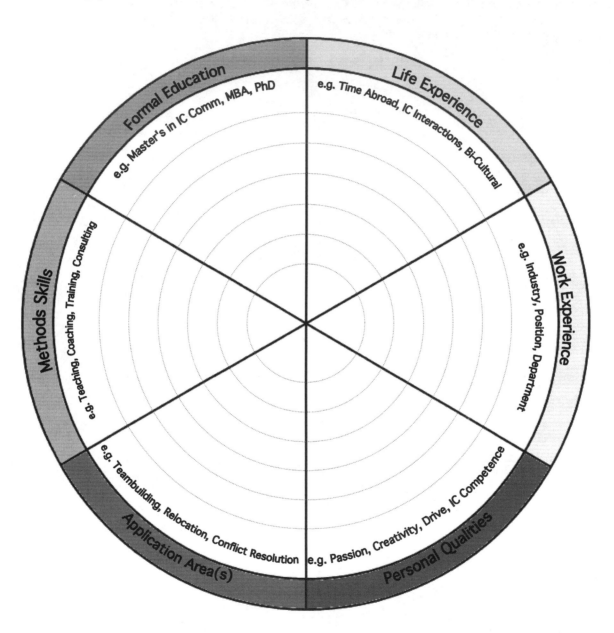

Formal Education
e.g. Master's in IC Comm, MBA, PhD

Life Experience
e.g. Time Abroad, IC Interactions, Bi-Cultural

Methods Skills
e.g. Teaching, Coaching, Training, Consulting

Work Experience
e.g. Industry, Position, Department

Application Area(s)
e.g. Teambuilding, Relocation, Conflict Resolution

Personal Qualities
e.g. Passion, Creativity, Drive, IC Competence

Step 4: Create an Action Plan

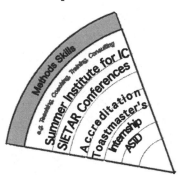

Brainstorm. Spend a few minutes brainstorming all the ways you can develop in each area. Write all the ideas that come to mind for each area of the wheel. Be creative. Consider both traditional and unconventional ways in which you can develop skills in each. Seek the input of others for additional ideas.

Compare. Focus in on the career and the specific profession or job you are seeking. In which three areas do you have the greatest skill gap between your experience and the experience needed for a given job? Write these in the first column. *Not sure yet what profession within the field you want to pursue? No problem. Just look then to the three areas where you are lacking the most experience overall.*

Evaluate. Now return to your list of brainstormed development opportunities. Ask yourself:
1. Which of these opportunities will likely help me advance the most in the field? *Mark these with a star (★).*
2. Which of these opportunities can I realistically act on within the next 1-3 years? *Mark these opportunities with a check mark (✓).*

Act. After reviewing which opportunities will help you most and which you can realistically act on, make an action plan for your development within the next year, following the example provided for method skills.

My Action Plan

My Goal:	*Example:* *Develop my group training skills (methods skills)*			
How I Plan to Do This:	*Attend the Summer Institute for Intercultural Communication in 2013*			
Specific Actions I Will Need to Take:	• *Seek funding and sponsorship from my organization* • *Identify the best course to take* • *Apply for academic credit*			
My First Step Being:	*Introduce idea to my boss*			
Which I Will Take By:	*Next Friday during my regular check-in meeting*			

EDITORS

The editors are highly experienced professionals who travel the globe on a regular basis to build the cultural competence of individuals and organizations. They are both active researchers and writers, educators, and facilitators, and bring a healthy and needed balance between the academic and practitioner worlds.

Kate Berardo

Kate Berardo is a consultant, facilitator, and coach who helps individuals and organizations to be more effective at a global level. Her core competencies include leadership development, diverse team building, international transitions, and global skill building, and she has work experience in over 18 countries with individuals from roughly 50 countries.

Kate runs her own business and also partners with select intercultural management firms in industries such as pharmaceutical, biotech, high-tech, energy, education, automotive, banking, manufacturing, media, and communications. She interacts at all organizational levels, from staff to senior executives, to reduce miscommunication, build trust, and increase effectiveness.

Kate also has experience teaching international business management courses at the university level and developing educational curricula. She is continually involved in the design and development of effective learning tools and is a frequent presenter at international conferences on the dynamics of culture and leadership in organizations. Her best-known research has focused on profiling the intercultural field as well as debunking the popular U-curve model of adjustment. She has coauthored *Putting Diversity to Work: How to Successfully Lead a Diverse Workforce* (Mississauga, Canada: Crisp Learning, 2004), *Cultural Detective Self-Discovery*, and *Cultural Detective Bridging Cultures* (www.culturaldetective.com).

In 2003 Kate founded the website Culturosity (www.culturosity.com) to help build awareness of cultural differences. She holds a distinguished master's in intercultural communication from the University of Bedfordshire, United Kingdom, and is a summa cum laude graduate of Northwestern University. She is certified in the Myers-Briggs Type Indicator, Argonaut-Online, and the International Profiler, and is an active committee member of the Society for Intercultural Education, Training, and Research. She has lived in the United States, United Kingdom, Japan, France, Spain, and Denmark.

Kate's work has been the subject of media worldwide, including CNN's *Business Traveler* and the Dubai, United Arab Emirates, daily *Gulf News*.

Darla K. Deardorff

Darla K. Deardorff is executive director of the Association of International Education Administrators, a national professional organization based at Duke University, where she is a research scholar in education. In addition, she is an adjunct professor at North Carolina State University and the University of North Carolina at Chapel Hill, visiting faculty at Leeds-Metropolitan

University in the United Kingdom, and is on faculty of the Summer Institute of Intercultural Communication in Portland, Oregon. Darla is also an educator with Duke Corporate Education and founder of ICC Global, a global network on intercultural competence for researchers and intercultural practitioners. She receives numerous invitations from around the world (including Europe, Latin America, Africa, and Asia) to speak on her research on intercultural competence and assessment and is a noted global expert on these topics. She has published widely on international education and intercultural learning/assessment and is editor of *The SAGE Handbook of Intercultural Competence* (Thousand Oaks, CA: Sage, 2009), coeditor of *The SAGE Handbook of International Higher*

Education (Thousand Oaks, CA: Sage, 2012), and coauthor of *Beneath the Tip of the Iceberg* (Ann Arbor: University of Michigan Press, 2011).

She has worked in the international education field for nearly 20 years and previously held positions at North Carolina State University and University of North Carolina at Chapel Hill where she has had experience in study abroad, international student services, cultural programming, and teaching and training in English as a Second Language. She is also an English as a Second Language instructor and teacher trainer with over 12 years of experience and has lived, taught, and worked in Germany, Japan, and Switzerland. Darla is an experienced cross-cultural trainer and coach and conducts training for nonprofits, corporations, and educational institutions. She completed a study with UNESCO on comparative perspectives on intercultural competence, which led to invited talks at United Nations events in Azerbaijan and Qatar.

Darla is a graduate of North Carolina State with a master's and doctorate in education, and her doctoral dissertation was on the definition and assessment of intercultural competence, which has drawn national and international attention, and her intercultural competence models developed through the research are being used by such organizations as the Bertelsmann Foundation in Germany, Cariplo Foundation in Italy, and Sodexo. Darla is a certified administrator/trainer of the Intercultural Development Inventory, the Global Competencies Inventory, Intercultural Edge, and Intercultural Effectiveness Scale.

CONTRIBUTORS

AFS Interkulturelle Begegnungen e.V. (AFS)

AFS is an international, nongovernmental, nonprofit, voluntary-based organization. Worldwide, AFS offers programs in more than 80 countries with more than 13,000 participants annually. AFS Germany provides school exchange, host family programs, and voluntary services in about 40 countries. The aim of all AFS exchange programs is to foster tolerance and understanding through exchanges between different cultures, leading to a process of intercultural learning. This exercise was created by a group of 12 volunteers from Germany and the United States who worked on intercultural materials for host families in the United States and Germany. The Intercultural Learning Department of AFS Germany can be reached at Annette.Gisevius@afs.org

Arasaratnam, Lily A.

Lily A. Arasaratnam, PhD, is director of master of arts (Christian studies) at Alphacrucis College and an honorary associate at Macquarie University, Sydney, Australia. Her primary area of expertise is in intercultural communication competence. Formerly an assistant professor at Oregon State University, Lily now teaches and conducts intercultural training in Australia, New Zealand, and the United States.

Bennett, Janet M.

Janet Bennett is executive director and cofounder of the Intercultural Communication Institute (ICI) and ICI director of the Master of Arts in Intercultural Relations Program. For 12 years Janet was the chair of the Liberal Arts Division at Marylhurst College, where she developed innovative academic programs for adult degree students. As a trainer and consultant, Janet designs and conducts intercultural and diversity training for colleges and universities, corporations, social service agencies, health care organizations, and international aid agencies. She teaches in the Training and Development Program at Portland State University and has published numerous articles on the subjects of intercultural training and adjustment processes. She coedited the third edition of the *Handbook of Intercultural Training* (Thousand Oaks, CA: Sage, 2003). She can be reached at jbennett@intercultural.org.

Berardo, Kate

Kate Berardo is a facilitator, coach, and consultant who specializes in global leadership development, communications, and diverse teams. Kate helps individuals and teams increase effectiveness, reduce miscommunication, and build stronger working relationships. She has worked in more than 18 countries, working with individuals from over 50 nations, and has been the subject of media worldwide, including CNN's *Business Traveler* and the *Gulf News*. She is the founder of Culturosity.com, coauthor of *Putting Diversity to Work* (Mississauga, Canada: Crisp Learning, 2004), and author of the *Cultural Detective Self-Discovery* and *Bridging Cultures* (www.culturaldetective.com). She holds a distinguished masters in intercultural communication and has lived in the United States, Spain, Japan, France, the United Kingdom, and Denmark. Kate can be reached at kate@culturosity.com.

Bourassa, Emma

Emma Bourassa is an English as a Second Language/ Teacher of English as a Second Language (ESL/TESL) instructor and faculty developer at Thompson Rivers University in Kamloops, Canada. Emma's experience of becoming a foreign student to understand the experience of living in another culture has led to the further exploration of cultural interactions (successful and not) beyond language exchanges. The development of visual models to explore and learn about cultural communication styles and intercultural learning has been used with ESL and TESL students and faculty. She can be reached at: ebourassa@tru.ca.

Chutnik, Monika

Monika Chutnik works as trainer and consultant in the area of leadership and culture. Having gained considerable experience in the corporate environment, Monika runs her own company etta Consulting and Training for Business, offering intercultural services in central and eastern Europe. She contributes to developing intercultural awareness in Poland as president of the Society for Intercultural Education, Training, and Research Polska and observes closely the intricacies of working in virtual teams, which she finds an exciting training area. Polish in origin, her working languages are also English and German. Monika holds an MA in sociology and an MSc in people management. She can be reached at www.ettaconsult.eu or www.monikachutnik.pl.

Deardorff, Darla K.

Darla K. Deardorff is a teacher, trainer, coach, researcher, and consultant who specializes in intercultural competence development and assessment. She is executive director of the Association of International Education Administrators, based at Duke University. In addition, she is an adjunct professor at North Carolina State University and the University of North Carolina at Chapel Hill, is on the faculty of the Summer Institute for Intercultural Communication in Portland, Oregon, and is founder of ICC Global. She receives numerous invitations from around the world to speak and give workshops on intercultural competence, global leadership, and assessment (including Europe, Latin America, Africa, and Asia) and is a noted expert and consultant on these topics. She has published widely on topics in international education and intercultural learning/assessment, including *The SAGE Handbook of Intercultural Competence* (Thousand Oaks, CA: Sage, 2009). She holds a master's and doctorate from North Carolina State University, where she focused on international education. The intercultural competence models developed from her research are being used worldwide. She can be reached at d.deardorff@duke.edu.

Di Tullio, Laura

Laura Di Tullio is a cross-cultural training consultant. A native of Cuneo, Italy, Laura has worked as a freelance and full-time terminologist in Italy, Belgium, and the United States. In the last 15 years, she has gained international experience living, studying and working abroad, and has acquired knowledge of different cultures and languages. Her past experiences naturally resulted in her interest in cross-cultural communication and training. She holds an MA in translation and terminology management. Apart from Italian, she speaks fluent English, French, and minimal Spanish. She can be reached at lditullio30@hotmail.com

Draheim, Kristin

Kristin Draheim holds an MA in intercultural communication from the European University Viadrina in Germany as well as a magister of cultural science from the Adam Mickiewicz University in Poland. Currently she works as a project coordinator at European University Viadrina's Center for Intercultural Learning and is pursuing a PhD on the facilitation of processes in intercultural teams. Since 2004 she has worked as a trainer for American Field Service and other organizations and since 2008 also designs and conducts training sessions for her own company. Her main training subjects are diversity management, team building in intercultural contexts, studying abroad and culture shock, working in intercultural teams, and dealing with conflicts in intercultural teams. She can be reached at info@draheim-dialog.de.

Evanuik, Jennifer

Jennifer Evanuik has worked in the Office of International Education at the Georgia Institute of Technology since March 2007. She is currently assistant director of the International Plan and has previously advised exchange programs. Among her responsibilities is the coordination of intercultural communication orientations and reentry seminars for study abroad students. She holds a BS in French from the Pennsylvania State University and an MEd in social and comparative analysis of education from the University of Pittsburgh. She can be reached at jcevanuik@yahoo.com.

Feldman, Jeanne

Jeanne Feldman specializes in deepening cross-cultural communication internationally. She develops and leads business communication workshops for French- and English-speaking managers who need to communicate internationally. Her goal is to enable them to find their true message and deliver it clearly. To do this, they often need to see and then bridge cultural differences.

In addition, Jeanne works with university students at Sciences Po in France to prepare them for the business world or for advanced studies abroad in English. She can be contacted at contact@jeanne-feldman.com.

Fertelmeyster, Tatyana

Tatyana Fertelmeyster is a facilitator, trainer, and consultant specializing in intercultural issues. Tatyana received an MA in journalism from Moscow State University in Russia and an MA in counseling from Northeastern Illinois University. She has done extensive postgraduate work in intercultural communication and diversity. She has conducted training programs for a variety of groups and organizations throughout the United States as well as in Europe. Tatyana is a coauthor of the Russian version of the training tool Cultural Detective. She is a faculty member at the Summer Institute for Intercultural Communication in Portland, Oregon, and is a past president of the Society for Intercultural Education, Training, and Research (SIETAR-USA). She can be reached at connecting.differences@gmail.com.

Goddard, David

David Goddard has 20 years' experience with diverse clients in Europe, Asia, and the United States as a cross-cultural consultant and coach. His key interest areas are leadership, teamwork, collaboration, and cross-cultural communication. David is a keen traveler and enjoys experiencing other cultures. He works at Pertec Consulting in Helsinki and is currently translating Pentti Sydänmaanlakka's latest book *Continuous Renewal: Leading Creativity and Innovation*.

Gregersen-Hermans, Jeanine

Jeanine Gregersen-Hermans is director of marketing and communications and spokesperson of the Executive Board at Maastricht University, Netherlands. She is the appointed director of the Maastricht Education and Research Center in Bangalore, India. Jeanine is a graduate of Radboud University Nijmegen and has worked at Wageningen University and for the Network of Universities from the Capitals of Europe (UNICA) in Brussels. Jeanine is a member of the editorial board of the Journal of Studies in International Education. She taught at various European universities and presented at conferences worldwide. Jeanine is a recipient of the Bo Gregersen Award of

the European Association of International Education (EAIE). She is an EAIE senior trainer and serves as a member of the General Council of the EAIE and its professional development committee. Jeanine is an honorary member of IROICA, the standing committee for internationalization of the European Association of Life Science Universities. She can be reached at j.gregersen@maastrichtuniversity.nl.

Hiller, Gundula Gwenn

Gundula Gwenn Hiller is director of the Center for Intercultural Learning at the European University Viadrina in Frankfurt/Oder on the German-Polish border in East Germany. She received a BMW Life Award for Intercultural Learning in 2008 for a program on students' development of intercultural competences. Her research areas are intercultural competence in higher education and training methods. In addition to her research, she teaches in different intercultural master programs, including the Master of Intercultural Communication Studies Program at the European University Viadrina. She can be reached at hiller@europa-uni.de.

Ibrahim DeVries, Basma

Basma Ibrahim DeVries, PhD, is professor of communication studies at Concordia University in St. Paul, Minnesota, where she specializes in teaching intercultural and interpersonal communication courses, incorporating service learning into courses, leading student travel courses, and facilitating campuswide intercultural competence-building sessions. She is coauthor (with Dianne Hofner Saphiere and Barbara Kappler Mikk) of *Communication Highwire: Leveraging the Power in Diverse Communication Styles* (Boston, MA: Nicholas Brealey, 2005) and *Cultural Detective: Egypt* (www.culturaldetective.com). Basma is on the faculty at the Summer Institute for Intercultural Communication. Basma trains and consults with corporate, educational, and community clients on a wide range of intercultural topics. She can be reached at askbasma@gmail.com.

Jicheva, Maria

Maria Jicheva is a partner in Coghill and Beery International. She is an intercultural communication and management specialist with a background in business and adult learning. Maria has lived and worked in various cultures through diplomatic postings and business assignments. She combines her international business and teaching background with Myers Briggs and solution focus training to coach individuals and teams with cross-cultural communication, motivation and conflict resolution issues. Maria was born in Bulgaria and received her MA and BA degrees from the University of Sofia, Bulgaria, her MBA from the American International University in London, and diploma in intercultural management at the University of Cambridge, England. Maria has published numerous articles on intercultural communication and cross-cultural adaptation. She can be reached at Jicheva@coghillbeery.com.

Kappler Mikk, Barbara

Barbara Kappler Mikk, PhD, directs intercultural training and programs at International Student and Scholar Services (ISSS) at the University of Minnesota. She has taught and trained at the university since 1989 and specializes in facilitating team and large-group discussions and in designing interactive intercultural learning opportunities. She is coauthor of *Maximizing Study Abroad* (University of Minnesota, Board of Regents, 2006), a series of guides for students, language instructors, and program coordinators. *Communication Highwire: Leveraging the Power in Diverse Communication Styles* (Boston, MA: Nicholas Brealey, 2005) coauthored with Dianne Hofner Saphiere and Basma Ibrahim DeVries, provides concrete strategies for understanding and improving communication disconnects across cultures. Barbara is on the faculty at the Summer Institute for Intercultural Communication and is a member of the graduate faculty with the College of Education and Human Development. She is active in Minneapolis public school classrooms as a volunteer. Barbara can reached at bkappler@umn.edu.

Katz, Lothar

Lothar Katz is a management adviser in the field of international business and founder of the cross-cultural consultancy Leadership Crossroads. As a former vice president and general manager of a Fortune 500 company, he led business organizations on four continents and later helped numerous companies and other organizations improve their management effectiveness and business results. A native of Germany, Lothar teaches or has taught international business leadership, negotiation, and project management at

several universities in the United States. He is the author of *Negotiating International Business* (Charleston, SC: BookSurge, 2006), lives in the United States, Germany, and Spain, and can be reached at lk@leadershipcrossroads.com.

La Brack, Bruce

Bruce La Brack is professor emeritus of anthropology and international studies, University of the Pacific, Stockton, California. For three decades he headed Pacific's innovative and integrated orientation and reentry programs for study abroad. He also served as director of the Pacific Institute for Cross-Cultural Training and chair of the Master of Arts in Intercultural Relations Program. He is a senior faculty member of the Summer Institute for Intercultural Communication and is the author and primary editor of the website *What's Up With Culture?* (www.pacific.edu/culture), a free Internet resource for preparing U.S. American study abroad participants. He can be reached at blabrack@pacific.edu.

Longatan, Nancy

Nancy Longatan is a trainer and writer who specializes in topics related to cross-cultural communication and surviving culture shock. She has worked in humanitarian assistance programs in Nepal, leadership training in Japan, overseas personnel recruitment in the United States, and rural development in the Philippines, as well as consulting with sojourners moving from and to many other cultures. She has articles in publications in Barbados, Nepal, Japan, the United Kingdom, the Philippines and the United States, as well as on the web. She has taught an online class in cross-cultural communication and culture shock and can be reached at longatann@gmail.com.

Matheusen, Fanny

Fanny Matheusen is a teacher, trainer, and consultant, working with the Centre for Intercultural Management and International Communication at the University of Mechelen, Belgium. She teaches intercultural communication and diversity management and works at the University Colleges of Mechelen and Antwerp in a variety of professional training and education settings. Her other areas of interest are gender, international cooperation, and climate change. She can be reached at fanny.matheusen@gmail.com.

Merryfield, Merry

Merry Merryfield is professor of social studies and global education at Ohio State University. Author of numerous publications on global education, she studies teacher decision making in global education, online versus face-to-face cross-cultural learning, and global citizenship education. She can be reached at merryfield.1@osu.edu.

Nam, Kyoung-Ah

Kyoung-Ah Nam is an assistant professor at the School of International Service at American University in Washington, DC. She holds a PhD from the University of Minnesota and has extensive experience in international education, intercultural communications, training, consulting, and public relations in North America and in Asia. An active member of the Society for Intercultural Education Training and Research and the International Academy for Intercultural Research, her focus areas include study abroad, intercultural training for international faculty and teaching assistants, expatriate adjustment, and global leadership development. She has worked in diverse organizational contexts including Aperian Global, Ogilvy & Mather, Radio Free Asia, Samsung, the United Nations, and UNESCO. Originally from Korea, she has worked and/or traveled in more than 35 countries over the last 15 years working with clients and students from Asia, Europe, Africa, and North America. She can be reached at nam0701@gmail.com.

Nevalainen, Lisa

Lisa Nevalainen is assistant director in the Office of Education Abroad at the University of North Carolina at Charlotte. Her EdM with a concentration in international education is from the Harvard Graduate School of Education, and she is an alumna of Mount Holyoke College. Her first significant experiences in participating and organizing cross-cultural training took place at International House in New York where she was a programs coordinator. She can be reached at Lisa.Nevalainen@uncc.edu.

Nowicka, Marta

Marta Nowicka runs her own training and consulting company, Global Competence, and is an intercultural trainer and coach. She is also an Insights Discovery licensed practitioner and provides a wide range of soft skills trainings based on the Insights model. Marta holds an MA in psychology and an MA in business management and marketing. She has business experience in the hospitality and translation industries where she worked in sales and marketing. Marta is active in the Society for Intercultural Education Training and Research Polska and coordinates the Warsaw Regional Group. For more about Marta, see www.globalcompetence.pl. She can be reached at marta.nowicka@globalcompetence.pl.

Pineda, Kimberly

Kimberly Pineda is a bilingual health educator for Valley Health focusing on training staff in intercultural competence and health care communication. In addition, she works with program development for culturally and linguistically diverse patients and language access services. Pineda also facilitates training for academic, governmental, business, and community service agencies. Previously she led the International Cross-Cultural Center at Shenandoah University and had the privilege of working with students representing 50 different countries. Pineda holds a master's in intercultural relations from the University of the Pacific and Intercultural Communication Institute and a bachelor's in Spanish from Shenandoah University. She can be reached at kpineda@alumni.su.edu.

Pollack, Stephanie

Stephanie Pollack, MA, is an interculturally and artistically focused experiential educator, trainer, facilitator, writer, and consultant. Stephanie has 20 years of experience working in a variety of cultures and environments on six continents. With her business, Creative Facilitations, she develops and leads innovative organizational and individual transformation processes, retreats, training sessions, educational programs, and community-building events around the globe. Clients include Royal Caribbean Cruises (The Scholar Ship), University of Virginia, Mercy Corps, Bioneers, and the Georgia O'Keeffe Museum. Stephanie is passionate about combining the arts and interactive on-your-feet methods to inspire aha moments for cultural proficiency, conflict prevention, team building, leadership development, and healing. She can be reached at Stephanie@CreativeFacilitations.com.

Pusch, Margaret "Peggy" D.

Margaret "Peggy" D. Pusch is associate director of the Intercultural Communication Institute in Portland, Oregon, which sponsors the Summer Institute for Intercultural Communication (SIIC) and a master's program with the University of the Pacific. Peggy is a cross-cultural trainer and consultant, author, and editor. She cofounded and was president of Intercultural Press for over 15 years, was president of the Association of International Educators (NAFSA), and was executive director of the Society for Intercultural Education Training and Research USA. Peggy is the recipient of numerous intercultural awards including Senior Interculturalist Award from the International Society for Intercultural Education, Training, and Research in 1988. She can be reached at mdpusch @pobox.com.

Ramsey, Sheila

Sheila Ramsey is a founding partner of Personal Leadership Seminars and principal of the Crestone Institute. She works with leaders all over the world enabling them to move beyond habit, receive inspiration from all sources, and welcome possibilities to bring forth the best in themselves and others and create life-enhancing systems. She has been a professor of communication in Japan and was on the faculty of the Summer Institute of Intercultural Communication. Her consultancies take her to Asia, Europe, the Balkans, the Middle East, and Africa with such diverse clients as Daimler A.G., U.S. Department of State, and the United Nations. She has been a professional photographer, a potter's apprentice in Japan, and is currently a visual artist living in Crestone, a small village in the mountains of Colorado.

Rao, Nagesh

Nagesh Rao is a teacher, storyteller, dancer, statistician, poet, and a proud father of two daughters. His many marginal experiences—first as a Kannadiga in a Tamil State; an accountant in an artist's soul; then, for 20-odd years, an East Indian in Mississippi, Michigan, Ohio, and New Mexico; and now a nonresident Indian back in India—give him a wealth of stories and theories to share about the many Indias, about discovery of oneself and others, and about how to be an effective change agent. Nagesh is also director and professor at Mudra Institute of Communications, Ahmedabad, India. He can be reached at raojirao@ yahoo.com.

Schaetti, Barbara F.

Barbara Schaetti is a founding partner of Personal Leadership Seminars and principal consultant of Transition Dynamics. She works globally with people and organizations seeking to translate intercultural knowledge into intercultural competence, and advocates for personal practices that help people stay inspired even when confronted by difference and the unexpected. A second-generation global nomad/Adult Third Culture Kid (ATCK) and a dual national, Barbara had lived in 10 countries on five continents by the age of 22. She is a member of the faculty of the Intercultural Communication Institute, coauthor of *Cultural Detective: Blended Culture* (www.cultural detective.com), and is author or coauthor of books, chapters, and articles on such topics as multicultural identity development, expatriate and repatriate families, cultural and geographic transitions, and the power and the practice of the methodology of personal leadership. Barbara is based in Seattle, Washington.

Simons, George

George Simons is president of George Simons International, a consulting network specializing in intercultural communication and teamwork. He is creator and editor in chief of diversophy®, learning instruments for developing intercultural competence in face-to-face training as well as online. He also serves as an associate director of diversophy® France, an organization whose mission is to deliver intercultural training based on diversophy® and the Cultural Detective tools in Francophone countries. As a member of governing boards of the Society for Intercultural Education Training and Research (SIETAR) Europa and France, he has worked at enhancing the interculturalist's role by developing professional standards and effective social networks for SIETAR membership and those interested in intercultural matters. He can be contacted at diversophy@gmail.com.

Trompenaars, Fons

As founder and director of Trompenaars Hampden-Turner, an intercultural management firm, Fons Trompenaars has spent over 20 years helping Fortune 500 leaders and professionals manage and solve their business and cultural dilemmas to increase global effectiveness and performance. Fons began his career at Royal Dutch Shell Group in 1981, where he met his partner, Charles Hampden Turner, with whom he has pioneered the seven dimensions of culture and dilemma reconciliation into a powerful approach for reconciling cultural differences. Fons's interest in cultural differences began at home, where he grew up speaking French and Dutch. He studied economics at the Free University of Amsterdam and later earned a PhD from Wharton School, University of Pennsylvania, with a dissertation on differences in conceptions of organizational structure in various cultures. Author of numerous books, his most recent is *Riding the Waves of Innovation: Harness the Power of Global Culture to Drive Creativity and Growth* (New York, NY: McGraw-Hill, 2010).

Wasilewski, Jacqueline

Jacqueline Wasilewski carries seven lines of history in her bones. She has worked with Native American and Hispanic communities in the United States, worked on informal education in Ecuador and Papua New Guinea, and for 17 years taught intercultural communication and conflict resolution at International Christian University in Tokyo. Since 1985 she has also worked with Structured Dialogic Design (SDD), a computer-assisted, structured dialogue process for complex problem solving by diverse stakeholders. She used this process in her Northeast Asian Dialogue Project, funded by the Japanese Ministry of Education, that brought together Japanese, Chinese, Korean, and Russian students and civil society members to address intercultural relations in the region. She can be reached at jwashi@aol.com.

Watanabe, Gordon

Gordon Watanabe is a founding partner of Personal Leadership Seminars and consults in corporate, education, and other organizational settings (most recently in the farm credit banking system). He is professor emeritus in education and was special assistant to the president for intercultural relations at Whitworth University. He is a member of the faculty of the Intercultural Communication Institute and is a member of its board of directors. Gordon's work focus is on the critical role of deep self-understanding in successful cross-cultural negotiations and intercultural team building. From his background as a third-generation Japanese American and his years working with international and U.S. minority students, Gordon is often called to be a cultural bridge, facilitating intercultural challenges between individuals and groups. He is also a qualified Intercultural Development Inventory facilitator. Gordon lives in Spokane, Washington.

White, Maureen

Maureen White currently designs and facilitates intercultural programs in the Office of International Programs at the University of North Carolina at Charlotte. Her experiences include teaching English in the United States and abroad, serving as the English for Speakers of Other Languages (ESOL) coordinator for a nonprofit literacy organization and conducting cultural and educational programs for groups at the high school and university levels as well as for mid-career professionals. She can be reached at mwhite93@uncc.edu.

Woźniak, Maja

Maja Woźniak completed her master's in intercultural communication studies at the European University Viadrina, Frankfurt, Germany. Born in Poland and raised in Germany, she interacted across cultures at an early age, which made her curious about the cause and impact of diverse cultural traditions, communication styles, and underlying values. Following this interest, she combined theoretical and practical knowledge through travel, living abroad, and formal studies. In May 2011 she completed two years working in Cyprus as a producer for international congresses and German summits at Marcus Evans, Ltd. After 25 years, she has returned to her country of origin as part of a highly intercultural team at Google Poland sp. z o.o. She can be reached at wozniak maja@gmx.de.

Wuebbeler, Rita

Rita Wuebbeler is founder of Interglobe Cross-Cultural Business Services, an international training and consulting firm based in Toronto, Canada, and Atlanta, Georgia. Rita helps leaders of global organizations and global virtual teams reach their highest performance potential. She conducts cultural awareness programs for international business leaders and coaches global executives in maximizing their leadership skills. A native German with a master's degree in applied linguistics, Rita spent the first two and a half decades of her life in Europe before moving to North America. After living in the United States for over 20 years, she now resides in Canada. Rita can be reached at rwuebbeler@interglobeweb.net.

INDEX